LIFE A

A GUIDEBOOK FOR THE PILGRIM LIFE

LIFE AT ITS BEST

A GUIDEBOOK FOR THE PILGRIM LIFE

EUGENE H. PETERSON
AUTHOR OF THE MESSAGE

ZONDERVAN™
GRAND RAPIDS, MICHIGAN 49530

ZONDERVAN™

Life At Its Best

ISBN 0 007 11119-3

The Journey first published in the USA in 1980 by InterVarsity Press and in Great Britain in 1989 by Marshall Morgan and Scott, under the title *A Long Obedience in the Same Direction*

A catalogue record for this book is available from the British Library.
ISBN 0 551 01753-8

The Quest first published in the United States of America in 1983 by InterVarsity Press under the title *Run with the Horses* and in Great Britain in 1995 by Marshall Pickering

A catalogue record for this book is available from the British Library.
ISBN 0 551 02981-1

The Gift first published in the USA in 1993 by Wm B. Eerdmans Publishing Co. and in Great Britain in 1995 by Marshall Pickering

A catalogue record for this book is available from the British Library.
ISBN 0 551 02978-1

Interior design by Beth Shagene

Printed and bound in the United Kingdom

02 03 04 05 06 07 08 /❖ OMN/ 10 9 8 7 6 5 4 3 2 1

Contents

THE JOURNEY

A GUIDEBOOK FOR THE PILGRIM LIFE

For Lu and Peter
Companions in the Long Obedience

Contents

1

Discipleship

'How Will You Compete with Horses?'

If you have raced with men on foot, and they have wearied you, how will you compete with horses?

JEREMIAH 12:5

The essential thing 'in heaven and earth' is . . . that there should be long obedience in the same direction; there thereby results, and has always resulted in the long run, something which has made life worth living.

FRIEDRICH NIETZSCHE, BEYOND GOOD AND EVIL

THIS WORLD IS NO FRIEND TO GRACE. A PERSON WHO MAKES a commitment to Jesus Christ as Lord and Saviour does not find a crowd immediately forming to applaud the decision nor old friends spontaneously gathering around to offer congratulations and counsel. Ordinarily there is nothing directly hostile, but an accumulation of puzzled disapproval and agnostic indifference constitutes, nevertheless, surprisingly formidable opposition.

An old tradition sorts the difficulties we face in the life of faith into the categories of world, flesh and devil.[1] We are, for the most part, well warned of the perils of the flesh and the wiles of the devil. Their temptations have a definable shape and maintain an historical continuity. That doesn't make them any easier to resist; it does make them easier to recognize.

The world, though, is protean: each generation has the world to deal with in a new form. *World* is an atmosphere, a mood.[2] It is nearly as hard for a sinner to recognize the world's temptations as it is for a fish to discover impurities in the water. There is a sense, a feeling, that things aren't right, that the environment is not whole, but just what it is eludes analysis. We know that the spiritual atmosphere in which we live erodes faith, dissipates hope and corrupts love, but it is hard to put our finger on what is wrong.

TOURISTS AND PILGRIMS

One aspect of *world* that I have been able to identify as harmful to Christians is the assumption that anything worthwhile can be acquired at once. We assume that if something can be done at all, it can be done quickly and efficiently. Our attention spans have been conditioned by thirty-second commercials. Our sense of reality has been flattened by thirty-page abridgments.

It is not difficult in such a world to get a person interested in the message of the gospel; it is terrifically difficult to sustain the interest. Millions of people in our culture make decisions for Christ, but there is a dreadful attrition rate. Many claim to have been born again, but the evidence for mature Christian discipleship is slim. In our kind of culture anything, even news about God, can be sold if it is packaged freshly; but when it loses its novelty, it goes on the garbage heap. There is a great market for religious experience in our world; there is little enthusiasm for the patient acquisition of virtue, little inclination to sign up for a long apprenticeship in what earlier generations of Christians called holiness.

Religion in our time has been captured by the tourist mindset. Religion is understood as a visit to an attractive site to be made when we have adequate leisure. For some it is a weekly jaunt to church. For others, occasional visits to special services. Some, with a bent for religious entertainment and sacred diversion, plan their lives around special events like retreats, rallies and conferences. We go to see a new personality, to hear a new truth, to get a new experience and so, somehow, expand our otherwise humdrum lives. The religious life is defined as the latest and the newest: Zen, faith-healing, human potential, parapsychology, successful living, choreography in the chancel, Armageddon. We'll try anything – until something else comes along.

I don't know what it has been like for pastors in other cultures and previous centuries, but I am quite sure that for a pastor in Western culture in the latter part of the twentieth century the aspect of *world* that makes the work of leading Christians in the way of faith most difficult is what Gore Vidal has analyzed as 'today's passion for the immediate and the casual.'[3] Everyone is in a hurry. The persons whom I lead in worship, among whom I counsel, visit, pray, preach, and teach, want short cuts. They want me to help them fill out the form that will get them instant credit (in eternity). They are impatient for results. They have adopted the lifestyle of a tourist and only want the high points. But a pastor is not a tour guide. I have no interest in telling apocryphal religious stories at and around dubiously identified sacred sites. The Christian life cannot mature under such conditions and in such ways.

Friedrich Nietzsche, who saw this area of spiritual truth, at least, with great clarity wrote, 'The essential thing "in heaven and earth" is . . . that there should be long obedience in the same direction; there thereby results, and has always resulted in the long run, something which has made life worth living'[4] It is this 'long obedience in the same direction' which the mood of the world does so much to discourage.

In going against the stream of the world's ways there are two biblical designations for people of faith that are extremely useful: *disciple* and *pilgrim. Disciple (mathetes)* says we are people who spend our lives apprenticed to our master, Jesus Christ. We are in a growing-learning relationship, always. A disciple is a learner, but not in the academic setting of a schoolroom, rather at the work site of a craftsman. We do not acquire information about God but skills in faith.

Pilgrim (parepidemos) tells us we are people who spend our lives going someplace, going to God, and whose path for getting there is the way, Jesus Christ. We realize that 'this world is not my home' and set out for the 'Father's house'. Abraham, who 'went out', is our archetype. Jesus, answering Thomas' question, 'Lord, we do not know where you are going; how can we know the way?' gives us directions: 'I am the way, and the truth, and the life; no one comes to the Father, but by me' (Jn 14:5-6). The letter to the Hebrews defines our program: 'Therefore, since we are surrounded by so great a cloud of witnesses, let us lay aside every weight, and sin which clings so closely, and let us run with perseverance the race that is set before us, looking to Jesus the pioneer and perfecter of our faith' (Heb 12:1-2).

A Dog-eared Songbook

In the pastoral work of training people in discipleship and accompanying them in pilgrimage, I have found, tucked away in the Hebrew Psalter, an old dog-eared songbook. I have used it to provide continuity in guiding others in the Christian way, and directing people of faith in the conscious and continuous effort which develops into maturity in Christ. The old songbook is called, in Hebrew, *šire hamm*ᵉ*lot̲* – the Songs of Ascents. The songs are the psalms numbered 120 through 134 in the book of Psalms.

These fifteen psalms were likely sung, possibly in sequence, by Hebrew pilgrims as they went up to Jerusalem to the great worship festivals. Jerusalem was the highest city geographically in Palestine, and so all who travelled there spent much of their time ascending.[5] But the ascent was not only literal, it was also a metaphor: the trip to Jerusalem acted out a life lived upward toward God, an existence that advanced from one level to another in developing maturity. What Paul described as 'the upward call of God in Christ Jesus' (Phil 3:14).

Three times a year faithful Hebrews made that trip (Ex 23:14-17; 34:22-24). The Hebrews were a people whose salvation had been accomplished in the exodus, whose identity had been defined at Sinai and whose preservation had been assured in the forty years of wilderness wandering. As such a people they regularly climbed the road to Jerusalem to worship. They refreshed their memories of God's saving ways at the Feast of Passover in the spring; they renewed their commitments as God's covenanted people at the Feast of Pentecost in early summer; they responded as a blessed community to the best that God had for them at the Feast of Tabernacles in the autumn. They were a redeemed people, a commanded people, a blessed people. These foundational realities were preached and taught and praised at the annual feasts. Between feasts the people lived these realities in daily discipleship until the time came to go up to the mountain city again as pilgrims to renew the covenant.

This picture of the Hebrews singing these fifteen psalms as they left their routines of discipleship and made their way from towns and villages, farms and cities, as pilgrims up to Jerusalem has become embedded in the Christian devotional imagination. It is our best background for understanding life as a faith-journey.

We know that our Lord from a very early age 'went up' to Jerusalem for the annual feasts (Lk 2:41-42). We continue to identify with the first disciples who 'were on the road, going up to Jerusalem, and Jesus was walking ahead of them; and they were amazed, and those who followed were afraid' (Mk 10:32). We also are amazed and afraid for there is wonder upon unexpected wonder on this road, and there are tearful spectres to be met. Singing the fifteen psalms is a way both to express the amazing grace and to quiet the anxious fears.

There are no better 'songs for the road' for those who travel the way of faith in Christ, a way that has so many continuities with the way of Israel. Since many (not all) essential items in Christian discipleship are incorporated in these songs, they provide a way to remember who we are and where we are going. I have not sought to produce scholarly expositions of these psalms but to offer practical meditations which use these tunes for stimulus, encouragement and guidance. If we learn to sing them well, they can be a kind of vade mecum for a Christian's daily walk.

Between the Times

Paul Tournier, in *A Place for You,* describes the experience of being in between – between the time we leave home and arrive at our destination; between the time we leave adolescence and arrive at adulthood; between the time we leave doubt and arrive at faith.[6] It is like the time when a trapeze artist lets go the bars and hangs in midair, ready to catch another support: it is a time of danger, of expectation, of uncertainty, of excitement, of extraordinary aliveness.

Christians will recognize how appropriately these psalms may be sung between the times: between the time we leave the world's environment and arrive at the Spirit's assembly; between the time we leave sin and arrive at holiness; between the time we leave home on a Sunday morning and arrive in church with the company of God's people; between the time we leave the works of the law and arrive at justification by faith. They are songs of transition, brief hymns that provide courage, support and inner direction for getting us to where God is leading us in Jesus Christ.

Meanwhile the world whispers, 'Why bother? There is plenty to enjoy without involving yourself in all that. The past is a graveyard; ignore it; the future is a holocaust; avoid it. There is no payoff for discipleship; there is no destination for pilgrimage. Get God the quick way; buy instant charisma.' But other voices speak, if not more attractively, at least more truly. Thomas Szasz, in his therapy and writing, has attempted to revive respect for what he calls the 'simplest and most ancient of human truths: namely, that life is an arduous and tragic struggle; that what we call 'sanity' – what we mean by 'not being schizophrenic' – has a great deal to do with competence, earned by struggling for excellence; with compassion, hard won by confronting conflict; and with modesty and patience, acquired through silence and suffering.'[7] His testimony validates the decision of those who commit themselves to explore the world of the Psalms of Ascents, who mine them for wisdom and sing them for cheerfulness.

These psalms were no doubt used in such ways by the multitudes Isaiah described as travelling 'up to the mountain of the Lord, to the house of the God of Jacob; that he may teach us his ways and that we may walk in his paths' (Is 2:3). They are also evidence of what Isaiah promised when he said, 'You shall have a song as in the night when a holy feast is kept; and gladness of heart, as when one sets out to the sound of the flute to go to the mountain of the Lord, to the Rock of Israel' (Is 30:29).

Everyone who travels the road of faith requires assistance from time to time. We need cheering up when spirits flag; we need direction when the way is unclear. One of Paul Goodman's 'little prayers'[8] expresses our needs.

On the highroad to death
trudging, not eager to get
to that city, yet the way is
still too long for my patience

– teach me a travel song,
Master, to march along
as we boys used to shout
when I was a young scout.

For those who choose to live no longer as tourists, but as pilgrims, the Psalms of Ascents combine all the cheerfulness of a travel song, with the practicality of a guidebook and map. Their unpretentious brevity is excellently described by William Faulkner. 'They are not monuments, but footprints. A monument only says, "At least I got this far," while a footprint says, "This is where I was when I moved again."'[9]

2

Repentance

'Woe Is Me, that I Sojourn in Meshech'

In my distress I cry to the Lord,
that he may answer me:
'Deliver me, O Lord,
from lying lips,
from a deceitful tongue.'

What shall be given to you?
And what more shall be done to you,
you deceitful tongue?
A warrior's sharp arrows,
with glowing coals of the broom tree!

Woe is me, that I sojourn in Meshech,
that I dwell among the tents of Kedar!
Too long I have had my dwelling
among those who hate peace.
I am for peace;
but when I speak,
they are for war!

PSALM 120

Before a man can do things there must be things he will not do.

MENCIUS

PEOPLE SUBMERGED IN A CULTURE SWARMING WITH LIES AND malice feel like they are drowning in it: they can trust nothing they hear, depend on no one they meet. Such dissatisfaction with the world as it is is preparation for travelling in the way of Christian discipleship. The dissatisfaction, coupled with a longing for peace and truth, can set us on a pilgrim path of wholeness in God.

A person has to be thoroughly disgusted with the way things are to find the motivation to set out on the Christian way. As long as we think that the next election might eliminate crime and establish justice or another scientific breakthrough might save the environment or another pay raise might push us over the edge of anxiety into a life of tranquillity, we are not likely to risk the arduous uncertainties of the life of faith. A person has to get fed up with the ways of the world before he, before she, acquires an appetite for the world of grace.

Psalm 120 is the song of such a person, sick with the lies and crippled with the hate, a person doubled up in pain over what is going on in the world. But it is not a mere outcry, it is pain that penetrates through despair and stimulates a new beginning - a journey to God which becomes a life of peace.

The fifteen Psalms of Ascents describe elements common to all those who apprentice themselves to the Lord Christ and who travel in the Christian way. The first of them is the prod which gets them going. It is not a beautiful song - there is nothing either hauntingly melancholy or lyrically happy in it. It is harsh, it is discordant. But it gets things started.

Life Without Error

In my distress is the opening phrase. The last word is *war.* Not a happy song, but an honest and necessary one.

Men are set against each other. Women are at each other's throats. We are taught rivalry from the womb. The world is restless, always spoiling for a fight. No one seems to know how to live in healthy relationships. We persist in turning every community into a sect, every enterprise into a war. We realize, in fugitive moments, that we were made for something different and better – 'I am for peace' – but there is no confirmation of that realization in our environment, no encouragement of it in our experience. 'I am for peace; but when I speak, they are for war!'

The distress that begins and ends the song is the painful awakening to the no longer avoidable reality that we have been lied to. The world, in fact, is not as it has been represented to us. Things are not all right as they are, and they are not getting any better.

We have been told the lie ever since we can remember: that human beings are basically nice and good. Everyone is born equal and innocent and self-sufficient. The world is a pleasant, harmless place. We are born free. If we are in chains now, it is someone's fault, and we can correct it with just a little more intelligence or effort or time.

How we can keep on believing this after so many centuries of evidence to the contrary is difficult to comprehend, but nothing we do or nothing anyone else does to us seems to disenchant us from the spell of the lie. We keep expecting things to get better, somehow. And when they don't we whine like spoiled children who don't get their way. We accumulate resentment that stores up in anger and erupts in violence. Convinced by the lie that what we are experiencing is unnatural, an exception, we devise ways to escape the influence of what other people do to us by getting away on a vacation as often as we can. When the vacation is over we get back into the flow of things again, our naiveté renewed that everything is going to work out all right – only to once more be surprised, hurt, bewildered when it doesn't. The lie ('everything is O.K.') covers up and perpetuates the deep wrong, disguises the violence, the war, the rapacity.

Christian consciousness begins in the painful realization that what we had assumed was the truth is in fact a lie. Prayer is immediate: 'Deliver me, O Lord, from lying lips, from a deceitful tongue.' Rescue me from the lies of advertisers who claim to know what I need and what I desire, from the lies of entertainers who promise a cheap way to joy, from the lies of politicians who pretend to instruct me in power and morality, from the lies of psychologists who offer to shape my behaviour and my morals so that I will live long, happily and successfully, from the lies of religionists who 'heal the wounds of this people lightly,' from the lies of moralists who pretend to promote me to the office of captain of my fate, from the lies of pastors who 'leave the commandment of God, and hold fast the tradition of men' (Mk 7:8). Rescue me from the person who tells me of life and omits Christ, who is wise in the ways of the world and ignores the movement of the Spirit.

The lies are impeccably factual. They contain no errors. There are no distortions or falsified data. But they are lies all the same because they claim to tell us who we are and omit everything about our origin in God and our destiny in God. They talk about the world without telling us that God made it. They tell us about our bodies without telling us that they are temples of the Holy Spirit. They instruct us in love without telling us about the God who loves us and gave himself for us.

Lightning Illuminates the Crossroads

The single word *Lord* occurs only once in this psalm, but it is the clue to the whole. God, once admitted to the consciousness, fills the entire horizon. God, revealed in his creative and redemptive work, exposes all the lies. The moment the word *God* is uttered, the world's towering falsehood is exposed – we see the truth. The truth about me is that God made and loves me. The truth about those sitting beside me is that God made them and loves them, and that each one is therefore my neighbour. The truth about the world is that God rules and provides for it. The truth about what is wrong with the world is that I and the neighbour sitting beside me have sinned in refusing to let God be for us, over us and in us. The truth about what is at the centre of our lives and of our history is that Jesus Christ was crucified on the cross for our sins and raised from the tomb for our salvation and that we can participate in new life as we believe in him, accept his mercy, respond to his love, attend to his commands.

John Baillie wrote, 'I am sure that the bit of the road that most requires to be illuminated is the point where it forks.'[1] The psalmists *Lord* is a lightning flash illuminating just such a crossroads. Psalm 120 is the decision to take one way as over against the other. It is the turning point marking the transition from a dreamy nostalgia for a better life to a rugged pilgrimage of discipleship in faith, from complaining about how bad things are to pursuing all things good. This decision is said and sung on every continent in every language. The decision has been realized in every sort of life in every century in the long history of mankind. The decision is quietly (and sometimes not so quietly) announced from thousands of Christian pulpits all over the world each Sunday morning. The decision is witnessed by millions in homes, factories, schools, businesses, offices and fields every day of every week. The people who make the decision and take delight in it are the people called Christians.

A No That Is a Yes

The first step toward God is a step away from the lies of the world. It is a renunciation of the lies we have been told about ourselves and our neighbours and our universe. 'Woe is me, that I sojourn in Meshech, that I dwell among the tents of Kedar! Too long have I had my dwelling among those who hate peace.' Meshech and Kedar are place names: Meshech a far-off tribe, thousands of miles from Palestine in southern Russia; Kedar a wandering Bedouin tribe of barbaric reputation along Israel's borders. They represent the strange and the hostile. Paraphrased, the cry is, 'I live in the midst of hoodlums and wild savages; this world is not my home and I want out.'

The usual biblical word describing the no we say to the world's lies and the yes we say to God's truth is *repentance*. It is always and everywhere the first word in the Christian life. John the Baptist's preaching was, 'Repent, for the kingdom of heaven is at hand' (Mt 3:2). Jesus' first preaching was the same: 'Repent, for the kingdom of heaven is at hand' (Mt 4:17). Peter concluded his first sermon with 'Repent, and be baptized' (Acts 2:38). In the last book of the Bible the message to the seventh church is 'be zealous and repent' (Rev 3:19).

Repentance is not an emotion. It is not feeling sorry for your sins. It is a decision. It is deciding that you have been wrong in supposing that you could manage your own life and be your own god; it is deciding that you were wrong in thinking that you had, or could get, the strength, education and training to make it on your own; it is deciding that you have been told a pack of lies about yourself and your neighbours and your world. And it is deciding that God in Jesus Christ is telling you the truth. Repentance is a realization that what God wants from you and what you want from God are not going to be achieved by doing the same old things, thinking the same old thoughts. Repentance is a decision to follow Jesus Christ and become his pilgrim in the path of peace.

Repentance is the most practical of all words and the most practical of all acts. It is a feet-on-the-ground kind of word. It puts a person in touch with the reality which God creates. Elie Weisel, in referring to the stories of the Hasidim, says that in the tales by Israel of Rizhim one motif comes back again and again: a traveller loses his way in the forest; it is dark and he is afraid. Danger lurks behind every tree. A storm shatters the silence. The fool looks at the lightning, the wise man at the road that lies – illuminated – before him.[2]

Whenever we say no to one way of life that we have long been used to, there is pain. But when the way of life is, in fact, a way of death, a way of war, the quicker we leave it the better. There is a condition that sometimes develops in our bodies called adhesions – parts of our internal organs become attached to other parts. The condition has to be corrected by a surgical procedure – a decisive intervention. The procedure hurts, but the results are healthy. As the Jerusalem Bible puts verses 3-4, 'How will he [God] pay back the false oath of a faithless tongue? With war arrows hardened over red-hot charcoal!' Emily Dickinson's spare sentence is an epigraph: 'Renunciation – the piercing virtue!'

God's arrows are judgments aimed at provoking repentance. The pain of judgment, called down against the evildoers could turn them also from their deceitful and violent ways to join our pilgrim on the way of peace. Any hurt is worth it that puts us on the path of peace, setting us free for the pursuit, in Christ, of eternal life. It is the action that follows the realization that history is not a blind alley, and guilt not an abyss. It is the discovery that there is always a way that leads out of distress – a way that begins in repentance, or turning to God. Whenever we find God's people living in distress there is always someone who provides this hope-charged word, showing the reality of a different day: 'In that day there will be a highway from Egypt to Assyria, and the Assyrian will come into Egypt, and the Egyptians into Assyria, and the Egyptians will worship with the Assyrians' (Is 19:23-25). All Israel knew of Assyria was war – the vision shows them at worship. Repentance is the catalytic agent for the change. Dismay is transformed into what a later prophet would describe as gospel.

The whole history of Israel is set in motion by two such acts of world rejection, which freed the people for an affirmation of God: 'the rejection of Mesopotamia in the days of Abraham and the rejection of Egypt in the days of Moses.'[3] All the wisdom and strength of the ancient world was in Mesopotamia and Egypt. But Israel said no to it. Despite the prestige, the vaunted and uncontested greatness, there was something foundationally alien and false in those cultures: 'I am for peace; but when I speak, they are for war!' Mesopotamian power and Egyptian wisdom were strength and intelligence divorced from God, put to the wrong ends and producing all the wrong results.

Modern interpretations of history are variations on the lies of the Mesopotamians and Egyptians in which, as Abraham Heschel describes it, 'man reigns supreme, with the forces of nature as his only possible adversaries. Man is alone, free, and growing stronger. God is either nonexistent or unconcerned. It is human initiative that makes history, and it is primarily by force that constellations change. Man can attain his own salvation.'[4]

So Israel said no and became a pilgrim people, picking a path of peace and righteousness through the battlefields of falsehood and violence, finding a path to God through the labyrinth of sin.

We know that Israel, in saying that no, did not miraculously return to Eden and live in primitive innocence, or mystically inhabit a heavenly city and live in supernatural ecstasy. They worked and played, suffered and sinned in the world as everyone else did, and as Christians still do. But they were now *going* someplace – they were going to God. The truth of God explained their lives, the grace of God fulfilled their lives, the forgiveness of God renewed their lives, the love of God blessed their lives. The no released them to a freedom that was diverse and glorious. The judgment of God invoked against the people of Meshech and Kedar was, in fact, a sharply worded invitation to repentance, asking them to join in the journey.

Among the more fascinating pages of American history are those that tell stories of the immigrants to these shores in the nineteenth century. Thousands upon thousands of people, whose lives in Europe had become mean and poor, persecuted and wretched, left. They had heard of a place where a new start could be made and had reports of a land where the environment was a challenge instead of an oppression. The stories continue to be told in many families, keeping alive the memory of the event that made an American out of what was a German or an Italian or Scot.

My grandfather left Norway eighty years ago in the midst of a famine. His wife and ten children remained behind until he could return and get them. He came to Pittsburgh and worked in the steel mills for two years until he had enough money to go back and get his family. When he returned with them he didn't stay in Pittsburgh although it had served his purposes well enough the first time, but he travelled on to Montana, plunging into new land, looking for a better place.

In all these immigrant stories there are mixed parts of escape and adventure; the escape from an unpleasant situation; the adventure of a far better way of life, free for new things, open for growth and creativity. Every Christian has some variation on this immigrant plot to tell.

'Woe is me, that I sojourn in Meshech, that I dwell among the tents of Kedar! Too long have I had my dwelling among those who hate peace.' But we don't have to live there any longer. Repentance, the first word in Christian immigration, sets us on the way to travelling in the light. It is a rejection that is also an acceptance, a leaving that develops into an arriving, a no to the world that is a yes to God.

3

Providence

'Keep You from All Evil'

I lift up my eyes to the hills.
From whence does my help come?
My help comes from the Lord,
who made heaven and earth.

He will not let your foot be moved,
he who keeps you will not slumber.
Behold, he who keeps Israel
will neither slumber nor sleep.

The Lord is your keeper;
the Lord is your shade
on your right hand.
The sun shall not smite you by day,
nor the moon by night.

The Lord will keep you from all evil;
he will keep your life.
The Lord will keep
your going out and your coming in
from this time forth and for evermore.

Psalm 121

> *But to deviate from the truth for the sake of some prospect of hope of our own can never be wise, however slight that deviation may be. It is not our judgement of the situation which can show us what is wise, but only the truth of the World of God. Here alone lies the promise of God's faithfulness and help. It will always be true that the wisest course for the disciple is always to abide solely by the Word of God in all simplicity.*
>
> DIETRICH BONHOEFFER

THE MOMENT WE SAY NO TO THE WORLD AND YES TO God all our problems are solved, all our questions answered, all our troubles over. Nothing can disturb the tranquillity of the soul at peace with God. Nothing can interfere with the blessed assurance that all is well between me and my Saviour. Nothing and no one can upset the enjoyable relationship which has been established by faith in Jesus Christ. We Christians are among that privileged company of persons who don't have accidents, who don't have arguments with our spouses, who aren't misunderstood by our peers, whose children do not disobey us.

If any of those things should happen – a crushing doubt, a squall of anger, a desperate loneliness, an accident that puts us in the hospital, an argument that puts us in the doghouse, a rebellion that puts us on the defensive, a misunderstanding that puts us in the wrong – it is a sign that something is wrong with our relationship with God. We have, consciously or unconsciously, retracted our yes to God; and God, impatient with our fickle faith, has gone off to take care of someone more deserving of his attention.

Is that what you believe? If it is, I have some incredibly good news for you. You are wrong.

To be told that we are wrong is sometimes an embarrassment, even a humiliation. We want to run and hide our heads in shame. But there are times when finding out we are wrong is sudden and immediate relief, and we can lift up our heads in hope. No longer do we have to keep doggedly trying to do something that isn't working.

A few years ago I was in my backyard with my lawn mower tipped on its side. I was trying to get the blade off so that I could sharpen it. I had my biggest wrench attached to the nut, but couldn't budge it. I got a four-foot length of pipe and slipped it over the wrench handle to give me leverage, and was leaning on that – still unsuccessfully. Next I took a large rock and was banging on the pipe. By this time I was beginning to get emotionally involved with my lawn mower. Then my neighbour walked over and said that he had a lawn mower like mine once and that, if he remembered correctly, the threads on the bolt went the other way. I reversed my exertions and, sure enough, the nut turned easily. I was glad to have been wrong. I was saved from frustration and failure. I would never have got the job done, no matter how hard I tried, doing it my way.

Psalm 121 is a quiet voice, gently and kindly telling us that we are, perhaps, wrong in the way we are going about the Christian life, and then, very simply, showing us the right way. As such it is the necessary sequel to the previous psalm which gets us started on the Christian way. It put a name to the confused and bewildering feelings of alienation and distrust that made us dissatisfied and restless in a way of life that ignores or rejects God, and prodded us into the repentance that renounces the 'devil and all his works' and affirms the way of faith in Jesus Christ.

But no sooner have we plunged, expectantly and enthusiastically, into the river of Christian faith than we get our noses full of water and come up coughing and choking. No sooner do we confidently stride out on to the road of faith than we trip on an obstruction and fall to the hard surface, bruising our knees and elbows. For many, the first great surprise of the Christian life is in the form of troubles we meet. Somehow it is not what we had supposed: we had expected something quite different; we had our minds set on Eden or New Jerusalem. We are rudely awakened to something very different and we look around for help, scanning the horizon for someone who will give us aid: 'I lift up my eyes to the hills. From whence does my help come?'

Psalm 121 is the neighbour coming over and telling us we are doing it the wrong way, looking in the wrong place for help. Psalm 121 is addressed to those of us who, 'disregarding God, gaze to a distance all around them, and make long and devious circuits in quest of remedies to their troubles.'[1]

Travellers' Advisory

Three possibilities for harm to travellers are referred to in the psalm. A person travelling on foot can, at any moment, step on a loose stone and sprain his ankle. A person travelling on foot, under the protracted exposure to a hot sun, can become faint with sunstroke. And a person travelling for a long distance on foot, under the pressures of fatigue and anxiety, can become emotionally ill, which was described by ancient writers as moonstroke (or by us as *lunacy*).

We can update the list of dangers. Provisions for law and order can break down with dismaying ease: a crazed person with a handgun or piece of explosive can turn the computerized travel plans of three hundred air passengers into instant anarchy. Disease can break through our pharmaceutical defences and invade our bodies with crippling pain and death.

An accident – in an automobile, from a stepladder, on an athletic field – can without warning interrupt our carefully laid plans. We take precautions by learning safety rules, fastening our seat belts and taking out insurance policies. But we cannot guarantee security.

In reference to these hazards the psalm says, 'He will not let your foot be moved . . . The sun shall not smite you by day, nor the moon by night.' Are we to conclude then that Christians never sprain their ankles, never get sunstroke, never have any emotional problems? That is what it sounds like. Yet we know plenty of instances to the contrary. Some of the best Christians I know have sprained their ankles, have fainted, have been over-wrought with anxiety. Put that way, either I'm wrong (these people I thought were Christians really weren't and therefore the psalm doesn't apply to them) or the psalm is wrong (God doesn't do what the psalm claims).

Help from the Hills?

But neither the psalm nor our experience are so easily disposed of. A psalm which has enjoyed high regard among Christians so long, must have truth in it that is verified in Christian living. Let's return to the psalm: the person set on the way of faith gets into trouble, looks around for help ('I lift up my eyes to the hills') and asks a question: 'From whence does my help come?' As this person of faith looks around at the hills for help, what is he, what is she, going to see?

Some magnificent scenery for one thing. Is there anything more inspiring than a ridge of mountains silhouetted against the sky? Does any part of this earth promise more in terms of majesty and strength, of firmness and solidity, than the mountains? But a Hebrew would see something else. During the time this psalm was written and sung, Palestine was overrun with popular pagan worship. Much of this religion was practiced on hilltops. Shrines were set up, groves of trees were planted, sacred prostitutes both male and female were provided; persons were lured to the shrines to engage in acts of worship that would enhance the fertility of the land, would make you feel good, would protect you from evil. There were nostrums, protections, spells and enchantments against all the perils of the road. Do you fear the sun's heat? Go to the sun priest and pay for protection against the sun god. Are you fearful of the malign influence of moonlight? Go to the moon priestess and buy an amulet. Are you haunted by the demons that can use any pebble under your foot to trip you? Go to the shrine and learn the magic formula to ward off the mischief. From whence shall my help come? from Baal? from Asherah? from the sun priest? from the moon priestess?[2]

They must have been a shabby lot: immoral, diseased, drunken – frauds and cheats all. The legends of Baal are full of the tales of his orgies, the difficulty of rousing him out of a drunken sleep to get his attention. Elijah taunting the priests of Baal ('Perhaps he is asleep and must be awakened,' 1 Kgs 18:27) is the evidence. But shabby or not, they promised help. A traveller in trouble would hear their offer.

That is the kind of thing a Hebrew, set out on the way of faith twenty-five hundred years ago, would have seen on the hills. It is what disciples still see. A person of faith encounters trial or tribulation and cries out, 'Help.' We lift our eyes to the hills, and offers of help, instant and numerous, appear. 'From whence does my help come?' From the hills? No. 'My help comes from the Lord, who made heaven and earth.'

A look to the hills for help ends in disappointment. For all their majesty and beauty, for all their quiet strength and firmness, they are, finally, just hills. And for all their promises of safety against the perils of the road, for all the allurements of their priests and priestesses, they are, all, finally, lies. As Jeremiah put it: 'Truly the hills are a delusion, the orgies on the mountains' (Jer 3:23).[3]

And so Psalm 121 says no. It rejects a worship of nature, a religion of stars and flowers, a religion that makes the best of what it finds on the hills; instead it looks to the Lord who made heaven and earth. Help comes from the Creator, not from the creation. The Creator is always awake: he will not slumber or sleep. Baal took long naps, and one of the jobs of the priests was to wake him up when someone needed his attention – and they were not always successful. The Creator is Lord over time: he 'will keep your going out and your coming in,' your beginnings and your endings. He is with you when you set out on your way; he is still with you when you arrive at your destination. You don't need to, in the meantime, get supplementary help from the sun or the moon. The Creator is Lord over all natural and supernatural forces: he made them. Neither sun, moon nor rocks have any spiritual power. They are not able to inflict evil upon us: we need not fear any supernatural assault from any of them. 'The Lord will keep you from all evil.'

The promise of the psalm – and both Hebrews and Christians have always read it this way – is not that we shall never stub our toes, but that no injury, no illness, no accident, no distress will have evil power over us, that is, will be able to separate us from God's purposes in us.

No literature is more realistic and honest in facing the harsh facts of life than the Bible. At no time is there the faintest suggestion that the life of faith exempts us from difficulties. What it promises is preservation from all the evil in them. On every page of the Bible there is recognition that faith encounters troubles. The sixth petition in the Lord's Prayer is 'Lead us not into temptation, but deliver us from evil.' That prayer is answered every day, sometimes many times a day, in the lives of those who walk in the way of faith. St Paul wrote, 'No temptation has overtaken you that is not common to man. God is faithful, and he will not let you be tempted beyond your strength, but with the temptation will also provide the way of escape, that you may be able to endure it' (1 Cor 10:13).

Five times in Psalm 121 God is referred to by the personal name *Lord.* Six times he is described as the *keeper.* He is not an impersonal executive that gives orders from on high; he is our present help every step of the way we travel. Do you think the way to tell the story of the Christian way is to describe its trials and tribulations? It is not. It is to name and to describe God who preserves, accompanies and rules us.

All the water in all the oceans cannot sink a ship unless it gets inside. Nor can all the trouble in the world harm us unless it gets within us. That is the promise of the psalm: 'The Lord will keep you from all evil.' Not the demon in the loose stone, not the fierce attack of the sun god, not the malign influence of the moon goddess – not any of these can separate you from God's call and purpose. From the time of your repentance that got you out of Kedar and Meshech to the time of your glorification with the saints in heaven, you are safe: 'The Lord will keep you from all evil.' None of the things that happen to you, none of the troubles you encounter, have any power to get between you and God, dilute his grace in you, divert his will from you (see Rom 8:28, 31-32).

The only serious mistake we can make when illness comes, when anxiety threatens, when conflict disturbs our relationships with others is to conclude that God has got bored of looking after us and has shifted his attention to a more exciting Christian, or that God has become disgusted with our meandering obedience and decided to let us fend for ourselves for a while, or that God has become too busy fulfilling prophecy in the Middle East to take time now to sort out the complicated mess we have got ourselves into. That is the *only* serious mistake we can make. It is the mistake that Psalm 121 prevents: the mistake of supposing that God's interest in us waxes and wanes in response to our spiritual temperature.

The great danger of Christian discipleship is that we should have two religions: a glorious, biblical Sunday gospel that sets us free from the world, that in the cross and resurrection of Christ makes eternity alive in us, a magnificent gospel of Genesis and Romans and Revelation; and, then, an everyday religion that we make do with during the week between the time of leaving the world and arriving in heaven. We save the Sunday gospel for the big crises of existence. For the mundane trivialities – the times when our foot slips on a loose stone, or the heat of the sun gets too much for us, or the influence of the moon gets us down – we use the everyday religion of the *Reader's Digest* reprint, advice from a friend, an Ann Landers column, the huckstered wisdom of a talk-show celebrity. We practice patent-medicine religion: we know that God created the universe and has accomplished our eternal salvation. But we can't believe that he condescends to watch the soap opera of our daily trials and tribulations; so we purchase our own remedies for that. To ask him to deal with what troubles us each day is like asking a famous surgeon to put iodine on a scratch.

But Psalm 121 says that the same faith that works in the big things works in the little things. The God of Genesis 1 who brought light out of darkness is also the God of this day who keeps you from all evil.

Travelling Companion

The Christian life is not a quiet escape to a garden where we can walk and talk uninterruptedly with our Lord; not a fantasy trip to a heavenly city where we can compare our blue ribbons and gold medals with others who have made it to the winner's circle. To suppose that, or to expect that, is to turn the nut the wrong way. The Christian life is going to God. In going to God Christians travel the same ground that everyone else walks on, breathe the same air, drink the same water, shop in the same stores, read the same newspapers, are citizens under the same governments, pay the same prices for groceries and petrol, fear the same dangers, are subject to the same pressures, get the same distresses, are buried in the same ground.

The difference is that each step we walk, each breath we breathe, we know we are preserved by God, we know we are accompanied by God, we know we are ruled by God; and therefore no matter what doubts we endure or what accidents we experience, the Lord will preserve us from evil, he will keep our life. We know the truth of Luther's hymn: 'And though this world, with devils filled, should threaten to undo us, we will not fear, for God hath willed His truth to triumph through us. The prince of darkness grim, we tremble not for him; his rage we can endure, for Lo! his doom is sure; one little word shall fell him.' We Christians believe that life is created and shaped by God and that the life of faith is a daily exploration of the constant and countless ways in which God's grace and love are experienced.

Psalm 121, learned early and sung repeatedly in the walk with Christ, clearly defines the conditions under which we live out our discipleship, which, in a word, is God. Once we get this psalm in our hearts it will be impossible for us to gloomily suppose that being a Christian is an unending battle against ominous forces that at any moment may break through and overpower us. Faith is not a precarious affair of chance escape from satanic assaults. It is the solid, massive, secure experience of God who keeps all evil from getting inside us, who keeps our life, who keeps our going out and our coming in from this time forth and forevermore.

4

Worship

'Let Us Go to the House of the Lord!'

I was glad when they said to me,
'Let us go to the house of the Lord!'
Our feet have been standing
within your gates, O Jerusalem!

Jerusalem, built as a city
which is bound firmly together,
to which the tribes go up,
the tribes of the Lord,
as was decreed for Israel,
to give thanks to the name of the Lord.
There thrones for judgment were set,
the thrones of the house of David.

Pray for the peace of Jerusalem!
'May they prosper who love you!
Peace be within your walls,
and security within your towers!'
For my brethren and companions' sake
I will say, 'Peace be within you!'
For the sake of the house of the Lord our God,
I will seek your good.

PSALM 122

> *There is something morally repulsive about modern activistic theories which deny contemplation and recognize nothing but struggle. For them not a single moment has value in itself, but is only a means for what follows.*
>
> NICHOLAS BERDYAEV

ONE OF THE AFFLICTIONS OF PASTORAL WORK HAS BEEN TO listen, with a straight face, to all the reasons people give for not going to church: 'My mother made me when I was little.' 'There are too many hypocrites in the church.' 'It's the only day I have to sleep in.' There was a time when I responded to such statements with simple arguments that exposed them as flimsy excuses. Then I noticed that it didn't make any difference. If I showed the inadequacy of one excuse, three more would pop up in its place. So I don't respond anymore. I listen (with a straight face) and go home and pray that that person will one day find the one sufficient reason for going to church, which is God. I go about my work hoping that what I do and say will be usable by the Holy Spirit to create in that person a determination to worship God in a Christian community.

Many people do: they decide to worship God, faithfully and devoutly. It is one of the important acts in a life of discipleship. And what is far more interesting than the reasons (excuses) people give for not worshiping, is discovering the reasons why they do.

Psalm 122 is the song of a person who decides to go to church and worship God. It is a sample of the complex, diverse and worldwide phenomenon of worship that is common to all Christians. It is an excellent instance of what happens when a person worships.

Psalm 122 is third in the sequence of the Psalms of Ascents. Psalm 120 is the psalm of repentance – the no that gets us out of an environment of deceit and hostility and sets us on our way to God. Psalm 121 is the psalm of trust – a demonstration of how faith resists patent-medicine remedies to trials and tribulations and determinedly trusts God to work out his will and 'keep you from all evil' in the midst of difficulty. Psalm 122 is the psalm of worship – an example of what people of faith everywhere and always do: gather to an assigned place and worship their God.

An Instance of the Average

The first line catches many by surprise. 'I was glad when they said to me, "Let us go to the house of the Lord!"' But it shouldn't. Worship is the most popular thing that Christians do. A great deal of what we call Christian behaviour has become part of our legal system and is embedded in our social expectations, both of which have strong coercive powers. If we removed all laws from society and eliminated all consequences for antisocial acts, we don't know how much murder, how much theft, how much perjury and falsification would take place. But we do know that much of what we commonly describe as Christian behaviour is not volitional at all – it is enforced.

But worship is not forced. Everyone who worships does so because he or she wants to. There are, to be sure, a few temporary coercions – children and spouses who attend church because another has decided that they must. But these coercions are short-lived, a few years at most. Most Christian worship is voluntary. An excellent way to test people's values is to observe what we do when we don't *have* to do anything, how we spend our leisure time, how we spend our extra money.

Even in a time when church attendance is not considered to be on the upswing, the numbers are impressive. There are more people at worship on any given Sunday, for instance, than are at all the football games or on the golf links or fishing or taking walks in the woods. Worship is the single most popular act in this land.

So when we hear the psalmist say, 'I was glad when they said to me, "Let us go to the house of the Lord."' we are not listening to the phony enthusiasm of a propagandist drumming up business for worship; we are witnessing what is typical of most Christians in most places at most times. This is not an exception to which we aspire; it is an instance of the average.

A Framework

Why do we do it? Why is there so much voluntary and faithful worship by Christians? Why is it that we never find a Christian life without, in the background somewhere, an act of worship, never find Christian communities without also finding Christian worship? Why is it that worship is the common background to all Christian existence and that is so faithfully and willingly practiced? The psalm singles out three items: worship gives us a workable structure for life; worship nurtures our needs to be in relationship with God; worship centres our attention on the decisions of God.

Worship gives us a workable structure for life. The psalm says, 'Jerusalem, built as a city which is bound firmly together, to which the tribes go up, the tribes of the Lord.' Jerusalem, for a Hebrew was *the* place of worship (only incidentally was it the geographical centre of the country and the political seat of authority). The great worship festivals to which everyone came at least three times a year were held in Jerusalem. In Jerusalem everything that God said was remembered and celebrated. When you went to Jerusalem, you encountered the great foundational realities: God created you, God redeemed you, God provided for you. In Jerusalem you saw in ritual and heard proclaimed in preaching the powerful history-shaping truth that God forgives our sins and makes it possible to live without guilt and with purpose. In Jerusalem all the scattered fragments of experience, all the bits and pieces of truth and feeling and perception were put together in a single whole.

The King James Version translates this sentence, 'Jerusalem is builded as a city that is compact together.' Earlier, Coverdale had translated the phrase, 'That is at unity with itself.' The city itself was a kind of architectural metaphor for what worship is: all the pieces of masonry fit compactly, all the building stones fit harmoniously. There were no loose stones, no leftover pieces, no awkward gaps in the walls or towers. It was well built, compactly built, skillfully built, 'at unity with itself'.

What is true architecturally is also true socially, for the sentence continues, '... to which the tribes go up, the tribes of the Lord.' In worship all the different tribes functioned as a single people in harmonious relationship. In worship though we have come from different places and out of various conditions, we are demonstrably after the same things, saying the same things, doing the same things. With all our differing levels of intelligence and wealth, background and language, rivalries and resentments, still, in worship we are gathered into a single whole. Outer quarrels and misunderstandings and differences pale into insignificance as the inner unity of what God builds in the act of worship is demonstrated.

When a person is confused and things refuse to fit together, he sometimes announces a need to get out of the noise and turbulence, to get away from all the hassle and 'get my head together'. When he succeeds in doing this we call that person 'put together'. All the parts are there, nothing is left out, nothing is out of proportion, everything fits into a workable frame.

As I entered a home to make a pastoral visit, the person I came to see was sitting at a window embroidering a piece of cloth held taut over an oval hoop. She said, 'Pastor, while waiting for you to come I realized what's wrong with me – I don't have a frame. My feelings, my thoughts, my activities – everything is loose and sloppy. There is no border to my life. I never know where I am. I need a frame for my life like this one I have for my embroidery.'

How do we get that framework, that sense of solid structure so that we know where we stand and are therefore able to do our work easily and without anxiety? Christians go to worship: week by week we enter the place compactly built, 'to which the tribes go up' and get a working definition for life: the way God created us, the ways in which he leads us. We know where we stand.

A Command

Another reason Christians keep returning to worship is that it nurtures our need to be in relationship with God. Worship is the place where we obey the command to praise God: 'as was decreed for Israel, to give thanks to the name of the Lord.' This command runs right down the centre of all Christian worship. A decree. A word telling us what we ought to do; and what we ought to do is praise.

When we sin and mess up our lives, we find that God doesn't go off and leave us – he enters into our trouble and saves us. That is good, an instance of what the Bible calls gospel. We discover reasons and motivations for living in faith and find that God is already helping us to do it – and that is good. Praise God! 'A Christian,' wrote Augustine, 'should be an alleluia from head to foot.' That is the reality. That is the truth of our lives. God made us, redeems us, provides for us. The natural, honest, healthy, logical response to that is praise to God. When we praise we are functioning at the centre, we are in touch with the basic, core reality of our being.

But very often we don't feel like it, and so we say, 'It would be dishonest for me to go to a place of worship and praise God when I don't feel like it. I would be a hypocrite.' The psalm says, I don't care whether you feel like it or not: as was *decreed,* 'give thanks to the name of the Lord.'

I have put great emphasis on the fact that Christians worship because they want to, not because they are forced to. But I have never said that we worship because we *feel* like it. Feelings are great liars. If Christians only worshipped when they felt like it, there would be precious little worship that went on. Feelings are important in many areas, but completely unreliable in matters of faith. Paul Scherer is laconic: 'The Bible wastes very little time on the way we feel.'[1] We live in what one writer has called the 'age of sensation'.[2] We think that if we don't *feel* something there can be no authenticity in *doing* it. But the wisdom of God says something different, namely, that we can *act* ourselves into a new way of feeling much quicker than we can *feel* ourselves into a new way of acting. Worship is an *act* which develops feelings for God, not a *feeling* for God which is expressed in an act of worship. When we obey the command to praise God in worship, our deep, essential need to be in relationship with God is nurtured.

A Word of God

A third reason we keep engaging in regular acts of worship is that in it our attention is centred on the decisions of God.

Our psalm describes worship as the place where 'thrones for judgment were set, the thrones of the house of David.' The biblical word *judgment* means 'the decisive word by which God straightens things out and puts things right.' Thrones of judgment are the places that that word is announced. Judgment is not a word *about* things, describing them; it is a word which *does* things, putting love in motion, applying mercy, nullifying wrong, ordering goodness. This word of God is everywhere in worship. In the call to worship we hear God's first word to us; in the benediction we hear God's last word to us; in the Scripture lessons we hear God speaking to our fathers; in the sermon we hear that word re-expressed to us; in the hymns, which are all to a greater or lesser extent paraphrases of Scripture, the Word of God makes our prayers articulate. Every time we worship our minds are informed, our memories refreshed with the judgments of God, we are familiarized with what God says, what he has decided, the ways he is working out our salvation.

There is simply no place where these can be done as well as in worship. If we stay at home by ourselves and read the Bible, we are going to miss a lot, for our reading will be unconsciously conditioned by our culture, limited by our ignorance, distorted by unnoticed prejudices. On worship we are part of 'the large congregation' where all the writers of Scripture address us, where hymn writers use music to express truths which touch us not only in our heads but in our hearts, where the preacher who has just lived through six days of doubt, hurt, faith and blessing with the worshippers, speaks the truth of Scripture in the language of the congregation's present experience. We want to hear what God says and what he says to us: worship is the place where our attention is centred on these personal and decisive words of God.

Peace and Security

Worship, even for those who are most faithful at it, takes up a small percentage of a person's life, an hour or so a week at most. Does it make any difference to the rest of the week? The final words of Psalm 122 say that it does: 'Pray for the peace of Jerusalem! "May they prosper who love you! Peace be within your walls, and security within your towers!" For my brethren and companions' sake I will say, "Peace be within you!" For the sake of the house of the Lord our God, I will seek your good.' Here we have prayers that overflow the bounds of worship and create new relationships in the city, in society.

The first word, *pray,* is a transition into the everyday world. It is not the word ordinarily used in formal worship, but the everyday Hebrew word for 'ask.' It is not improperly translated 'pray' for when we ask from God we pray. But the asking is not a formal prayer in the sanctuary; it is an informal asking as we go about our business between Sundays. It is the word Hebrews would use to ask for a second helping of potatoes if still hungry, or for directions if lost.

Worship does not satisfy our hunger for God – it whets our appetite. Our need for God is not taken care of by engaging in worship – it deepens. It overflows the hour and permeates the week. The need is expressed in a desire for peace and security. Our everyday needs are changed by the act of worship. We are no longer living from hand to mouth, greedily scrambling through the human rat race to make the best we can out of a mean existence. Our basic needs suddenly become worthy of the dignity of creatures made in the image of God: peace and security. The words *shalom* and *shalvah,* play on the sounds in Jerusalem, *jerushalom,* the place of worship.

Shalom, peace, is one of the richest words in the Bible. You can no more define it by looking up its meaning in the dictionary than you can define a person by his social security number. It gathers all aspects of wholeness that result from God's will being completed in us. It is the work of God that, when complete, releases streams of living water in us and pulsates with eternal life. Every time Jesus healed, forgave or called someone, we have a demonstration of *shalom*.

And *shalvah,* security. It has nothing to do with insurance policies or large bank accounts or stockpiles of weapons. The root meaning is leisure – the relaxed stance of one who knows that everything is all right because God is over us, with us and for us in Jesus Christ. It is the security of being at home in a history that has a cross at its centre. It is the leisure of the person who knows that every moment of our existence is at the disposal of God, lived under the mercy of God.

Worship initiates an extended, daily participation in peace and security so that we share in our daily rounds what God initiates and continues in Jesus Christ.

A Pause to Sharpen a Tool

We live in a pragmatic age and are reluctant to do anything if its practical usefulness cannot be demonstrated. It is inevitable that we ask regarding worship, is it worth it? Can you justify the time and energy and expense involved in gathering Christians together in worship? Well, 'Look at the mower in the summer's day, with so much to cut down ere the sun sets. He pauses in his labour – is he a sluggard? He looks for his stone, and begins to draw it up and down his scythe, with rink-atink, rink-atink, rink-atink. Is that idle music – is he wasting precious moments? How much he might have mowed while he has been ringing out those notes on his scythe! But he is sharpening his tool, and he will do far more when once again he gives his strength to those long sweeps which lay the grass prostrate in rows before him.'[3]

5

Service

'Our Eyes Look to the Lord Our God'

To thee I lift up my eyes,
O thou who art enthroned
in the heavens!
Behold, as the eyes of servants
look to the hand of their master,
as the eyes of a maid
to the hand of her mistress,
so our eyes look to the Lord our God,
till he have mercy upon us.

Have mercy upon us, O Lord, have mercy upon us,
for we have had more than enough of contempt.
Too long our soul has been sated
with the scorn of those who are at ease,
the contempt of the proud.

PSALM 123

In general terms, service is a willing, working, and doing in which a person acts not according to his own purposes or plans but with a view to the purpose of another person and according to the need, disposition, and direction of others. It is an act whose freedom is limited and determined by the other's freedom, an

> *act whose glory becomes increasingly greater to the extent that the doer is not concerned about his own glory but about the glory of the other. . . . It is* ministerium Verbi divini, *which means, literally, 'a servant's attendance on the divine Word.' The expression 'attendance' may call to mind the fact that the New Testament concept of* Diakonos *originally meaning 'a waiter'. [We] must wait upon the high majesty of the divine Word, which is God himself as he speaks in his action.*
>
> KARL BARTH

AS A PERSON GROWS AND MATURES IN THE CHRISTIAN WAY, it is necessary to acquire certain skills. One is service. The skill is so difficult to acquire and liable to so many misunderstandings that it is necessary to single it out for special attention from time to time.

Psalm 123 is an instance of service. In this, as so often in the psalms, we are not instructed in what to do, we are provided an instance of what is done. A psalm is not a lecture; it is a song. In a psalm we have the observable evidence of what happens when a person of faith goes about the business of believing and loving and following God. We don't have a rule book defining the action, we have a snapshot of the players playing the game. In Psalm 123 we observe that aspect of life of discipleship that takes place under the form of a servant.

IF GOD IS GOD AT ALL

'To thee I lift up my eyes, O thou who art enthroned in the heavens!' Service begins with an upward look to God. God is over us. He is above us. The person of faith looks up to God, not at him or down on him. The servant assumes a certain posture, a stance. If he or she fails to take that posture, attentive responsiveness to the master's commands will be hard.

It is easy to get the wrong idea, for when a person becomes a Christian there is a new sense of confident ability and assured power. Furthermore we are provided promises which tell us to go ahead: 'Ask, and it will be given you; seek, and you will find; knock and it will be opened to you' (Lk 11:9). God presents himself to us in the history of Jesus Christ as a servant: with that before us it is easy to assume the role of master and begin ordering him around. God is not a servant to be called into action when we are too tired to do something ourselves, not an expert to be called on when we find we are ill equipped to handle a specialized problem in living. Paul Scherer writes scathingly of people who lobby around in the courts of the Almighty for special favours, plucking at his sleeve, pestering him with our requests. God is not a buddy that we occasionally ask to join us at our convenience or for our diversion. God did not become a servant so that we could order him around but so that we could join him in a redemptive lifestyle.

Too often we think of religion as a far-off, mysteriously run bureaucracy to which we apply for assistance when we feel the need. We go to a local branch office and direct the clerk (sometimes called a pastor) to fill out an order for God. Then we go home and wait for God to be delivered to us according to the specifications that we have set down. But that is not the way it works. And if we thought about it for two consecutive minutes, we would not want it to work that way. If God is God at all, he must know more about our needs than we do; if God is God at all, he must be more in touch with the reality of our thoughts, our emotions, our bodies than we are; if God is God at all, he must have a more comprehensive grasp of the interrelations in our families and communities and nations than we do.

'O thou who art enthroned in the heavens!' When the Bible uses that phrase, and it does use it frequently, it is not saying anything about geography or space. Biblical writers are neither geographers nor astronomers – they are theologians. They describe with profound accuracy the relation between God and persons like you and me, a relationship between the Creator and the creature; they coordinate our knowledge of the God who loves us with our experience of being loved; they tell the story of the God who leads us through difficulties and document it with our experience of being guided. We are not presented with a functional god who will help us out of jams or an entertainment god who will lighten tedious hours. We are presented with the God of exodus and Easter, the God of Sinai and Calvary. If we want to understand God, we must do it on his terms. If we want to see God the way he really is, we must look to the place of authority – to Scripture and to Jesus Christ.

And do we really want it any other way? I don't think so. We would very soon become contemptuous of a god whom we could figure out like a puzzle or learn to use like a tool. No, if God is worth our attention at all, he must be a God we can look up to – a God we *must* look up to: 'To thee I lift up my eyes, O thou who art enthroned in the heavens!'

The moment we look up to God (and not over at him, or down on him) we are in the posture of servitude.

'Have Mercy Upon Me'

A second element in service has to do with our expectation. What happens when we look up to God in faith? There is an awesome mystery in God that we can never completely penetrate. We cannot define God; we cannot package God. But that doesn't mean that we don't know anything about God. It doesn't mean that we are completely at sea with God, never knowing what to expect, nervously on edge all the time, wondering what he might do.

We know very well what to expect, and what we expect is mercy. Three times the expectation is articulated in Psalm 123: 'Our eyes look to the Lord our God, till he have mercy upon us. Have mercy upon us, O Lord, have mercy upon us.'

The basic conviction of a Christian is that God intends good for us and that he will get his way in us. He does not treat us according to our deserts, but according to his plan. He is not a police officer on patrol, watching over the universe, ready to club us if we get out of hand or put us in jail if we get obstreperous. He is a potter, working with the clay of our lives, forming and reforming until, finally, he has shaped a redeemed life, a vessel fit for the kingdom.

'Have mercy upon us': the prayer is not an attempt to get God to do what he is unwilling, otherwise, to do, but a reaching out to what we know that he does do, an expressed longing to receive what God is doing in and for us in Jesus Christ. In obedience we pray *have mercy upon us* instead of 'give us what we want'. We pray *have mercy upon us,* and not 'reward us for our goodness so our neighbours will acknowledge our superiority'. We pray *have mercy upon us* and not 'punish us for our badness so we will feel better'. We pray *have mercy upon us* and not 'be nice to us because we have been such good people'.

We live under the mercy. God does not treat us as alien others, lining us up so that he can evaluate our competence or our usefulness or our worth. He rules, guides, commands, loves us as children whose destinies he carries in his heart.

The word *mercy* means that the upward look to God in the heavens does not expect God to stay in the heavens, but to come down, to enter our condition, to accomplish the vast enterprise of redemption, to fashion, in us, his eternal salvation. 'The root meaning "to stoop", "to be inclined", has been conjectured.'[1] Servitude is not a vague woolgathering in the general direction of God and not a cringing, cowering terror under the lash of God. Servitude is specific in its expectation, and what it expects is mercy.

Urgent Service

A third element in the servant life is urgency: 'Have mercy upon us, for we have had more than enough of contempt. Too long our soul has been sated with the scorn of those who are at ease, the contempt of the proud.'

The experience of servitude is recurrent through history. And the experience has never been happy. The psalmist lived in a culture in which the slave and the servant were institutionalized, as they have been at different times in world history. As far as we can tell, it has never worked very well. Power breeds oppression. Masters get lazy and become scornful of those under them. The cry 'too long our soul has been sated with the scorn of those who are at ease, the contempt of the proud' is believable. The psalm is part of a vast literature of outcry, a longing for deliverance from oppression.

We live in a similar slavery. True, we have, in our country, abolished the institutionalized forms of slavery and all but eliminated a servant class, but the experience of servitude is still among us and is as oppressive as ever. Freedom is on everyone's lips. Freedom is announced and celebrated. But not many feel or act free. Evidence? We live in a nation of complainers and a society of addicts. Everywhere we turn we hear complaints: I can't spend my money the way I want; I can't spend my time the way I want; I can't be myself; I'm under the control of others all the time. And everywhere we meet the addicts – addiction to alcohol and drugs, to compulsive work habits and to obsessive consumption. We trade masters; we stay enslaved.

The Christian is a person who recognizes that our real problem is not in achieving freedom but in learning service under a better master. The Christian realizes that every relationship that excludes God becomes oppressive. Recognizing and realizing that, we urgently want to live under the mastery of God.

For such reasons all Christian service involves urgency. Servitude is not a casual standing around waiting for orders. It is never desultory; it is urgent need: 'Speak Lord, for thy servant hears.' And the gospel is the good news that the words of God, commanding new life in us, are already in our ears; 'he who has ears to hear, let him hear.'

Reasonable Service

The best New Testament commentary on this psalm is in the final section of Paul's letter to the Romans, chapters 12-16. The section begins with this sentence: 'I appeal to you therefore, brethren, by the mercies of God, to present your bodies as a living sacrifice, holy and acceptable to God, which is your spiritual worship' (12:1). The psalm's emphasis on actual, physical service (not a spiritual intention, not a desire to be of service) is picked up in the invitation to present our *bodies.* The motivation for service (not coerced, not demanded) is picked up in the phrase 'by the mercy'. But most significant are the remarkable last two words, *logiken latreian,* which another translation renders 'reasonable service'. Service, that is, that makes sense. The word *latreia,* means 'service', the work one does on behalf of the community. But it also is the base of our word *liturgy,* the service of worship which we render to God. And it is precisely that service that is logical, reasonable. That service we render to God (in worship) is extended into specific acts which serve others. We learn a relationship – an attitude towards life, a stance – of servitude before God, and then we are available to be of use to others in acts of service.

The psalm has nothing in it about serving others. It concentrates on being servant to God. Its position is that if the attitude of servanthood is learned, by attending to God as Lord, then serving others will develop as a very natural way of life. Commands will be heard to be hospitable, to be compassionate, to visit the sick, to help and to heal (commands which Paul assembles in Romans 12-16 and many other places) and carried out with ease and poise.

As we live out the implications of a life of service, we are provided with continuous encouragement and example by Jesus Christ who said, 'Do you know what I have done to you? You call me Teacher and Lord; and you are right, for so I am. If I then, your Lord and Teacher, have washed your feet, you also ought to wash one another's feet. For I have given you an example, that you also should do as I have done to you. Truly, truly, I say to you, a servant is not greater than his master; nor is he who is sent greater than he who sent him. If you know these things, blessed are you if you do them' (Jn 13:12-17).

The Freest Person on Earth

God's people are everywhere and always encouraged to work for the liberation of others, helping to free them from every form of bondage – religious, economic, cultural, political – that sin uses to stunt or thwart or cramp their lives. Their promises and fulfillments of freedom are antiphonal throughout Scripture. The glorious theme has extensive documentation in the lives of the people of God. But there are also, sadly, numerous instances in our society of persons who, having been given their freedom, have at once squandered it, using it as 'an opportunity for the flesh' (Gal 5:13), ending in a worse slavery. For freedom is the freedom to live as persons in love for the sake of God and neighbour, not a licence to grab and push. It is the opportunity to live at our best, 'little less than God' (Ps 8:5), not as unruly beasts. The work of liberation must therefore be accompanied by instruction in the use of liberty as children of God who 'walk by the Spirit' (Gal 5:25). Those who parade the rhetoric of liberation but scorn the wisdom of service do not lead people into the glorious liberty of the children of God but into a cramped and covetous squalor.

As Psalm 123 prays the transition from oppression ('the contempt of the proud') to freedom ('have mercy upon us') to a new servitude ('as the eyes of servants look to the hand of their master . . . so our eyes look to the Lord'), it puts us in the way of learning how to use our freedom most appropriately, under the lordship of a merciful God. The consequences are all positive. I have never yet heard a servant Christian complain of the oppressiveness of his servitude. I have never yet heard a servant Christian rail against the restrictions of her service. A servant Christian is the freest person on earth.

6

Help

'We Have Escaped as a Bird from the Snare'

If it had not been the Lord who was on our side,
let Israel now say –
if it had not been the Lord who was on our side,
when men rose up against us,
then they would have swallowed us up alive,
when their anger was kindled against us;
then the flood would have swept us away,
the torrent would have gone over us;
then over us would have gone
the raging waters.

Blessed be the Lord,
who has not given us
as prey to their teeth!
We have escaped as a bird
from the snare of the fowlers;
the snare is broken,
and we have escaped!

Our help is in the name of the Lord,
who made heaven and earth.

Psalm 124

> *God is almost intolerably careless about crosses and swords, arenas and scaffolds, about all the 'evils' and all the 'plagues'. His caring doesn't mean that he goes in for upholstering!*
>
> PAUL SCHERER

I WAS AT A RED CROSS BLOODMOBILE TO DONATE MY ANNUAL pint, and being asked a series of questions by a nurse to see if there was any reason for disqualification. The final question on the list was, 'Do you engage in hazardous work?' I said, 'Yes'. She was interrupted from her routine and looked up, a little surprised, for I was wearing a clerical collar by which she could identify me as a pastor. Her hesitation was only momentary: she smiled, ignored my answer and marked the no on her questionnaire, saying, 'I don't mean *that* kind of hazardous.'

I would like to have continued the conversation, comparing what she supposed I meant by hazardous with what I did in fact mean by it. But that was not the appropriate time and place. There was a line of people waiting for their turn at the needle. There are, though, appropriate times and places for just such conversations, and one of them is when Christians encounter Psalm 124. Psalm 124 is a song of hazard – and of help. Among the Psalms of Ascents, sung by the people of God on the way of faith, this is one which better than any other describes the hazardous work of all discipleship and declares the help which is always experienced at the hand of God.

A CLERK IN THE COMPLAINTS DEPARTMENT OF HUMANITY

The first lines of the psalm twice describe God as 'the Lord who was on our side'. The last line is, 'Our help is in the name of the Lord, who made heaven and earth.' God is on our side. God is our help.

Statements like that are red flags to some people. They provoke challenges. I, confident and assured in the pulpit, can announce, 'The Lord is on our side. . . . Our help is in the name of the Lord.' But no sooner am I out of the pulpit than someone is saying to me, 'Look, I wish you would be a little more careful about your pronouns. How do you get this *our* . . . ? The Lord might be on *your* side, he might be *your* help. But he is not *mine*. Listen to this . . .' Through the week I get case histories of family tragedy and career disappointment, along with pessimistic recounts of world events. The concluding line is a variation on the theme: 'How do you explain that, you who are so sure that God is on my side?'

I am put on the spot of being God's defender. I am expected to explain God to his disappointed clients. I am thrust into the role of a clerk in the complaints department of humanity, asked to trace down bad service, listen sympathetically to aggrieved patrons, try to put right any mistakes that I can and apologize for the rudeness of the management.

But if I accept any of those assignments I misunderstand my proper work, for God doesn't need me to defend him. He doesn't need me for a press secretary, explaining to the world that he didn't really say what everyone thought they heard in that interview with Job, or that the quotation of his word by St Paul was taken out of context and needs to be understood against the background paper that Isaiah wrote.

The proper work for the Christian is witness, not apology, and Psalm 124 is an excellent model. It does not argue God's help; it does not explain God's help; it is a testimony of God's help in the form of a song. The song is so vigorous, so confident, so bursting with what can only be called reality, that it fundamentally changes our approach and our questions. No longer does it seem of the highest priority to ask, 'Why did this happen to me? Why do I feel left in the lurch?' Instead we ask, 'How does it happen that there are people who sing with such confidence, "God is our help"?' The psalm is data that must be accounted for and the data are so solid, so vital, have so much more substance and are so much more interesting than the other things we hear through the day that it must be dealt with before we can go back to the whimpering complaints.

'If it had not been the Lord who was on our side, let Israel now say – if it had not been the Lord who was on our side, when men rose up against us, then they would have swallowed us up alive, when their anger was kindled against us; then the flood would have swept us away, the torrent would have gone over us; then over us would have gone the raging waters.' The witness is vivid and contagious. One person announces the theme, everyone joins in. God's help is not a private experience; it is a corporate reality – not an exception that occurs among isolated strangers, but the norm among the people of God.

God's help is described by means of two illustrations. The people were in danger of being swallowed up alive; and they were in danger of being drowned by a flood. The first picture is of an enormous dragon or sea monster. Nobody has ever seen a dragon, but everyone (especially children) knows they exist. Dragons are projections of our fears, horrible constructions of all that might hurt us. A dragon is total evil. A peasant confronted by a magnificent dragon is completely outclassed. There is no escape: the dragon's thick skin, fiery mouth, lashing serpentine tail, and insatiable greed and lust sign an immediate doom. The second picture, that of the flood, is a picture of sudden disaster. In the Middle East, watercourses which have eroded the countryside are all interconnected by an intricate, gravitational system. A sudden storm fills these little gullies with water, they feed into one another, and in a very few minutes a torrential flash flood is produced. Persons who live in these desert areas are endangered during the rainy season by such unannounced catastrophies. There is no escaping. One minute you are well and happy and making plans for the future; the next minute the entire world is disarranged by a catastrophe.

The psalmist is not a person talking about the good life, how God has kept him out of all difficulty. This person has gone through the worst – the dragon's mouth, the flood's torrent – and finds himself intact. He was not abandoned but helped. The final strength is not in the dragon or in the flood but in 'the Lord who was on our side'.

We can, of course, avoid dealing with this by employing a cheap back-of-the-hand cynicism. It is inevitable, in one sense, that we should respond with some cynicism to enthusiasm. Advertisers are routinely so dishonest with us that we train ourselves to keep our distance from any who speak with passion and excitement for fear they will manipulate us. We see Pete Rose or Robert Young or Joe Dimaggio speaking on behalf of a product and inwardly discount the witness; we know the words were written by a highly paid copywriter and that the testimonial was done for a handsome fee. In the midst of that kind of world we come on the lines, 'If it had not been the Lord who was on our side, when men rose up against us, then they would have swallowed us up alive . . .' and we say, 'Vigorous poetry! Well done! But who was your copywriter, and how much did they pay you to say it?'

The only cure for that kind of cynicism is to bring it out in the open and deal with it. If it is left to work behind the scenes in our hearts, it is a parasite on faith, enervates hope and leaves us anaemic in love. Don't hesitate to put the psalm (or any other Scripture passage) under the searchlight of your disbelief! The reason many of us do not ardently believe in the gospel is that we have never given it a rigorous testing, thrown our hard questions at it, faced it with our most prickly doubts.

Subjected to our most relentless and searching criticism, Psalm 124 will, I think, finally convince us of its honesty. There is no literature in all the world that is more true to life and more honest than the Psalms, for here we have warts-and-all religion. Every skeptical thought, every disappointing venture, every pain, every despair that we can face is lived through and integrated into a personal, saving relationship with God, which relationship also has in it acts of praise, blessing, peace, security, trust and love.

Good poetry survives not when it is pretty or beautiful or nice but when it is true: accurate and honest. The Psalms are great poetry and have lasted not because they appeal to our fantasies and our wishes but because they are confirmed in the intensities of honest and hazardous living. Psalm 124 is not a selected witness, inserted like a commercial into our lives to testify that life goes better with God; it is not part of a media blitz to convince us that God is superior to all the other gods on the market. It is not a press release but honest prayer.

The people who know this psalm best and who have tested it out and used it often (that is, the people of God who are travellers on the way of faith, singing it in all kinds of weather) tell us that it is credible, that it fits into what we know of life lived in faith.

Hazardous Work

Christian discipleship is hazardous work. I hope the Red Cross nurse did not think that I was referring to my pastoral work as hazardous. My work, as such, is no more difficult than anyone else's. Any work done faithfully and well is difficult. It is no harder for me to do my job well than for any other person, and no less. There are only easy tasks which can be done faithfully or erratically, with joy or resentment. And there is no room for any of us, pastors or grocers, accountants or engineers, typists or gardeners, physicians or teamsters, to speak in tones of self-pity of the terrible burdens of our work.

What is hazardous in my life is my work as a Christian. Every day I put faith on the line. I have never seen God. In a world where nearly everything can be weighed, explained, qualified, subjected to psychological analysis and scientific control I persist in making the centre of my life a God whom no eye hath seen, nor ear heard, whose will no one can probe. That's a risk.

Every day I put hope on the line. I don't know one thing about the future. I don't know what the next hour will hold. There may be sickness, personal or world catastrophe. Before this day is over I may have to deal with death, pain, loss, rejection. I don't know what the future holds for me, for those whom I love, for my nation, for this world. Still, despite my ignorance and surrounded by tinny optimists and cowardly pessimists, I say that God will accomplish his will and cheerfully persist in living in the hope that nothing will separate me from Christ's love.

Every day I put love on the line. There is nothing I am less good at than love. I am far better in competition than in love. I am far better at responding to my instincts and ambitions to get ahead and make my mark than I am at figuring out how to love another. I am schooled and trained in acquisitive skills, in getting my own way. And yet, I decide, every day, to set aside what I can do best and attempt what I do very clumsily – open myself to the frustrations and failures of loving, daring to believe that failing in love is better than succeeding in pride.

All that is hazardous work; I live on the edge of defeat all the time. I have never done any of those things to my (or anyone else's) satisfaction. I live in the dragon's maw and at the flood's edge. 'How very hard it is to be/A Christian! Hard for you and me.'[1]

The psalm, though, is not about hazards but about help. The hazardous work of discipleship is not the subject of the psalm but only its setting. The subject is help: 'Blessed be the Lord, who has not given us as prey to their teeth! We have escaped as a bird from the snare of the fowlers; the snare is broken, and we have escaped! Our help is in the name of the Lord, who made heaven and earth.' Hazards or no hazards, the fundamental reality we live with is 'The Lord who was on our side . . . Our help is in the name of the Lord.'

When we are first in it, our consciousness of hazard is total: like a bird trapped in a snare. All the facts add up to doom. There is no way out. And then, unaccountably, there is a way out. The snare breaks and the bird escapes. Deliverance is a surprise. Rescue is a miracle. 'Blessed be the Lord, who has not given us as prey to their teeth!'

How God wants us to sing like this! Christians are not fussy moralists who cluck their tongues over a world going to hell; Christians are people who praise the God who is on our side. Christians are not pious pretenders in the midst of a decadent culture; Christians are robust witnesses to the God who is our help. Christians are not fatigued outcasts who carry righteousness as a burden in a world where the wicked flourish; Christians are people who sing 'Blessed be the Lord, who has not given us as prey to their teeth!'

Enlarged Photographs of Ordinary Objects

The final sentence, 'Our help is in the name of the Lord, who made heaven and earth,' links the God who created heaven and earth to the God who helps us personally. It takes the majesty of the one who pulled a universe into order and beauty, and finds this God involved in the local troubles of a quite ordinary person.

A friend showed me a series of pictures that he had taken. The subject matter consisted exclusively of household items found in an ordinary kitchen: a match stick, a pin, the edge of a knife. Household utensils are not ordinarily thought of as possessing much beauty, but all of these photographs of very ordinary objects were quite astonishingly beautiful. The beauty was suddenly visible because the photographs had all been made through a magnifying lens. Small, ugly, insignificant items were blown into great size and we could see what we had overlooked in our everyday routine. And it turned out that what we had overlooked was careful, planned details which produced exquisite beauty.

I remember particularly well the photograph of a highly magnified brillo pad. Nothing in the kitchen seems quite as ordinary or quite as lacking in aesthetic appeal. When possible we keep them hidden under the sink. No one would think of hanging one on a nail or a hook for people to admire. Yet under magnification the brillo pad is one of the most beautiful of kitchen items. The swirl of fine wire is pleasing to the eye. The colours of blue fade in and out of the soap film. What we assume is not worth looking at twice, and best kept in an obscure place, is, on examination, a beautiful construction.

Psalm 124 is a magnification of the items of life that are thought to be unpleasant, best kept under cover, best surrounded with silence lest they clutter our lives with unpleasantness; the dragon's mouth, the flood's torrent, the snare's entrapment; suffering, catastrophe, disaster. They are a very real part of life, and they constitute a dominating, fearful background for many. We look for relief among experts in medicine and psychology, and go to museums to get a look at beauty. Psalm 124 is an instance of a person who digs deeply into the trouble and finds there the presence of God who is on our side. In the details of the conflict, the majestic greatness of God becomes revealed in the minuteness of a personal history. Faith develops out of the most difficult aspects of our existence, not the easiest. The person of faith is not a person who has been born, luckily, with a good digestion and sunny-disposition. The assumption by outsiders that Christians are naive or protected is the opposite of the truth: Christians know more about the deep struggles of life than others, more about the ugliness of sin.

A look into the heavens can bring a breathtaking sense of wonder and majesty, and, if a person is a believer, a feeling of praise to the God who made heaven and earth. The psalm looks in the other direction. It looks into the troubles of history, the anxiety of personal conflict and emotional trauma. And it sees there the God who is on our side, God our help. The close look, the microscopic insight into the dragon's terrors, the flood's waters and the imprisoning trap, sees the action of God in deliverance.

We speak our words of praise in a world that is hellish; we sing our songs of victory in a world where things get messy; we live our joy among people who neither understand nor encourage us. But the content of our lives is God, not man. We are not scavenging in the dark alleys of the world, poking in its rubbish bins for a bare subsistence. We are travelling in the light, towards God who is rich in mercy and strong to save. It is Christ, not culture, that defines our lives. It is the help we experience, not the hazards we risk, that shape our days.

7

Security

'The Lord Is Round about His People'

Those who trust in the Lord are like Mount Zion,
which cannot be moved, but abides for ever.
As the mountains are round about Jerusalem,
so the Lord is round about his people,
from this time forth and for evermore.
For the sceptre of wickedness shall not rest
upon the land allotted to the righteous,
lest the righteous put forth
their hands to do wrong.
Do good, O Lord, to those who are good,
and to those who are upright in their hearts!
But those who turn aside upon their crooked ways
the Lord will lead away with evildoers!
Peace be in Israel!

Psalm 125

Judea was designed to produce in her inhabitants the sense of seclusion and security, though not to such a degree as to relieve them from the attractions of the great world, which throbbed closely past, or to relax in them those habits of discipline, vigilance, and valour, which are the necessary elements of a nation's character. In the position of Judea there was not enough to tempt her people to put their confidence in herself; but there was enough to encourage them to defend their freedom and a strenuous life. And while the isolation of their land was sufficient to confirm their calling to a discipline and destiny separate from other peoples, it was not so complete as to keep them in ignorance of the world or to release them from those temptations to mix with the world, in combating which their discipline and destiny could alone be realized.

GEORGE ADAM SMITH

CLIMBING IS DIFFICULT. THE TUG OF GRAVITY IS CONSTANT. There are barriers to be surmounted and hazards to be met. Ordinarily, though, with a moderate amount of determination and stamina, people complete the climb they begin. But sometimes the foothold gives way and there is a slide backwards.

The Rocky Mountains, where our family loves to hike in the summer, are mostly sedimentary rock. There are places where the rock, under the impact of ice and water, erodes to a loose, crumbly stuff called scree. A misstep there can send you cascading down a mountain slope for hundreds of feet.

Backslider was a basic word in the religious vocabulary that I learned as I grew up. *Exempla* were on display throughout the town: people who had made a commitment of faith to our Lord, were active in our little church and who lost their footing on the ascent to Christ and backslid.

My Uncle Harry was a backslider. He was a warm, ardent Christian. In his middle years, on the basis of a mere wisp of rumour, he acquired hundreds of acres of useless land. Not long afterwards the Department of Interior decided to build a hydroelectric dam on that land. Suddenly my uncle was a rich man. The excitement of making money got into his blood; attendance at worship became infrequent. He became impatient with his children and with me, his nephew. His work habits became compulsive. That is when I first heard *backslider* applied to someone I knew. He died of high blood pressure and a heart attack. Everyone in his family visibly relaxed.

Two girls, older than I, whom I very much admired, attractive and vivacious, went away to college. They returned for vacation wearing brighter lipstick and shorter skirts. From the pew in front of me on a Sunday morning I heard the stage whispers between two grandmotherly types: 'Do you think they have backslidden?' One is now a pastor's wife near Philadelphia, the other a missionary, with her husband, in Ethiopia.

Backsliding was everywhere and always an ominous possibility. Warnings were frequent and the sad consequences on public display. The mood was anxious and worried. I was taught to take my spiritual temperature every day, or at least every week; if it was not exactly 'normal', there was general panic. I got the feeling that backsliding was not something you *did*, it happened to you. It was an accident that intruded on the unwary or an attack that involved the undefended.

Later in life, as I read Scripture for myself, and still later when as a pastor I had the responsibility for guiding the spiritual development of others, I acquired a very different way of looking at the conditions under which the Christian walks the way of discipleship. In both the Scriptures and the pastoral traditions of the church I found a background of confidence, a leisured security, among persons of faith.

Someone Else Built the Fortress

The emphasis of Psalm 125 is not on the precariousness of the Christian life but on its solidity. Living as a Christian is not walking a tightrope without a safety net high above a breathless crowd, many of whom would like nothing better than the morbid thrill of seeing you fall; it is sitting secure in a fortress.

The psalm uses familiar geography to demonstrate the truth: 'Those who trust in the Lord are like Mount Zion, which cannot be moved, but abides for ever. As the mountains are round about Jerusalem, so the Lord is round about his people, from this time forth and for evermore.' Jerusalem was set in a saucer of hills. It was the safest of cities because of the protective fortress these hills provided. Just so is the person of faith surrounded by the Lord. Better than a city wall, better than a military fortification is the presence of the God of peace. Geographically the city of Jerusalem had 'borders and bulwarks of extraordinary variety and intricacy'[1] which illustrated and enforced the reality of God's secure love and care.

City life in the ancient world was dangerous. The outside world was filled with roaming marauders, ready to attack at any sign of weakness. Constant vigilance was a prerequisite for community life and for the development of the arts of civilization. Cities needed elaborate and extensive defence systems to make them safe. An immense effort was expended on building walls and digging moats.

We still live in that kind of world and we still build those defences although the forms have changed somewhat. The process is not only political but personal. The outer world is only an extension of an inner, spiritual world. Psychologists who observe us talk of the elaborate security systems (Sullivan) and the defence mechanisms (Freud) that we use to protect ourselves.

People of faith have the same needs for protection and security as anyone else. We are no better than others in that regard. What is different is that we find that we don't have to build our own: 'God is our refuge and strength, a very present help in trouble' (Ps 46:1). 'As the mountains are round about Jerusalem, so the Lord is round about his people.' We don't always have to be looking over our shoulder lest evil overtake us unawares. We don't always have to keep our eyes on our footsteps lest we slip, inadvertently, on a temptation. God is at our side. He is, as another psalmist put it, 'behind and before' (139:5). And when it comes down to it, do we need anything more than our Lord's prayer for us: 'Holy Father, keep them in thy name. . . . I do not pray that thou shouldst take them out of the world, but that thou shouldst keep them from the evil one' (Jn 17:11, 15)? With a prayer like that offered to the Father on our behalf, are we not secure?

A Saw-toothed History

All the same, we do become anxious, we do slip into fearful moods, we become uncertain and insecure. The confident, robust faith that we desire and think is our destiny is qualified by recurrent insecurities. Singing Psalm 125 is one way Christians have to develop confidence and banish insecurity. The psalm makes its mark not by naively whistling when life is dark but by honestly facing the typical insecurities that beset us and putting them in their place.

One threat to our security comes from feelings of depression and doubt. The person of faith is described in this psalm as one who 'cannot be moved, but abides for ever.' But I am moved. I am full of faith one day and empty with doubt the next. I wake up one morning full of vitality, rejoicing in the sun; the next day I am grey and dismal, faltering and moody.

'Cannot be moved' – nothing could be less true of me. I can be moved by nearly anything: sadness, joy, success, failure. I'm a thermometer and go up and down with the weather.

A couple of years ago a friend introduced me to the phrase *the saw-toothed history of Israel.* Israel was up one day and down the next. One day they were marching in triumph through the Red Sea, singing songs of victory, the next they were grumbling in the desert because they missed having Egyptian steak and potatoes for supper. One day they were marching around Jericho blowing trumpets and raising hearty hymns, and the next they were plunged into an orgy at some Canaanite fertility shrine. One day they are with Jesus in the upper room, listening in rapt attention to his commands and receiving his love, the next they are stamping around and cursing in the courtyard, denying they ever knew him.

But all the time, as we read that saw-toothed history, we realize something solid and steady: they are always God's people. God is steadfastly with them, in mercy and judgment, insistently gracious. We get the feeling that everything is done in the sure, certain environment of the God who redeems his people. And as we learn that, we learn to live not by our feelings about God but by the facts of God. I refuse to believe my depressions; I choose to believe in God. If I break my leg I do not become less a person. My wife and children do not repudiate me. Neither when my faith fractures nor my feelings bruise does God cast me off and reject me.

My feelings are important for many things. They are essential and valuable. They keep me aware of much that is true and real. But they tell me next to nothing about God or my relation to God. My security comes from who God is, not from how I feel. Discipleship is a decision to live by what I know about God, not by what I *feel* about him or myself or my neighbours. 'As the mountains are round about Jerusalem, so the

Lord is round about his people.' The image that announces the dependable, unchanging, safe, secure existence of God's people comes from geology, not psychology.

A Damoclean Sword

Another source of uncertainty is in our pain and suffering. Unpleasant things happen to us. We lose what we think we cannot live without. Pain comes to those whom we love, and we conclude that there is no justice. Why does God permit this? Anxiety seeps into our hearts. We have the precarious feeling of living under a Damoclean sword. When will the axe fall on me? If such a terrible thing could happen to my friend who is so good, how long until I get mine?

The psalmist knows all this! Sickness and death, despair and persecution. He is familiar with the rape and pillage of military invasion, and the famine and earthquake of natural disaster. Psalm 125 was written by a person who did not have anaesthetics in his hospital, aspirin in his medicine chest and whose government did not have hundreds of billions of dollars to spend on national defence. Pain and suffering were most certainly in his daily life. Why did they not destroy his confidence?

The answer is in these words: 'For the scepter of wickedness shall not rest upon the land alloted to the righteous, lest the righteous put forth their hands to do wrong.' The key word is *rest:* abide there permanently and finally. Israel had more than its share of oppression: the scepter of wickedness was on her time and time again: Pharaoh, the Philistines, Tiglath-Pileser, Sennacherib, Nebuchadnezzar, Caesar. To an outsider it must have looked much of the time as if wicked rule was permanent. From the inside the witness of faith said that it was not: 'The sceptre of wickedness shall not rest upon the land alloted to the righteous, lest the righteous put forth their hands to do wrong.'

If the evil is permanent, if there is no hope for salvation, even the most faithful and devout person will break, '. . . put forth their hands to do wrong.' But God does not permit that to happen. Danger and oppression are never too much for faith. They were not too much for Job, they were not too much for Jeremiah and they were not too much for Jesus. Evil is always temporary. 'The worst does not last.'[2] Nothing counter to God's justice has any eternity to it. Paul's witness was, 'God is faithful, and he will not let you be tempted beyond your strength, but with the temptation will also provide the way of escape, that you may be able to endure it' (1 Cor 10-13). 'He knows when to say, It is enough.'[3]

A Non-negotiable Contract

The third threat to the confidence that is promised to the Christian is the known possibility of defection. The general truth under which the Christian lives in this regard is 'once saved always saved.' Once you are a Christian there is no way of getting out of it. It is a non-negotiable contract. Once you have signed you cannot become a free agent again, no matter what the commissioner or the Supreme Court rules.

However true that is generally, and I think it is, there are exceptions. It would seem that if God will not force us to faith in the first place, he will not keep us against our will, finally. Falling away is possible. We know of Judas. We know of Hymenaeus and Alexander who 'made shipwreck of their faith' (1 Tim 1:19-20). These are the ones described in the psalm 'who turn aside upon their crooked ways.'[4] The way of discipleship gets difficult, they see an opening through the trees that promises a softer, easier path. Distracted and diverted, they leave and never return.

If it is possible to defect, how do I know that I won't – or even worse, that I haven't? How do I know that I have not already lost faith, especially during those times when I am depressed or have one calamity after another piled on me.

Such insinuated insecurities need to be confronted directly and plainly: it is not possible to drift unconsciously from faith to perdition. We wander like lost sheep, true; but he is a faithful shepherd who pursues us relentlessly. We have our ups and downs, zealously believing one day and gloomily doubting the next, but he is faithful. We break our promises, but he doesn't break his. Discipleship is not a contract in which if we break our part of the agreement he is free to break his; it is a covenant in which he establishes the conditions and guarantees the results.

Certainly, you may quit if you wish. You may say no to God. It's a free faith. You may choose the crooked way. He will not keep you against your will. But it is not the kind of thing you fall into by chance or slip into by ignorance. Defection requires a deliberate sustained and determined act of rejection.

All the persons of faith I know are sinners, doubters, uneven performers. We are secure not because we are sure of ourselves but because we trust that God is sure of us. The opening phrase of the psalm is 'those who trust in the Lord' – not those who trust in their performance, in their morals, in their righteousness, in their health, in their pastor, in their doctor, in their president, in their economy, in their nation – 'those who trust in the Lord.' Those who decide that God is for us and will make us whole eternally.

Mountain Climbers Roped Together

When I was a child I walked about a mile to school each day with my two best friends. Along a quarter of that distance there was a railway track. When we came to that stretch we always walked on the rails. Each of us wanted to make it all the way without falling off, but didn't want the others to similarly succeed. We would throw things at each other to upset balance, or say things to divert attention, cry out that the train was coming, or announce that there was a dead body in the ditch. There are some who have supposed that this is what Christian living is, teetering and wobbling along that rail, taunted by the devil and his angels. With some skill and a lot of luck we might just make it to heaven, but it's an uncertain business at best.

Psalm 125 says that is not the way it is at all. Being a Christian is like sitting in the middle of Jerusalem, fortified and secure. 'First we are established and then entrenched; settled, and then sentinalled: made like a mount, and then protected as if by mountains.'[5] And so the last sentence is, 'Peace be in Israel!' A colloquial, but in the context accurate, translation would be, 'Relax.' We are secure. God is running the show. Neither our feelings of depression nor the facts of suffering nor the possibilities of defection are evidence that God has abandoned us. There is nothing more certain than that he will accomplish his salvation in our lives and perfect his will in our histories. Three times in his great Sermon, Jesus, knowing how easily we imagine the worst, repeats the reassuring command, 'Do not be anxious. . . .' (Mt 6:25, 31, 34). Our life with God is a sure thing.

When mountain climbers are in dangerous terrain, on the face of a cliff or on the slopes of a glacier, they rope themselves together. Sometimes one of them slips and falls – backslides. But not everyone falls at once, and so those who are still on their feet are able to keep the backslider from falling away completely. And of course, in any group of climbers, there is a veteran and experienced climber in the lead, identified for us in the letter to the Hebrews as 'Jesus, who leads us in our faith and brings it to perfection' (Heb 12:2 JB).

Travelling in the way of faith and climbing the ascent to Christ may be difficult, but it is not worrisome. The weather may be adverse but it is never fatal. We may slip and stumble and fall, but the rope will hold us.

8

Joy

'Our Mouth Was Filled with Laughter'

When the Lord restored the fortunes of Zion,
we were like those who dream.
Then our mouth was filled with laughter,
and our tongue with shouts of joy;
then they said among the nations,
'The Lord has done great things for them.'
The Lord has done great things for us;
we are glad.

Restore our fortunes, O Lord,
like the watercourses in the Negeb!
May those who sow in tears
reap with shouts of joy!
He that goes forth weeping,
bearing the seed for sowing,
shall come home with shouts of joy,
bringing his sheaves with him.

Psalm 126

> *I have read that during the process of canonization the Catholic Church demands proof of joy in the candidate, and although I have not been able to track down chapter and verse I like the suggestion that dourness is not a sacred attribute.*
>
> PHYLLIS MCGINLEY

ELLEN GLASGOW, IN HER AUTOBIOGRAPHY, TELLS OF HER FATHER who was a Presbyterian elder, full of rectitude and rigid with duty: 'He was entirely unselfish, and in his long life he never committed a pleasure.'[1] Peter Jay, in a recent political column in the *Baltimore Sun,* described the sober intensity and the personal austerities of one of our Maryland politicians, then threw in this line: 'He dresses like a Presbyterian.'

I know there are Christians, so-called, who never crack a smile and who can't abide a joke, and I suppose Presbyterians contribute their quota. But I don't meet very many of them. The stereotype as such is a big lie created, presumably, by the devil. One of the delightful discoveries along the way of Christian discipleship is how much enjoyment there is, how much laughter you hear, how much sheer fun you find.

In Phyllis McGinley's delightful book *Saint-Watching* there is this story: 'Martin Luther's close friend was Philipp Melanchthon, author of the Augsburg Confession. Melanchthon was a cool man where Luther was fervid, a scholar opposed to a doer, and he continued to live like a monk even after he had joined the German reformation. . . . One day Luther lost patience with Melanchthon's virtuous reserve, "For heaven's sake," he roared, "why don't you go out and sin a little? God deserves to have something to forgive you for!"'[2]

A Consequence Not a Requirement

'Our mouth was filled with laughter, and our tongue with shouts of joy.' That is the authentic Christian note, a sign of those who are on the way of salvation. Joy is characteristic of Christian pilgrimage. It is the second in Paul's list of the fruits of the Spirit (Gal 5:22). It is the first of Jesus' signs in the Gospel of John (turning water into wine). It was said of the Hasid, Levi-Yitzhak of Berditchev: 'His smiles were fraught with greater meaning than his sermons.'[3] The same thing can be said of much of the Bible: its smiles carry more meaning than its sermons.

That is not to say that joy is a moral requirement for Christian living. Some of us experience things that are full of sadness and pain. Some of us descend to low points in our lives when joy seems to have permanently departed. We must not in such circumstances or during such times say, 'Well, that's the final proof that I am not a good Christian. Christians are supposed to have their mouths filled with laughter and tongues with shouts of joy; and I don't. I'm not joyful, therefore I must not be a Christian.'

Joy is not a requirement of Christian discipleship, it is a consequence. It is not what we have to acquire in order to experience life in Christ; it is what comes to us when we are walking in the way of faith and obedience.

We come to God (and to the revelation of God's ways) because none of us have it within ourselves, except momentarily, to be joyous. Joy is a product of abundance; it is the overflow of vitality. It is life working together harmoniously. It is exuberance. Inadequate sinners as we are, none of us can manage that for very long.

We try to get it through entertainment. We pay someone to make jokes, tell stories, perform dramatic actions, sing songs.

We buy the vitality of another's imagination to divert and enliven our own poor lives. The enormous entertainment industry in our land is a sign of the depletion of joy in our culture. Society is a bored, gluttonous king employing a court jester to divert it after an overindulgent meal. But that kind of joy never penetrates our lives, never changes our basic constitution. The effects are extremely temporary – a few minutes, a few hours, a few days at most. When we run out of money, the joy trickles away. We cannot make ourselves joyful. Joy cannot be commanded, purchased or arranged.

But there is something we can do. We can decide to live in response to the abundance of God, and not under the dictatorship of our own poor needs. We can decide to live in the environment of a living God and not our own dying selves. We can decide to centre ourselves in the God who generously gives and not in our own egos which greedily grab. One of the certain consequences of such a life is joy, the kind expressed in Psalm 126.

Joy: Past, Present, Future

The centre sentence in the psalm is, 'We are glad' (v. 3). The words on one side of that centre (vv. 1-2) are in the past tense, the words on the other side (vv. 4-6) in the future tense. Present gladness has past and future. It is not an ephemeral emotion. It is not a spurt of good feelings that comes when the weather and the stock market are both right on the same day.

The background for joy is only alluded to here, but the words trigger vast memories: 'When the Lord restored the fortunes of Zion . . . then our mouth was filled with laughter, and our tongue with shouts of joy; then they said among the nations, "The Lord has done great things for them." The Lord has done great things for us; we are glad.'

What were the 'great things'? On nearly any page of the Bible we find them. There is the story of God's people in a long, apparently interminable servitude under the shadows of the Egyptian pyramids and the lash of harsh masters. And then, suddenly and without warning, it was over. One day they were making 'bricks without straw' and the next they were running up the far slopes of the Red Sea, shouting the great song, 'I will sing to the Lord, for he has triumphed gloriously; the horse and his rider he has thrown into the sea. The Lord is my strength and my song, and he has become my salvation; this is my God, and I will praise him, my father's God, and I will exalt him' (Ex 15:1-2).

We turn over a few pages and find the story of David. There were years of wilderness guerrilla warfare against the Philistines, a perilous existence with moody, manic King Saul, a painful groping through the guilt of murder and adultery, then in his old age chased from his throne by his own son and forced to set up a government in exile. And, at the end, his song. It begins with gratitude: 'The Lord is my rock, and my fortress, and my deliverer'; it ends in confidence, 'The Lord lives; and blessed be my rock.' In the centre there is a rocket burst of joy: 'Yea, by thee I can crush a troop, and by my God I can leap over a wall' (2 Sm 22:2, 47, 30).

We turn a few more pages and find the terrible story of the Babylonian captivity. Israel experienced the worst that can come to any of us: rape in the streets, cannibalism in the kitchens, neighbours reduced to bestiality, a six-hundred-mile forced march across a desert, the taunting mockeries by the captors. And then, incredibly – joy. Beginning with the low, gentle words, 'Comfort, comfort my people, says your God. Speak tenderly to Jerusalem, and cry to her that her warfare is ended, that her iniquity is pardoned' (Is 40:1-2). And then the swelling reassurances of help: 'When you pass through the waters I will be with you. . . . Fear not' (43:2-5). The sounds combine and surge to a proclamation: 'How beautiful upon the mountains are the feet of him who brings good tidings. . . . Hark, your watchmen lift up their voice, together they sing for joy' (52:7-8). The gratitude and gladness builds and soars. There is a sea-change into joy,

'When the Lord restored the fortunes of Zion, we were like those who dream.' Each act of God was an impossible miracle. There was no way it could have happened, and it did happen. 'We were like those who dream.' We nurture these memories of laughter, these shouts of joy. We fill our minds with the stories of God's acts. Joy has a history. Joy is the verified, repeated experience of those involved in what God is doing. It is as real as a date in history, as solid as a stratum of rock in Palestine. Joy is nurtured by living in such a history, building on such a foundation.

Joyful Expectation

The other side of 'we are glad' (vv. 4-6) is in the future tense. Joy is nurtured by anticipation. If the joy-producing acts of God are characteristic of our past as God's people, they will also be characteristic of our future as his people. There is no reason to suppose that God will arbitrarily change his way of working with us. What we have known of him, we will know of him. Just as joy builds on the past, it borrows from the future. It expects certain things to happen.

Two images fix the hope: The first is 'Restore our fortunes, O Lord, like the watercourses in the Negeb!' The Negeb, south of Israel, is a vast desert. The watercourses of the Negeb are a network of ditches cut into the soil by wind and rain erosion. For most of the year they are baked dry under the sun, but a sudden rain makes the desert ablaze with blossoms.

With such suddenness long years of barren waiting are interrupted by God's invasion of grace into our lives.

The second image is 'May those who sow in tears reap with shouts of joy! He that goes forth weeping, bearing the seed for sowing, shall come home with shouts of joy, bringing his sheaves with him.' The hard work of sowing seed in what looks like perfectly empty earth has, as every farmer knows, a time of harvest. All suffering, all pain, all emptiness, all disappointment is seed: sow it in God, he will, finally, bring a crop of joy from it.

It is clear in Psalm 126 that the one who wrote it and those who sang it were no strangers to the dark side of things. They carried the painful memory of exile in their bones and the scars of oppression on their backs. They knew the deserts of the heart and the nights of weeping. They knew what it meant to sow in tears.

One of the most interesting and remarkable things that Christians learn is that laughter does not exclude weeping. Christian joy is not an escape from sorrow. Pain and hardship still come, but they are unable to drive out the happiness of the redeemed.

A common but futile strategy for achieving joy is trying to eliminate things that hurt: get rid of pain by numbing the nerve ends, get rid of insecurity by eliminating risks, get rid of disappointments by depersonalizing your relationships. And then try to lighten the boredom of such a life by buying joy in the form of vacations and entertainment. There isn't a hint of that in Psalm 126.

Laughter is a result of living in the midst of God's great works ('when the Lord restored . . . our mouth was filled with laughter'). Enjoyment is not an escape from boredom but a plunge by faith into God's work ('he that goes forth weeping, bearing the seed for sowing, shall come home with shouts of joy, bringing his sheaves with him'). There is plenty of suffering on both sides, past and future. The joy comes because God knows how to wipe away tears, and, in his resurrection work, create the smile of new life. Joy is what God gives, not what we work up. Laughter is the delight that things are working together for good to them that love God, not the giggles that betray the nervousness of a precarious defence system. The joy that develops in the Christian way of discipleship is an overflow of spirits that comes from feeling good not about yourself but about God. We find that his ways are dependable, his promises sure.

This joy is not dependent on our good luck in escaping hardship. It is not dependent on our good health and avoiding pain. Christian joy is actual in the midst of pain, suffering, loneliness and misfortune. St Paul is our most convincing witness to this. One of his great, characteristic words is *rejoice.* The word is tympanic, resonating through every movement of his life: 'We rejoice in our sufferings, knowing that suffering produces endurance, and endurance produces character, and character produces hope, and hope does not disappoint us, because God's love has been . . . given to us. . . . We also rejoice in God through our Lord Jesus Christ, through whom we have now received our reconciliation' (Rom 5:3-5, 11). That is the fulfillment of the prayer, 'Restore our fortunes, O Lord, like the watercourses in the Negeb!'

And then out of his prison cell we hear Paul's trumpeting conclusion to his Philippian letter: 'Rejoice in the Lord always; again I will say, Rejoice. Let all men know your forbearance. The Lord is at hand' (Phil 4:4-5). There is no grim, Greek Stoicism in that; it is a robust, Welsh hymn, striding from sorrow into song. It is the end result of the petition: 'May those who sow in tears reap with shouts of joy!' The witness is repeated over and over again, through the generations and has scattered representatives through every community of Christians.

The psalm does not give us this joy as a package or as a formula, but there are some things it does do. It shows up the tinniness of the world's joy and affirms the solidity of God's joy. It reminds us of the accelerating costs and diminishing returns of those who pursue pleasure as a path toward joy. It introduces us to the way of discipleship which has consequences in joy. It encourages us in the way of faith to both experience and share joy. It tells us the story of God's acts which put laughter into people's mouths and shouts on their tongues. It repeats the promises of a God who accompanies his wandering, weeping children until they arrive home, exuberant, 'bringing in the sheaves'. It announces the existence of a people who assemble to worship God and disperse to live to God's glory, whose lives are bordered on one side by a memory of God's acts and the other by hope in God's promises, and who along with whatever else is happening are able to say, at the centre, 'We are glad.'

9

Work

'Unless the Lord Builds the House'

Unless the Lord builds the house,
those who build it labour in vain.
Unless the Lord watches over the city,
the watchman stays awake in vain.
It is in vain that you rise up early and go late
to rest,
eating the bread of anxious toil;
for he gives to his beloved sleep.

Lo, sons are a heritage from the Lord,
the fruit of the womb a reward.
Like arrows in the hand of a warrior
are the sons of one's youth.
Happy is the man who has
his quiver fill of them!
He shall not be put to shame
when he speaks with his enemies in the gate.

Psalm 127

> *The first great fact which emerges from our civilization is that today everything has becomes 'means'. There is no longer an 'end'; we do not know whither we are going. We have forgotten our collective ends, and we possess great means: we set huge machines in motion in order to arrive nowhere.*
>
> JACQUES ELLUL

THE GREATEST WORK PROJECT OF THE ANCIENT WORLD IS A story of disaster. The unexcelled organization and enormous energy that were concentrated in building the Tower of Babel resulted in such a shattered community and garbled communication that civilization is still trying to recover. Effort, even if the effort is religious (perhaps *especially* when the effort is religious), does not in itself justify anything.

One of the tasks of Christian discipleship is to learn how to 'do the works you did at first' (Rv 2:5) and absolutely refuse to 'work like the devil'. Work is a major component in most lives. It is unavoidable. It can be either good or bad, an area where our sin is magnified or where our faith matures. For it is the nature of sin to take good things and twist them, ever so slightly, so that they miss the target to which they were aimed, the target of God. One requirement of discipleship is to learn the ways in which sin skews our nature and submit what we learn to the continuing will of God so that we are reshaped through the days of our obedience.

Psalm 127 shows both the right way and the wrong way to work. It posts a warning and provides the example which guide Christians in work that is done to the glory of God.

Babel or Buddhist

Psalm 127 first posts a warning about work: 'Unless the Lord builds the house, those who build it labour in vain. Unless the Lord watches over the city, the watchman stays awake in vain. It is in vain that you rise up early and go late to rest, eating the bread of anxious toil; for he gives to his beloved sleep.'

Some people have read these verses and paraphrased them to read like this: 'You don't have to work hard to be a Christian. You don't have to put yourself out at all. Go to sleep. God is doing everything that needs to be done.' St Paul had to deal with some of these people in the church at Thessalonica. They were saying that since God had done everything in Christ there was nothing more for them to do. If all effort ends up in godless confusion (as it did with the people at Babel) or in hypocritic self-righteousness (as had happened among the Pharisees), the obvious and Christian solution is to quit work and wait for the Lord to come. With a magnificent redeemer like our Lord Jesus Christ and a majestic God like our Father in heaven, what is there left to do? And so they sat around, doing nothing.

Meanwhile they lived 'by faith' off their less spiritual friends. Unfriendly critics might have called them freeloaders. Paul became angry and told them to get to work: 'We hear that some of you are living in idleness, mere busybodies, not doing any work. Now such persons we command and exhort in the Lord Jesus Christ to do their work in quietness and to earn their own living. Brethren, do not be weary in well-doing' (2 Thes 3:11-13). How did they dare to reinterpret the gospel into a rationalization for sloth when he, Paul, from whom they had learned the gospel, 'worked night and day, that we might not burden any of you' (1 Thes 2:9).

The Christian has to find a better way to avoid the sin of Babel than by imitating the lilies of the field, who 'never toil nor spin'. The pretentious work which became Babel and its pious opposite which developed at Thessalonica are displayed today on the broad canvasses of Western and Eastern cultures respectively.

Western culture takes up where Babel left off and deifies human effort as such. The machine is the symbol of this way of life that attempts to control and manage. Technology promises to give us control over the earth and over other people. But the promise is not fulfilled: lethal automobiles, ugly buildings and ponderous bureaucracies ravage the earth and empty lives of meaning. Structures become more important than the people who live in them. Machines become more important than the people who use them. We care more for our possessions with which we hope to make our way in the world than with our thoughts and dreams which tell us who we are in the world.

Eastern culture, on the other hand, is a variation on the Thessalonican view. There is a deep-rooted pessimism regarding human effort. Since all work is tainted with selfishness and pride, the solution is to withdraw from all activity into pure being. The symbol of such an attitude is the Buddha – an enormous fat person sitting cross-legged, looking at his own navel. Motionless, inert, quiet. All trouble comes from doing too much; therefore, do nothing. Step out of the rat race. The world of motion is evil, so quit doing everything. Say as little as possible; do as little as possible; finally, at the point of perfection, you will say nothing and do nothing. The goal is to withdraw absolutely and finally from action, from thought, from passion.

The two cultures are in collision today and many think that we must choose between them. But there is another option: Psalm 127 shows a way to work which is neither sheer activity nor pure passivity. It doesn't glorify work as such and it doesn't condemn work as such. It doesn't say, 'God has a great work for you to do; go and do it.' Nor does it say, 'God has done everything; go fishing.' If we want simple solutions in regard to work we can become workaholics or dropouts. If we want to experience the fullness of work, we will do better to study Psalm 127.

In the Beginning God Worked

The premise of the psalm for all work is that God works: 'Unless the Lord builds the house. . . . Unless the Lord watches over the city. . . .' The condition *unless* presupposes that God does work: he builds; he watches.

The main difference between Christians and others is that we take God seriously and they do not. We really do believe that he is the central reality of all existence. We really do pay attention to what he is and to what he does. We really do order our lives in response to that reality and not to some other. Paying attention to God involves a realization that he works.

The Bible begins with the announcement, 'In the beginning God created . . .' not 'sat majestic in the heavens,' and not 'was filled with beauty and love'. He created. He *did* something. He *made* something. He fashioned heaven and earth. The week of creation was a week of work. The days are described not by their weather conditions and not by their horoscope readings: Genesis 1 is a journal of work. We live in a universe and in a history where God is working. Before anything else, work is an activity of God. Before we go to the sociologists for a description of work or to the psychologists for insight into work or the economists for an analysis of work, we must comprehend the biblical record: God works. The work of God is defined and described in the pages of Scripture. We have models of creation, acts of redemption, examples of help and compassion, paradigms of comfort and salvation. One of the reasons that Christians read Scriptures repeatedly and carefully is to find out just how God works in Jesus Christ so that we can work in the name of Jesus Christ.

In every letter St Paul wrote he demonstrated that a Christian's work is a natural, inevitable and faithful development out of God's work. Each of his letters concludes with a series of directives which guide us into the kind of work that participates in God's work. The curse of some people's lives is not work, as such, but senseless work, vain work, futile work, work that takes place apart from God, work that ignores the *unless.* Christian discipleship, by orienting us in God's work and setting us in the mainstream of what God is already doing, frees us from the compulsiveness of work. Hilary of Tours taught that every Christian had to be constantly vigilant against what he called *'Irreligiosa solicitudo pro Deo'* – a blasphemous anxiety to do God's work for him.[1]

Our work goes wrong when we lose touch with the God who works 'his salvation in the midst of the earth.' It goes wrong both when we work anxiously and when we don't work at all, when we become frantic and compulsive in our work (Babel) and when we become indolent and lethargic in our work (Thessalonica). The foundational truth is that work is good. If God does it, it must be all right. Work has dignity: there can be nothing degrading about work if God works. Work has purpose: there can be nothing futile about work if God works.

Effortless Work

The psalm not only posts a warning, it gives an example: 'Lo, sons are a heritage from the Lord, the fruit of the womb a reward. Like arrows in the hand of a warrior are the sons of one's youth. Happy is the man who has his quiver full of them! He shall not be put to shame when he speaks with his enemies in the gate.'

In contrast to the anxious labour that builds cities and guards possessions, the psalm praises the effortless work of making children. Opposed to the strenuous efforts of persons who, in doubt of God's providence and mistrust of man's love, seek their own gain by godless struggles is the gift of children, born not through human effort, but through the miraculous process of reproduction which God has created among us. The example couldn't have been better chosen. What do we do to get sons? Very little. The entire miracle of procreation and reproduction requires our participation, but hardly in the form of what we call our work. We did not make these marvellous creatures that walk and talk and grow among us. We participated in an act of love which was provided for us in the structure of God's creation.

Jesus leads us to understand the psalmist's 'sons' in terms representative of all intimate and personal relationships. He himself did not procreate children, yet by his love he made us all sons and daughters (Mt 12:46-50). His job description was 'My Father is working still, and I am working' (Jn 5:17). By joining Jesus and the psalm we learn a way of work which does not acquire things or amass possessions but responds to God and develops relationships. People are at the centre of Christian work. In the way of pilgrimage we do not drive cumbersome Conestoga wagons loaded down with baggage over endless prairies. We travel light. The character of our work is shaped not by accomplishments or possessions but in the birth of relationships: 'Sons are a heritage from the Lord.' We invest our energy in people. Among those around us we develop sons and daughters, sisters and brothers even as our

Lord did with us: 'Happy is the man who has his quiver full of them!'

For it makes very little difference how much money Christians carry in their wallets or purses. It makes little difference how our culture values and rewards our work ... *unless.* For our work creates neither life nor righteousness. Relentless, compulsive work habits ('the bread of anxious toil') which our society rewards and admires are seen by the psalmist as a sign of weak faith and assertive pride, as if God could not be trusted to accomplish his will, as if we could rearrange the universe by our own effort.

What does make a difference is the personal relationships that we create and develop. We learn a name; we start a friendship; we follow up on a smile – or maybe even on a grimace. Nature is profligate with its seeds, scattering them everywhere; a few of them sprout. Out of numerous handshakes and greetings, some germinate and grow into a friendship in Christ. Christian worship gathers the energy and focuses the motivation which transform us from consumers who use work to get things into people who are intimate and in whom work is a way of being in creative relationship with another. Such work can be done within the structure of any job, career or profession. As Christians do the jobs and tasks assigned to them in what the world calls work, we learn to pay attention to and practice what God is doing in love and justice, in helping and healing, in liberating and cheering.

The first people to sing this psalm had expended much effort to get to Jerusalem. Some came great distances and overcame formidable difficulties. Would there be a tendency among the pilgrims to congratulate one another on their successful journeys, to swell with pride in their accomplishment, to trade stories of their experiences? Would there be comparisons on who made the longest pilgrimage, the fastest pilgrimage, who had brought the most neighbours, who had come the most times? Then, through the noise of the crowd someone would strike up the tune, 'Unless the Lord. . . .' The pilgrimage is not at the centre; the Lord is at the centre. No matter how hard they struggled to get there, no matter what they did in the way of heroics – fending off bandits, clubbing lions and crushing wolves – that is not what is to be sung. Psalm 127 insists on a perspective in which our effort is at the periphery and God's work is at the centre.

10

Happiness

'You Shall Be Happy, and It Shall Be Well with You'

Blessed is every one who fears the Lord,
who walks in his ways!
You shall eat the fruit of the labour of your hands;
you shall be happy, and it shall be well with you.

Your wife will be like a fruitful vine
within your house;
your children will be like olive shoots
around your table.
Lo, thus shall the man be blessed
who fears the Lord.

The Lord bless you from Zion!
May you see the prosperity of Jerusalem
all the days of your life!
May you see your children's children!
Peace be upon Israel!

PSALM 128

Joy, which was the small publicity of the pagan, is the gigantic secret of the Christian.

G. K. CHESTERTON

THERE IS A GENERAL ASSUMPTION PREVALENT IN THE WORLD that it is extremely difficult to be a Christian. While it is true that many don't completely disqualify themselves. They do modify their claims: *ordinary* Christians they call themselves. They respect the church, worship fairly regularly, try to live decently. But they also give themselves somewhat generous margins to allow for the temptations and pressures put upon them by the world. To *really* be on the way of faith, take with absolute *seriousness* all that the Bible says – well, that requires a predisposition to saintliness, extraordinary will power and an unspecified number of nameless austerities that they are quite sure they cannot manage.

But this is as far from the truth as the east is from the west. The easiest thing in the world is to be a Christian. What is hard is to be a sinner. Being a Christian is what we were created for. The life of faith has the support of an entire creation and the resources of a magnificent redemption. The structure of this world was created by God so we could live in it easily and happily as his children. The history we walk in has been repeatedly entered by God, most notably in Jesus Christ, first to show us and then to help us live full of faith and exuberant with purpose. In the course of Christian discipleship we discover that without Christ we were doing it the hard way and that with Christ we are doing it the easy way. It is not Christians who have it hard, but non-Christians.

PROMISES AND PRONOUNCEMENTS

Blessing is the word that describes this happy state of affairs. Psalm 128 features the word. The psalm begins with three descriptive promises: 'Blessed is every one who fears the Lord, who walk in his ways!' 'You shall eat the fruit of the labour of your hands.' 'You shall be happy [Hebrew, *blessed*], and it shall be well with you.' It concludes with three vigorous pronouncements: 'The Lord bless you from Zion!' 'May you see the prosperity of Jerusalem all the days of your life!' 'May you see your children's children!' Sandwiched between those promises and pronouncements is an illustration of blessing: 'Your wife will be like a fruitful vine within your house; your children will be like olive shoots around your table. Lo, thus shall the man be blessed who fears the Lord.'[1]

That all adds up to a good life – a life that is bound on one side by promises of blessing, on the other side by pronouncements of blessing and which experiences blessings between those boundaries.

The Bible is one long exposition of this blessing. In Genesis, God, having completed the work of creation by making man male and female, 'blessed them' (Gn 1:28). He called Abraham and promised, 'I will make of you a great nation, and I will bless you, and make your name great, so that you will be a blessing' (Gn 12:2). Each of the twelve tribes of Israel receives a special blessing which identifies its particular characteristic of vitality (Gn 49). David, who in so many ways embodied the intensities and and joys of faith was 'richer in blessing than any other Israelite' – a long series of blessings, not without sorrow to be sure, but always brimming with life. Jesus, in his introduction to his Sermon on the Mount, identifies the eight key qualities in the life of a person of faith and announces each one with the word *blessed.* He makes it clear that the way of discipleship is not a reduction in what we already are, not an attenuation of our lives, not a subtraction from what we are used to. He will rather expand our capacities and fill us up with life so that we overflow with joy. The conclusion of the Bible is that great, thunderous book of Revelation in which there are seven salvos of blessing (1:3; 14:13; 16:15; 19:9; 20:6; 22:7, 14). The blessings cannonade back and forth across the battlefield on which Christ completed his victory over sin and establishes his eternal rule. 'The whole book stands in the framework of the blessing of those who attain to and keep the blessed revelation of the mysteries of God (1:3 confirmed in 22:7).'[2]

As we read this story of blessing and familiarize ourselves with the men and women who are experiencing God's blessing, we realize that it is not something external or ephemeral. Not a matter of having a good day, not an occasion run of luck. It is an 'inner strength of the soul and the happiness it creates, . . . the vital power, without which no living being can exist. Happiness cannot be given to a person as something lying outside him. . . . The action of God does not fall outside but at the very center of the soul; that which it gives us is not something external, but the energy, the power of creating it. . . . The blessing thus comprises the power to live in its deepest and most comprehensive sense. Nothing which belongs to action and to making life real can fall outside the blessing. . . . Blessing is the vital power, without which no living being can exist.'[3]

It is this that fills and surrounds the person who is on the way of faith.

Sharing in Life

The illustration that forms the centre of the psalm shows how the blessing works: 'Your wife will be like a fruitful vine within your house; your children will be like olive shoots around your table.' The illustration is, as we would expect, conditioned by Hebrew culture in which the standard signs of happiness were a wife who had many children and children who gathered and grew around the table: fruitful vine and olive shoots. This illustration is just that, an example which we need not reproduce exactly in order to experience blessing. (We, for instance, don't try to have as many children as possible – and try to get them to stay at home for all their lives!) But the meaning is still with us: blessing has inherent in it the power to increase. It functions by the sharing and delight in life. 'Life consists in the constant meeting of souls, which must share their contents with each other. The blessed gives to the others, because strength instinctively pours from him and up around him. . . . The characteristic of blessing is to multiply.'[4]

John Calvin, preaching to his congregation in Geneva, Switzerland, pointed out to his parishioners that we must develop better and deeper concepts of happiness from those held by the world which makes a happy life to consist in 'ease, honours, and great wealth.'[5] Psalm 128 helps us do that. Too much of the world's happiness depends on taking from one to satisfy another. To increase my standard of living, someone in another part of the world must lower his. The worldwide crisis of hunger that we face today is a result of that method of pursuing happiness. Industrialized nations acquire appetites for more and more luxuries and higher and higher standards of living, and increasing numbers of people are made poor and hungry. It doesn't have to be that way. The experts on the world hunger problem say that there is enough to go around right now. We don't have a production problem. We have the agricultural capability to produce enough food. We have the transportation technology to distribute the food. But we have a greed problem: if I don't grab mine while I can, I might not be happy. The hunger problem is not going to be solved by government or by industry, but in church, among Christians who learn a different way to pursue happiness.

Christian blessing is a realizing that 'it is more blessed to give than to receive.' As we learn to give and to share, our vitality increases and the people around us become 'fruitful vines' and 'olive shoots' around our tables.

The blessings that are promised to, pronounced upon and experienced by Christians, do not of course exclude difficulties. The Bible never indicates that. But the difficulties are not inherent in the faith: they come from the outside in the form of temptations, seductions, pressures. Not a day goes by but what we have to deal with that ancient triple threat that Christians in the Middle Ages summarized under the headings of the world, the flesh, and the devil: the world – the society of proud and arrogant mankind that defies and tries to eliminate God's rule and presence in history; the flesh – the corruption that sin has introduced into our very appetites and instincts; and the devil – the malignant will that tempts and seduces us away from the will of God. We have to contend with all of that. We are in a battle. There is a fight of faith to be waged. But the way of faith itself is in tune with what God has done and is doing. The road we travel is the well-travelled road of discipleship. It is not a way of boredom or despair or confusion. It is not a miserable groping, but a way of blessing.

Travelling by the Roads

There are no tricks involved in getting in on this life of blessing, and no luck required. We simply become Christians and begin the life of faith. We acknowledge God as our maker and lover, and accept Christ as the means by which we can be in living relationship with God. We accept the announced and proclaimed truth that God is at the centre of our existence, find out how he has constructed this world (his creation), how he has provided for our redemption, and proceed to walk in that way. In the plain words of the psalm: 'Blessed is every one who fears the Lord, who walk in his ways!'

'Fears the Lord.' *Reverence* might be a better word. Awe. The Bible isn't interested in whether we believe in God or not. It assumes that everyone more or less does. What it is interested in is the response we have toward him: will we let God be as he is, majestic and holy, cast and wondrous, or will we always be trying to whittle him down to the size of our small minds, insist on confining him within the boundaries we are comfortable with, refuse to think of him other than in images that are convenient to our lifestyle? But then we are not dealing with the God of creation and the Christ of the cross, but with a dime-store reproduction of something made in our image, usually for commercial reasons. To guard against all such blasphemous chumminess with the Almighty, the Bible talks of the fear of the Lord – not to scare us but to bring us to awesome attention before the overwhelming grandeur of God, to shut up our whining and chattering and stop our running and fidgeting so that we can really see him as he is and listen to him as he speaks his merciful, life-changing words of forgiveness.

'Walk in his ways.' We not only let God be God as he really is, but we start doing the things for which he made us. We take a certain route; we follow certain directions; we do specified things. There are ethical standards to follow, there are moral values to foster, there are spiritual disciplines to practice, there is social justice to pursue, there are personal relationships to develop. None of it is difficult to understand. 'Mere ethics,' quipped Austin Farrer once, 'call for no such august or mysterious explanation; next to plumbing, morality is social convenience number one. . . .'[6]

Because of the ambiguities of the world we live in and the defects in our own wills, we will not do any of this perfectly and without fault. But that isn't the point. The way is plain – walk in it. Keeping the rules and obeying the commands is only common sense. People who are forever breaking the rules, trying other roads, attempting to create their own system of values and truth from scratch, spend most of their time calling up someone to get them out of trouble and help repair the damages, and then ask the silly question, 'What went wrong?' As H. H. Farmer said, 'If you go against the grain of the universe you get splinters.'

Some who read Psalm 128 will say, 'Of course, that's the way it is with me. Doesn't everyone feel that?' and others will only be puzzled by how anyone could sing such a cheerful song in such a messed-up world. John Henry Newman once explained it this way: 'If I want to travel north and all the roads are cut to the east, of course I shall complain of the roads. I shall find nothing but obstacles; I shall have to surmount walls, and cross rivers, and go round about, and after all fail of my end.' Such is the conduct of those who are trying to achieve some meaning in their lives, pursuing their right to happiness, but refusing to take the well-travelled roads that lead there. They are trying to get to Mount Zion but ignore all the signposts and compass readings, and stubbornly avoid the trails as they bushwack their way through wilderness. 'Do you not see that they necessarily must meet with thwartings, crossings, disappointments, and failure?' They go mile after mile, watching in vain for their destination, but never sighting it. 'And then they accuse religion of interfering with what they consider their innocent pleasures and wishes.' But religion is only an inconvenience to those who are traveling against the grain of creation, at cross-purposes with the way which leads to redemption.[7]

Everyone wants to be happy, to be blessed. Too many people are willfully refusing to pay attention to the one who wills our happiness and ignorantly supposing that the Christian way is a harder way to get what they want than doing it on their own. But they are wrong. God's ways and God's presence are where we experience the happiness that lasts. Do it the easy way: 'Blessed is every one who fears the Lord, who walks in his ways!'

11

Perseverance

'Yet They Have Not Prevailed against Me'

'Sorely have they afflicted me from my youth,'
let Israel now say –
'Sorely have they afflicted me from my youth,
yet they have not prevailed against me.
The plowers plowed upon my back;
they made long their furrows.'
The Lord is righteous;
he has cut the cords of the wicked.
May all who hate Zion
be put to shame and turned backward!
Let them be like the grass on the housetops,
which withers before it grows up,
with which the reaper does not fill his hand
or the binder of sheaves his bosom,
while those who pass by do not say,
'The blessing of the Lord be upon you!
We bless you in the name of the Lord!'

Psalm 129

> *Patience is drawing on underlying forces; it is powerfully positive, though to a natural view it looks like just sitting it out. How would I persist against positive eroding forces if I were not drawing on invisible forces? And patience has a positive tonic effect on others; because of the presence of the patient person, they revive and go on, as if he were the gyroscope of the ship providing a stable ground. But the patient person himself does not enjoy it.*
>
> PAUL GOODMAN

STICK-TO-IT-IVENESS IS ONE OF THE MORE INELEGANT WORDS in the language, but I have a special fondness for it nevertheless. I heard the word a great deal when I was young, mostly, as I recall, from my mother. I was a creature of sudden but short-lived enthusiasms. I had a passion for building model aeroplanes, and then one day, mysteriously, all desire left and the basement was littered with half-finished models. Then stamp-collecting became an all-consuming hobby. I received an immense stamp album for Christmas, joined a philatelic club, acquired piles and piles of stamps and then one day, unaccountably, the interest left me. The album gathered dust and the mounds of stamps were left unmounted. Next it was horses. Each Saturday morning my best friend and I would ride our bikes to a dude ranch two miles from town, get horses and ride up into the Montana foothills imagining we were Merriweather Lewis and William Clark, or, less pretentiously, Gene Autry and the Lone Ranger. And then, overnight, that entire world vanished and in its place was – girls.

It was during these rather frequent transitions from one enthusiasm to another that I was slapped with the reprimand,

'Eugene, you have no stick-to-it-iveness. You never finish anything.' Years later I learned that the church had a fancier word for the same thing: *perseverance.* I have also found that it is one of the marks of Christian discipleship and have learned to admire those who exemplified it. Along the way Psalm 129 has become included in my admiration.

TOUGH FAITH

'"Sorely they have afflicted me from my youth," let Israel now say – "Sorely they have afflicted me from my youth, yet they have not prevailed against me."' The people of God are tough. For long centuries those who belong to the world have waged war against the way of faith, and they have yet to win. They have tried everything, but none of it has worked. They have tried persecution and ridicule, torture and exile, but the way of faith has continued healthy and robust: 'Sorely have they afflicted me from my youth, yet they have not prevailed against me.'

Do you think of Christian faith as a fragile style of life that can flourish only when the weather conditions are just right, or do you see it as a tough perennial that can stick it out through storm and drought, survive the trampling of careless feet and the attacks of vandals? Here is a biblical writer's view: 'He grew up before him like a young plant, and like a root out of dry ground. . . . He was despised and rejected by men; a man of sorrows, and acquainted with grief. . . . He was oppressed, and he was afflicted.' It is a portrait of extreme rejection and painful persecution. What can come of such a poor, precarious beginning? Not much, it would seem. Yet look at the results: 'He shall see his offspring, he shall prolong his days; the will of the Lord shall prosper in his hand; he shall see the fruit of the travail of his soul and be satisfied; by his knowledge shall the righteous one, my servant, make many to be accounted righteous; and he shall bear their iniquities' (Is 53). The person of faith outlasts all the oppressors. Faith lasts.

We remember the way it was with Jesus. His ministry began with forty days of temptation in the desert and concluded in that never to be forgotten night of testing and trial in Gethsemane and Jerusalem. Has anyone ever experienced such a relentless, merciless pounding from within and from without? First there were the cunning attempts to get him off the track, every temptation disguised as a suggestion for improvement, offered with the best of intentions to help Jesus in the ministry on which he had so naively and innocently set out. Then, at the other end, when all the temptations had failed, that brutal assault when his body was turned into a torture chamber. And we know the result: an incomprehensible kindness ('Father, forgive them ...'), an unprecedented serenity ('Father, into thy hands I commit my spirit') and – resurrection.

And Paul. His life recklessly caromed from adversity to persecution and back to adversity. In one passage he looks back and summarizes: 'I have been beaten times without number. I have faced death again and again. I have been beaten the regulation thirty-nine stripes by the Jews five times. I have been beaten with rods three times. I have been stoned once. I have been shipwrecked three times. I have been twenty-four hours in the open sea. In my travels I have been in constant danger from rivers, from bandits, from my own countrymen, and from pagans. I have faced danger on the high seas, danger among false Christians. I have known drudgery, exhaustion, many sleepless nights, hunger and thirst, fasting, cold and exposure. Apart from all external trials I have the daily burden of responsibility for all the churches. Do you think anyone is weak without my feeling his weakness? Does anyone have his faith upset without my burning indignation?' (2 Cor 11:23-29 Phillips). None of that had the power to push Paul off his path. None of it convinced him that he was on the wrong way. None of it persuaded him that he had made the wrong choice years earlier on the Damascus Road. At the end of his life, among the last words he wrote, is this sentence: 'Straining forward to what lies ahead, I press on toward the goal for the prize of the upward call of God in Christ Jesus' (Phil 3:13-14).

Stick-to-it-iveness. Perseverance. Patience. The way of faith is not a fad that is taken up in one century only to be discarded in the next. It lasts. It is a way that works. It has been tested thoroughly.

Cut Cords, Withered Grass

There is an interesting line in Psalm 129 that provides a detail that is both fascinating and useful. The sentence is, 'The Lord is righteous; he has cut the cords of the wicked.' The previous verse provides the context for understanding the lines, 'The plowers plowed upon my back; they made long their furrows.' Picture Israel, the person of faith, lying stretched out, prone. The enemies hitch up their oxen and ploughs and begin cutting long furrows in the back of Israel. Long gashes cut into the skin and flesh, back and forth systematically, like a farmer working a field. Imagine the whole thing: the blood, the pain, the back-and-forth cruelty. And then, suddenly, the realization that there was no more hurting. The oxen were still tramping back and forth, the oxherds were still shouting their commands, but the ploughs were not working. 'The Lord is righteous; he has cut the cords of the wicked.' The harness cords, connecting plough to oxen, have been severed. The ploughs of persecution aren't working, and the oxherds haven't even noticed! They plod back and forth, unaware that their opposition is worthless. They are wasting their time and energy. The wicked oxherds are comic figures, solemnly and efficiently doing their impressive work, proudly puffed with self-importance thinking of what they are accomplishing historically on the back of Israel. If they ever looked behind them (which they never do – their stiff necks make that exercise too painful), they would see that their bluster and blasphemy are having no results at all: 'The Lord ... has cut the cords of the wicked.'

The concluding illustration in the psalm tells a similar truth. Opposition to the people of faith is like grass on the housetops. Palestinian houses were flat topped; dirt was spread upon the roofs for insulation. Seeds would sprout and grow from this dirt but the grass didn't last; the thin soil couldn't support it. By midday the grass withered. No harvest there. No reapers upon the roofs. No one going along the road would ever look up and shout out, 'Great harvest you have there. God's blessing upon you!' The illustration is a cartoon, designed to bring a smile to the people of faith.

The life of the world that is opposed or indifferent to God is barren and futile. It is ploughing a field, thinking you are tramping all over God's people and cutting his purposes to ribbons, but unaware that long ago your plough was disengaged. It is naively thinking you might get a harvest of grain from that shallow patch of dirt on your rooftop. The way of the world is peppered with brief enthusiasms, like that grass on the roof, spring up so wonderfully and without effort, but as quickly withering. The way of the world is catalogued with proud, God-defying purposes, unharnessed from eternity, and therefore worthless and futile.

The Passion of Patience

There is one phrase in this psalm that good taste would prefer to delete but that honesty must deal with: 'May all who hate Zion be put to shame and turned backward!' Anger seethes and pulses in the wounds. A sense of wrong has been festering. Accumulated resentment wants vindication.

However much we feel the inappropriateness of this kind of thing in a man or woman of faith, we must also admit to its authenticity. For who does not experience flashes of anger at those who make our way hard and difficult? There are times in the long obedience of Christian discipleship when we get tired and fatigue draws our tempers short. At such times to see someone flitting from one sensation to another, quitting on commitments, ducking responsibilities, bouncing from one enthusiasm to another provokes our anger – and sometimes it piques our envy. No matter that we are, on other grounds, convinced that their adulteries are an admission of boredom, that their pleasures are the shallowest of distractions from which they must return to worsening anxieties and an emptier loneliness. Still, even when we know we are doing good work which has a good future, the foolery and the enmity of these others make a hard day harder, and anger flares.

We can't excuse the psalmist for getting angry on the grounds that he was not yet a Christian, for he had Leviticus to read: 'You shall not hate your brother in your heart. . . . You shall not take vengeance or bear any grudge against the sons of your own people, but you shall love your neighbour as yourself' (Lv 19:17-18). And he had Exodus: 'If you meet your enemy's ox or his ass going astray, you shall bring it back to him. If you see the ass of one who hates you lying under its burden, you shall refrain from leaving him with it, you shall help him to lift it up' (Ex 23:4-5). And he had Proverbs: 'Do not rejoice when your enemy falls, and let not your heart be glad when he stumbles' (Prv 24:17). When Jesus said 'love your enemies', he added nothing to what this psalmist already had before him.

So we will not make excuses for the psalmists vindictiveness. What we will do is admire its energy, for it is apathetic, sluggish neutrality that is death to perseverance, acts like a virus in the bloodstream and enervates the muscles of discipleship. The person who makes excuses for the hypocrites and rationalizes the excesses of the wicked, who loses a sense of opposition to sin, who obscures the difference between faith and denial, grace and selfishness – *that* is the person to be wary of. For if there is not all that much difference between the way of faith and the ways of the world, there is not much use in making any effort to stick to it. We drift on the tides of convenience. We float on fashions.

It is in the things that we care about that we are capable of expressing anger. A parent sees a child dart out into a roadway and narrowly miss being hit by a car, and angrily yells at the child, at the driver – at both. The anger may not be the most appropriate expression of concern, but it is evidence of concern. Indifference would be somehow inhuman.

And so here. The psalms are not sung by perfect pilgrims. They made their mistakes, just as we make ours. *Perseverance* does not mean 'perfect'. It means that we keep going. We do not quit when we find that we are not yet mature and that there is a long journey still before us. We get caught yelling at our wives, at our husbands, at our friends, at our employers, at our employees, at our children. Our yelling (though not all of it!) means we care about something: we care about God; we care about the ways of the kingdom; we care about morality, about justice, about righteousness. The way of faith centres and absorbs our lives and when someone makes the way difficult, throws stumbling blocks in the path of the innocent, creates difficulties for those young in faith and unpracticed in obedience, there is anger: 'May all who hate Zion be put to shame and turned backwards!'

For perseverance is not resignation, putting up with things the way they are, staying in the same old rut year after year after year, or being a doormat for people to wipe their feet on. Endurance is not a desperate hanging on but a travelling from strength to strength. There is nothing fatigued or humdrum in Isaiah, nothing flatfooted in Jesus, nothing jejune in Paul. Perseverance is triumphant and alive. The psalmist lived among prophets and priests who dealt with his vindictive spirit and nurtured him towards a better way of treating the wicked than calling down curses on them, learning what Charles Williams once described as the 'passion of patience'. We are in a similar apprenticeship. But we will not learn it by swallowing our sense of outrage on one hand, or, on the other, excusing all wickedness as a neurosis. We will do it by offering up our anger to God who trains us in creative love.

God Sticks with Us

The cornerstone sentence of Psalm 129 is, 'The Lord is righteous.' When the Bible says that God is righteous it is not saying that he is always right (although it, of course, assumes that) but that he is always in right relation to us. The word does not mean that he corresponds to some abstract ideal of the right, it speaks of a personal right relationship between Creator and his creation. '... Righteous is out and out a term denoting relationship, and that it does this in the sense of referring to a real relationship between two parties ... and not to the relationship of an object under consideration to an idea.'[1]

That the 'Lord is righteous' is the reason that Christians can look back over a long life, crisscrossed with cruelties, unannounced tragedies, unexpected setbacks, sufferings, disappointments, depressions – look back across all that and see it as a road of blessing and make a song out of what we see. 'Sorely have they afflicted me from my youth, yet they have not prevailed against me.' God sticks to his relationship. He establishes a personal relationship with us and stays with it. The central reality for Christians is the personal, unalterable, persevering commitment that God makes to us. Perseverance is not the result of *our* determination, it is the result of God's faithfulness. We survive in the way of faith not because we have extraordinary stamina but because God is righteous. Christian discipleship is a process of paying more and more attention to God's righteousness and less and less attention to our own; finding the meaning of our lives not by probing our moods and motives and morals but by believing in God's will and purposes; making a map of faithfulness of God, not charting the rise and fall of our enthusiasms. It is out of such a reality that we acquire perseverance.

This is what the writer of the New Testament letter to the Hebrew Christians did. He sang a litany of people who lived by faith, that is, people who centred their lives on the righteous God who stuck by them through thick and thin in such a way that they were able to persevere. They lived with uncommon steadiness of purpose and with a most admirable integrity. None of them lived without sin. They all made their share of mistakes and engaged in episodes of disobedience and rebellion. But God stuck with them so consistently and surely that they learned how to stick with God. Out of the litany comes this call: 'Let us run with perseverance the race that is set before us, looking to Jesus the pioneer and perfector of our faith, who for the joy that was set before him endured the cross, despising the shame, and is seated at the right hand of the throne of God' (Heb 12:1-2).

Some of those early Christians to whom he wrote had been complaining, apparently, that life was too rough for them. They couldn't hold out any longer (complaints that are, from time to time, heard in every congregation). They didn't see the use in believing in a God they never saw, serving a God who didn't give them what they want, trusting a God who let babies die and good people suffer. There is just a touch of irony in the words their pastor addressed to them: 'In your struggle against sin you have not yet resisted to the point of shedding your blood.' Quit your complaining. Take a look at the pilgrim road and see where you have come from and where you are going. Take up the refrains of the great song. '"Sorely have they afflicted us from our youth," Let Israel now say' – come now, all of you sing it – '"Sorely have they afflicted us from our youth, yet they have not prevailed against us."'

Purposes Last

The reason why our childhoods were one enthusiasm after another was that we hadn't yet found an organizing centre for our lives and a goal that would demand our all and our best. The Christian faith is the discovery of that centre in the righteous God. Christian discipleship is a decision to walk in his ways, steadily and firmly, and then finding that the way integrates all our interests, passions and gifts, our human needs and our eternal aspirations. It is the way of life we were created for. There are endless challenges in it to keep us on the growing edge of faith; there is always a righteous God with us to make it possible for us to persevere.

In Charles Williams's delightful, brief drama, *Grab and Grace,* there is a dialogue between Grace and a man who is dabbling in religion, trying out different experiences, 'into yoga one week, buddhism the next, spiritualism the next'. Grace mentions the Holy Spirit. The man says,

'The Holy Spirit? Good. We will ask him to come while I am in the mood, which passes so quickly and then all is so dull.'

And Grace answers:

'Sir, purposes last.'

12

Hope

'I Wait for the Lord, My Soul Waits'

Out of the depths I cry to thee, O Lord!
Lord, hear my voice!
Let thy ears be attentive
to the voice of my supplications!

If thou, O Lord, shouldst mark iniquities,
Lord, who could stand?
But there is forgiveness with thee,
that thou mayest be feared.

I wait for the Lord, my soul waits,
and in his word I hope;
my soul waits for the Lord
more than watchmen for the morning,
more than watchmen for the morning.

O Israel, hope in the Lord!
For with the Lord there is steadfast love,
and with him is plenteous redemption.
And he will redeem Israel
from all his iniquities.

Psalm 130

Hope is a projection of the imagination; so is despair. Despair all too readily embraces the ills it foresees; hope is an energy and arouses the mind to explore every possibility to combat them. . . . In response to hope the imagination is aroused to picture every possible issue, to try every door, to fit together even the most heterogeneous pieces in the puzzle. After the solution has been found it is difficult to recall the steps taken – so many of them are just below the level of consciousness.

THORNTON WILDER

TO BE HUMAN IS TO BE IN TROUBLE. JOB'S ANGUISH IS OUR epigraph: 'Man is born to trouble as the sparks fly upward.' Suffering is a characteristic of the personal. Animals can be hurt, but they do not suffer. The earth can be ravaged, still it cannot suffer. Man and woman, alone in the creation, suffer. For suffering is pain *plus:* physical or emotional pain *plus* the awareness that our own worth as people is threatened, that our own value as creatures made in the dignity of God is called into question, that our own destiny as eternal souls is jeopardized. Are we to be, finally, nothing? Are we to be discarded? Are we to be rejects in the universe and thrown onto the rubbish dump of humanity because our bodies degenerate or our emotions malfunction or our minds become confused or our families find fault with us or society avoids us? Any one of these things or, as is more likely, a combination of them, can put us in what Psalm 130 calls the depths.

A Christian is a person who decides to face and live through suffering. If we do not make that decision, we are endangered on every side. A man or woman of faith who fails to acknowledge and deal with suffering becomes, at last, either a cynic or a melancholic or a suicide. Psalm 120 grapples mightily with suffering, sings its way through it, and provides usable experience for those who are committed to travelling the way of faith to God through Jesus Christ.

Giving Dignity to Suffering

The psalm begins in pain: 'Out of the depths I cry to thee, O Lord! Lord, hear my voice! Let thy ears be attentive to the voice of my supplications!' The psalm is anguished prayer.

By setting the anguish out in the open and voicing it as a prayer, the psalm gives dignity to our suffering. It does not look on suffering as something slightly embarrassing which must be hushed up and locked in a closet (where it finally becomes a skeleton) because this sort of thing shouldn't happen to a real person of faith. And it doesn't treat it as a puzzle that must be explained, and therefore turn it over to theologians or philosophers to work out an answer. Suffering is set squarely, openly, passionately, before God. It is acknowledged and expressed. It is described and lived.

If the psalm did nothing more than that, it would be a prize, for it is difficult to find anyone in our culture who will respect us when we suffer. We live in a time when everyone's goal is to be perpetually healthy and constantly happy, and if any one of us fails to live up to the standards that are advertised as normative, we are labelled as a problem to be solved and a host of well-intentioned people rush to try out various cures on us. Or we are looked on as an enigma to be unravelled in which case we are subjected to endless discussions in which our lives are examined by zealous researchers for the clue that will account for our lack of health or happiness. Ivan Illich, in a recent interview, said: 'You know, there is an American myth that denies suffering and the sense of pain. It acts as if they *should* not be, and hence it devalues the *experience* of suffering. But this myth denies our encounter with reality.'[1]

The gospel offers a different view of suffering: in suffering we enter *the depths;* we are at the heart of things; we are near to where Christ was on the cross. P. T. Forsyth wrote: 'The depth is simply the height inverted, as sin is the index of moral grandeur. The cry is not only truly human, but divine as well. God is deeper than the deepest depth in man. He is holier than our deepest sin is deep. There is no depth so deep to us as when God reveals his holiness in dealing with our sin. . . . [And so] think more of the depth of God than the depth of your cry. The worst thing that can happen to a man is to have no God to cry to out of the depth.'[2]

Israel teaches us to respond to suffering as reality, not deny it as illusion, and leads us to face it with faith, not avoid it out of terror. The psalm in this way is representative of Israel which 'took a supremely realistic view of life's sufferings and dangers, saw herself as exposed to them vulnerably and without defence, and showed little talent for fleeing from them into ideologies of any kind. Rather, concepts of her faith directed her to bring these actual experiences of her daily life into connection with Jahweh. In her older period, indeed, she lacked any aptitude for the doctrinaire: she possessed, rather, an exceptional strength to face up even to negative realities, to recognize and not to repress them, even when she was spiritually unable to master them in any way. It is to this realism, which allowed every event its own inevitability and validity . . . that the narrative art of the OT, especially in its earlier form, owes its darksome grandeur.'[3]

And so we find in Psalm 130 not so much as a trace of those things that are so common among us, which rob us of our humanity when we suffer and make the pain so much more terrible to bear. No glib smart answers. No lectures on our misfortunes in which we are hauled into a classroom and given graduate courses in suffering. No hasty, Band-Aid treatments covering up our trouble so that the rest of society does not have to look at it. Neither prophets nor priests nor psalmists offer quick cures for the suffering; we don't find any of them telling us to take a vacation, use this drug, get a hobby. Nor do they ever engage in publicity cover-ups, the plastic smile propaganda campaigns that hide trouble behind a billboard of positive thinking. None of that: the suffering is held up and proclaimed – and prayed.

Not that Christians celebrate suffering – we don't make a religion out of it. We are not masochists who think we are being holy when we are hurting, who think personal misery is a sign of exceptional righteousness. There is some suffering in which we get involved that is useless and unnecessary; but there is adequate common-sense wisdom in Christian ways which prevents us from suffering for the wrong reasons if only we will pay attention to it. Henri Nouwen wrote, 'Many people suffer because of the false supposition on which they have based their lives. That supposition is that there should be no fear or loneliness, no confusion or doubt. But these sufferings can only be dealt with creatively when they are understood as wounds integral to our human condition. Therefore ministry is a very *confronting* service. It does now allow people to live with illusions of immortality and wholeness. It keeps reminding others that they are mortal and broken, but also that with the recognition of this condition, liberation starts.'[4] George MacDonald put it with epigrammatic force when he wrote, 'The Son of God suffered unto the death, not that men might not suffer, but that their sufferings might be like His.'[5]

The second important thing that Psalm 130 does is to immerse the suffering in God – all the suffering is spoken in the form of prayer, which means that God is taken seriously as a personal and concerned being. There are sentences in the psalm which show specific knowledge of the character of God as a personal redeemer: God is personal so that we may have an intimate relation with him; God is redeemer so that we may be helped by him. This is *meaning to* our lives and there is *salvation for* our lives, a truth summed up by Forsyth when he said, 'Our very pain is a sign of God's remembrance of us, for it would be much worse if we were left in ghastly isolation.'[6]

Eight times the name of God is used in the psalm. We find, as we observe how God is addressed, that he is understood as one who forgives sin, who comes to those who wait and hope for him, who is characterized by steadfast love and plenteous redemption, and who will redeem Israel. God makes a difference. God acts positively toward his people. God is not indifferent. He is not rejecting. He is not ambivalant or dilatory. He does not act arbitrarily in fits and starts. He is not stingy, providing only for bare survival. Karl Barth describes God in this regard: 'The free inclination of God to His creature, denoted in the Biblical witness by grace, takes place under the presupposition that the creature is in distress and that God's intention is to espouse his cause and to grant him assistance in his extremity. Because grace, the gracious love of God, consists in this inclination, it is, and therefore God himself is, merciful; God's very being is mercy. The mercy of God lies in His readiness to share in sympathy the distress of another, a readiness which springs from His inmost nature and stamps all His being and doing. It lies, therefore, in His will, springing from the depths of His nature and characterizing it, to take the initiative Himself for the removal of this distress. For the fact that God participates in it by sympathy implies that He is really present in its midst, and this means again that He wills that it should not be, that He wills therefore to remove it.'[7]

And this, of course, is why we are able to face, acknowledge, accept and live through suffering, for we know that it can never be ultimate, it can never constitute the bottom line. God is at the foundation and God is at the boundaries. God seeks the hurt, maimed, wandering and lost. God woos the rebellious and confused. If God were different than he is, not one of us would have a leg to stand on: 'If thou, O Lord, shouldst mark iniquities, Lord, who could stand? But there is forgiveness with thee, that thou mayest be feared.' Because of the forgiveness we have a place to stand. We stand in confident awe before God, not in terrorized despair.

Employed to Wait

Such are the two great realities of Psalm 130: suffering is real, God is real. Suffering is a mark of our existential authenticity; God is proof of our essential and eternal humanity. We accept suffering; we believe in God. The acceptance and the belief both come from 'the depths'.

But there is more than a description of reality here, there is a procedure for participating in it. The programme is given in two words: *wait* and *hope.* The words are at the centre of the psalm. 'I wait for the Lord, my soul waits, and in his word I hope; my soul waits for the Lord more than watchmen for the morning, more than watchmen for the morning. O Israel, hope in the Lord!'

The words *wait* and *hope* are connected with the image of the watchmen waiting through the night for the dawn. The connection provides important insights for the person in trouble who asks, 'But surely, there is something for me to do!' The answer is yes, there is something for you to do, or more exactly there is someone you can be; be a watchman.

A watchman is an important person, but he doesn't do very much. The massive turning of the earth, the immense energies released by the sun – all that goes on apart from him. He does nothing to influence or control such things: he is a watchman. He knows the dawn is coming; there are no doubts concerning that. Meanwhile he is alert to dangers, he comforts restless children or animals until it is time to work or play again in the light of day.

I was once a watchman. I worked from 10 P.M. until 6 A.M. in a building in New York City. My work as a night watchman was combined with that of elevator operator, but the elevator work petered out about midnight. After that I sat and read, dozed or studied. There were assorted night people in the neighbourhood who would stop in through the night hours and visit with me: strange, bizarre people with wonderful stories. I will never know how much of what I heard from them was fact and how much fiction: a failed millionaire obsessed with communist plots responsible for his demise, a South American adventurer now too old to tramp the remote jungles and mountains, a couple of streetwalkers who on slow nights would sit and talk about God and the worth of their souls.

I did that for an entire year. I stayed awake, I studied, I learned. I visited and gossiped. And I waited for the dawn. Dawn always came. The people who employed me though it was worth several dollars an hour for me to wait through the night and watch for the morning. But I never did anything, never constructed anything, never made anything happen. I waited. I hoped.

If I had not known that there were others in charge of the building, I might not have been content to just be a watchman and collect my pay. If I were not confident that the building had an owner who cared about it, if I did not know that there was a building engineer who kept it in good order and repair, if I did not know that there were hundreds of people in the building who were going about their work everyday quite capably . . . if I had not known these things, I might not have been so relaxed in making idle gossip with women of the night and old men of storied pasts.

Nor would the psalmist have been content to be a watchman if he were not sure of God. The psalmist's and the Christian's waiting and hoping is based on the conviction that God is actively involved in his creation and vigorously at work in redemption.

Waiting does not mean doing nothing. It is not fatalistic resignation. It means going about our assigned tasks, confident that God will provide the meaning and the conclusions. It is not compelled to work away at keeping up appearances with a bogus spirituality. It is the opposite of desperate and panicky manipulations, of scurrying and worrying.

And hoping is not dreaming. It is not spinning an illusion of fantasy to protect us from our boredom or our pain. It means a confident alert expectation that God will do what he said he will do. It is imagination put in the harness of faith. It is a willingness to let him do it his way and in his time. It is the opposite of making plans that we demand that God put into effect, telling him both how and when to do it. That is not hoping in God but bullying God. 'I wait for the Lord, my soul waits, and in his word I hope; my soul waits for the Lord more than watchmen for the morning, more than watchmen for the morning.'

An Eye Specialist and a Painter

When we suffer we attract counsellors as money attracts thieves. Everybody has an idea of what we did wrong to get ourselves into such trouble and a prescription for what we can do to get out of it. We are flooded first with sympathy and then with advice, and when we don't come around quickly we are abandoned as a hopeless case. But none of that is what we need. We need hope. We need to know that we are in relation to God. We need to know that suffering is part of what it means to be human and not something alien. We need to know where we are and where *God* is. We need an eye specialist rather, than, say, a painter. A painter tries to convey to us with the aid of his brush and palette a picture of the world as he sees it; an ophthalmologist tries to enable us to see the world as it really is.

There is a passage in George MacDonald's novel *The Princess and Curdie* that tells us that when Curdie reaches the castle, he sees the great staircase and he knows that to reach the tower he must go farther. The narrator takes the occasion to say that 'those who work well in the depths more easily understand the heights, for indeed in their true nature they are one and the same.'[8]

For the person who suffers, has suffered, or will suffer Psalm 130 is essential equipment, for it convinces us that the big difference is not in what people suffer but in the way they suffer. ('The same shaking that makes fetid water stink makes perfume issue a more pleasant odour.'[9]) The psalm does not exhort us to put up with suffering; it does not explain it or explain it away. It is, rather, a powerful demonstration that our place in the depths is not out of bounds from God. We see that whatever or whoever got us in trouble cannot separate us from God, for 'there is forgiveness with thee'. We are persuaded that God's way with us is redemption and that the redemption, not the suffering, is ultimate.

The depths have a bottom; the heights are boundless. Knowing that, we are helped to go ahead and learn the skills of waiting and hoping by which God is given room to work out our salvation and develop our faith while we fix our attention on his ways of grace and resurrection.

13

Humility

'My Eyes Are Not Raised Too High'

O Lord, my heart is not lifted up,
my eyes are not raised too high;
I do not occupy myself with things
too great and too marvelous for me.
But I have calmed and quieted my soul,
like a child quieted at its mother's breast;
like a child that is quieted is my soul.

O Israel, hope in the Lord
from this time forth and for evermore.

Psalm 131

Humility is the obverse side of confidence in God, whereas pride is the obverse side of confidence in self.

John Baillie

CHRISTIAN FAITH NEEDS CONTINUOUS MAINTENANCE. IT requires attending to. 'If you leave a thing alone you leave it to a torrent of change. If you leave a white post alone it will soon be a black post.'[1]

Every spring in my neighbourhood a number of people prune their bushes and trees. It is an annual practice with people who care about growing things. It is also one of those acts which an outsider, one who does not understand how growth works, almost always misunderstands, for it always looks like an act of mutilation. It appears that you are ruining the plant, when, in fact, you are helping it. We have a rosebush that hasn't been pruned for several years. When it first bloomed the roses were full and vigorous. Last summer the plant was larger than ever. The vines ranged up to the roof on a trellis I had made. I anticipated more roses than ever. But I was disappointed. The blossoms were small and scrawny. The branches had grown too far from their roots. The plant couldn't grow a good blossom. It needed a good pruning.

Psalm 131 is a maintenance psalm. It is functional to the person of faith as pruning is functional to the gardener: it gets rid of that which looks good to those who don't know any better, and reduces the distance between our hearts and their roots in God.

The two things that Psalm 131 prunes away are unruly ambition and infantile dependency, what we might call getting too big for our breeches, and refusing to cut the apron strings. Both of these tendencies can easily be supposed to be virtues, especially by those who are not conversant with Christian ways.

If we are not careful, we will be encouraging the very things that will ruin us. We are in special and constant need of expert correction. We need pruning. Jesus said, 'Every branch of mine that bears no fruit, he takes away, and every branch that does bear fruit he prunes, that it may bear more fruit' (Jn 15:2). More than once our Lord the Spirit has used Psalm 131 to do this important work among his people. As we gain a familiarity with and understanding of the psalm, he will be able to use it that way with us 'that we may bear more fruit.'

Aspiration Gone Crazy

'O Lord, my heart is not lifted up, my eyes are not raised too high; I do not occupy myself with things too great and too marvellous for me. But I have calmed and quieted my soul.'

These lines are enormously difficult for us to comprehend – not that they are difficult to understand with our minds, for the words are all plain, but difficult to grasp with our emotions, feeling their truth. All cultures throw certain stumbling blocks in the way of those who pursue gospel realities. It is sheerest fantasy to suppose that we would have had an easier time of it as Christian believers if we were in another land or another time. It is no easier to be a Chinese Christian than to be a Spanish Christian than to be a Russian Christian than to be a Brazilian Christian than to be an American Christian – nor more difficult. The way of faith deals with realities in whatever time or whatever culture.

But there are differences from time to time and from place to place which cause special problems. For instance, when an ancient temptation or trial becomes an approved feature in the culture, a way of life that is expected and encouraged, Christians have a stumbling block put before them that is hard to recognize for what it is, for it has been made into a monument, gilded with bronze and bathed in decorative lights. It has become an object of veneration. But the plain fact is that it is right in the middle of the road of faith, obstructing discipleship. For all its fancy dress and honoured position it is still a stumbling block.

One temptation that has received this treatment in Western civilization, with some special flourishes in America, is ambition. Our culture encourages and rewards ambition without qualification. We are surrounded by a way of life in which betterment is understood as expansion, as acquisition, as fame. Everyone wants to get more. To be on top, no matter what it is the top of, is admired. There is nothing recent about the temptation. It is the oldest sin in the book, the one that got Adam thrown out of the garden and Lucifer tossed out of heaven. What is fairly new about it is the general admiration and approval that it receives.

The old story of Doctor Faustus used to be well known and appreciated as a warning. John Faustus became impatient with the limitations placed upon him in his study of law, of medicine, of theology. No matter how much he learned in these fields he found he was always in the service of something greater than he was – of justice, of healing, of God. He chafed in the service and wanted out: he wanted to be in control, to break out of the limits of the finite. So he became adept in magic by which he was able to defy the laws of physics, the restrictions of morality and relations with God and use his knowledge in these fields for his own pleasures and purposes. In order to bring it off, though, he had to make a pact with the devil which permitted him to act for the next twenty-four years in a godlike way – living without limits, being in control instead of being in relationship, exercising power instead of practising love. But at the end of the twenty-four years was damnation.

For generations this story has been told and retold by poets and playwrights and novelists (Goethe, Marlowe, Mann) warning people against abandoning the glorious position of being a person created in the image of God and attempting the foolhardy adventure of trying to be a god on our own. But now something alarming has happened. There have always been Faustian characters, people in the community who embarked on a way of arrogance and power; now our entire culture is Faustian. We are caught up in a way of life which, instead of delighting in finding out the meaning of God and searching out the conditions in which human qualities can best be realized, recklessly seeks ways to circumvent nature, arrogantly defies personal relationships and names God only in curses. The legend of Faustus, useful for so long in pointing out the folly of a god-defying pride, now is practically unrecognizable because the assumptions of our whole society (our educational models, our economic expectations, even our popular religion) are Faustian.

It is difficult to recognize pride as a sin when it is held up on every side as a virtue, urged as profitable, and rewarded as an achievement. What is described in Scripture as the basic sin, the sin of taking things into your own hands, being your own god, grabbing what is there while you can get it, is now described as basic wisdom: improve yourself by whatever means you are able; get ahead regardless of the price, take care of me first. For a limited time it works. But at the end the devil has his due. There is damnation.

It is additionally difficult to recognize unruly ambition as a sin because it has a kind of superficial relationship to the virtue of aspiration – an impatience with mediocrity, and a dissatisfaction with all things created until we are at home with the Creator, the hopeful striving for the best God has for us – the kind of thing Paul expressed: 'I press on toward the goal for the prize of the upward call of God in Christ Jesus' (Phil 3:14). But if we take the energies that make for aspiration and remove God from the picture, replacing him with our own crudely sketched self-portrait, we end up with ugly arrogance. Robert Browning's fine line on aspiration, 'A man's reach should exceed his grasp, or what's a heaven for?' has been distorted to 'Reach for the skies and grab everything that isn't nailed down.' Ambition is aspiration gone crazy. Aspiration is the channeled, creative energy that moves us to growth in Christ, shaping goals in the Spirit. Ambition takes these same energies for growth and development and uses them to make something tawdry and cheap, sweatily knocking together a Babel when we could be vacationing in Eden. Calvin comments, 'Those who yield themselves up to the influence of ambition will soon lose themselves in a labyrinth of perplexity.'[2]

Our lives are only lived well when they are lived in terms of their creation, with God loving and us being loved, with God making and us being made, with God revealing and us understanding, with God commanding and us responding. Being a Christian means accepting the terms of creation, accepting God as our maker and redeemer, and growing day by day into an increasingly glorious creature in Christ, developing joy, experiencing love, maturing in peace. By the grace of Christ we experience the marvel of being made in the image of God. If we reject this way the only alternative is to attempt the hopelessly fourth-rate, embarrassingly awkward imitation of God made in the image of man.

Both revelation and experience (Genesis and Goethe) show it to be the wrong way, and so the psalmist is wise to see it and sing, 'O Lord, my heart is not lifted up, my eyes are not raised too high; I do not occupy myself with things too great and too marvellous for me. But I have calmed and quieted my soul.' I will not try to run my own life or the lives of others; that is God's business, I will not pretend to invent the meaning of the universe; I will accept what God has shown its meaning to be; I will not noisily strut about demanding that I be treated as the centre of my family or my neighbourhood or my work, but seek to discover where I fit and do what I am good at. The soul, clamorously crying out for attention and arrogantly parading its importance, is calmed and quieted so that it can be itself, truly.

As Content as a Child

But if we are not to be proud, clamorous, arrogant persons, what are we to be? Mousey, cringing, insecure ones? Well, not quite. Having realized the dangers of pride, the sin of thinking too much of ourselves, we are suddenly in danger of another mistake, that of thinking too little of ourselves. There are some who conclude that since the great Christian temptation is to try to be everything, the perfect Christian solution is to be nothing. And so we have the problem of the doormat Christian and the dishrag saint: the person upon whom everyone walks and wipes their feet, the person who is used by others to clean up the mess of everyday living and then discarded. These people then compensate for their poor lives by weepily clinging to God, hoping to make up for the miseries of everyday life by dreaming of luxuries in heaven.

Christian faith is not neurotic dependency but childlike trust. We do not have a God who forever indulges our whims but a God whom we trust with our destinies. The Christian is not a naive, innocent infant who has no identity apart from a feeling of being comforted and protected and catered to but a person who has discovered an identity that is given by God which can be enjoyed best and fully in a voluntary trust in

God. We do not cling to God desperately out of fear and the panic of insecurity; we come to him freely in faith and love.

Our Lord gave us the picture of the child as a model for Christian faith (Mk 10:14-16) not because of the child's helplessness but because of the child's willingness to be led, to be taught, to be blessed. God does not reduce us to a set of Pavlovian reflexes in which we mindlessly worship and pray and obey on signal; he establishes us with a dignity in which we are free to receive his word, his gifts, his grace.

The psalm shows great genius at this point and describes a relationship which is completely attractive. The translators of the Jerusalem Bible have retained the literalism of the Hebrew metaphor: 'Enough for me to keep my soul tranquil and quiet like a child in its mother's arms, as content as a child that has been weaned.' The last phrase, 'as a child that has been weaned,' creates a completely new, unguessed reality. The Christian is 'not like an infant crying loudly for his mother's breast, but like a weaned child that quietly rests by his mother's side, happy in being with her. . . . No desire now comes between him and his God; for he is sure that God knows what he needs before he asks him. And just as the child gradually breaks off the habit of regarding his mother only as a means of satisfying his own desires and learns to love her for her own sake, so the worshipper after a struggle has reached an attitude of mind in which he desires God for himself and not as a means of fulfilment of his own wishes. His life's centre of gravity has shifted. He now rests no longer in himself but in God.'[3]

The transition from a sucking infant to a weaned child, from squalling baby to quiet son or daughter, is not smooth. It is stormy and noisy. It is no easy thing to quieten yourself: sooner may a person calm the sea or rule the wind or tame a tiger, than quieten oneself. It is pitched battle. The baby is denied expected comforts and flies into rages or sinks into sulks. There are sobs and struggles. The infant is facing its first great sorrow and it is in sore distress. But 'to the weaned child his mother is his comfort though she has denied him comfort. It is a blessed mark of growth out of spiritual infancy when we can forgo the joys which once appeared to be essential, and can find our solace in him who denies them to us.'[4]

Many who have travelled this way of faith have described the transition from an infantile faith that grabs at God out of desperation to a mature faith that responds to God out of love . . . 'as content as a child that has been weaned.' Often our conscious Christian lives do begin at points of desperation, and God, of course, does not refuse to meet our needs. There are heavenly comforts that break through our despair and persuade us that 'all will be well and all manner of things will be well.' The early stages of Christian belief are not infrequently marked with miraculous signs and exhilarations of spirit. But as discipleship continues the sensible comforts gradually disappear. For God does not want us neurotically dependent upon him but willingly trustful in him. And so he weans us. The period of infancy will not be sentimentally extended beyond what is necessary. The time of weaning is very often noisy and marked with misunderstandings: 'I no longer feel like I did when I was first a Christian. Does that mean I am no longer a Christian? Has God abandoned me? Have I done something terribly wrong?'

The answer is, 'Neither: God hasn't abandoned you and you haven't done anything wrong. You are being weaned. The apron strings have been cut. You are free to come to God or not come to him. You are, in a sense, on your own with an open invitation to listen and receive and enjoy our Lord.'

The last line of the psalm addresses this quality of newly acquired freedom: 'O Israel, hope in the Lord from this time forth and for evermore.' Choose to be with him; elect his presence; aspire to his ways; respond to his love.

The Plain Way

When Charles Spurgeon preached this psalm he said that it 'is one of the shortest Psalms to read, but one of the longest to learn.'[5] We are always, it seems, reeling from one side of the road to the other as we travel in the way of faith. At one turning of the road we are presented with awesome problems and terrifying emergencies. We rise to the challenge, take things into our own hands to become master of the situation, telling God, 'Thank you, but get lost. We'll take care of this one ourselves.' At the next turning we are overwhelmed and run in a panic to some kind of infantile religion that will solve all our problems for us, freeing us of the burden of thinking and the difficulty of choosing. We are, alternately, rebellious runaways and whining babies. Worse, we have numerous experts, so-called, encouraging us to pursue one or the other of these ways.

The experts in our society who offer to help us have a kind of general-staff mentality, from which massive, top-down solutions are issued to solve our problems. Then when the solutions don't work, we get mired in the nothing-can-be-done swamp. We are first incited into being grandiose and then intimidated into being infantile. But there is another way, the plain way of quiet, Christian humility. We need pruning. Cut back to our roots, we then learn this psalm and discover the quietness of the weaned child, the tranquillity of maturing trust. It is such a minute psalm that many have overlooked it, but for all its brevity and lack of pretence it is essential. For every Christian encounters problems of growth and difficulties of development.

A number of years ago Peter Marin made an incisive observation that was very much in the spirit of Psalm 131. 'There are cultural conditions,' he wrote, 'for which there are no solutions, turnings of the soul so profound and complex that no system can absorb or contain them. How could one have 'solved' the Reformation? Or first-century Rome? One makes accommodations and adjustments, one dreams about the future and makes plans to save us all, but in spite of all that, because of it, what seems more important are the private independent acts that become more necessary every day: the ways we find as private persons to restore to one another the strengths we should have now – whether to make the kind of revolution we need or to survive the repression that seems likely . . . what saves us as men and women is always a kind of witness: the quality of our own acts and lives.'[6]

And that is what Psalm 131 nurtures: a quality of calm confidence and quiet strength which knows the difference between unruly arrogance and faithful aspiration, knows how to discriminate between infantile dependency and childlike trust, and chooses to aspire and to trust – and to sing, 'Enough for me to keep my soul tranquil and quiet like a child in its mother's arms, as content as a child that has been weaned.'

14

Obedience

'How He Swore to the Lord'

Remember, O Lord, in David's favour,
all the hardships he endured;
how he swore to the Lord
and vowed to the Mighty One of Jacob,
'I will not enter my house
or get into my bed;
I will not give sleep to my eyes
or slumber to my eyelids,
until I find a place for the Lord,
a dwelling place for the Mighty One of Jacob.'

Lo, we heard of it in Ephrathah,
we found it in the fields of Jaar.
'Let us go to his dwelling place;
let us worship at his footstool!'

Arise, O Lord, and go to thy resting place,
thou and the ark of thy might.
Let thy priests be clothed with righteousness,
and let thy saints shout for joy.
For thy servant David's sake
do not turn away the face of thy anointed one.

The Lord swore to David a sure oath
from which he will not turn back:
'One of the sons of your body
I will set on your throne.
If your sons keep my covenant
and my testimonies which I shall teach them,
their sons also for ever
shall sit upon your throne.'

For the Lord has chosen Zion;
he has desired it for his habitation:
'This is my resting place for ever;
here I will dwell, for I have desired it.
I will abundantly bless her provisions;
I will satisfy her poor with bread.
Her priests I will clothe with salvation,
and her saints will shout for joy.
There I will make a horn to sprout for David;
I have prepared a lamp for my anointed,
His enemies I will clothe with shame,
but upon himself his crown will shed its lustre.'

PSALM 132

True knowledge of God is born out of obedience.

JOHN CALVIN

AN INCIDENT TOOK PLACE A FEW YEARS AGO THAT HAS acquired the force of a parable for me. I had a minor operation on my nose and was in my hospital room recovering. Even though the surgery was minor, the pain was great and I was full of misery. Late in the afternoon a man was assigned to the other bed in my room. He was to have a tonsillectomy the next day. He was young, about twenty-two years old, good looking and friendly. He came over to me, put out his hand, and said, 'Hi, my name is Kelly. What happened to you?' I was in no mood for friendly conversation, did not return the handshake, grunted my name and said that I had had my nose broken. He got the message that I did not want to talk, pulled the curtain between our beds and let me alone. Later in the evening his friends were visiting and I heard him say, 'There's a man in the next bed who is a prize fighter; he got his nose broken in a championship fight.' He went on to embellish the story for the benefit of his friends.

Later in the evening as I was feeling better. I said, 'Kelly, you misunderstood what I said. I'm not a prize fighter. The nose was broken years ago in a basketball game and I am just now getting it fixed.'

'Well, what then do you do?'

'I'm a pastor.'

'Oh,' he said and turned away; I was no longer an interesting subject.

In the morning he woke me: 'Peterson, Peterson – wake up.' I groggily came awake and asked what he wanted. 'I want you to pray for me; I'm scared.' And so, before he was taken to surgery, I went to his bedside and prayed for him.

When he was brought back a couple of hours later, a nurse came and said, 'Kelly, I am going to give you an injection that should take care of any pain that you might have.'

In twenty minutes or so he began to groan, 'I hurt. I can't stand it. I'm going to die.'

I rang for the nurse and, when she came, said, 'Nurse, I don't think that shot did any good; why don't you give him another one.' She didn't acknowledge my credentials for making such a suggestion, told me curtly that she would oversee the medical care of the patient, turned on her heel and, a little abruptly, left. Meanwhile Kelly continued to vent his agony.

After another half an hour he began to hallucinate, and having lost touch with reality began to shout. 'Peterson, pray for me; can't you see I'm dying! Peterson, pray for me.' His shouts brought nurses and doctors and orderlies running. They held him down and quietened him with the injection that I had prescribed earlier.

The parabolic force of the incident is this: when the man was scared he wanted me to pray for him, and when the man was crazy he wanted me to pray for him, but in between, during the hours of so-called normalcy, he didn't want anything to do with a pastor. What Kelly betrayed *in extremis* is all many people know of religion: a religion to help them with their fears but which is forgotten when the fears are taken care of; a religion made of moments of craziness but which is remote and shadowy in the clear light of the sun and in the routines of every day. The most religious places in the world, as a matter of fact, are not churches but battlefields and mental hospitals. You are much more likely to find passionate prayer in a foxhole than in a church pew; and you will certainly find more otherworldly visions and supernatural voices in a mental hospital than you will in a church.

Stable not Petrified

Nevertheless we Christians don't go to either place to nurture our faith. We don't deliberately put ourselves in places of fearful danger to evoke heartfelt prayer, and we don't put ourselves in psychiatric wards so we can be around those who clearly see visions of heaven and hell, and distinctly hear the voice of God. What most Christians do is come to church, a place that is fairly safe and moderately predictable. For we have an instinct for health and sanity in our faith. We don't seek out death-defying situations, and we avoid mentally unstable teachers. But in doing that we don't get what some people seem to want very much, namely, a religion that makes us safe at all costs, certifying us as inoffensive to our neigbours and guaranteeing us as good credit risks to the banks. It would be simply awful to find that as we grew in Christ we became dull, that as we developed in discipleship we became like Anthony Trollope's Miss Thorne, whose 'virtues were too numerous to describe, and not sufficiently interesting to deserve description.'

We want a Christian faith that has stability but is not petrified; that has vision but is not hallucinatory. How do we get both the sense of stability and the spirit of adventure, the ballast of good health and the zest of true sanity? How do we get the adult maturity to keep our feet on the ground and retain the childlike innocence to make the leap of faith?

Psalm 132 is one of the oldest psalms in the Bible. It was included in the Psalms of Ascents to develop just those aspects of life under God and in Christ which my sometime friend Kelly lacked and which we all need.

It is a psalm of David's obedience, of 'how he swore to the Lord and vowed to the Mighty One of Jacob.' The psalm shows obedience as a lively, adventurous response of faith, that is rooted in historical fact and reaching into a promised hope.

Obedience with a History

The first half of Psalm 132 is the part that roots obedience in fact and keeps our feet on the ground. The psalm takes a single incident out of the past, the history of the ark of the covenant, and reminisces over it: 'Lo, we heard of it in Ephrathah, we found it in the fields of Jaar. "Let us go to his dwelling place; let us worship at his footstool!" Arise, O Lord, and go to thy resting place, thou and the ark of thy might.'

The ark of the covenant was a box approximately forty-five inches long, twenty-seven inches broad and twenty-seven inches deep, constructed of wood and covered with gold. Its lid of solid gold was called the mercy seat. Two cherubim, angel-like figures at either end, framed the space around the central mercy seat from which God's word was heard. It had been made under the supervision of Moses (Ex 25:10-22) and was a symbol of the presence of God among his people. The ark had accompanied Israel from Sinai, through the wilderness wanderings, and had been kept at Shiloh from the time of the conquest. In a battle the ark had been captured by the enemy Philistines and was a trophy of war displayed in the Philistine cities until it became a problem to them (the story is told in 1 Samuel 4-7) and was returned to Israel to the village of Kiriath-jearim (7:1-2) where it rested until David came to get it and place it in honour in Jerusalem where it later became enshrined in Solomon's Temple.

The history of the ark was, for the Hebrews, a kind of theological handbook. It provided an account of the presence of God among the people. Its history showed the importance of having God with you and the danger of trying to use God or carry him around. And so the ark itself was important in that it emphasized that God was with his people, and that God was over and above his people (for God quite obviously was not in the box). The ark was the symbol not the reality. When the ark was treated as a talisman, as a curio or as a magical device with which to manipulate God, everything went wrong. God cannot be contained or used.

The psalm does not retell this history, it only remembers the history. There is only enough here to trigger the historical memories of the people. For the rich symbolism of the ark was everyday stuff to them. Its extensive and intricate history was common knowledge, much as the story of Jesus is to Christians. With promptings from the psalm the story would come alive for them again, especially the part that tells of the time that David rediscovered the ark in an obscure village and determined to set it at the centre of Israelite life, restoring an old unity to the life of the people of God in adoration and worship. 'Lo, we heard of it in Ephrathah, we found it in the fields of Jaar.' News had come to David of where the ark was; he vowed to get it and was obedient to his vow. He gathered his people to himself and said: 'Let us go to his dwelling place; let us worship at his footstool.' He went to the ark and brought it up to Jerusalem in festive parade: 'Arise, O Lord, and go to thy resting place, thou and the ark of thy might. Let thy priests be clothed with righteousness, and let thy saints shout for joy.' As the song was sung we are told that 'David danced before the Lord with all his might. . . . So David and all the house of Israel brought up the ark of the Lord with shouting, and with the sound of the horn' (2 Sm 6:14-15).

As this old ark song is resung now by the people of God on pilgrimage, historical memories are renovated and relived: there is a vast, rich reality of obedience beneath the feet of disciples. They are not the first persons to ascend these slopes on their way of obedience to God, and they will not be the last. Up these same roads, along these same paths, the ark had been carried, accompanied by a determined and expectant people. It had been carried in both good and bad ways. They would remember the time they carried it in panic ('I'm scared! Pray for me!'), superstitiously as a secret weapon against the Philistines. *That* ended in calamity. They would also remember the Davidic parade of awed adoration and dancing celebration as obedience was tuned into worship. Christians tramp well-worn paths: obedience has a history.

This history is important for without it we are at the mercy of whims. Memory is a data bank we use to evaluate our position and make decisions. With a biblical memory we have two thousand years of experience from which to make the off-the-cuff responses that are required each day in the life of faith. If we are going to live adequately and maturely as the people of God, we need more data to work from than our own experience can give us.

What would we think of a pollster who issued a definitive report on how the American people felt about a new television special, only to discover later that he had interviewed only one person who had seen only ten minutes of the programme? We would dismiss the conclusions as frivolous. Yet that is exactly the kind of evidence that too many Christians accept as the final truth about many much more important matters – matters such as answered prayer, God's judgment, Christ's forgiveness, eternal salvation. The only person they consult is themselves and the only experience they evaluate is the most recent ten minutes. But we need other experiences, the community of experience of brothers and sisters in the church, the centuries of experience provided by our biblical ancestors. A Christian who has David in his bones, Jeremiah in his bloodstream, Paul in his fingertips and Christ in his heart will know how much and how little value to put on his own momentary feelings and the experience of the past week.

To remain willfully ignorant of Abraham wandering in the desert, the Hebrews enslaved in Egypt, David battling the Philistines, Jesus arguing with the Pharisees and Paul writing to the Corinthians is like saying, 'I refuse to remember that when I kicked that black dog last week he bit my leg.' If I don't remember it, in the next fit of anger I will kick him again and get bitten again. Biblical history is a good memory for what doesn't work. It is also a good memory for what does work –

like remembering what you put in the soup that made it taste so good so that you can repeat and enjoy the recipe on another day; or remembering the short cut through the city to the ocean that saved you from being tied up in traffic and got you to the beach two hours earlier.

A Christian with a defective memory has to start everything from scratch and spends far too much of his or her time backtracking, repairing, starting over. A Christian with a good memory avoids repeating old sins, knows the easiest way through complex situations and instead of starting over each day continues what was begun in Adam. Psalm 132 activates faith's memory so that obedience will be sane. 'Each act of obedience by the Christian is a modest proof, unequivocal for all its imperfection, of the reality of what he attests.'[1]

Hope: A Race towards God's Promises

But Psalm 132 doesn't just keep our feet on the ground, it also gets them off the ground. It is not only a solid foundation in the past; it is a daring leap into the future. For obedience is not a stodgy plodding in the ruts of religion, it is a hopeful race towards God's promises. The second half of the psalm has a propellent quality to it. The psalmist is not an antiquarian, revelling in the past for its own sake, but a traveller using what he knows of the past to get to where he is going – to God.

For all its interest in history the Bible never refers to the past as 'the good old times.' The past is not, for the person of faith, a restored historical site that we tour when we are on vacation; it is a field that we plow and harrow and plant and fertilize and work for a harvest.

The second half of Psalm 132 takes seriously what God said to David and how David responded (matters that are remembered in the ark narrative) and uses them to make a vision of the reality that is in the future of faith: 'I will abundantly bless her provisions; I will satisfy her poor with bread. Her priests I will clothe with salvation, and her saints will shout for joy. There I will make a horn to sprout for David; I have prepared a lamp for my anointed. His enemies I will clothe with shame, but upon himself his crown will shed its luster.' All the verb tenses are future. Obedience is fulfilled by hope.

Now none of these hopes is unrelated to or detached from actual history: each develops from what a person with a good memory knows happened.

'I will abundantly bless her provisions; I will satisfy her poor with bread.' The devout mind goes back to those years in the wilderness when God gave water from the rock, manna from the ground and quail from the skies, and fashions a hope for abundant, eternal providence.

'Her priests I will clothe with salvation, and her saints will shout for joy.' No other people knew so much of salvation as Israel. The priests renewed the knowledge and applied it to daily life at every gathering of worship – occasions that were always marked with joy – renewing the life of redemption. Has any other people had such a good time with their faith as Israel? From Moses's song at the edge of the Red Sea with Miriam and the women accompanying with tambourines to the victorious trumpets that shook and finally tumbled the walls of Jericho, to the robust hymns of David that we continue to sing in our churches today, the joy has overflowed.

'There I will make a horn to sprout for David; I have prepared a lamp for my anointed.' The horn was a sign of strength. The hope is that its brightness will provide a light for the path of the one who represents God's presence, a light we now identify with revelation in Scripture and in Christ.

'His enemies I will clothe with shame, but upon himself his crown will shed its luster.' The shame of God's enemies and the glory of God's king will finally be decisive. The triumph will be complete. Evil will lie sprawling in defeat, righteousness will flourish in victory. That is an agenda that hope writes for obedience.

Psalm 132 cultivates a hope that gives wings to obedience, a hope that is consistent with the reality of what God has done in the past but is not confined to it. All the expectations listed in Psalm 132 have their origin in an accurately remembered past. But they are not simply repetitions of the past projected into the future. They are developments *out* of it, with new features of their own.

Christians who master Psalm 132 will be protected from one danger, at least, that is ever a threat to obedience: the danger that we should reduce Christian existence to ritually obeying a few commandments that are congenial to our temperament and convenient to our standard of living. It gives us, instead, a vision into the future so that we can see what is right before us. If we define the nature of our lives by the mistake of the moment or the defeat of the hour or the boredom of the day, we will define it wrongly. We need roots in the past to give obedience ballast and breadth; we need a vision of the future to give obedience direction and goal. And they must be connected. There must be an organic unity between them. If we never learn how to do this, extend the boundaries of our lives beyond the dates enclosed by our birth and death and acquire an understanding of God's way as something larger and more complete than the anecdotes in our private diaries, we will forever be missing the point of things by making headlines out of something that ought to be tucked away on page 37 in section C of the newspaper, or putting into the classified ads something that should be getting a full-page colour advertisement – mistaking a sore throat for a descent into hell. ('Peterson, pray for me!') For Christian faith cannot be comprehended by examining an instamatic flash picture which has caught a pose of beauty or absurdity, ecstacy or terror; it is a full revelation of a vast creation and a grandly consummated redemption. Obedience is doing what God tells us to do in it.

The Strength to Stand; the Willingness to Leap

In such ways Psalm 132 cultivates the memory and nurtures the hope that lead to mature obedience. It protects us from a religion that is ignorant of the ways of God and so keeps us prey to every fear that thrusts itself upon us. It guards us from a religion riot with fantasies and nightmares because it has become disassociated from the promises of God. It develops a strong sense of continuity with the past and a surging sense of exploration into the future. It is the kind of thing we sing to stay normal without becoming dull, to walk upright in the middle of the road without getting stuck in a long rut of mediocrity. Its words prod us to reach into the future without losing touch with daily reality. Its rhythms stimulate us to new adventures in the Spirit without making us lunatics. For Christian living demands that we keep our feet on the ground; it also asks us to make a leap of faith.

A Christian who stays put is no better than a statue. A person who leaps about constantly is under suspicion of being not a man but a jumping jack. What we require is obedience – the strength to stand and the willingness to leap, and the sense to know when to do which. Which is exactly what we get when an accurate memory of God's ways is combined with a lively hope in his promises.

15

Community

'Like the Precious Oil upon the Head'

Behold, how good and pleasant it is
when brothers dwell in unity!
It is like the precious oil upon the head,
running down upon the beard,
upon the beard of Aaron,
running down on the collar of his robes!
It is like the dew of Hermon,
which falls on the mountains of Zion!
For there the Lord has commanded the blessing,
life for evermore.

PSALM 133

All actual life is encounter.

MARTIN BUBER

WHETHER WE LIKE IT OR NOT, THE MOMENT WE CONFESS Jesus Christ as our Lord and Saviour, that is, from the time we become a Christian, we are at the same time a member of the Christian church . . . even if we do not permit our name to be placed on a church roll, even if we refuse to identify ourselves with a particular congregation and share responsibilities with them, even if we absent ourselves from the worship of a congregation. Our membership in the church is a corollary of our faith in Christ. We can no more be a Christian and have nothing to do with the church than we can be a person and not be in a family. Membership in the church is a basic spiritual fact for those who confess Christ as Lord. It is not an option for those Christians who happen, by nature, to be more gregarious than others. It is part of the fabric of redemption.

There are Christians, of course, who never put their names down on a membership list; there are Christians who refuse to respond to the call to worship each Sunday; there are Christians who say, 'I love God but I hate the church.' But they are members all the same, whether they like it or not, whether they acknowledge it or not. For God never makes private, secret salvation deals with people. His relationships with us are personal, true: intimate, yes; but private, no. We are a family in Christ. When we become Christians, we are among brothers and sisters in faith. No Christian is an only child.

But, of course, just because we are a family of faith does not mean that we are one big happy family. The people we encounter as brothers and sisters in faith are not always nice people. They do not stop being sinners the moment they begin believing in Christ. They don't suddenly metamorphose into brilliant conversationalists, exciting companions and glowing inspirations. Some of them are cranky, some of them dull and others (if the truth be spoken) a drag. But at the same time our Lord tells us that they are brothers and sisters in faith. If God is my father, then this is my family.

So the question is not, 'Am I going to be a part of a community of faith?' but, 'How am I going to live in this community of faith?' God's children do different things. Some run away from it and pretend that the family doesn't exist. Some move out and get an apartment on their own from which they return to make occasional visits, nearly always showing up for the parties and bring a gift to show that they really do hold the others in fond regard. And some would never dream of leaving but cause others to dream it for them for they are always criticizing what is served at the meals, quarreling with the way the housekeeping is done and complaining that the others in the family are either ignoring or taking advantage of them. And some determine to find out what God has in mind by placing them in this community called a church, learn how to function in it harmoniously and joyously and develop the maturity that is able to share and exchange God's grace with those who might otherwise be viewed as nuisances.

Not Like Paying Taxes

Psalm 133 presents what we are after: 'Behold, how good and pleasant it is when brothers dwell in unity!' The psalm puts into song what is said and demonstrated throughout Scripture and church: community is essential. Scripture knows nothing of the solitary Christian. People of faith are always members of a community. Creation itself was not complete until there was community. Adam needing Eve before humanity was whole. God never works with individuals in isolation, but always with people in community.

This is the biblical datum, and that with which we must begin. Jesus worked with twelve disciples and lived with them in community. The church was formed when one hundred twenty people were 'all together' in one place (Acts 2:1 and again in 5:12). When some early Christians were dropping out of the community and pursuing private interests, a pastor wrote to them urging them to nurture their precious gift of community, 'not neglecting to meet together, as is the habit of some, but encouraging one another, and all the more as you see the Day drawing near' (Heb 10:25). The Bible knows nothing of a religion that is defined by what a person does inwardly in the privacy of thought or feeling, or apart from others on lonely retreat. When Jesus was asked what the great commandment was, he said, 'Love the Lord your God with all your heart, and with all your soul, and with all your mind,' and then immediately, before anyone could go off and make a private religion about it ('I come to the garden alone . . .') riveted it to another: 'A second is like it, You shall love your neighbour as yourself' (Mt 22:34-40).

Christians make this explicit in their act of worship each week by gathering as a community: other people are unavoidably present. As we come to declare our love for God we must face the unlovely and lovely fellow sinners whom God loves and commands us to love. This must not be treated as something to put up with, one of the inconvenient necessities of faith in the way that paying taxes is an inconvenient consequence of living in a secure and free nation. It is not only necessary; it is desirable that our faith have a social dimension, a human relationship: 'Behold, how good and pleasant it is when brothers dwell in unity!'

For centuries this psalm was sung on the road as throngs of people made the ascent to Jerusalem for festival worship. Our imaginations readily reconstruct those scenes. How great to have everyone sharing a common purpose, travelling a common path, striving towards a common goal, that path and purpose and goal being God. How much better than making the long trip alone: 'How good, how delightful it is for all to live together like brothers' (JB).

Two Ways to Avoid Community

But if living in community is necessary and desirable, it is also enormously difficult.[1] There is a clue to the nature of the difficulty in the simile 'like brothers.'

Many Christians have some firsthand experience of what it means to live 'like brothers'. Brothers fight. And sisters fight. The first story in the Bible about brothers living together is the story of Cain and Abel. And it is a murder story. Significantly, their fight was a religious fight, a quarrel over which of them loved God best. The story of Joseph and his brothers follows a few pages later, in which Joseph, envied by the rest, is sold into Egypt as a slave. David and his brothers fare no better and add to the evidence of discord. Even Jesus and his brothers are evidence of disharmony rather than peace. The one picture we have of them shows the brothers misunderstanding Jesus and trying to drag him away from his messianic work because they are convinced that he is crazy.

Those who have acquired their knowledge of human relationships by reading psychology books instead of the Bible find the case histories on this subject under the chapter entitled 'Sibling Rivalry'. But most of what is there is only a footnote to what the Scripture says: children fight a lot; each brother is quick to take offence if he doesn't get his own way; each sister wants a major share of the parents' attention.

Children are ordinarily so full of their own needs and wants that they look at a brother and sister not as an ally but as a competitor. If there is only one pork chop on the plate and three of us who want it, I will no longer look at my brother and sister as delightful dinner companions but as difficult rivals. Much of the literature of the world (novels, plays, poetry) documents this: living together 'like brothers' means, in actual practice, endless squabbles, murderous quarrels and angry arguments. And so if we are going to sing 'how delightful it is for all to live together like brothers', we will not do it by being left by ourselves, following our natural bent. If we do, we will only get into a big fight, and the only delightful thing about it will be the pleasure the spectators get in watching us bloody each other's noses.

Living together in a way that evokes the glad song of Psalm 133 is one of the great and arduous tasks before Christ's people. Nothing requires more attention and energy. It is easier to do almost anything else. It is far easier to deal with people as problems to be solved than to have anything to do with them in community. If a person can be isolated from the family (from husband, from wife, from parents, from children, from neighbours) and then be professionally counselled, advised and guided without the complications of all those relationships, things are very much simpler. But if such practices are engaged in systematically, they become an avoidance of community. Christians are a community of people who are visibly together at worship, but who remain in relationship through the week in witness and service. 'In the beginning is the relation.'[2]

Another common way to avoid community is to turn the church into an institution. In this way people are treated not on the basis of personal relationships but in terms of impersonal functions. Goals are set that will catch the imagination of the largest numbers of people; structures are developed that will accomplish the goal through planning and organization. Organizational planning and institutional goals become the criteria by which the community is defined and evaluated. In the process the church becomes less and less a community, that is, people who pay attention to each other, ('brothers living together'), and more and more a collectivism of 'contributing units.'

Every community of Christians is imperiled when either of these routes are pursued: the route of defining others as problems to be solved, the way one might repair an automobile; the route of lumping persons together in terms of economic ability or institutional effectiveness, the way one might run a bank. Somewhere between there is community – a place where each person is taken seriously, learns to trust others, depend on others, be compassionate with others, rejoice with others. 'Behold, how good and pleasant it is when brothers dwell in unity!'

Each Other's Priest

There are two poetic images in Psalm 133 that are instinct with insights in the work of encouraging and shaping a good and delightful life together in Christ. The first image describes community as 'precious oil upon the head, running down . . . upon the beard of Aaron, running down on the collar of his robes!'

The picture comes from Exodus 29 where instructions are given for the ordination of Aaron and other priests. After sacrifices were prepared, Aaron was dressed in the priestly vestments. Then this direction is given: 'you shall take the anointing oil, and pour it on his head and anoint him. . . . Thus you shall ordain Aaron and his sons' (Ex 29:7, 9).

Oil, throughout Scripture, is a sign of God's presence, a symbol of the Spirit of God. The oil glistens, picks up the warmth of sunlight, softens the skin, perfumes the person. (Gerard Manley Hopkins, extolling God's grandeur in creation, uses a similar image in his line, 'It gathers to a greatness, like the ooze of oil crushed.'[3]) There is a quality of warmth and ease in God's community which contrasts with the icy coldness and hard surfaces of people who jostle each other in mobs and crowds.

But more particularly here the oil is an anointing oil, marking the person as a priest. Living together means seeing the oil flow over the head, down the face, through the beard, onto the shoulders of the other – and when I see that I know that my brother, my sister, is my priest. When we see the other as God's anointed, our relationships are profoundly affected.

No one has realized this more perceptively in our time than Dietrich Bonhoeffer. He wrote, 'Not what a man is in himself as a Christian, his spirituality and piety, constitutes the basis of our community. What determines our brotherhood is what that man is by reason of Christ. Our community with one another consists solely in what Christ has done to both of us.'[4] And what he has done is anoint us with his Spirit. We are set apart for service to one another. We mediate to one another the mysteries of God. We represent to one another the address of God. We are priests who speak God's Word and share Christ's sacrifice. 'The Christian needs another Christian who speaks God's Word to him. He needs him again and again when he becomes uncertain and discouraged, for by himself he cannot help himself without belying the truth. He needs his brother man as a bearer and proclaimer of the divine word of salvation. He needs his brother man as a bearer and proclaimer of the divine word of salvation. He needs his brother solely because of Jesus Christ.

The Christ in his own heart is weaker than the Christ in the word of his brother; his own heart is uncertain, his brother's is sure.'[5]

In the second image, the community is 'like the dew of Hermon, which falls on the mountains of Zion!' Hermon, the highest mountain in that part of the world, rose to a height of over nine thousand feet in the Lebanon range, north of Israel. Anyone who has slept overnight in high alpine regions knows how heavy the dew is at such altitudes. When you wake in the morning, you are drenched. This heavy dew, which was characteristic of each new dawn on the high slopes of Hermon, is extended by the imagination to the hills of Zion – a copious dew, fresh and nurturing in the drier barren Judean country. The alpine dew communicates a sense of morning freshness, a feeling of fertility, a clean anticipation of growth.

Important in any community of faith is an ever-renewed sense of expectation in what God is doing with our brothers and sisters in the faith. We refuse to label the others as one thing or another. We refuse to predict our brother's behaviour, our sister's growth. Each person in the community is unique, each is specially loved and particularly led by the Spirit of God. How can I presume to make conclusions about anyone? How can I pretend to know your worth or your place? Margaret Mead, who makes learned and passionate protests against the ways modern culture flattens out and demoralizes people, wrote, 'No recorded cultural system has ever had enough different expectations to match all the children who were born within it.'[6]

A community of faith flourishes when we view each other with this expectancy, wondering what God will do today in this one, in that one. When we are in a community with those Christ loves and redeems, we are constantly finding out new things about them. They are new persons each morning, endless in their possibilities. We explore the fascinating depths of their friendship, share the secrets of their quest. It is impossible to be bored in such a community, impossible to feel alienated among such people.

The oil flowing down Aaron's beard communicates a sense of warm, priestly relationship. The dew descending down Hermon's slops communicates a sense of fresh and expectant newness. Oil and dew. The two things that make life together delightful.

Rousing Good Fellowship

The last line of the psalm concludes that the good and delightful life together is where 'the Lord has commanded the blessing, life for evermore.'

Christians are always attempting and never quite succeed at getting a picture of the life everlasting. When we try to imagine it, we only banalize it. And then, having scrawled an uninteresting and amateurish sketch using the paint pots of an impoverished faith, we announce that we are not so sure we want to spend eternity in a place like that. Maybe we would prefer the rousing good fellowship of hell.

There is just a hint thrown out in Psalm 133 of heaven (a hint that is expanded into a grand vision in Revelation 4-5), that turns that on its head: the rousing good fellowship is in heaven. Where relationships are warm and expectancies fresh we are already beginning to enjoy the life together that will be completed in our life everlasting. Which means that heaven is like nothing quite so much as a good party. Assemble in your imagination all the friends that you enjoy being with most, the companions that evoke the deepest joy, your most stimulating relationships, the most delightful of shared experiences, the people with whom you feel completely alive – *that* is a hint at heaven, 'for there the Lord has commanded the blessing, life for evermore.'

April 9, 1945

One of the best, maybe *the* best, book written in this century on the meaning of living together as a family of faith is *Life Together* by Dietrich Bonhoeffer. The book begins with the words of the psalm, 'Behold, how good and how pleasant it is for brethren to live together in unity!' The text was with Bonhoeffer all his life. His first publication, a doctoral dissertation at age twenty-one, was titled, 'The Communion of the Saints.' His book *The Cost of Discipleship* has been a handbook to a vast company of twentieth-century Christians on pilgrimage. During the Nazi years he led a fugitive community of seminarians, living with them in a daily quest to discover for themselves the meaning of being a family in Christ and training them in the pastoral ministries that would lead others into that fellowship of a common life. It was during this period that he wrote *Life Together.*

During the last years of the Third Reich he was imprisoned by Adolf Hitler. But even then prison walls did not separate him from his brothers and sisters in Christ. He prayed for them and wrote letters to them, deepening the experience of community in Christ. And then he was killed. Even as his life had been an exploration of the first line of Psalm 133, his death was an exposition of the last line in which 'the Lord has commanded the blessing, life for evermore.'

> The time was April 9th, 1945. The prison doctor at Flossenburg wrote this report: 'On the morning of the day, some time between five and six o'clock, the prisoners . . . were led out of their cells and the verdicts read to them. Through the half-open door of a room in one of the huts I saw Pastor

> Bonhoeffer, still in his prison clothes, kneeling in fervent prayer to the Lord his God. The devotion and evident conviction of being heard that I saw in the prayer of this intensely captivating man, moved me to the depths.' So the morning came. Now the prisoners were ordered to strip. They were led down a little flight of steps under the trees to the secluded place of execution. There was a pause.... Naked under the scaffold in the sweet spring woods, Bonhoeffer knelt for the last time to pray. Five minutes later, his life was ended.... Three weeks later Hitler committed suicide. In another month the Third Reich had fallen. All Germany was in chaos and communications were impossible. No one knew what had happened to Bonhoeffer. His family waited in anguished uncertainty in Berlin. The report of his death was first received in Geneva and then telegraphed to England. On July 27th his aged parents, as was their custom, turned on their radio to listen to the broadcast from London. A memorial service was in progress. The triumphant measures of Vaughan Williams' 'For all the Saints' rolled out loud and solemn from many hundred voices. Then a single German was speaking in English, 'We are gathered here in the presence of God to make thankful remembrance of the life and work of his servant Dietrich Bonhoeffer, who gave his life in faith and obedience to His holy word....'[7]

In such a way one man showed in his life and death, even as we can in the communities we live in and lead, the rich and continuing truths of Psalm 133: 'Behold, how good and pleasant it is when brothers dwell in unity! ... For there the Lord has commanded the blessing, life for evermore.'

16

Blessing

'Lift Up Your Hands'

Come, bless the Lord,
all you servants of the Lord,
who stand by night in the house of the Lord!
Lift up your hands to the holy place,
and bless the Lord!

May the Lord bless you from Zion,
he who made heaven and earth!

PSALM 134

Not seldom in this life; when, on the right side, fortune's favourites sail close by us, we, though all adroop before, catch somewhat of the rushing breeze, and joyfully feel our bagging sails fill out.

HERMAN MELVILLE

THE STORY OF CHARLES COLSON TELLS OF ELECTION NIGHT 1972 when President Nixon describes a familiar scene in the interior life of what could be anyone. There had been months of struggle, of strategy, of sacrifice. It had all paid off in a landslide victory. He was in the place that he had always wanted to be. The picture Colson draws of that night has three figures in it: Halderman, arrogant and sullen; Nixon, restless and gulping Scotch; and Colson feeling let down, deflated, '. . . a deadness inside me.' Three men at the power pinnacle of the world and not a single note of joy discernible in the room. 'If someone had peered in on us that night from some imaginary peephole in the ceiling of the President's office, what a curious sight it would have been: a victorious President, grumbling over words he would grudgingly say to his fallen foe; his chief of staff angry, surly, and snarling; and the architect of his political strategy sitting in numbed stupor.'[1]

The experience is not uncommon. We work hard for something, get it and then find we don't want it. We struggle for years to get to the top and find life there thoroughly boring. Colson wrote, 'Being part of electing a President was the fondest ambition of my life. For three long years I had committed everything I had, every ounce of energy to Richard Nixon's cause. Nothing else mattered. We had had no time together as a family, no social life, no vacations.'[2] And then, having in his hands what he had set out for, he found he couldn't enjoy it.

For some the goal is an academic degree; for some a career position; for some a certain standard of living; for some acquiring a possession, getting married, having a child, landing a job, visiting a country, meeting a celebrity. But having got what we had always wanted, we find that we have forgotten what we wanted at all. We are less fulfilled than ever, and only conscious of 'a deadness inside me.'

Stand, Stoop, Stay

In Psalm 120, the first of the Psalms of Ascents, we saw the theme of *repentance* developed. The word in Hebrew is *t^e^shubah,* a turning away from the world and a turning towards God; the initial move in a life-goal set on God. It was addressed to the person at the crossroads, inviting each of us to make the decision to set out on the way of faith. Each of the psalms that followed has described a part of what takes place along this pilgrim way among people who have turned to God and follow him in Christ. We have discovered in these psalms beautiful lines, piercing insights, dazzling truths, stimulating words. We have found that the world in which these psalms are sung is a world of adventure and challenge, of ardour and meaning. We have realized that while there are certainly difficulties in the way of faith, it cannot, by any stretch of the imagination, be called dull. It requires everything that is in us; it enlists all our desires and abilities; it gathers our total existence into its songs. But when we get to where we are going, what then? What happens at the end of faith? What takes place when we finally arrive? Will we be disappointed?

Psalm 134, the final Psalm of Ascents, provides the evidence. The way of discipleship that begins in an act of repentance *(t^e^shubah)* concludes in a life of praise *(b^e^rakah)*. It doesn't take long to find the key word and controlling thought in the psalm: *bless* the Lord, *bless* the Lord, the Lord *bless* you.

There are two words which are translated 'blessed' in our Bibles. One is *ashre,* which describes the having-it-all-together sense of well-being that comes when we are living in tune with creation and redemption. It is what Psalm 1 announces and what Psalm 128 describes. It is what we experience when God blesses us. The word in Hebrew 'is used only of men, never of God, (and) in the NT there are only two instances in which it is used of God (*makarios* in 1 Tm 1:11; 6:15).'[3] The other word is *b*ᵉ*rakah.* It describes what God does to us and among us: he enters into covenant with us, he pours out his own life for us, he shares the goodness of his Spirit, the vitality of his creation, the joys of his redemption. He empties himself among us and we get what he is. That is *blessing.* When the first word is *t*ᵉ*shubah* the last word is *b*ᵉ*rakah.*

God gets down on his knees among us; gets on our level and shares himself with us. He does not reside afar off and send us diplomatic messages, he kneels among us. That posture is characteristic of God. The discovery and realization of this is what defines what we know of God as *good* news – God shares himself generously and graciously. 'Whichever form the blessing takes, it implies an exchange of the contents of the soul.'[4] God enters into our need, he anticipates our goals, he 'gets into our skin' and understands us better than we do ourselves. Everything we learn about God through Scripture and in Christ tells us that he knows what it is like to change a nappy for the thirteenth time in the day, have a report over which we have worked long and carefully gather dust on somebody's desk for weeks and weeks, find our teaching treated with scorn and indifference by children and youth, discover that the integrity and excellence of our work has been overlooked and the shoddy duplicity of another's rewarded with a promotion. A book on God has for its title *The God Who Stands, Stoops, and Stays.* That summarizes the posture of blessing: God stands – he is foundational and dependable; God stoops – he kneels to our level and meets us where we are; God stays – he sticks with us through hard times and good, sharing his life with us in grace and peace.

And because God blesses us, we bless God. We respond with that which we have received. We participate in the process which God has initiated and continues. We who are blessed, bless. When the word is used for what people do, it has, in Scripture, the sense of 'praise and gratitude for blessing received.'[5] The people who learn what it is like to receive the blessing, persons who travel the way of faith experiencing the ways of grace in all kinds of weather and over every kind of terrain, become good at blessing. In Israel this became 'the distinctive expression of the practice of religion.'[6] In Judaism to this day all forms of prayer which begin with praise of God are called *b^erakoth,* that is, blessings.[7]

An Invitation and a Command

There is no better summarizing and concluding word in all of Scripture than the word *blessing.* It describes what we most prize in God's dealing with us and what is most attractive when we evaluate our way of living. Every act of worship concludes with a benediction. Psalm 134 features the word in a form that might be called an invitational command: 'Come, bless the Lord . . . Lift up your hands . . . and bless the Lord!'

The persons who first sang this song had been travelling, literally, the roads that led to Jerusalem. Now they had arrived and were at the temple to worship God in festival celebration. Some would have been on the road for days, some for weeks, in some instances, perhaps, for months. Now they were at the end of the road. What will happen? What will they feel? What will they do? Will there be the 'deadness inside'?

Read in one way the sentence is an invitation: 'Come, bless the Lord.' The great promise of being in Jerusalem is that all might join in the rich temple worship. You are welcome now to do it. Come and join in. Don't be shy. Don't hold back. Did you have a fight with your wife on the way? That's all right. You are here now. Bless the Lord. Did you quarrel with your neighbour while making the trip? Forget it. You are here now. Bless the Lord. Did you lose touch with your children while coming and aren't sure just where they are now? Put that aside for the moment. They have their own pilgrimage to make. You are here. Bless the Lord. Are you ashamed of the feelings you had while travelling? the grumbling you indulged in? the resentment you harboured? Well, it wasn't bad enough to keep you from arriving, and now that you are here, bless the Lord. Are you embarrassed at the number of times you quit and had to have someone pick you up and carry you along? No matter. You are here. Bless the Lord.

The sentence is an invitation; it is also a command. Having arrived at the place of worship, will we now sit around and tell stories about the trip? Having got to the big city, will we spend our time here as tourists, visiting the bazaars, window-shopping and trading? Having checked Jerusalem off our list of things to do, will we immediately begin looking for another challenge, another holy place to visit? Will the Temple be a place to socialize, receive congratulations from others on our achievement, a place to share gossip and trade stories, a place to make business contacts that will improve our prospects back home? But that is not why you made the trip: bless the Lord. You are here because the Lord blessed you. Now you bless the Lord.

Our stories may be interesting but they are not the point. Our achievements may be marvellous but they are not germane. Our curiosity may be understandable but it is not relevant. Bless the Lord. 'When the perfect comes, the imperfect will pass away' (1 Cor 13:10). Bless the Lord. Do that for which you were created and redeemed; lift your voices in gratitude; enter into the community of praise and prayer that anticipates the final consummation of faith in heaven. Bless the Lord.

Feelings Don't Run the Show

We are invited to bless the Lord; we are commanded to bless the Lord. And then someone says, 'But I don't feel like it. And I won't be a hypocrite. I can't bless the Lord if I don't feel like blessing the Lord. It wouldn't be honest.'

The biblical response to that is, 'Lift up your hands to the holy place, and bless the Lord!' You can lift up your hands regardless of how you feel; it is a simple motor movement. You may not be able to command your heart, but you can command your arms. Lift your arms in blessing; just maybe your heart will get the message and be lifted up also in praise. We are psychosomatic beings; body and spirit are intricately interrelated. Go through the motions of blessing God and your spirit will pick up the cue and follow along. 'For why do men lift their hands when they pray? Is it not that their hearts may be raised at the same time to God?'[8]

It isn't quite the same thing, and there are many differences in detail, but there is a broad similarity between the directions in the psalm and the contemporary movement known as 'behaviour modification' – which in a rough-and-ready way means that you can act yourself into a new way of being. Find the right things to do, practice the actions and other things will follow. 'Lift up your hands to the holy place, and bless the Lord.' Act your gratitude; pantomime your thanks; you will become that which you do.

Many think that the only way to change your behaviour is to first change your feelings. We take a pill to alter our moods so that we won't kick the dog. We turn on music to soothe our emotions so that our conversation will be less abrasive. But there is an older wisdom that puts it differently: by changing our behaviour we can change our feelings. One person says, 'I don't like that man; therefore I will not speak to him. When and if my feelings change, I will speak.' Another says, 'I don't like that person; therefore I am going to speak to him.' The person, surprised at the friendliness, cheerfully responds and suddenly friendliness is shared. One person says, 'I don't feel like worshipping; therefore I am not going to church. I will wait till I feel like it and then I will go.' Another says, 'I don't feel like worshipping; therefore I will go to church and put myself in the way of worship.' In the process she finds herself blessed and begins, in turn, to bless.

Most probably the people who were first addressed by this command were the professional leaders of worship in the Jerusalem Temple, the Levites ('who stand by night in the house of the Lord'). They worked in shifts around the clock during festival time, and through the night some of them were always on duty. The great danger in those hours was that the worship would be listless and slovenly. 'What can you expect at three o'clock in the morning.' 'No excuses,' says the psalm singer, 'your feelings might be flat but you can control your muscles: lift up your hands.' Humphrey Bogart once defined a professional as a person who 'did a better job when he didn't feel like it.' That goes for a Christian too. Feelings don't run the show. There is a reality deeper than our feelings. Live by that. Eric Routley thinks that, colloquially, to bless means to 'speak well of.'[9] The Lord has spoken well of you; now you speak well of him.

Taking God Seriously but Not Ourselves

It is as easy to find instances of people who bless in Christian ranks as it is to find examples of people who curse in the world's.

Karl Barth is one of my favourites. He is one of the great theologians of all time, but the really attractive thing about him is that he was a man who blessed God. His mind was massive, his learning immense, his theological industry simply staggering. He wrote a six-million-word, seven-thousand-page, twelve-volume dogmatics plus forty or fifty other books and several hundred learned articles. Impressive as that is, what is far more impressive, to me at least, is what he called *dankbarkeit.* Gratitude. Always and everywhere we aware that Barth was responding to God's grace; there is a chuckle rumbling underneath his most serious prose; there is a twinkle on the edges of his eyes – always. He never took himself seriously and always took God seriously and therefore was full of cheerfulness, exuberant with blessing. Speaking of his own work as a theologian he said. 'The theologian who has no joy in his work is not a theologian at all. Sulky faces, morose thoughts and boring ways of speaking are intolerable in this science.'[10]

He was on a bus in Basel, the Swiss city in which he lived and taught for so many years. A man came and sat beside him, a tourist. Barth struck up a conversation, 'You are a visitor, yes? And what do you want to see in our city?' The man said, 'I would like to see the great theologian, Karl Barth. Do you know him?' 'Oh, yes,' said Barth, 'I shave him every morning.' The man went away satisfied, telling his friends that he had met Barth's barber.

Because he refused to take himself seriously and decided to take God seriously he burdened neither himself nor those around him with the gloomy, heavy seriousness of ambition or pride or sin or self-righteousness. Instead, the lifting up of hands, the brightness of blessing.

Charles Dickens described one of his characters as a person 'who called her rigidity religion.'[11] We find that kind of thing far too often, but, thankfully, we do not find it in Scripture. In Scripture we find Jesus concluding his parable of the lost sheep with the words, 'I tell you, there will be more joy in heaven over one sinner who repents' (Lk 15:7). Not relief, not surprise, not self-satisfied smugness. And certainly not the 'deadness inside me'. But joy. Blessing is at the end of the road. And that which is at the end of the road influences everything that takes place along the road. The end shapes the means. As Catherine of Siena said, 'All the way to heaven is heaven.' A joyful end requires a joyful means. Bless the Lord.

The Chief End

I have a friend who is dean in a theological seminary where men and women are being trained to be pastors. Sometimes he calls one of these people into his office and says something like this: 'You have been around here for several months now and I have had an opportunity to observe you. You get good grades, seem to take your calling to ministry seriously, work hard and have clear goals. But I don't detect any joy. You don't seem to have any pleasure in what you are doing. And I wonder if you should not reconsider your calling into ministry. For if a pastor is not in touch with joy, it will be difficult to teach or preach convincingly that the news is good. If you do not convey joy in your demeanour and gestures and speech, you will not be an authentic witness for Jesus Christ. Delight in what God is doing is essential in our work.'

The first question in the Westminster Shorter Catechism is 'What is the chief end of man?' What is the final purpose?

What is the main thing about us? Where are we going, and what will we do when we get there? The answer is, 'To glorify God and enjoy him forever.'

Glorify. Enjoy. There are other things involved in Christian discipleship. The Psalms of Ascents have shown some of them. But it is extremely important to know the one thing that overrides everything else. The main thing is not work for the Lord; it is not suffering in the name of the Lord; it is not witnessing to the Lord; it is not teaching Sunday School for the Lord; it is not being responsible for the sake of the Lord in the community; it is not keeping the Ten Commandments; not loving your neighbour; not observing the golden rule. 'The chief end of man is to glorify God and enjoy him forever.' Or, in the vocabulary of Psalm 134, 'Bless the Lord.'

'*Charis* always demands the answer *eucharistia* (that is, grace always demands the answer of gratitude). Grace and gratitude belong together like heaven and earth. Grace evokes gratitude like the voice of an echo. Gratitude follows grace as thunder follows lightning.'[12] God is personal reality to be enjoyed. We are so created and so redeemed that we are capable of enjoying him. All the movements of discipleship arrive at a place where joy is experienced. Every step of assent towards God develops the capacity to enjoy. Not only is there, increasingly, more to be enjoyed, there is steadily the acquired ability to enjoy it.

Best of all, we don't have to wait until we get to the end of the road before we enjoy what is at the end of the road. So, 'Come, bless the Lord.... The Lord bless you!'

> May it be our blessedness, as years go on, to add one grace to another, and advance upward, step by step, neither neglecting the lower after attaining the higher, nor aiming at the higher before attaining the lower. The first grace is faith, the last is love; first comes zeal, afterwards comes loving-kindness; first

comes humiliation, then comes peace; first comes diligence, then comes resignation. May we learn to mature all graces in us; fearing and trembling, watching and repenting, because Christ is coming; joyful, thankful and careless of the future, because he is come.[13]

Notes

Chapter 1

[1] *The Book of Common Prayer* (New York: The Church Pension Fund, 1945), p. 276.

[2] Amos T. Wilder writes, 'World means more than "mankind fallen away from God" . . . The world is created and loved by God, and Christ has come to save it. But it is ephemeral, subject to decay and death; moreover, it has fallen under the control of the evil one, and therefore into darkness.' *The Interpreter's Bible,* ed. George Arthur Buttrick (Nashville: Abingdon, 1952), XII, 238.

[3] Gore Vidal, *Matters of Fact and Fiction* (New York: Random House, 1977), p. 86.

[4] Friedrich Nietzsche, *Beyond Good and Evil,* trans. Helen Zimmern (London: 1907), Section 188, pp. 106-9.

[5] There is no independent documentation that the Psalms of Ascents were used thus, and therefore no consensus among scholars that they were associated with the pilgrimage journeys to Jerusalem. The connection is conjectural but not at all fanciful. Commentators, both Jewish and Christian, have interpreted these psalms in this framework.

[6] Paul Tournier, *A Place for You* (New York: Harper & Row, 1968), p. 163.

[7] Thomas Szasz, *Schizophrenia, The Sacred Symbol of Psychiatry* (Garden City: Doubleday, 1978), p. 72.

[8] Paul Goodman, *Little Prayers and Finite Experience* (New York: Harper & Row, 1972), p. 16.

[9] William Faulkner, quoted in Sam di Bonaventura's Program Notes to Elie Siegmeister's Symphony No. 5, Baltimore Symphony Concert, 5 May 1977.

Chapter 2

[1] John Baillie, *Invitation to Pilgrimage* (New York: Chas. Scribner's and Sons, 1942), p. 8.

[2] Elie Weisel, *Souls on Fire* (New York: Vintage, 1973), p. 154.

[3] Abraham Heschel, *The Prophets* (New York: Harper & Row, 1962), pp. 71-72.

[4] Ibid., p. 190.

CHAPTER 3

[1] John Calvin, *Commentary on the Psalms* (Grand Rapids: Eerdmans, 1949), V.63.

[2] Johannes Pedersen describes the situation thus: 'The sun and the moon, which meant so much for the maintenance of order in life, often became independent gods among the neighbouring peoples or became part of the nature of other gods. Job expressly denies having kissed his hand to these mighty beings (". . . if I have looked at the sun when it shone, or the moon moving in splendour, and my heart had been secretly enticed, and my mouth has kissed my hand; this also would be an iniquity to be punished by the judgment, for I should have been false to God above"). And in a judgment prophecy it is said that Yahweh will visit all the host of heaven on high, and the kings on earth, and the sun and the moon shall be put to shame, when Yahweh shall reign in Zion ("Then the moon shall be confounded and the sun ashamed; for the lord of hosts will reign on Mount Zion and in Jerusalem." Isaiah 24:33).' *Israel, It's Life and Culture* (London: Oxford University Press, 1926), III-IV, 635.

[3] There are, of course, numerous instances when hills and mountains are used as a metaphor for the strength and majesty of God; for instance, Ps 3:4; 24:3; 43:4; 48:1.

CHAPTER 4

[1] Paul Scherer, *The Word God Sent* (New York: Harper & Row, 1965), p. 166.

[2] Herbert Hendin, *The Age of Sensation* (New York: Norton, 1975), p. 325.

[3] Charles Spurgeon, quoted in H. Thielicke, *Encounter with Spurgeon* (Philadelphia: Fortress, 1963), p. 11.

CHAPTER 5

[1] Walther Zimmerli, '*charis,*' in Gerhard Kittel, ed., *Theological Dictionary of the New Testament,* IX (Grand Rapids: Eerdmans, 1974), 377.

CHAPTER 6

[1] Robert Browning, 'Easter Day,' in *The Poems and Plays of Robert Browning* (New York: Random House, 1934), p. 503.

CHAPTER 7

[1] George Adam Smith, *Historical Geography of the Holy Land* (London: Collins, 1966), p. 178.

[2] Gilbert Highet, *Man's Unconquerable Mind* (New York: Columbia University Press, 1954), p. 24.

[3] Alexander Maclaren, *The Psalms* (New York: A. C. Armstrong and Son, 1908), II, 316.

[4] A better translation is that by Mitchell Dahood: 'But those tottering for their devious ways . . .' By repointing the Hebrew consonants he finds the psalmist using the same word as in verse 1 (*mwt*) and so contrasting the one who trusts in God and is 'not moved' with the one who refused to trust in God and therefore 'totters'. *Psalms III* (Garden City: Doubleday, 1970), p. 214.

[5] Charles Spurgeon, *The Treasure of David* (Grand Rapids: Zondervan, 1950), VI, 59.

CHAPTER 8

[1] Ellen Glasgow, *The Woman Within* (New York: Harcourt, Brace and Co., 1954), p. 15.

[2] Phyllis McGinley, *Saint-Watching* (New York: Viking, 1969), pp. 113-14.

[3] Elie Weisel, p. 100.

CHAPTER 9

[1] Hilary of Tours, quoted in G. A. Studdert-Kennedy, *The Word and The Work* (London: Hodder and Stoughton, 1965), p. 33.

CHAPTER 10

[1] Two hebrew words are translated 'blessed' in this psalm. The word used in verse 1-2 (*'ašre*) describes the sense of happiness and wholeness that comes from living in good relationship with God. The word used in verses 4-5 (*barak*) describes what God does as he shares his abundant life with us in a relationship of salvation.

[2] F. Hauck, '*makarios,*' in *Theological Dictionary of the New Testament,* IV (1967), 369.

[3] Pedersen, I, 182-99.

[4] Ibid., pp. 193, 211.

[5] Calvin, V, 115.

[6] Austin Farrer, *The Brink of Mystery* (London: SPCK, 1976), p. 52.

[7] W. D. White, ed., *The Preaching of John Henry Newman* (Philadelphia: Fortress, 1969), p. 77.

CHAPTER 11

[1] H. Cremer, quoted in Gerhard von Rad, *Theology of the Old Testament* (New York: Harper & Row, 1962), I, 371.

CHAPTER 12

[1] Sally Cunnen, 'Listening to Illich,' *The Christian Century,* 29 Sept. 1976.

[2] P. T. Forsyth, *The Cure of Souls* (Grand Rapids: Eerdmans, 1971), p. 128.

[3] Van Rad, I, 384.

[4] Henri J. M. Nouwen, *The Wounded Healer* (New York: Doubleday, 1972), p. 95.

[5] George MacDonald, *Unspoken Sermons, First Series,* quoted in frontispiece of C. S. Lewis, *The Problem of Pain* (New York: Macmillan, 1953).

[6] Forsyth, p. 113.

[7] Karl Barth, *Church Dogmatics* (Edinburgh: T & T Clark, 1957), II/I, 369.

[8] George MacDonald quoted in Denos Donogue, *New York Review of Books,* 21 Dec. 1967.

[9] Augustine, *The City of God* (New York: Doubleday, 1958), p. 46.

CHAPTER 13

[1] Gilbert Keith Chesterton, *Orthodoxy* (New York: John Lane, 1909), p. 212.

[2] Calvin, V, 140.

[3] Artur Weiser, *The Psalms* (Philadelphia: Westminster, 1962), p. 777.

[4] Spurgeon, VI, 137.

[5] Ibid., p. 136.

[6] Peter Marin, *Saturday Review of Literature,* 19 Sept. 1970, p. 73.

CHAPTER 14

[1] Barth, IV/3, second half, 670.

CHAPTER 15

[1] Philip Slater, in his searching study of the way Americans live together says that all of us have a desire and need for community – 'the wish to live in trust and fraternal cooperation with one's fellows in a total and visible collective entity. It is easy to produce examples of the many ways in which Americans attempt to minimize, circumvent, or deny the interdependence upon which all human societies are based. We seek a private house, a private means of transportation, a private garden, a private laundry, self-service stores, and do-it-yourself skills of every kind. An enormous technology seems to have set itself the task of making it unnecessary for one human being ever to ask anything of another in the course of going about his daily business ... we seek more and more privacy, and feel more and more alienated and lonely when we get it ... our encounters with others tend increasingly to be competitive as a result of the search for privacy. We less and less often meet our fellow man to share and exchange, and more and more often encounter him as an impediment or a nuisance: making the highway crowded when we are rushing somewhere, cluttering and littering the beach or park or wood, pushing in front of us at the supermarket, taking the last parking place, polluting our air and water, building a highway through our house, blocking our view, and so on. Because we have cut off so much communication with each other we keep bumping into each other, and thus a higher and higher percentage of our interpersonal contacts are abrasive.' *Pursuit of Loneliness* (Boston: Beacon, 1970), pp. 7-8.

[2] Martin Buber, *I and Thou* (New York: Charles Scribner's Sons, 1970), p. 62.

[3] *Poems and Prose of Gerard Manley Hopkins* (Baltimore: Penguin, 1953), p. 27.

[4] Dietrich Bonhoeffer, *Life Together* (New York: Harper and Brothers, 1954), p. 25.

[5] Ibid., p.23.

[6] Margaret Mead, *Culture and Commitment* (Garden City: Natural History Press/Doubleday, 1970), p. 17.

[7] Mary Bosenquet, *The Life and Death of Dietrich Bonhoeffer* (New York: Harper & Row, 1968), pp. 15-16.

CHAPTER 16

[1] Charles Colson, *Born Again* (New York: Bantam Books, 1976), p. 10.

[2] Ibid., p. 7.

[3] George Arthur Buttrick, ed., *Interpreter's Dictionary of the Bible* (Nashville: Abingdon, 1962), I, 445.

[4] Pedersen, I-II, 202.

[5] *Interpreter's Dictionary*, I, 446.

[6] B. Duhm, *Das Buch Hiob* (1897), p.12, quoted in Hermann W. Beyer, *'eulogeō,'* in *Theological Dictionary of the New Testament*, II (1964), 758.

[7] Ibid., p. 760.

[8] Calvin, p. 168.

[9] Eric Routley, *Ascent to the Cross* (London: SCM Press Ltd., 1962), p. 72.

[10] Barth, II/I, 656.

[11] Charles Dickens, *Great Expectations* (New York, Heritage, 1939), p. 198.

[12] Barth, IV/I, 41.

[13] John Henry Newman, *The Preaching of John Henry Newman*, ed. W. E. White (Philadelphia: Fortress Press, 1969), p. 211.

THE QUEST

FOR LIFE AT ITS BEST

For Eric also the son of a priest

Contents

I will run
in the way of thy commandments
when thou enlargest
my understanding!

PSALM 119:32

1

How Will You Compete with Horses?

If you have raced with men on foot, and they have wearied you,
how will you compete with horses?
And if in a safe land you fall down,
how will you do in the jungle of the Jordan?

JEREMIAH 12:5

My grievance with contemporary society is with its decrepitude. There are few towering pleasures to allure me, almost no beauty to bewitch me, nothing erotic to arouse me, no intellectual circles or positions to challenge or provoke me, no burgeoning philosophies or theologies and no new art to catch my attention or engage my mind, no arousing political, social, or religious movements to stimulate or excite me. There are no free men to lead me. No saints to inspire me. No sinners sinful enough to either impress me or share my plight. No one human enough to validate the 'going' lifestyle. It is hard to linger in that dull world without being dulled.

I stake the future on the few humble and hearty lovers who seek God passionately in the marvelous, messy world of redeemed and related realities that lie in front of our noses.

WILLIAM MCNAMARA[1]

THE PUZZLE IS WHY SO MANY PEOPLE LIVE SO BADLY. NOT SO wickedly, but so inanely. Not so cruelly, but so stupidly. There is little to admire and less to imitate in the people who are prominent in our culture. We have celebrities but not saints. Famous entertainers amuse a nation of bored insomniacs. Infamous criminals act out the aggressions of timid conformists. Petulant and spoiled athletes play games vicariously for lazy and apathetic spectators. People, aimless and bored, amuse themselves with trivia and trash. Neither the adventure of goodness nor the pursuit of righteousness gets headlines.

Modern man is 'a bleak business,' says Tom Howard. 'To our chagrin we discover that the declaration of autonomy has issued not in a race of free, masterly men, but rather in a race that can be described by its poets and dramatists only as bored, vexed, frantic, embittered, and sniffling.'[2]

This condition has produced an odd phenomenon: individuals who live trivial lives and then engage in evil acts in order to establish significance for themselves. Assassins and hijackers attempt the gigantic leap from obscurity to fame by killing a prominent person or endangering the lives of an airplane full of passengers. Often they are successful. The mass media report their words and display their actions. Writers vie with one another in analyzing their motives and providing psychological profiles on them. No other culture has been as eager to reward either nonsense or wickedness.

If, on the other hand, we look around for what it means to be a mature, whole, blessed person, we don't find much.

These people are around, maybe as many of them as ever, but they aren't easy to pick out. No journalist interviews them. No talk show features them. They are not admired. They are not looked up to. They do not set trends. There is no cash value in them. No Oscars are given for integrity. At year's end no one compiles a list of the ten best-lived lives.

A Thirst for Wholeness

All the same, we continue to have an unquenchable thirst for wholeness, a hunger for righteousness. When we get thoroughly disgusted with the shams and cretins that are served up to us daily as celebrities, some of us turn to Scripture to satisfy our need for someone to look up to. What does it mean to be a real man, a real woman? What shape does mature, authentic humanity take in everyday life?

When we do turn to Scripture for help in this matter we are apt to be surprised. One of the first things that strikes us about the men and women in Scripture is that they were disappointingly nonheroic. We do not find splendid moral examples. We do not find impeccably virtuous models. That always comes as a shock to newcomers to Scripture: Abraham lied; Jacob cheated; Moses murdered and complained; David committed adultery; Peter blasphemed.

We read on and begin to suspect intention: a consistent strategy to demonstrate that the great, significant figures in the life of faith were fashioned from the same clay as the rest of us. We find that Scripture is sparing in the information that it gives on people while it is lavish in what it tells us about God. It refuses to feed our lust for hero worship. It will not pander to our adolescent desire to join a fan club. The reason is, I think, clear enough. Fan clubs encourage secondhand living. Through pictures and memorabilia, autographs and tourist visits, we associate with someone whose life is (we think) more exciting and glamorous than our own. We find diversion from our own humdrum existence by riding on the coattails of someone exotic.

We do it because we are convinced that we are plain and ordinary. The town or city that we live in, the neighborhood we grew up in, the friends we are stuck with, the families or marriages that we have – all seem undramatic. We see no way to be significant in such settings, with such associations, so we surround ourselves with evidence of someone who is. We stock our fantasies with images of a person who is living more adventurously than we are. And we have enterprising people around who provide us (for a fee, of course) with the material to fuel the fires of this vicarious living. There is something sad and pitiful about the whole business. But it flourishes nonetheless.

Scripture, however, doesn't play that game. Something very different takes place in the life of faith: each person discovers all the elements of a unique and original adventure. We are prevented from following in another's footsteps and are called to an incomparable association with Christ. The Bible makes it clear that every time that there is a story of faith, it is completely original. God's creative genius is endless. He never, fatigued and unable to maintain the rigors of creativity, resorts to mass-producing copies. Each life is a fresh canvas on which he uses lines and colors, shades and lights, textures and proportions that he has never used before.

We see *what* is possible: anyone and everyone is able to live a zestful life that spills out of the stereotyped containers that a sin-inhibited society provides. Such lives fuse spontaneity and purpose and green the desiccated landscape with meaning. And we see *how* it is possible: by plunging into a life of faith, participating in what God initiates in each life, exploring what God is doing in each event. The persons we meet on the pages of Scripture are remarkable for the intensity with which they live Godwards, the thoroughness in which all the details of their lives are included in God's word to them, in God's action in them. It is these persons, who are conscious of participating in what God is saying and doing, who are most human, most alive. These persons are evidence that none of us is required to live 'at this poor dying rate' for another day, another hour.

AN IMAGE OF MAN

This two-edged quality of Scripture – the capacity to intensify a passion for excellence combined with an indifference to human achievement as such – strikes me with particular force in the book of Jeremiah.

Cleanth Brooks wrote, 'One looks for an image of man, attempting in a world increasingly dehumanized to realize himself as a man – to act like a responsible moral being, not to drift like a mere thing.'[3] Jeremiah, for me, is such an 'image of man,' a life of excellence, what the Greeks called *aretē*. In Jeremiah it is clear that the excellence comes from a life of faith, from being more interested in God than in self, and has almost nothing to do with comfort or esteem or achievement. Here is a person who lived life to the hilt, but there is not a hint of human pride or worldly success or personal achievement in the story. Jeremiah arouses my passion for a full life. At the same time he firmly shuts the door against attempts to achieve it through self-promotion, self-gratification or self-improvement.

It is enormously difficult to portray goodness in an attractive way; it is much easier to make a scoundrel interesting. All of us have so much more experience in sin than in goodness that a writer has far more imaginative material to work with in presenting a bad character than a good person. In novels and poems and plays most of the memorable figures are either villains or victims. Good people, virtuous lives, mostly seem a bit dull. Jeremiah is a stunning exception. For most of my adult life he has attracted me. The complexity and intensity of his person caught and kept my attention. The captivating quality in the man is his goodness, his virtue, his excellence. He lived at his best. His was not a hot-house piety, for he lived through crushing storms of hostility and furies of bitter doubt. There is not a trace of smugness or complacency or naiveté in Jeremiah – every muscle in his body was stretched to the limits by fatigue, every thought in his mind subjected to rejection, every feeling in his heart put through fires of ridicule. Goodness in Jeremiah was not 'being nice'. It was something more like *prowess.*

Jeremiah has thus served personal needs. But he has also been of pastoral importance, and the personal and pastoral interests converge. As a pastor I encourage others to live at their best and provide guidance in doing it. But how do I do this without inadvertently inciting pride and arrogance? How do I stimulate an appetite for excellence without feeding at the same time a selfish determination to elbow anyone aside who gets in the way? Insistent encouragement is given by many voices today for living a better life. I welcome the encouragement. But the counsel that accompanies the encouragement has introduced no end of mischief into our society, and I am in strenuous opposition to it. The counsel is that we can arrive at our full humanness by gratifying our desires. It has been a recipe for misery for millions.[4] The biblical counsel in these matters is clear: 'not my will but thine be done.' But how do I guide people to deny self without having that misunderstood as encouraging them to be doormats on which people wipe their feet? The difficult pastoral art is to encourage people to grow in excellence and to live selflessly, at one and the same time to lose the self and find the self. It is paradoxical, but it is not impossible. And Jeremiah is preeminent among those who have done it – a fully developed self (and therefore extraordinarily attractive) and a thoroughly selfless person (and therefore maturely wise). In conversations, in lectures, on retreats, in sermons, Jeremiah has, for twenty-five years now, been example and mentor for me.

A Quest for the Best

We live in a society that tries to diminish us to the level of the antheap so that we scurry mindlessly, getting and consuming. It is essential to take counteraction. Jeremiah is counteraction: a well-developed human being, mature and robust, living by faith. My procedure here is to select the biographical parts of the book of Jeremiah and reflect on them personally and pastorally in the context of present, everyday life. More is known of the life of Jeremiah than of any other prophet, and his life is far more significant than his teaching.[5] It is noteworthy, I think, that when people were trying to account for Jesus, Jeremiah was one of the names put forward (Mt 16:14). By enlisting the devout imagination in meditatively perusing these pages of Scripture, I hope to stir up a dissatisfaction with anything less than our best. I want to provide fresh documentation that the only way that any one of us can live at our best is in a life of radical faith in God. Every one of us needs to be stretched to live at our best, awakened out of dull moral habits, shaken out of petty and trivial busy-work. Jeremiah does that for me. And not only for me. Millions upon millions of Christians and Jews have been goaded and guided toward excellence as they have attended to God's word spoken to and by Jeremiah.

I have arranged the passages that I have chosen for reflection in roughly chronological order. The book of Jeremiah is not itself arranged chronologically, and there is far more in it than biography. That means that readers not infrequently puzzle over transitions and wrestle to find the appropriate settings for the sayings. I have not attempted to sort out these puzzles or explain the difficulties. Nor have I described the complex international historical background of the times, a knowledge of which is an immense help in reading Jeremiah. That would be to write another kind of book and a much longer one. For readers who want to extend their understanding of Jeremiah and be guided through the text in detail, I recommend three books: R. K. Harrison, *Jeremiah and Lamentations* (Inter Varsity Press) for a good, readable introduction into the world and text of Jeremiah; John A. Thompson, *The Book of Jeremiah* (Eerdmans) for a more advanced, detailed treatment; and John Bright, *Jeremiah* (Doubleday) for the most complete study of the prophet and the prophecy.

Competing with Horses

Vitezslav Gardavsky, the Czech philosopher and martyr who died in 1978, took Jeremiah as his 'image of man' in his campaign against a society that carefully planned every detail of material existence but eliminated mystery and miracle, and squeezed all freedom from life. The terrible threat against life, he said in his book *God Is Not Yet Dead*, is not death, nor pain, nor any variation on the disasters that we so obsessively try to protect ourselves against with our social systems and personal stratagems. The terrible threat is 'that we might die earlier than we really do die, before death has become a natural necessity. The real horror lies in just such a *premature* death, a death after which we go on living for many years.'[6]

There is a memorable passage concerning Jeremiah's life when, worn down by the opposition and absorbed in self-pity, he was about to capitulate to just such a premature death. He was ready to abandon his unique calling in God and settle for being a Jerusalem statistic. At that critical moment he heard the reprimand: 'If you have raced with men on foot, and they have wearied you, how will you compete with horses? And if in a safe land you fall down, how will you do in the jungle of the Jordan?' (Jer 12:5). Biochemist Erwin Chargaff updates the questions: 'What do you want to achieve? Greater riches? Cheaper chicken? A happier life, a longer life? Is it power over your neighbors that you are after? Are you only running away from your death? Or are you seeking greater wisdom, deeper piety?'[7]

Life is difficult, Jeremiah. Are you going to quit at the first wave of opposition? Are you going to retreat when you find that there is more to life than finding three meals a day and a dry place to sleep at night? Are you going to run home the minute you find that the mass of men and women are more interested in keeping their feet warm than in living at risk to the glory of God? Are you going to live cautiously or courageously? I called you to live at your best, to pursue righteousness, to sustain a drive toward excellence. It is easier, I know, to be neurotic. It is easier to be parasitic. It is easier to relax in the embracing arms of The Average. Easier, but not better. Easier, but not more significant. Easier, but not more fulfilling. I called you to a life of purpose far beyond what you think yourself capable of living and promised you adequate strength to fulfill your destiny. Now at the first sign of difficulty you are ready to quit. If you are fatigued by this run-of-the-mill crowd of apathetic mediocrities, what will you do when the real race starts, the race with the swift and determined horses of excellence? What is it you really want, Jeremiah, do you want to shuffle along with this crowd, or run with the horses?

It is understandable that there are retreats from excellence, veerings away from risk, withdrawals from faith. It is easier to define oneself minimally ('a featherless biped') and live securely within that definition than to be defined maximally ('little less than God') and live adventurously in that reality. It is unlikely, I think, that Jeremiah was spontaneous or quick in his reply to God's question. The ecstatic ideals for a new life had been splattered with the world's cynicism. The euphoric impetus of youthful enthusiasm no longer carried him. He weighed the options. He counted the cost. He tossed and turned in hesitation. The response when it came was not verbal but biographical. His life became his answer, 'I'll run with the horses.'

2

Jeremiah

The words of Jeremiah, the son of Hilkiah, of the priests who were in Anathoth in the land of Benjamin, to whom the word of the LORD came . . .

JEREMIAH 1:1-2

What's in a name? The history of the human race is in names. Our objective friends do not understand that, since they move in a world of objects which can be counted and numbered. They reduce the great names of the past to dust and ashes. This they call scientific history. But the whole meaning of history is in the proof that there have lived people before the present time whom it is important to meet.

EUGEN ROSENSTOCK-HUESSY[1]

THE FIRST THING THAT I CAN REMEMBER WANTING TO BE when I grew up was an Indian fighter. Only a couple of generations before I was born the area in which I grew up was Indian country. I could walk from my house into the foot-hills of the Rocky Mountains in about twenty minutes. On most Saturdays through my boyhood years I carried a lunch with me and roamed for the day in those hills, exploring forests and streams, imagining myself matching wits with treacherous Indians.

If anyone would have pressed me to account for what I was doing on those rambles, I'm not sure I could have done it, but the feelings are still sharp and vivid in my memory: a feeling of adventure in the wilderness in contrast to the protected and prosaic life in the town; a feeling of goodness in contest with evil, for in those days the only Indian stories I had heard featured them scalping innocent travelers.

All the great stories of the world elaborate one of two themes: that all life is an exploration like that of the *Odyssey* or that all life is a battle like that of the *Iliad.* The stories of Odysseus and Achilles are archetypal. Everyone's childhood serves up the raw material that is shaped by grace into the life of mature faith.

I had most of my facts wrong on those wonderful Saturdays. The wilderness that I thought I was exploring was owned by the Great Northern Railroad and was already plotted for destruction by executives in a New York City skyscraper; the Indians that I supposed were darkly murderous were, I learned later, noble and generous, themselves victims of rapacious early settlers. My facts were wrong; all the same there were two things essentially right about what I experienced. One, there was far more to existence than had been presented to me in home and school, in the streets and alleys of my town, and it was important to find out what it was, to reach out and explore. Two, life was a contest of good against evil and the battle was for the highest stakes – the winning of good over evil, of blessing over malignity. Life is a continuous exploration of ever more reality. Life is a constant battle against everyone and anything that corrupts or diminishes its reality.

After a few years of wandering those hills and never finding any Indians, I realized that there was not much of a market any longer for Indian fighters. I was forced to abandon that fantasy, and I did it readily enough when the time came, for I have always found that realities are better in the long run than fantasies. At the same time I found myself under pressure to abandon the accompanying convictions that life is an adventure and that life is a contest. I was not, and am not, willing to do that.

Some people as they grow up become less. As children they have glorious ideas of who they are and of what life has for them. Thirty years later we find that they have settled for something grubby and inane. What accounts for the exchange of childhood aspiration to the adult anemia?

Other people as they grow up become more. Life is not an inevitable decline into dullness; for some it is an ascent into excellence. It was for Jeremiah. Jeremiah lived about sixty years. Across that life span there is no sign of decay or shriveling. Always he was pushing out the borders of reality, exploring new territory. And always he was vigorous in battle, challenging and contesting the shoddy, the false, the vile.

How did he do it? How do I do it? How do I shed the fantasies of boyhood and simultaneously increase my hold on the realities of life? How do I leave the childish yet keep the deeply accurate perceptions of the child – that life is an adventure, that life is a contest?

What's in a Name?

The book of Jeremiah begins with a personal name, *Jeremiah*. Seven more personal names follow: Hilkiah, Benjamin, Josiah, Amon, Judah, Jehoiakim, Zedekiah. The personal name is the most important part of speech in our language. The cluster of personal names that opens the book of Jeremiah strikes exactly the right note for what is most characteristic of Jeremiah: the personal in contrast to the stereotyped role, the individual in contrast to the blurred crowd, the unique spirit in contrast to generalized cultural moods. The book in which we find this most memorable record of what it means to be human in the fullest, most developed sense, begins with personal names.

Naming focuses the essential. The act of naming, an act that occurs early in everyone's life, has enormous significance. We are named. From that sextant a life course is plotted on the oceans of reality in pursuit of righteousness. Eugen Rosenstock-Huessy has mined the meaning of naming: 'The name is the state of speech in which we do not speak of people or things or values, but in which we speak *to* people, things, and values. . . . The name is the right address of a person under which he or she will respond. The original meaning of language was this very fact that it could be used to make people respond.'[2]

At our birth we are named, not numbered. The name is that part of speech by which we are recognized as a person. We are not classified as a species of animal. We are not labeled as a compound of chemicals. We are not assessed for our economic potential and given a cash value. We are named. What we are named is not as significant as *that* we are named.

Jeremiah's impressive stature as a human being – Ewald calls him the 'most human prophet'[3] – and the developing vitality of that humanness for sixty years have their source in his naming, along with the centered seriousness with which he took his name and the names of others. 'To be called by his true name is part of any listener's process of becoming his true self. We have to receive a name by others; this is part of the process of being fully born.'[4] Jeremiah was named and immersed in names. He was never reduced to a role or absorbed into a sociological trend or catapulted into a historical crisis. His identity and significance developed from the event of naming and his response to naming. The world of Jeremiah does not open with a description of the scenery or a sketch of the culture but with eight personal names.

Any time that we move from personal names to abstract labels or graphs or statistics, we are less in touch with reality and diminished in our capacity to deal with what is best and at the center of life. Yet we are encouraged on every side to do just that. In many areas of life the accurate transmission of our social-security number is more important than the integrity with which we live. In many sectors of the economy the title that we hold is more important than our ability to do certain work. In many situations the public image that people have of us is more important than the personal relations that we develop with them. Every time that we go along with this movement from the personal to the impersonal, from the immediate to the remote, from the concrete to the abstract, we are diminished, we are less. Resistance is required if we will retain our humanity.

'It is a spiritual disaster,' warned Thomas Merton, 'for a man to rest content with his exterior identity, with his passport picture of himself. Is his life merely in his finger-prints?'[5] But passport pictures, more likely than not, are preferred, even required, in most of our dealings in the world.

In preparing for travel to another continent I applied for a passport. I presented my birth certificate with the application. The clerk in the post office to whom I presented the document was a man I had known by name for nineteen years. He refused the application: I had not presented the original birth certificate but a photocopy. I brought in the original; that also was rejected; it had to be embossed. I wrote to the state in which I was born and purchased an embossed copy. All this time I was dealing with a person who knew my name and had observed my life in the community for nineteen years. That personal, firsthand knowledge was rejected in favor of an impersonal document.

I think that I can reconstruct the steps that result in such procedures. There is danger of foreign espionage. Our government has a responsibility for keeping our nation safe. It would be unreliable to depend on the personal loyalty and knowledge of a post-office worker to determine identities. Insisting on an embossed birth certificate is a way of guarding against forgeries.

In my situation the procedure was not so much frustrating as amusing. But the incident itself, a minor inconvenience, is symptomatic of a major danger to our humanity: if I am frequently and authoritatively treated impersonally, I begin to think of myself the same way. I consider myself in terms of how I fit into the statistical norms; I evaluate myself in terms of my usefulness; I assess my worth in response to how much others want me or don't want me. In the process of going along with such procedures I find myself defined by a label, squeezed into a role, functioning at the level of my social-security number. It requires assertive, lifelong effort to keep our names in front. Our names are far more important than trends in the economy, far more important than crises in the cities, far more important than breakthroughs in space travel. For a name addresses the uniquely human creature. A name recognizes that I am this person and not another.

No one can assess my significance by looking at the work that I do. No one can determine my worth by deciding the salary they will pay me. No one can know what is going on in my mind by examining my school transcripts. No one can know me by measuring me or weighing me or analyzing me. Call my name.

A Way of Hoping

Names not only address what we are, the irreplaceably human, they also anticipate what we become. Names call us to become who we will be. A lifetime of growth and development is announced by a name. Names *mean* something. A personal name designates what is irreducibly personal; it also calls us to become what we are not yet.

The meaning of a name is not discovered through scholarly etymology or through meditative introspection. It is not validated by bureaucratic approval. And it certainly is not worked up through the vanity of public relations. The meaning of a name is not in the dictionary, not in the unconscious, not in the size of the lettering. It is in *relationship* – with God. It was the Jeremiah 'to whom the word of the LORD came' who realized his authentic and eternal being.

Naming is a way of hoping. We name a child after someone or some quality that we hope he or she will become – a saint, a hero, an admired ancestor. Some parents name their children trivially after movie stars and millionaires. Harmless? Cute? But we do have a way of taking on the identities that are prescribed for us. Millions live out the superficial sham of the entertainer and the greedy exploitiveness of the millionaire because, in part, significant people in their lives cast them in a role or fantasized an illusion and failed to hope a human future for them.

When I take an infant into my arms at the baptismal font and ask the parents, 'What is the Christian name of this child?' I am not only asking, 'Who is this child I am holding?' but also, 'What do you want this child to become? What are your visions for this life?' George Herbert knew the evocative power of naming when he instructed his fellow pastors in sixteenth-century England that at baptism they 'admit no vain or idle names.'[6]

Yoknapatawpha County, Mississippi, is the region created by novelist William Faulkner to show the spiritual and moral condition of life in our times. An examination of the men and women who live there is a powerful incentive to the imagination to realize both the comic and tragic aspects of what is going on among us as we make it (or don't make it) through life. One of the children is named Montgomery Ward. Montgomery Ward Snopes.[7] It is the perfect name for the child being trained to be a successful consumer. If you want your child to grow up getting and spending, using available leisure in the shopping malls, proving virility by getting things, that is the right name: Montgomery Ward Snopes, patron saint of the person for whom the ritual of shopping is the new worship, the department store the new cathedral, and the advertising page the infallible Scripture.

One of the supreme tasks of the faith community is to announce to us early and clearly the kind of life into which we can grow, to help us set our sights on what it means to be a human being complete. Not one of us, at this moment, is complete. In another hour, another day, we will have changed. We are in process of becoming either less or more. There are a million chemical and electrical interchanges going on in each of us this very moment. There are intricate moral decisions and spiritual transactions taking place. What are we becoming? Less or more?

John, writing to an early community of Christians, said, 'Beloved, we are God's children now; it does not yet appear what we shall be, but we know that when he appears we shall be like him, for we shall see him as he is' (1 Jn 3:2). We *are* children; we *will be* adults. We can see what we are now; we are children of God. We don't yet see the results of what we are becoming, but we know the goal, to be like Christ, or, in Paul's words, to arrive at 'mature manhood, to the measure of the stature of the fulness of Christ' (Eph 4:13). We do not deteriorate. We do not disintegrate. We *become.*

William Stafford was once asked in an interview, 'When did you decide to be a poet?' He responded that the question was put wrongly: everyone is born a poet – a person discovering the way words sound and work, caring and delighting in words. I just kept on doing, he said, what everyone starts out doing. 'The real question is why did the other people stop?'[8]

Jeremiah kept on doing what everybody starts out doing, being human. And he didn't stop. For sixty years and more he continued to live into the meaning of his name. The exact meaning of *Jeremiah* is not certain: it may mean 'the LORD exalts'; it may mean 'the LORD hurls'. What is certain is that 'the LORD,' the personal name of God, is in his name.

On the day that their son was born, Hilkiah and his wife named him in anticipation of the way that God would act in his life. In hope they saw the years unfolding and their son as one in whom the Lord would be lifted up: *Jeremiah* – the Lord is exalted. Or, in hope they saw into the future and anticipated their son as a person whom God would hurl into the community as a javelin-representative of God, penetrating the defenses of selfishness with divine judgment and mercy: *Jeremiah* – the Lord hurls. Either way, it is clear that God is in the name. Jeremiah's life was compounded with God's action. Jeremiah's parents saw their child as a region of being in which the human and divine would integrate. The life of God in some way or other (exalting? hurling?) would find expression in this child of theirs. Naming is not a whim; it is a lever of hope against the future. And the 'hope is not a dream but a way of making dreams become reality' (Cardinal L. J. Suenens).

No child is just a child. Each is a creature in whom God intends to do something glorious and great. No one is only a product of the genes contributed by parents. Who we are and will be is compounded with who God is and what he does. God's love and providence and salvation are comprised in the reality of our existence along with our metabolism and blood type and fingerprints.

Most names throughout Israel's history were compounded with the name of God. The names anticipated what each would be when he, when she, grew up. *Josiah,* God heals; *Jehoiakim,* the Lord raises up; *Zedekiah,* the Lord is righteous; *Jeremiah,* the Lord exalts, or the Lord hurls. Some of these people lived out the meaning of their names. Jeremiah and Josiah did. Others, like Jehoiakim and Zedekiah, were an embarrassment to their names, parodying with their lives the great promise of their names. Zedekiah had a glorious name; he betrayed it. Jehoiakim had a superb name; he abandoned it.

There were at least three categories into which Jeremiah could have quietly slipped, taking his place among the religious professionals of his day: prophet, priest or wise man. These were the accepted roles for persons who had concern for the things of God and the ways of humanity. Jeremiah's refusal to accept any of the available roles and his eccentric insistence on living out the identity of his name put him in conspicuous contrast to the eroded smoothness of those who were shaped by the expectations of popular opinion and who gathered content for their messages not by asking 'What is there to eat?' but 'What will Jones swallow?' His angular integrity exposed the shallow complacencies in which they lived. They were provoked and then enraged: 'Come, let us make plots against Jeremiah, for the law shall not perish from the priest, nor counsel from the wise, nor the word from the prophet. Come, let us smite him with the tongue, and let us not heed any of his words' (Jer 18:18). Priest and wise man and prophet alike felt that their professional well-being was threatened by Jeremiah's singularity. Panicked, they plotted his disgrace. Their 'law' and 'counsel' and 'word' were in danger of being exposed as pious frauds by Jeremiah's honest and passionate life.

The French talk of a *deformation professionelle* – a liability, a tendency to defect, that is inherent in the role one has assumed as say, a physician or a lawyer. The *deformation* to which prophets and priests and wise men are subject is to market God as a commodity, to use God to legitimize selfishness. It is easy and it is frequent. It happens without deliberate intent.

What I had not foreseen
Was the gradual day
Weakening the will
Leaking the brightness away . . .[9]

A personal name, not an assigned role, is our passbook into reality. It is also our continuing orientation in reality. Anything other than our name – title, job description, number, role – is less than a name. Apart from the name that marks us as uniquely created and personally addressed, we slide into fantasies that are out of touch with the world as it is and so we live ineffectively, irresponsibly. Or we live by the stereotypes in which other people cast us that are out of touch with the uniqueness in which God has created us, and so live diminished into boredom, the brightness leaking away.

Jeremiah – a name linked with the name and action of God. The only thing more significant to Jeremiah than his own being was God's being. He fought in the name of the Lord and explored the reality of God and in the process grew and developed, ripened and matured. He was always reaching out, always finding more truth, getting in touch with more of God, becoming more himself, more human.

3

Before

Before I formed you in the womb I knew you,
and before you were born I consecrated you;
I appointed you a prophet to the nations.

JEREMIAH 1:5

What science will ever be able to reveal to man the origin, nature and character of that conscious power to will and to love which constitutes his life? It is certainly not our effort, nor the effort of anyone around us, which set that current in motion. And it is certainly not our solicitude, nor that of any friend, which prevents its ebb or controls its turbulence. We can, of course, trace back through generations some of the antecedents of the torrent which bears us along; and we can, by means of certain moral and physical disciplines and stimulations, regularise or enlarge the aperture through which the torrent is released into us. But neither that geography nor those artifices help us in theory or in practice to harness the sources of life. My self is given to me far more than it is formed by me. Man, Scripture says, cannot add a cubit to his stature. Still less can he add a unit to the potential of his love, or accelerate by another unit

> *the fundamental rhythm which regulates the ripening of his mind and heart. In the last resort the profound life, the fontal life, the new-born life, escape our grasp entirely.*
>
> PIERRE TEILHARD DE CHARDIN[1]

I WAS SITTING AT THE COUNTER OF A DELICATESSEN IN BROOKLYN, eating a pastrami sandwich on Jewish rye and making small talk with the owner. After fifteen minutes or so of desultory conversation, neither of us saying much of interest to the other, he planted himself in front of me, assumed a pose of intense concentration and said, 'Don't tell me, you are from . . . let's see . . . you come frommmm . . . Nebraska.'

'No,' I said, 'I come from Montana.'

He was disappointed, 'I usually don't miss it by that far.'

The tempo of the conversation picked up. I learned that he took great pride in his ability to distinguish regional accents. Persons from all over the country, from all over the world, came into his store. He had a good ear. He developed fine skills in locating people's origins by listening to dialectical variations in their speech.

I was flattered to be the object of his curiosity. The only previous interest that I can recall shopkeepers having in me was getting my order straight and making sure I got the price right.

'Whaddal ya' have?'

'Hot pastrami on rye. How much?'

'Buck seventy-five.'

The language was informational and utilitarian. When it had done its work it either stopped or digressed into gossip. But for those few moments in that Brooklyn setting, someone listened to my words for something more than information;

the man was after *knowledge.* He wanted to know where I came from and what I had experienced that resulted in my pronouncing words just the way I did that day. I was not reduced to a customer with hunger pangs that could be turned into a profit. I had geographic particularity, linguistic idiosyncrasy. There was more to me than my biological needs and economic potential, and he was interested in it, or at least part of it.

In a journalistic age in which the only things that qualify as attention-getting are the immediate and the extraordinary, I am not used to being approached that way. In a commercial age in which each person is evaluated as an economic unit and time is money, I am not used to such leisurely attentiveness. But only this kind of attention allows me to express the many layers of humanness and the complex significance they have for who I am. Apart from the *before,* the *now* has little meaning. The *now* is only a thin slice of who I am; isolated from the rich deposits of *before,* it cannot be understood.

So biographers search through family archives. So psychiatrists recover repressed memories and ask about childhood impressions. So lovers rummage through the photograph albums for everything and anything about one another, knowing that every detail deepens comprehension and therefore deepens love. The *before* is the root system of the visible *now.* Our lives cannot be read as newspaper reports on current events; they are unabridged novels with character and plot development, each paragraph essential for mature appreciation.

Knowing that the fully developed, passionate humanity of Jeremiah necessarily had a complex and intricate background, we prepare to examine it. But we are brought up short. We are told next to nothing: three bare, unadorned background items – his father's name, Hilkiah; his father's vocation, priest; his place of birth, Anathoth. We want to know more. Without more information how can we gain an adequate understanding of the humanity of Jeremiah? We need to know the social and economic conditions of Anathoth so that we can trace the early influences on Jeremiah's passion for justice. We need to know whether the father was passive or assertive in order to evaluate the son's complex emotional life. We need to know if the mother was overly protective and when she weaned her son if we are to account for the incredible tenacity in the adult prophet. We need to know the teaching methods used by local wise men to distinguish between the original and conventional in Jeremiah's preaching and teaching. The questions pile up. Lack of evidence frustrates us. What we need is a break-through manuscript discovery in seventh century B.C. Anathoth, manuscripts containing anecdotes, statistics and letters – raw material for a reconstruction of the world into which Jeremiah was born.

We fantasize an archaeological scoop. Meanwhile what we have right before us turns out to be far more useful – a theological probe. Instead of being told what Jeremiah's parents were doing, we are told what his God was doing: 'Before I formed you in the womb I knew you, and before you were born I consecrated you; I appointed you a prophet to the nations' (Jer 1:5).

The First Move

Before Jeremiah knew God, God knew Jeremiah: 'Before I formed you in the womb I knew you.' This turns everything we ever thought about God around. We think that God is an object about which we have questions. We are curious about God. We make inquiries about God. We read books about God. We get into late night bull sessions about God. We drop into church from time to time to see what is going on with God. We indulge in an occasional sunset or symphony to cultivate a feeling of reverence for God.

But that is not the reality of our lives with God. Long before we ever got around to asking questions about God, God has been questioning us. Long before we got interested in the subject of God, God subjected us to the most intensive and searching knowledge. Before it ever crossed our minds that God might be important, God singled us out as important. Before we were formed in the womb, God knew us. We are known before we know.

This realization has a practical result: no longer do we run here and there, panicked and anxious, searching for the answers to life. Our lives are not puzzles to be figured out. Rather, we come to God, who knows us and reveals to us the truth of our lives. The fundamental mistake is to begin with ourselves and not God. God is the center from which all life develops. If we use our ego as the center from which to plot the geometry of our lives, we will live eccentrically.

All wise reflection corroborates Scripture here. We enter a world we didn't create. We grow into a life already provided for us. We arrive in a complex of relationships with other wills and destinies that are already in full operation before we are introduced. If we are going to live appropriately, we must be aware that we are living in the middle of a story that was begun and will be concluded by another. And this other is God.

My identity does not begin when I begin to understand myself. There is something previous to what I think about myself, and it is what God thinks of me. That means that everything I think and feel is by nature a response, and the one to whom I respond is God. I never speak the first word. I never make the first move.

Jeremiah's life didn't start with Jeremiah. Jeremiah's salvation didn't start with Jeremiah. Jeremiah's truth didn't start with Jeremiah. He entered the world in which the essential parts of his existence were already ancient history. So do we.

Sometimes when we are in close and involved conversation with three or four other people, another person joins the group and abruptly begins saying things, arguing positions and asking questions in complete ignorance of what has been said for the past two hours, oblivious to the delicate conversational balances that have been achieved. When that happens, I always want to say, 'Just shut up for a while, won't you? Just sit and listen until you get caught up on what is going on here. Get in tune with what is taking place, then we will welcome you into our conversation.'

God is more patient. He puts up with our interruptions; he backtracks and fills us in on the old stories; he repeats the vital information. But how much better it is if we take the time to get the drift of things, to find out where we fit. The story into which life fits is already well on its way when we walk into the room. It is an exciting, brilliant, multivoiced conversation. The smart thing is to find out the identity behind the voices and become familiar with the context in which the words are being used. Then, gradually, we venture a statement, make a reflection, ask a question or two, even dare to register an objection. It is not long before we are regular participants in the conversation in which, as it unfolds, we get to know ourselves even as we are known.

Choosing Sides

The second item of background information provided on Jeremiah is this: 'Before you were born I consecrated you.' *Consecrated* means set apart for God's side. It means that the human is not a cogwheel. It means that a person is not the keyboard of a piano on which circumstances play hit-parade tunes.[2] It means we are chosen out of the feckless stream of circumstantiality for something important that God is doing.

What is God doing? He is saving; he is rescuing; he is blessing; he is providing; he is judging; he is healing; he is enlightening. There is a spiritual war in progress, an all-out moral battle. There is evil and cruelty, unhappiness and illness. There is superstition and ignorance, brutality and pain. God is in continuous and energetic battle against all of it. God is for life and against death. God is for love and against hate. God is for hope and against despair. God is for heaven and against hell. There is no neutral ground in the universe. Every square foot of space is contested.

Jeremiah, before he was born, was enlisted on God's side in this war. He wasn't given a few years in which to look around and make up his mind which side he would be on, or even whether he would join a side at all. He was already chosen as a combatant on God's side. And so are we all. No one enters existence as a spectator. We either take up the life to which we have been consecrated or we traitorously defect from it. We cannot say, 'Hold it! I am not quite ready. Wait until I have sorted things out.'[3]

For a long time all Christians called each other 'saints.' They were all saints regardless of how well or badly they lived, of how experienced or inexperienced they were. The word *saint* did not refer to the quality or virtue of their acts, but to the kind of life to which they had been chosen, life on a battlefield. It was not a title given after a spectacular performance, but a mark of whose side they were on. The word *saint* is the noun form of the verb *consecrated* that gave spiritual shape to Jeremiah even before he had biological shape.

In the neighborhood in which I lived when I was in the first grade all the children were older than I. When we had neighborhood games and chose up sides, I was always the last one chosen. There was one time – it probably happened more than once, but this once sticks in my memory – that when everyone else had been chosen, I was left standing in the middle between the two teams. The captains argued over who was going to have to choose me. Having me, I suddenly realized, was a liability. As the argument raged between them I went from being a zero to a minus.

But not with God. Not a zero. Not a minus. I have a set-apart place that only I can fill. No one can substitute for me. No one can replace me. Before I was good for anything, God decided that I was good for what he was doing. My place in life doesn't depend on how well I do in the entrance examination. My place in life is not determined by what market there is for my type of personality.

God is out to win the world in love and each person has been selected in the same way that Jeremiah was, to be set apart to do it with him. He doesn't wait to see how we turn out to decide to choose or not to choose us. Before we were born he chose us for his side – consecrated us.

The Great Giveaway

The third thing that God did to Jeremiah before Jeremiah did anything on his own was this: 'I appointed you a prophet to the nations.' The word *appointed* is, literally, 'gave' *(nathan)* – I *gave* you as a prophet to the nations. God gives. He is generous. He is lavishly generous. Before Jeremiah ever got it together he was given away.

That is God's way. He did it with his own son, Jesus. He gave him away. He gave him to the nations. He did not keep him on display. He did not preserve him in a museum. He did not show him off as a trophy. 'God so loved the world that he gave his only Son, that whoever believes in him should not perish but have eternal life' (Jn 3:16).

And he gave Jeremiah away. I can hear Jeremiah objecting, 'Wait a minute. Don't be so quick to give me away. I've got something to say about this. I've got my inalienable rights. I have a few decisions about life that I am going to make myself.' Imagine God's response: 'Sorry, but I did it before you were even born. It's already done; you are given away.'

Some things we have a choice in, some we don't. In this we don't. It is the kind of world into which we were born. God created it. God sustains it. Giving is the style of the universe. Giving is woven into the fabric of existence. If we try to live by getting instead of giving, we are going against the grain. It is like trying to go against the law of gravity – the consequence is bruises and broken bones. In fact, we do see a lot of distorted, misshapen, crippled lives among those who defy the reality that all life is given and must continue to be given to be true to its nature.

There is a rocky cliff on the shoreline of the Montana lake where I live part of each summer. There are breaks in the rock face in which tree swallows make their nests. For several weeks one summer I watched the swallows in swift flight collect insects barely above the surface of the water then dive into the cavities in the cliff, feeding first their mates and then their new-hatched chicks. Near one of the cracks in the cliff face a dead branch stretched about four feet over the water. One day I was delighted to see three new swallows sitting side by side on this branch. The parents made wide, sweeping, insect-gathering circuits over the water and then returned to the enormous cavities that those little birds became as they opened their beaks for a feeding.

This went on for a couple of hours until the parents decided they had had enough of it. One adult swallow got alongside the chicks and started shoving them out toward the end of the branch – pushing, pushing, pushing. The end one fell off. Somewhere between the branch and the water four feet below, the wings started working, and the fledgling was off on his own. Then the second one. The third was not to be bullied. At the last possible moment his grip on the branch loosened just enough so that he swung downward, then tightened again, bulldog tenacious. The parent was without sentiment. He pecked at the desperately clinging talons until it was more painful for the poor chick to hang on than risk the insecurities of flying. The grip was released and the inexperienced wings began pumping. The mature swallow knew what the chick did not – that it would fly – that there was no danger in making it do what it was perfectly designed to do.

Birds have feet and can walk. Birds have talons and can grasp a branch securely. They can walk; they can cling. But *flying* is their characteristic action, and not until they fly are they living at their best, gracefully and beautifully.

Giving is what we do best. It is the air into which we were born. It is the action that was designed into us before our birth. *Giving* is the way the world is. God gives himself. He also gives away everything that is. He makes no exceptions for any of us. We are given away to our families, to our neighbors, to our friends, to our enemies – to the nations. Our life is for others. That is the way creation works. Some of us try desperately to hold on to ourselves, to live for ourselves. We look so bedraggled and pathetic doing it, hanging on to the dead branch of a bank account for dear life, afraid to risk ourselves on the untried wings of giving. We don't think we can live generously because we have never tried. But the sooner we start the better, for we are going to have to give up our lives finally, and the longer we wait the less time we have for the soaring and swooping life of grace.

Jeremiah could have hung on to the dead-end street where he was born in Anathoth. He could have huddled in the security of his father's priesthood. He could have conformed to the dull habits of his culture. He didn't. He believed what had been told him about his background, that God long before gave him away, and he participated in the giving, throwing himself into his appointment.

Dignity and Design

Many critical things happen before I am conceived and born that predetermine the reality that I experience: biological things that make me a biped that walks and not a fish that swims, geographic things that provide me a temperate zone instead of an ice age, scientific things that produce physicians to visit when I am sick and not witch-doctors, political things that make me a citizen in a democracy and not a serf on a feudal estate. But the most important things are what God did before I was conceived, before I was born. He knew me, therefore I am no accident; he chose me, therefore I cannot be a zero; he gave me, therefore I must not be a consumer.

There are frenzied efforts in our culture to salvage ruined self-esteem by bolstering people with reassurance and affirmation, by telling them that they are terrific, that they are number one, and that they had better treat themselves to a good time. The result is not larger persons but smaller ones – pygmy egos. But how do we acquire a sense of significance without puffing up the ego? How do we become important without becoming self-important, confident without being arrogant, dignified without looking ridiculous?

Jeremiah sets the pattern. Has anyone lived so well out of such deep reservoirs of dignity and design – no hollow piece of strutting straw! – as Jeremiah? He did it from a base of meditation on the awesome *before* of his life, and he lived *out of* this background and not *against* it. This, not Anathoth, was where he came from, and the accent in his speech betrays his origins to anyone with a sensitive ear.

It is difficult to cultivate this kind of depth-memory awareness. We get no help from our contemporaries who rarely go back further than the minutes of the previous meeting in an attempt to understand the agenda of their humanity. We are so used to considering everything through the prism of our current feelings and our most recent acquisitions that it is a radical change to consider the vast *before.* But if we would live well, it is necessary. Otherwise we live feebly and gropingly, blind to the glory that we are known, chosen and given away by God.

4

I Am Only a Youth

Then I said, 'Ah, Lord GOD! Behold, I do not know how to speak, for I am only a youth.' But the LORD said to me,
'Do not say, "I am only a youth";
for to all to whom I send you you shall go,
and whatever I command you you shall speak.
Be not afraid of them,
for I am with you to deliver you, says the LORD. . . .
Behold, I make you this day a fortified city, an iron pillar, and bronze walls, against the whole land, against the kings of Judah, its princes, its priests, and the people of the land.'

JEREMIAH 1:6-8, 18

'I am not made for perilous quests,' cried Frodo. 'I wish I had never seen the Ring! Why did it come to me? Why was I chosen?'

'Such questions cannot be answered,' said Gandalf. 'You may be sure that it was not for any merit that others do not possess; not for power or wisdom, at any rate. But you have been chosen and you must therefore use such strength and heart and wits as you have.'

J. R. R. TOLKIEN[1]

GOD ASKED JEREMIAH TO DO SOMETHING HE COULDN'T DO. Naturally, he refused. If we are asked to do something that we know that we cannot do, it is foolish to accept the assignment, for it soon becomes an embarrassment to everyone.

The job Jeremiah refused was to be a prophet. There are two interlaced convictions that characterize a prophet. The first conviction is that God is personal and alive and active. The second conviction is that what is going on right now, in this world at this time in history, is critical. A prophet is obsessed with *God*, and a prophet is immersed in the *now*. God is as real to a prophet as his next-door neighbor, and his next-door neighbor is a vortex in which God's purposes are being worked out.

The work of the prophet is to call people to live well, to live rightly – to be human. But it is more than a call to say something, it is a call to live out the message. The prophet must be what he or she says. The person as well as the message of the prophet challenges us to live up to our creation, to live into our salvation – to become all that we are designed to be.

We cannot be human if we are not in relation to God. We can be an animal and be unaware of God. We can be an aggregate of minerals and be unaware of God. But humanity requires relationship with God before it can be itself. 'As the scholastics used to say: *Homo non proprie humanus sed superhumanus est* – which means that to be properly human, you must go beyond the merely human.'[2]

A relationship with God is not something added on after we complete our basic growth, it is the essential core of that growth. Take that core out, and there is no humanity at all but only a husk, the appearance but not the substance of the human. Nor can we be human if we are not existing in the present, for the present is where God meets us. If we avoid the details of the actual present, we abdicate a big chunk of our humanity. Søren Kierkegaard parodies our inattentiveness to our immediate reality when he writes about the man who was caught up in things and projects and causes so abstracted from himself that he woke up one day and found himself dead.[3]

A prophet lets people know who God is and what he is like, what he says, and what he is doing. A prophet wakes us up from our sleepy complacency so that we see the great and stunning drama that is our existence, and then pushes us onto the stage playing our parts whether we think we are ready or not. A prophet angers us by rejecting our euphemisms and ripping off our disguises, then dragging our heartless attitudes and selfish motives out into the open where everyone sees them for what they are. A prophet makes everything and everyone seem significant and important – important because God made it, or him, or her; significant because God is actively, right now, using it, or him, or her. A prophet makes it difficult to continue with a sloppy or selfish life.

Pleading Inadequacy

No job is more important, for what is more important than a persuasive presentation of the invisible but living reality, God? And what is more important than a convincing demonstration of the eternal meaning of the visible, ordinary stuff of daily life? But important or not, Jeremiah refused. He was not qualified. He had not done well in the God courses in school. And he hadn't been around long enough to know how the world works. 'Ah, Lord GOD! Behold, I do not know how to speak, for I am only a youth.'

We are practiced in pleading inadequacy in order to avoid living at the best that God calls us to. How tired the excuses sound! I am only a youth; I am only a housewife; I am only a layman; I am only a poor preacher; I only have an eighth-grade education; I don't have enough time; I don't have enough training; I don't have enough confidence; or, with biblical precedence, 'Oh, my Lord, I am not eloquent' (Ex 4:10). Too much is being asked of us. We cannot cope. We cannot manage.

If we look at ourselves and are absolutely honest, we are always inadequate. Of course, we are not always honest. We fudge and cheat on the tests. We cover up a bit here; we bluff a bit there. We pretend to be more sure than we are.

> *Our race would not have gotten far,*
> *Had we not learned to bluff it out*
> *And look more certain than we are*
> *Of what our motion is about.*[4]

Life, in fact, *is* too much for us. This business of living in awareness and response to God, in attentive love to the people with us, and in reverent appreciation of the world round about exceeds our capacities. We aren't smart enough; we don't have enough energy; we can't concentrate adequately. We are apathetic, slouching and slovenly. Not all the time, to be sure. We have spurts of love, passionate risks of faith, impressive episodes of courageous caring. But then we slip back into indolence or greed. Soon we are back at the old stand, handing out the glib patter that fools others into thinking we are better than we really are. Sometimes we even deceive ourselves into thinking we are pretty nice people indeed. Jeremiah knew it all from the inside: 'the heart is deceitful above all things, and desperately corrupt' (Jer 17:9).

But a ruthless honesty will always leave us shattered by our inadequacy. The world is a frightening place. If we are not a little bit scared, we simply don't know what is going on. If we are pleased with ourselves, we either don't have very high standards or have amnesia in regard to the central reality, for 'it is a fearful thing to fall into the hands of the living God' (Heb 10:31). Pascal said, 'Fear not, provided you fear; but if you fear not, then fear.'[5]

There is an enormous gap between what we think we can do and what God calls us to do. Our ideas of what we can do or want to do are trivial; God's ideas for us are grand. God's call to Jeremiah to be a prophet parallels his call to us to be a person. The excuses we make are plausible; often they are statements of fact, but they are excuses all the same and are disallowed by our Lord, who says: 'Do not say, "I am only a youth"; for to all to whom I send you you shall go, and whatever I command you you shall speak. Be not afraid of them, for I am with you to deliver you, says the LORD.' The Lord then put forth his hand and touched Jeremiah's mouth, saying, 'Behold, I have put my words in your mouth. See, I have set you this day over nations and over kingdoms, to pluck up and to break down, to destroy and to overthrow, to build and to plant' (Jer 1:9-10).

The three pairs of verbs *(pluck up/break down, destroy/overthrow, build/plant)* are all-involving. In the way of faith we do not escape because it is too much for us; we plunge into it because we are commanded and equipped. It is not our feelings that determine our level of participation in life, nor our experience that qualifies us for what we will do and be; it is what God decides about us. God does not send us into the dangerous and exacting life of faith because we are qualified;

he chooses us in order to qualify us for what he wants us to be and do: 'I have put my words in your mouth . . . I have set you this day over nations.'

Eight verses down the page Jeremiah is no longer inadequate. 'And I, behold, I make you this day a fortified city, an iron pillar, and bronze walls, against the whole land, against the kings of Judah, its princes, its priests, and the people of the land. They will fight against you; but they shall not prevail against you, for I am with you, says the LORD, to deliver you' (Jer 1:18-19). Everything that we know about Jeremiah shows that this in fact happened. In a forty-year public ministry through the most confused and chaotic decades of Israel's entire history, Jeremiah was invincible. Inwardly he was in great agony many times, but he never swerved from his course. He was mocked cruelly and persecuted severely, but he never deviated from his position. There was enormous pressure on him to change, to compromise, to quit and to hide. He never did it. He was 'bronze walls.'

How did Jeremiah make the transition from the shuffling, excuse-making 'Ah, LORD, I am only a youth' to the 'iron pillar' career of accepting the assignment as prophet? God equipped Jeremiah for life by showing him two visions. The two visions led Jeremiah from enervating inadequacy to adrenalin-charged obedience.

A Rod of Almond

The first vision was of a rod of almond: '"Jeremiah, what do you see?" And I said, "I see a rod of almond." Then the LORD said to me, "You have seen well, for I am watching over my word to perform it"' (Jer 1:11-12).

The almond tree is one of the earliest trees to bloom in Palestine. Before it puts forth leaves, it puts forth blossoms, white and snowy. While the land is still chill from winter, the warm blossoms, untended and unforced, surprise us with a promise of spring. Every spring it happens again: the explosion of blossom in our forests and gardens before the leaves are out, before the grass is green. And we know what is coming next: migratory birds will soon be filling the air with song; leaves will festoon the trees with great banners of green; fruit will begin to develop. The blossom is a delight in itself, beautiful to look at, fragrant to smell. But it is more. It is anticipation. It is promise. Like words. 'I am watching over my word to perform it.' Words, like the almond blossom, are promises, anticipations of what is about to take place. They *become* something. 'The word *became* flesh.'

The vision is accented with a word play. The word *almond* and the word *watching* are nearly identical in Hebrew. 'What do you see, Jeremiah?' I see a *shaqed* ('almond'). 'Good! you see very well, for I am *shoqed* ('watching') my word to perform it. I am watching my word like a shepherd watching his flock. Not one of these words that you hear me speak will wander off. Not one will be lost. I'll bring each word to some kind of living completion.'

The method was audio-visual: a visual image joined to an auditory pun trained Jeremiah in hope. Every spring for the rest of his life the sight of the almond blossom, *shaqed*, would trigger the sound *shoqed* ('watching') in his memory ('I am watching over my word to perform it'), and for the rest of his life every time he heard the everyday word *shoqed* ('watching') spoken – and there could not have been many days when he did not – the visual image of the *shaqed* ('almond') would release all the life-enhancing, energy-releasing associations of spring.

There is no living the life of faith, whether by prophet or person, without some kind of sustaining vision like this. At some deep level we need to be convinced, and in some way or other we need periodic reminders, that no words are mere words. In particular, God's words are not mere words. They are promises that lead to fulfillments. God performs what he announces. God does what he says.

A Boiling Pot

The second vision was of a boiling pot: '"What do you see?" And I said, "I see a boiling pot, facing away from the north"' (Jer 1:13). The pot was tipped so that the scalding water was being spilled to the south. The village of Anathoth and the Jerusalem streets and courtyards were directly in the path of its flow.

The boiling water cascading down toward Israel is identified as enemy armies poised for an invasion (Jer 1:14-16). The nations to the north were boiling a kettle of war that was going to inundate the land with evil – murder and rape and pillage. The seething turbulence on the horizon was going to spill over into the pleasant hills of Judea. The enemy kings and officers, audacious and mocking, would camp right in front of the city gates and around the city walls. This imminent war is linked with God's judgment. The boiling water is going to wash the land. 'I believe in getting into hot water,' said G. K. Chesterton, 'it keeps you clean.'[6] The scalding judgment was coming because the people had abandoned a relationship of love with God and taken up with little religious rituals and picayune idolatries (Jer 1:16). The war would interrupt their inane and distracted, their soiled and silly lives and force them to attend to what is essential and eternal: life and death, God and humanity, faith and faithfulness, covenant and obedience.

The subject of the vision is negative (in contrast to the almond vision) but its message is positive, for its effect is to *contain* evil. The boiling pot is a container, located at a specific place on the compass.

Neither Jeremiah nor the people needed a vision to tell them that danger was gathering momentum in the north. Everybody knew that.[7] The Neo-Babylonian armies were on the move and no reasonably intelligent person could fail to be aware of it. It did, though, take a vision to see that the evil had limits. The boiling-pot vision named, located and limited the evil that was afflicting everyone with a kind of metaphysical paranoia.

Uninstructed and untrained we let evil seep through the atmosphere and through our emotions like a fog, obscuring the sharp outlines of reality and absorbing everything in its ominous, soggy gray. In such an atmosphere we are terrorized by every rumor, jumpy at every noise, edgy and anxious. It is certainly true that there is evil in the world - a great deal of it. And it is frightening. If we live realistically, with our eyes open, we see a lot of evil. Seeing all that evil, how can we relax? How can we engage in such undramatic counteractions as giving cups of cold water to thirsty strangers? The vision supplies the answer: the evil is not everything, and it is not everywhere. It is named. It has an origin and a finish. The evil that has its paralyzing grip on everyone is not a wild, uncontrollable evil; it is a carefully commanded judgment, with God as the commander. The boiling pot reduces evil to a location and a use. We cannot afford to be naive about evil - it must be faced. But we cannot be intimidated by it either. It will be used by God to bring good. For it is one of the most extraordinary aspects of the good news that God uses bad men to accomplish his good purposes. The great paradox of judgment is that evil becomes fuel in the furnace of salvation.

Uninstructed by this vision, or something like it, we lose our sense of proportion and are incapacitated for living in open and adventurous response to whatever comes to us through the day. If we forget that the newspapers are footnotes to Scripture and not the other way around, we will finally be afraid to get out of bed in the morning. Too many of us spend far too much time with the editorial page and not nearly enough with the prophetic vision. We get our interpretation of politics and economics and morals from journalists when we should be getting only information; the *meaning* of the world is most accurately given to us by God's Word.

The two visions, the blossoming almond branch and the pot of boiling water, were Jeremiah's Harvard and Yale. The single-image visions burned themselves deep into the retina of his faith. By means of these visions he kept his balance and sanity and passion in the theater of God's glory and through the holocaust of human sin. Whether he was ecstatic in the splendor or nauseated by the stench of evil, he kept his grip on reality, never retreating into a cave of self-pity, never shutting his eyes to the ugly evil around him, never cynically dismissive of the glory exploding around him.

The first vision convinced Jeremiah that the word of God bursts with wonders and that its wonders are not illusions. The second vision convinced Jeremiah that the world is very dangerous but that the danger is not catastrophic.

In order to be equipped to be what God calls us to be – prophet, person – and not be crippled all our lives by inadequacy, we need to know supremely these two subjects, God and world, and to be trained in them thoroughly. In both subjects first impressions and surface appearances are deceiving. We underestimate God and we overestimate evil. We don't see what God is doing and conclude that he is doing nothing. We see everything that evil is doing and think it is in control of everyone. The visions penetrate appearances. By means of the blossoming almond and the boiling pot we are trained to live with a keen edge of hope and to never be intimidated by evil. For if we are going to live in God's image, alive to all that is God, open and responsive to all he is doing, we must trust in his word, trust what we do not see. And if we are going to live in the world, attentive to each particularity, loving it through all the bad times without being repelled by it or afraid of it or conformed to it, we are going to have to face its immense evil, but know at the same time that it is a limited and controlled evil.

Vision-Shaped

Did the visions work? Do they? Jeremiah's life is evidence that the visions were the educational curriculum that directed development from an insecure youth to a solid, mature adult. Jeremiah was shaped by the visions, not by the fashions of the day, not by his feelings about himself. We know that he often felt terrible and that he was treated terribly. He often felt weak; he often was near despair. In fact, he was always strong. His emotions often failed him; his faith always held fast.

His strength was not achieved by growing calluses over his highly sensitive spirit. Throughout his life Jeremiah experienced an astonishing range of emotions. His spirit registered, it seems, everything. He was one of those finely tuned persons who pick up and respond to the slightest tremors around him. At the same time he was utterly impervious to assault and mockery, to persecution and opposition.

The thorough integration of strength and sensitivity, of firmness and feeling, is rare. We sometimes see sensitive people who are unstrung most of the time. They bleed profusely at the sight of blood. Their sensitivity incapacitates them for action in the rough-and-tumble cruelties of the world. In contrast others are rigid moralists, ramrod stiff with righteous rectitude. There is never any doubt about their dogmatically asserted position. But their principles are hammers that crack skulls and bruise flesh. The world makes a wide circuit around such persons. It is dangerous to be in their company for very long, for if they detect any mental weakness or moral wavering in us, we will be lucky to escape without at least a headache.

But not Jeremiah. Educated by the almond rod, his inward responsiveness to the personal, whether God or human, deepened and developed. Educated by the boiling pot, his outward capacity to deal with dehumanizing evil and to resist depersonalizing intimidation became invincible: 'a fortified city, an iron pillar, bronze walls.' Not bad for someone who started out as 'only a youth.'

5

Do Not Trust in These Deceptive Words

The word that came to Jeremiah from the LORD: 'Stand in the gate of the LORD's house, and proclaim there this word, and say, Hear the word of the LORD, all you men of Judah who enter these gates to worship the LORD. Thus says the LORD of hosts, the God of Israel, Amend your ways and your doings, and I will let you dwell in this place. Do not trust in these deceptive words: "This is the temple of the LORD, the temple of the LORD, the temple of the LORD."'

JEREMIAH 7:1-4

Jesus today has many who love his heavenly kingdom, but few who carry his cross; many who yearn for comfort, few who long for distress. Plenty of people he finds to share his banquet, few to share his fast. Everyone desires to take part in his rejoicing, but few are willing to suffer anything for his sake. There are many that follow Jesus as far as the breaking of bread, few as far as drinking the cup of suffering; many that revere his miracles, few that follow him in the indignity of his cross.

THOMAS À KEMPIS[1]

MANASSEH WAS THE WORST KING THE HEBREWS EVER HAD. He was a thoroughly bad man presiding over a totally corrupt government. He reigned in Jerusalem for fifty-five years, a dark and evil half century.

He encouraged a pagan worship that involved whole communities in sexual orgies. He installed cult prostitutes at shrines throughout the countryside. He imported wizards and sorcerers who enslaved the people in superstitions and manipulated them with their magic. The man could not do enough evil. There seemed to be no end to his barbarous cruelties. His capacity for inventing new forms of evil seemed bottomless. His appetite for the sordid was insatiable. One day he placed his son on the altar in some black and terrible ritual of witchcraft and burned him as an offering (2 Kings 21).

The great Solomonic temple in Jerusalem, resplendent in its holy simplicity, empty of any form of god so that the invisible God could be attended to in worship, swarmed with magicians and prostitutes. Idols shaped as beasts and monsters defiled the holy place. Lust and greed were deified. Murders were commonplace. Manasseh dragged the people into a mire far more stinking than anything the world had yet seen. The sacred historian's judgment was blunt: 'Manasseh seduced them to do more evil than the nations had done whom the LORD destroyed before the people of Israel' (2 Kgs 21:9).[2]

Jeremiah was born in the last decade of Manasseh's rule. This is the world in which Jeremiah learned to walk and talk and play. No worse environment in which to raise a child can be imagined. It was a slum society: 'On every side the wicked prowl, as vileness is exalted among the sons of men' (Ps 12:8).

Fifty-five years of such misrule brought the faith close to oblivion. Some old people remembered prophetic oracles and acts of true worship. Rumors of holiness were no doubt whispered about. Hidden pockets of faithful people maintained a fugitive existence. Then Manasseh died. His son Amon succeeded him. The people watched to see if things would change. They didn't. The evil continued. But the people had their stomachs full. They had reached the breaking point and could take no more. Amon was murdered. His eight-year-old son, Josiah, was put on the throne.

Josiah's Reforms

Now begins one of the most remarkable chapters in the story of these people who are our ancestors. Somehow in this boy king there was an innocence and uncorrupt spirit that God was able to use to bring new life to the land.

We wonder how Josiah got started, for he had no models to work from. Goodness originates at some deep level inaccessible to our investigations. When I see a large expanse of black asphalt parking lot, I sometimes think of Manasseh and Josiah. The asphalt is ugly and forbidding. A fresh green creation has been bulldozed into oblivion to make way for this sterile, monotonous surface. A harsh and brutal technology has obliterated a delicately nuanced life for the convenience of the worshipers of the god Mammon. But before long, cracks appear and grasses, wildflowers, even sprouting trees, push their way through. The underground forces of life break through the surface patina of death. Maintenance engineers patch and fill and seal to keep their surface intact and smooth. If they are inattentive for so much as a season or two, seemingly fragile but in fact formidable life reasserts itself.

I speak of the unremarked
Forces that split the heart
And make the pavement toss –
Forces concealed in quiet
People and plants . . .[3]

Mannasseh had covered the Holy Land with sodom-and-gomorrah asphalt. But the holy was not gone, only invisible. Josiah was one of the first shoots to break through the black bitumen. Out of some deep, intuitive longing for God that corrupt parents had not been able to quash, that an evil environment had not been able to annihilate, he asked questions: How could a better rule be established? What could he do as king to recover health and goodness in the garbage dump that was Jerusalem? He had to start some place. He started at the place of worship.

A people's lives are only as good as their worship. The temple in Jerusalem was the architectural evidence of the importance of God in the life of the people. All the lines of life crisscrossed in the temple. Meaning was established there. Values were created there. Worship defines life. If worship is corrupt, life will be corrupt. For fifty-seven years lust and violence in the temple had percolated into the streets and homes and villages of the nation. Josiah began by cleaning up the temple.

As the temple was being renovated and repaired, Hilkiah the priest found an old book there. The book was brought to Josiah and read aloud to him. It was the book of Deuteronomy. Imagine the impact of that reading. Here is Josiah, disgusted with the evil of his father and grandfather and determined to do something about it, but not knowing quite how. He had no blueprint, no direction, no counsel. The only thing he had inherited from his father and grandfather was fifty-seven years of evil. Now he had this powerful document about the love of God and our worship of him, clear definitions of what is right and wrong, and explicit directions on how to make moral decisions and conduct intelligent worship. In Josiah's ears the reading was 'a thunderclap of conscience.'[4]

The young king's response was swift and commanding. He immediately put into action everything that he read. Now that he knew what true worship was, he banished every vestige of false worship. The government-subsidized immorality was wiped out. The cult prostitutes who had special housing in the temple were turned out. The magicians and sorcerers who had set up shop in the temple precincts were scattered. Josiah dispersed his agents throughout the land announcing what was discovered in this scroll. Old altars were torn down and people were taught the way of faith. It was exciting, dramatic and glorious. 'Never had there been a reform so sweeping in its aims and so consistent in execution!'[5]

The muck of a half century of corruption was shoveled out of the city, out of the land. The place had been a religious zoo. At the old places of worship you could get any loathsome desire gratified, any murderous ambition licensed. There was a ritual and god or goddess for every whim. Under Manasseh religion was centered in what William James, in a memorable phrase, called the 'convulsive little ego'.[6] Religion was supernatural assistance to do whatever you wished: make money, insure a good harvest, feel good, murder the person you hate, get ahead of your neighbor. Now, under Josiah, religion centered in one holy God. Religion became what it must be but often is not – a way of discovering the meaning of life, of ordering justice in society, of finding direction toward goals of excellence, of acquiring the discipline to live with integrity, of realizing how God loves and of learning how to love God in return.

A Ringside Seat

Jeremiah had a ringside seat in the arena of this reform. It is hardly conceivable though that he remained a spectator. He was not the sort of person to stand on the sidelines. He helped. He participated in the reform with his preaching. We have fragments of his sermons.

'You have polluted the land,' he said, 'with your vile harlotry' (Jer 3:2). The people had abandoned the God who loved and called them into being and had given themselves in reckless prodigality to every god and goddess they met. Moral pollution works the same way as environmental pollution. The waste products of careless living work insidiously into the soil of thought and the streams of language, poisoning every part of society.

Jeremiah pleaded with them: 'Break up your fallow ground' (Jer 4:3). Superstition and idolatry form a tough crust that makes us insensitive and unreceptive to the word that God speaks in mercy and salvation. Ploughing is a metaphor for the repentance that prepares the ground of our hearts to receive what God has for us.

Jeremiah was scathing and sarcastic: 'What do you mean that you dress in scarlet . . . that you enlarge your eyes with paint? In vain you beautify yourself' (Jer 4:30). Do you think that by using cosmetics you can change your destiny? It is you yourselves who need to be changed.

Through it all Jeremiah conveyed hope: 'Stand by the roads, and look, and ask for the ancient paths, where the good way is; and walk in it, and find rest for your souls' (Jer 6:16). There *are* ancient paths, well-trodden and clearly marked, that lead to goodness and to God. The Scriptures – in this case the Deuteronomy scroll – map the roads. If we ignore them, we stumble over obstacles. Jeremiah's preaching was tireless in insisting on the plain, obvious truth: that God is among us, that we can and must live in faithful love with him.

Only Skin-deep Reform

The reform was accomplished. Everything that a king's commands could do was done: conspicuous crime was stopped; superstitious religion was sent packing; immoral worship was banned. But getting rid of evil does not make people good. It didn't take Jeremiah long to realize that the reform was only skin-deep. Everything had changed, but nothing had changed. The outward changes had been enormous; the inward changes were imperceptible.

It isn't long before we find Jeremiah standing in the gates of the Jerusalem temple preaching an odd sermon. This is the very temple that had been the focus for the impressive and successful reform. We would expect a note of congratulation, praising the people for cleaning up the place, getting rid of the wizards, banishing the cult prostitutes, making it safe to walk the street again without getting mugged or murdered. But we hear nothing like that. Everybody is coming to church, arriving at the temple to offer sacrifices just as they are commanded to do in the new best-selling book of Deuteronomy. Worship of the Lord is popular and enthusiastic. The throngs were euphoric: 'This is the temple of the LORD, the temple of the LORD, the temple of the LORD.'

And what is Jeremiah saying? This: 'Do not trust in these deceptive words: "This is the temple of the LORD, the temple of the LORD, the temple of the LORD."' The people stood in the holy place and spoke the current religious cliché and supposed that everything was just fine. They were in the right place, and they said the right words – but *they* were not right. The reform was necessary, but it was not enough. For religion is not a matter of arrangements or places or words, but of life and love, of mercy and obedience, of persons in a passion of faith.

Just when Jeremiah expected the people, free from the corruption of Manasseh, to launch into a life of faith using their energy in love, venturing into justice and peace, he arrives at the temple, and what does he find? He finds the people stupidly pleased with themselves and repeating the reform slogan 'temple of the LORD, temple of the LORD, temple of the LORD.' Jeremiah is irate.

Places are important – immensely important. Sites and buildings are places where we gather ourselves for fresh action and assemble ourselves for new endeavor. But standing in a church singing a hymn doesn't make us holy any more than standing in a barn and neighing makes us a horse.

And words are important – immensely important. What we say and the way we say it expresses what is most personal and intimate in us. But mindlessly repeating holy words no more creates a relationship than saying 'I love you' twenty times a day makes us skilled lovers.

Only because the reform was successful could this kind of thing happen. The temple was now clearly the Lord's temple and not a pagan shrine. When the people came they did not buy amulets, or visit the cult prostitute, or pay to get their fortune told – they worshiped the way they had been commanded by Moses. They were in the right place, saying the right thing. Yet Jeremiah calls their presence and the words there a lie.

Born Again, Born Again, Born Again

This sermon by Jeremiah is so important to us. It is especially important in times of success, when everything is going well, when the church is admired and church attendance swells.

We think everything is fine because the appearances are fine and the statistics are impressive. The church is never in so much danger as when it is popular and millions of people are saying 'I'm born again, born again, born again.'

Jeremiah is as concerned with the right place and the right words as anyone. He, after all, fought hard for this reform. But the right place and the right words are not the life of faith but only the opportunity for the life of faith. They can just as easily be used as a respectable front for a corrupt self. Jeremiah accused the people of just this, using God's temple as a front for a robber's den (Jer 7:11).

A robber's den is a secure place to hide between forays into the countryside to pillage weak and unprotected travelers. After these raids for plunder the robbers go back to the cave where they are safe. That is Jeremiah's accusation: 'You have found a safe place, haven't you! This nice, clean temple. You spend all week out in the world doing what you want to do, taking advantage of others, exploiting the weak, cursing the person who isn't pliable to your plans, and, then you repair to this place where everything is in order and protected and right.' Six hundred and fifty years later Jesus used Jeremiah's text in his 'spring cleaning' temple sermon (Mk 11:15-19) and Paul similarly warned Timothy of those who were 'holding the form of religion but denying the power of it' (2 Tm 3:5).

Jeremiah is specific in his arraignment: 'Will you steal, murder, commit adultery, swear falsely, burn incense to Baal, and go after other gods that you have not known, and then come and stand before me in this house, which is called by my name, and say, "We are delivered!" – only to go on doing all these abominations?' (Jer 7:9-10). Their religious performance was impeccable; their everyday life was rotten.

The outside is a lot easier to reform than the inside. Going to the right church and saying the right words is a lot easier than working out a life of justice and love among the people you work and live with. Showing up at church once a week and saying a hearty Amen is a lot easier than engaging in a life of daily prayer and Scripture meditation that develops into concern for poverty and injustice, hunger and war.

Images without Substance

Are the people who do this deliberately trying to pull the wool over the eyes of their neighbors and fake God into blessing them? Some are, but for most I don't think so. I don't think they are trying to get by with anything. I think they have lived for so long on the basis of outward appearances that they have no feel for inward reality. I think they were so impressed with the success of the reform that they thought that was all there was to it. We live in a culture where image is everything and substance nothing. We live in a culture where a new beginning is far more attractive than a long follow-through. Images are important. Beginnings are important. But an image without substance is a lie. A beginning without a continuation is a lie.

Jeremiah attempted to shock his people into a recognition of this obvious but avoided truth by sending them on a field trip to Shiloh: 'Go now to my place that was in Shiloh, where I made my name dwell at first, and see what I did to it for the wickedness of my people Israel' (Jer 7:12).

Shiloh was one of the most famous holy places in Hebrew history. Located at the center of the country, it had been the earliest focus for worship and consultation in Israel. When Joshua brought the people into the land after their deliverance from Egypt and forty years of wilderness wandering, Shiloh was where they assembled, set up the tabernacle and divided up the land among the twelve tribes. The revered ark of the covenant was kept at Shiloh. The great prophet Samuel spoke his words of counsel there. Shiloh was a magnificent beginning. Shiloh was a glorious image. But all Shiloh was now was a few piles of rocks in a field of weeds, as every traveler from Galilee to Jerusalem could see. Shiloh was the right place; at Shiloh the right words were spoken. But when the right place no longer launched a walk with God and when the right words no longer expressed love and faith, Shiloh was destroyed.

If it could happen to Shiloh, it can happen to Jerusalem – and any other place where people gather to worship God. It is not enough to be in the right place; it is not enough to say the right words; it is never enough until we are walking with God twenty-four hours a day everywhere we go, with everything we say an expression of love and faith.

A Lifelong Career

When I talk with people who come to me in preparation for marriage I often say, 'Weddings are easy; marriages are difficult.' The couple want to plan a wedding; I want to plan a marriage. They want to know where the bridesmaids will stand; I want to develop a plan for forgiveness. They want to discuss the music of the wedding; I want to talk about the emotions of the marriage. I can do a wedding in twenty minutes with my eyes shut; a marriage takes year after year after year of alert, wide-eyed attention.

Weddings are important. They are beautiful; they are impressive; they are emotional; sometimes they are expensive. We weep at weddings and we laugh at weddings. We take care to be at the right place at the right time and say the right words. Where people stand is important. The way people dress is significant. Every detail – this flower, that candle – is memorable. All the same, weddings are easy.

But marriages are complex and difficult. In marriage we work out in every detail of life the promises and commitments spoken at the wedding. In marriage we develop the long and rich life of faithful love that the wedding announces. The event of the wedding without the life of marriage doesn't amount to much. It hardly matters if the man and woman dress up in their wedding clothes and re-enact the ceremony every anniversary and say 'I'm married, I'm married, I'm married' if there is no daily love shared, if there is no continuing tenderness, no attentive listening, no inventive giving, no creative blessing.

Josiah's reform was like a wedding. Jeremiah's concern was with a marriage. It was a great achievement to repudiate Manasseh and establish the people in covenant with their God; but it was a lifelong career to embrace God's love and walk in his ways. The people celebrated Josiah's reform; they ignored Jeremiah's preaching. It is Jeremiah's lifelong achievement that the soggy religious mush of the masses never dulled his perceptions nor muted his insistent witness.

6

Go Down to the Potter's House

The word that came to Jeremiah from the LORD*: 'Arise, and go down to the potter's house, and there I will let you hear my words.' So I went down to the potter's house, and there he was working at his wheel. And the vessel he was making of clay was spoiled in the potter's hand, and he reworked it into another vessel, as it seemed good to the potter to do.*

JEREMIAH 18:1-4

It is indeed by analogy that I believe the mind makes its richest movements, and it is by analogy that I believe the mind makes its deepest use of what it has understood; or at any rate I believe this to be an appropriate way of looking at the labor of the mind in a society, like ours, without a fixed character, and operating under a revelation which turns out to have been imperfectly understood. It is through analogy, if at all, that the falcon can again hear the falconer, that things can come together again, and that again the center can hold.

R. P. BLACKMUR[1]

WILLI OSSA WAS AN ARTIST WHO WORKED AS A JANITOR AT night in a church on New York's West Side to support his wife and infant daughter. During the day he painted. German by birth, Willi grew up during the war years and then married an American girl, the daughter of an officer in the occupying army. I got to know Willi when I was a theological student working at the same church as an assistant pastor.

Willi liked to talk about religion; I liked to talk about art. We became friends. We got along well together and had long conversations. He decided to paint my portrait. I went to his house on West 92nd Street a couple of afternoons a week on my way to my work at the church and sat for thirty minutes or so for my portrait. He never permitted me to see what he was painting. Day after day, week after week, I sat while he painted. One day his wife came into the room and looked at the portrait now nearing completion and exclaimed in outrage, '*Krank, krank.*' I knew just enough German to know that she was saying, 'Sick! You paint him to look like a corpse!'

He answered, '*Nicht krank, aber keine Gnade*' – 'he's not sick; that is the way he will look when the compassion is gone, when the mercy gets squeezed out of him.'

A few half-understood phrases were enough for me to guess correctly, without seeing the portrait, what Willi was doing. We had often argued late into the night about the Christian faith. He hated the church. He thought Christians were hypocrites – all of them. He made a partial exception for me for friendship's sake. The Christians he had known had all collaborated with and blessed the Nazis. The Christians he had known were responsible for the death camps and the cremation of six million Jews. The Christians he had known had turned his beloved Germany into a pagan war machine. The word *Christian* was associated in Willi's experience with state church Christians who had been baptized and took communion and played Mozart all the while they led the nation into atrocities on a scale larger than anything the world had yet seen.

His argument was that the church squeezed the spirit and morality out of persons and reduced them to function in a bureaucracy where labels took the place of faces and rules took precedence over relationships. I would argue the other side. He would become vehement. Willi's English was adequate but not fluent; when he got excited he spoke German. 'But there is no mercy in the church, *keine Gnade,* no compassion.' He told me that I must never become a pastor. If I became a pastor, in twenty years I would be nothing but a hollow-eyed clerk good for nothing but desk work.

That was what he was painting day by day without my knowing it: a prophetic warning. A portrait not of what I was right then, but of what he was sure I would become if I persisted in the Christian way.

I have the portrait. I keep it in a closet and take it out to look at from time to time. The eyes are flat and empty. The face is gaunt and unhealthy. I was never convinced that what he painted was certain to happen – if I had been, I would not have become a pastor – but I knew it was possible. I knew that before I met Willi Ossa. I knew it from reading Scripture and from looking around me. But his artistic imagination created a portrait that was far more vivid than any verbal warning. The artist shows us what happens before it happens. The artist has eyes to connect the visible and the invisible and the skill to show us complete what we in our inattentive distraction see only in bits and pieces. So I look at that portrait, then look into the mirror and compare.

Master of Imagination

Jeremiah had an artistic imagination. It was one of the powerful imaginations in the history of our race. His imagination, used in the prophetic vocation, keeps us in touch with the reality of God and our essential lives. Jeremiah's imagination wakes us to the reality of God that permeates everything around us, shows us what our lives look like from the inside, and forces us to examine what we suppose we are doing and what God is doing in us.

Jeremiah, attentive and sensitive to God's direction, was commanded: 'Arise, and go down to the potter's house, and there I will let you hear my words.' God's task, through Jeremiah, is this: How can I get these people to take me seriously, right where they are? How can I get them to see that I am working, right now, silently and invisibly, but surely and eternally, in their lives and in their history? How can I get them to see the connections between what they are doing now and who they will be in ten years – in twenty years? How can I get them to see the continuities between what I did in Abraham and Moses and David and what they are now? How can I get them out of their tedious egos into my glorious will here and now? 'Go down to the potter's house.'

The great masters of the imagination do not make things up out of thin air; they direct our attention to what is right before our eyes. They then train us to see it whole – not in fragments but in context, with all the connections. They connect the visible and the invisible, the *this* with the *that.* They assist us in seeing what is around us all the time but which we regularly overlook. With their help we see it not as commonplace but as awesome, not as banal but as wondrous. For this reason the imagination is one of the essential ministries in nurturing the life of faith. For faith is not a leap out of the everyday but a plunge into its depths.

'Go down to the potter's house.' Go down to the shoemaker's shop. Go down to the butcher's stall. Go down to the grocer's stand. Go where the necessary, everyday work is taking place. In our community he would have sent his prophet to the gas station. In seventh-century Israel the potter's house was a fixture in every community. The potter was a craftsman the location of whose house everyone knew, whose activity was familiar to everyone, whose work was necessary for the maintenance of everyday life.

'So I went down to the potter's house, and there he was working at his wheel.' Jeremiah watches the potter at work. He is working at a wheel that has a formless mass of clay on it. He turns the wheel and with skilled fingers shapes the clay. A little pressure here, more there, a vessel begins to rise out of that shapeless lump.

Do you realize how significant pottery is? The invention of pottery set off a revolution. Before pottery there were only wandering tribes, following herds of animals, going from one food supply to another, forced here by drought, there by famine. There was no time to develop anything, no leisure to reflect on anything. It was hand-to-mouth existence, day-to-day survival. But the invention of pottery made it possible to store and carry. Then it was possible to stay in a place for a while because grain could be stored for next winter's meal and water carried. Then cooking could be done and merchandise transported. The invention of pottery signaled a revolution and the revolution was what we call civilization – the Neolithic Age.[2]

Try to imagine how life would change if we had no containers in which to store anything: no pots and pans, no bowls and dishes, no buckets and jugs, no cans and barrels, no cardboard boxes and brown paper bags, no grain silos and no oil storage tanks. Life would be reduced to what we could manage in a single day with what we could hold in our hands at one time. Pottery made it possible for communities to develop. Life was extended beyond the immediate, beyond the urgent.

The practical impact of the invention of pottery is immense. But there is something else that is just as important. No one has ever been able to make a clay pot that is *just* a clay pot. Every pot is also an art form. Pottery is always changing its shape as potters find new proportions, different ways to shape the pots in pleasing combinations of curves. There is no pottery that besides being useful does not also show evidence of beauty. Pottery is artistically shaped, designed, painted, glazed, fired. It is one of the most functional items in life; it is also one of the most beautiful.

No one in Jeremiah's time ever put a piece of pottery on the mantel just to look at, using it to give a touch of elegance to a bare shelf. But neither, and this is just as significant, did anyone use a piece of pottery just because it was useful – always there was evidence of an artist's hand in it.

It is difficult for us to grasp the significance of that combination, for we live in a quite different world. We commonly separate the useful and the beautiful, the necessary and the elegant. We use brown paper bags for containers to which no one bothers to give shape or color or design. After all, we only want something in which to get our groceries home. Then we buy paintings to beautify the walls of our homes. We build featureless office buildings and ugly factories for our necessary work, then we build museums to contain the objects of beauty. But there have been times in history when these things were done better, when the necessary and the beautiful were integrated, when, in fact, it was impossible to think of separating them. For Jeremiah this was certainly the case: there were no brown paper bags and there were no museums, but there was pottery. Everywhere. Useful and beautiful. Functionally necessary and artistically elegant at one and the same time with no thought that the two elements could be separated.

Jeremiah's imagination went to work as he stood before this potter with his lump of clay and his wheel. Jeremiah had seen potters at work all his life, but today he saw something else – he saw God at work making a people for his glory. A people of God. Persons created in the image of God. Necessary but not only necessary – each one also beautiful. And beautiful but not only beautiful – each one also necessary. Each human being is an inseparable union of necessity and freedom. There is no human being who is not useful with a part to play in what God is doing. And there is no human being who is not unique with special lines and colors and forms distinct from anyone else. All this came clear to Jeremiah in the potter's house: the brute fact of the clay, lumpish and inert, shaped for a purpose by the hands of the potter, and then, as it took shape, the realization of the uniquely designed individuality and wide-ranging usefulness it would acquire as a finished pot, painted and baked and glazed. God shapes us for his eternal purposes and he begins right here. The dust out of which we are made and the image of God into which we are made are one and the same.

The Pot Spoiled

And then the pot was spoiled: 'the vessel he was making of clay was spoiled in the potter's hand.'

Jeremiah knew all about that. He knew about spoiled vessels – men and women with impurities and blemishes that resist the shaping hand of the creator. He rubbed shoulders daily with people who were not useful: imperfections made their lives leak, holding neither wine nor water; a failure of proportion made their lives wobble or tip, unstable and undependable. Jeremiah had other words for it: sin, rebellion, self-will, wandering. But he had never had such a striking image for it.

Jeremiah continued to observe. What would the potter do now? Kick the wheel and go off in a sulk? Throw the clay at the cat and go to the market and purchase another brand? Neither. 'He reworked it into another vessel, as it seemed good to the potter to do.' God kneads and presses, pushes and pulls. The creative work starts over again, patiently, skillfully. God doesn't give up. God doesn't throw away what is spoiled. Under a different image, George Herbert saw and said the same thing, 'Storms are the triumph of his art.'[3]

Hope and Warning

Hope and warning join hands in this message: 'Behold, like the clay in the potter's hand, so are you in my hand, O house of Israel' (Jer 18:6). He expands in both directions: 'If that nation, concerning which I have spoken, turns from its evil, I will repent of the evil that I intended to do to it' (Jer 18:8). On the other hand, 'If it does evil in my sight, not listening to my voice, then I will repent of the good which I had intended to do to it' (Jer 18:10). No ominous prediction is set in concrete dooming us. No rosy promise is license to lazy indolence. 'The clay *can* frustrate the potter's intention and cause him to change it: as the quality of the clay determines what the potter can do with it, so the quality of a people determines what God will do with them.'[4]

The people refuse to respond, to participate, to willingly involve themselves in the shaping purposes of God: 'That is in vain! We will follow our own plans, and will every one act according to the stubbornness of his evil heart' (Jer 18:12). Do the people feel like they are stuck with their lives and will simply make the best (or worst!) of what is there? Jeremiah will not agree to their fatalism. He continues to preach. He continues to confront. His visit to the potter's house and his sermon about pottery-making are put to use in making the people responsive to the God who is mercifully shaping their lives into what is useful and beautiful. In such a setting even his judgments will be seen to be mercies.

In their recalcitrant, mulish unbelief the people will experience evil far beyond what they ever supposed possible, climaxing in the fall of Jerusalem and the Babylonian exile, but they will never be discarded.

God the Potter

This is one of Jeremiah's most powerful sermons. The image has captured the attention of people of faith everywhere. Not the least of the reasons for its effectiveness is that Jeremiah experienced it before he preached it. For no act of imagination, prophetic or artistic, is powerful if it is not wrought out of the inner life. This one had been working in Jeremiah's insides for a long time. The first word that Jeremiah heard from God was 'Before I formed you in the womb I knew you' (Jer 1:5). The verb *formed* is *yatzar.* Now, as Jeremiah is prepared to set an image before the people by which they can understand themselves in relation to their God, he stands in the house of the *yotzer,* the potter. The word by which Jeremiah first learned to understand his own life, *yatzar,* is the word which is now used to let the people understand their lives: God shaped Jeremiah;

God is shaping the people. God is a potter, a *yotzer,* working at his wheel on Jeremiah the lump of clay, on the people who are a lump of clay; he forms, *yatzar,* them. Jeremiah preaches to the people what he has lived himself.

All truth must be experienced personally before it is complete, before it is authentic. This truth, that God shapes us, that we are shaped by God, was Jeremiah's from the beginning. He had lived it in detail. He had been on that potter's wheel from before his birth. No word would mean more to Jeremiah than this one, *formed* by God. Jeremiah experienced his life as the created work of God. He was not a random accumulation of cells; he was formed by loving, skilled hands. He wasn't a potentiality of material just waiting for the lucky time when he could, by asserting his will, make something of his life; he was already made something by God, formed for his purposes.

The life of faith is very physical. Being a Christian is very much a matter of the flesh – of space and time and things. It means being thrown on the potter's wheel and shaped, our entire selves, into something useful and beautiful. And when we are not useful or beautiful we are reshaped. Painful, but worth it.

Willi Ossa's portrait shows me what I become if I drift from or deny a personal faith in a merciful God. Jeremiah's potter shows me what I become as I submit my life to the creative and merciful God. Our lives become the pottery that makes possible the emergence of civilization – what Jeremiah called the 'people of God,' what Jesus called the 'kingdom of God,' what Augustine called the 'city of God.' It is no longer every man for himself and the devil take the hindmost. We are containers, 'regions of being' in Heiddeger's words, in which love and salvation and mercy are conserved and shared. Everything is connected and makes sense now – the shape of creation and the shape of salvation, God's shaping hand and the shape of my life.

7

Pashhur Beat Jeremiah

Now Pashhur the priest, the son of Immer, who was chief officer in the house of the LORD, heard Jeremiah prophesying these things. Then Pashhur beat Jeremiah the prophet, and put him in the stocks that were in the upper Benjamin Gate of the house of the LORD. On the morrow, when Pashhur released Jeremiah from the stocks, Jeremiah said to him, 'The LORD does not call your name Pashhur, but Terror on every side.'

JEREMIAH *20:1-3*

Contrary to what might be expected, I look back on experiences that at the time seemed especially desolating and painful with particular satisfaction. Indeed, I can say with complete truthfulness that everything I have learned in my seventy-five years in this world, everything that has truly enhanced and enlightened my existence, has been through affliction and not through happiness, whether pursued or attained. In other words, if it ever were to be possible to eliminate affliction from our earthly existence by means of some drug or other medical mumbo jumbo . . . the result would not be to make life delectable, but to make it too banal and trivial to be endurable. This, of course, is what the Cross signifies. And it is the Cross, more than anything else, that has called me inexorably to Christ.

MALCOLM MUGGERIDGE[1]

MY FIRST ASSIGNMENT AFTER BEING ORDAINED AS A PASTOR almost finished me. I was called to be the assistant pastor in a large and affluent suburban church. I was glad to be part of such an obviously winning organization. After I had been there a short time, a few people came to me and asked that I lead them in a Bible study. 'Of course,' I said, 'there is nothing I would rather do.' We met on Monday evenings. There weren't many – eight or nine men and women – but even so that was triple the two or three that Jesus defined as a quorum. They were eager and attentive; I was full of enthusiasm. After a few weeks the senior pastor, my boss, asked me what I was doing on Monday evenings. I told him. He asked me how many people were there. I told him. He told me that I would have to stop.

'Why?' I asked.

'It is not cost-effective. That is too few people to spend your time on.'

I was told then how I should spend my time. I was introduced to the principles of successful church administration: crowds are important, individuals are expendable; the positive must always be accented, the negative must be suppressed. Don't expect too much of people – your job is to make them feel good about themselves and about the church. Don't talk too much about abstractions like God and sin – deal with practical issues. We had an elaborate music program, expensively and brilliantly executed. The sermons were seven minutes long and of the sort that Father Taylor (the sailor-preacher in Boston who was the model for Father Mapple in Melville's

Moby Dick) complained of in the transcendentalists of the last century: that a person could no more be converted listening to sermons like that than get intoxicated drinking skim milk.[2]

It was soon apparent that I didn't fit. I had supposed that I was there to be a pastor: to proclaim and interpret Scripture, to guide people into a life of prayer, to encourage faith, to represent the mercy and forgiveness of Christ at special times of need, to train people to live as disciples in their families, in their communities and in their work. In fact I had been hired to help run a church and do it as efficiently as possible: to be a cheerleader to this dynamic organization, to recruit members, to lend the dignity of my office to certain ceremonial occasions, to promote the image of a prestigious religious institution.

I got out of there as quickly as I could decently manage it. At the time I thought I had just been unlucky. Later I came to realize that what I experienced was not at all uncommon. Those contrasting expectations and the conflicts that grow out of them are a major theme in the history of religion.

Conflicting Expectations

Some people come to church looking for a way to make life better, to feel good about themselves, to see things in a better light. They arrange a ritual and hire a preacher to make that happen for them. Other people come to church because they want God to save and rule them. They accept the fact that there are temptations and sufferings and sacrifices involved in leaving a way of life in which they are in control and plunging into an uncertain existence in which God is in control. One group of people sees religion as a way to successful happy living; nothing that interferes with the success or interrupts the happiness will be tolerated. The other group sees religion as a way in which hurt, flawed and damaged persons become whole in relation to God; anything will be accepted (mockery, pain, renunciation, self-denial) in order to deepen and extend that reality.

One way is the way of enhancing what I want; the other way is a commitment of myself to become what God wants. Always and everywhere these contrasting expectations are in evidence. They are conspicuous in the experience of Jeremiah and collide in a noisy and dramatic confrontation one day in Jerusalem.

The Popular Preacher

In Jeremiah's lifetime there was a terrific revival of religion. The reform that King Josiah launched cleaned up the country and made the truth of God known and the worship of God popular. Jeremiah was one of the preachers of the reform. He was, no doubt, delighted that people were thronging the temple. He could hardly fail to be pleased that Scripture was once again known and preached.

The most popular preacher in Jerusalem during those years, though, was probably Pashhur. Pashhur was the chief overseer in the temple in Jerusalem, a man of prominence. When you saw him at the head of the flourishing religious establishment, the temple, you could not help feeling better. His enthusiasm was electric. When he stretched out his arms in blessing, everyone, from the least to the greatest, knew that they were included. Everyone loved to hear him: he was positive, affirmative, confident. He had the ability to draw out the best from everything. He was able to search the Scriptures and find texts that made the darkest days bright.

Living is difficult. There is much that goes wrong. We lay our plans carefully and things still go badly. We try to get ahead, but unaccountably something interferes, and we end up flat on our faces. Accidents. Weather. The general cussedness of life. Murphy's Law. In the midst of this there are some men and women who make it all seem better. There is a tone in their voices that dispels gloom. They have a smile that is infectious. They say that everything is going to be all right, and we believe them.

It is no small advantage to have a place to go from time to time for this kind of pick-up, to have a person who will perform this function for us – a place like the temple, a person like Pashhur. He saw the positive dimension in everything. He interpreted the current scene in such a way that anxieties were allayed and fears banished. Pashhur was a national asset. He had a host of imitators, prophets and priests and teachers who specialized in finding ways to massage the national psyche. Flannery O'Connor described one of their twentieth-century descendants: 'He is really a combination minister and masseur.'[3] Their favorite word was peace: 'Everything is going to be all right; God is working out his purposes in us; we are God's people; and he will bless all the people of the earth through us.' They celebrated the illustrious past – Moses the liberator, Joshua the conqueror, David the sweet psalmist of Israel, Solomon splendid in wisdom and riches. With such blood flowing in their veins the people knew they were members of an inviolable elect.

There were, to be sure, a few problems: an inordinate amount of crime, scandalous reports of injustice, a widening gap between the rich and the poor. And even though the religious life of the people had been cleaned up in public, it was an open secret that all the old fertility rites were being practiced in out-of-the-way places in the country ('beside every green tree, and on the high hills, on the mountains in the open country' – Jer 17:2-3). What the reform movement had managed mostly was to get the scandalous behavior out of sight and make church-going popular again.

But that did not daunt the positive thinking of Pashhur. The people loved him. They crowded the temple to be reassured by his sonorous baritone, to be cheered by his dazzling smile: 'God loves you. . . . Peace, peace, peace.'

Peace, Peace, but No Peace

There was one man in Jerusalem who was not impressed by Pashhur. Jeremiah couldn't stomach him. In angry exasperation Jeremiah cried out, 'From prophet to priest every one deals falsely. They have healed the wound of my people lightly, saying, "Peace, peace," when there is no peace' (Jer 8:10-11).

The task of a prophet is not to smooth things over but to make things right. The function of religion is not to make people feel good but to make them good. Love? Yes, God loves us. But his love is passionate and seeks faithful, committed love in return. God does not want tame pets to fondle and feed; he wants mature, free people who will respond to him in authentic individuality. For that to happen there must be honesty and truth. The self must be toppled from its pedestal. There must be pure hearts and clear intelligence, confession of sin and commitment in faith.

And peace? Yes, God gives peace. But it is not a peace that gets along with everyone by avoiding the hint of anything unpleasant. It is not a peace achieved by refusing to talk about painful subjects or touch sore spots. It is a peace that is hard won by learning to pray. There is evil to combat, apathy to defeat, dullness to challenge, ambition to confront. There are persons all around us, children and parents, youth and adults, who are being trampled and violated, who are being hurt and despised. Any preaching of peace that turns its back on these is a cruel farce.

There is nothing wrong with success, and there is nothing wrong with applause. It is not evidence of a sellout when a preacher has a crowd of people before him, and it is not proof of superficiality when a church is full. Nor, to take the other side, is it a sign of integrity that a man is persecuted and run out of town for what he says. He may, in fact, be a dangerous fraud. Nor can poverty be claimed as proof of courageous authenticity - the person may be simply incompetent. What is wrong is to evaluate the worth of words and deeds by their popularity. What is scandalous is to approve only what is applauded. What is disastrous is to assume that only the celebrated is genuine.

There are times when the truth will receive a wide hearing and times when it will not. Jesus had a congregation of five thousand one day and four women and two bored soldiers another. His message was the same both days. We must learn to live by the truth, not by our feelings, not by the world's opinion, not by what the latest statistical survey tells us is the accepted morality, not by what the advertisers tell us is the most gratifying lifestyle. We are trained in the biblical faith to take lightly what the experts say, the scholars say, the pollsters say, the politicians say, the pastors say. We are trained to listen to the Word of God, to test everything against what God reveals to us in Christ, to discover all meaning and worth by examining life in relation to God's will.

Despotic Egos

Jeremiah's task was to challenge the lies and speak the truth. Why do we so easily swallow the lies? Why do we find it so difficult to accept the truth? Because we are looking for bargains. We want shortcuts. There are no easy ways. There is only one way. If we are going to be complete human beings, we are going to have to do it with God. We will have to be rescued from these despotic egos that reduce us to something less than human. We will have to expose the life of self-centeredness and proclaim the truth of God-centeredness.

Jeremiah wanted his people to practice adoration of God – something full-blooded and soaring – instead of mincing around the temple preening themselves before the mirrors of self-admiration. He arranged for a conference with some of the leaders of the city. He took them three or four hundred yards south of the temple to the Valley of Hinnom at the site of Topheth. Child sacrifice had been carried out there and still was being done in secret. It was the garbage dump of the city. The place stank.

Jeremiah had a pottery water jug under his arm. He spoke his concern to the leaders. He told them that God had immense love and holy purposes for them. He said what he had said so many times, that a reform is useless if it does not change people's lives. It is no good polishing up the brass in the temple if the quality of people's lives is left unattended in their poverty. It is no good obeying the letter of the commands written in Deuteronomy if the spirit of love that permeates Deuteronomy is ignored. It is no good being enthusiastic over the great religious traditions if the people we don't like are treated like scum. It is no good adoring religious ceremony and ritual that make us feel good if the feelings never get connected with good actions. Truth is inward: we must experience within ourselves that which we profess. Truth is social: we must share with others what we profess. Statistics are a farce. Popularity is a smoke screen. All that matters is God.

Standing with these leaders in this place of dreadful reminders, Jeremiah accused them of going along with a religion that assured them of success in whatever they undertook at the same time that they were abandoning the God who called them to live in love and faith. He accused them of taking their religion from the world around them, making a religious ritual out of the gratification of lust, handing out religious formulas for financial prosperity. When he finished his short speech, Jeremiah broke the pottery decanter by throwing it to the ground: 'Thus says the LORD of hosts: So will I break this people and this city, as one breaks a potter's vessel, so that it can never be mended' (Jer 19:11).

Terror on Every Side

Word traveled fast. By the time Jeremiah got back to the temple area the city was buzzing. Pashhur, of course, heard. Pashhur as chief overseer of the temple was responsible for maintaining the successful operation. A man like Jeremiah was no help. Pashhur arrested him and put him in the stocks on the north side of the temple area. Jeremiah was humiliated, but not intimidated. He spoke as sharply as ever to Pashhur. Putting Jeremiah in the stocks confined him, but it did not silence him. He yelled at Pashhur, 'The LORD does not call your name Pashhur but *Magor-missabib,* Terror-on-every-side. Judgment is coming because of willful, selfish, entrenched sin, and all you do is sprinkle holy water on it. Babylon will invade this place and plunder everything and take the people captive. When that happens Pashhur, your name will be remembered as *Magormissabib,* Terror-on-every-side. It will be obvious then that you, not me, are responsible for disturbing the peace. The falseness of your preaching will be exposed, the hypocrisy of your success cult will be on display and because of it inescapable judgment. *Magor-missabib* indeed, Terror-on-every side.'

This wasn't the first time that Jeremiah had used that phrase. He had spoken it frequently enough so that it was associated with him. We have references to it in three other sermons (Jer 6:25; 46:5; 49:29). Putting the tag on Pashhur was, under the circumstances, futile. Pashhur was the honored chief officer of the temple, presiding over splendid rituals and applauded by crowds of people; Jeremiah was in the stocks – a laughingstock. That day, as people went to the temple and passed Jeremiah, someone picked up the phrase that he had used so often and turned it against him as a mocking nickname. Soon the crowd was chanting in derision of Jeremiah, 'There's old *Magor-missabib,* Terror-on-every-side.'[4]

Jeremiah's humiliation was complete: an object of ridicule in the stocks, taunted with the name *Magor-missabib.* The word that had been forged out of suffering and articulated out of concern for the perilous existence of his people was now a slogan of contempt: *Magor-missabib,* Terror-on-every-side; *Magor-missabib,* old fire-and-brimstone himself!

Bronze Walls

Unafraid of the stocks. Unintimidated by the taunts. Undeterred by humiliation, or embarrassment, or insecurity, or pain, or failure, or doubt. 'A fortified city, an iron pillar, and bronze walls' indeed!

We don't have to like it. Jeremiah didn't like it. He yelled at Pashhur, and after he yelled at Pashhur he yelled at God, angry, hurt and somewhat bewildered that all this was happening to him (Jer 20:7-10). He didn't like any of it, but he wasn't afraid of it because the most important thing in his life was God – not comfort, not applause, not security, but the living God. What he did fear was worship without astonishment, religion without commitment. He feared getting what he wanted and missing what God wanted. It is still the only thing worthy of our fear.

What a waste it would be to take these short, precious, eternity-charged years that we are given and squander them in cocktail chatter when we can be, like Jeremiah, vehemently human and passionate with God.

8

My Wound Incurable

O L*ORD*, *thou knowest;*
remember me and visit me, . . .
I did not sit in the company of merrymakers,
nor did I rejoice;
I sat alone, because thy hand was upon me,
for thou hadst filled me with indignation.
Why is my pain unceasing,
my wound incurable,
refusing to be healed?
Wilt thou be to me like a deceitful brook,
like waters that fail?

JEREMIAH *15:15, 17-18*

Talking to God, I felt, is always better than talking about God; those pious conversations – there's always a touch of self-approval about them.

THERESE OF LISIEUX[1]

INDISPUTABLY GREAT PERSONS AROUSE CURIOSITY. WHAT ARE they like on the inside? What do they do when they are not being watched? What goes on in their private lives? Our appetite for gossip, for confessions, for inside information is insatiable. For every person who reads the front page story on a politician's speech there are twenty who will read the gossip column that describes in delicious detail his companion at dinner the night before. We want, we say, to know what a person is *really* like. We are not content with the public image, the outer event, the external happening. We pounce on any detail, however insignificant, that might reveal what goes on behind the scenes in the heart.

Often this curiosity is a sniping pettiness that wants to cut people down to our size so that we will not be embarrassed in our own littleness. It is the kind of sleazy attitude that Harry Stack Sullivan found so disreputable: 'If I have to be a mole hill, by God there are going to be no mountains.' But there is an avid interest in the personal details of a great person's life that is healthy. It is the instinctive search for the essentially human that establishes a link of kinship with the rest of us.

What was Jeremiah really like? What did he do when he was alone? When no one was watching, how did he conduct himself? Where there was no audience to address, how did he behave? What did Jeremiah do when he was not staging confrontations with the religious leaders of Jerusalem? What did he do when he was not standing the people on their ears with his thundering prophecies? What did he do when he wasn't colliding with temple officials and upsetting the status quo? What did he do when he was not making headlines?

A Praying Prophet

There is a single, clear, straightforward answer to these questions: he prayed. Seven passages in the book of Jeremiah are labeled 'confessional.'[2] In each of these Jeremiah speaks in the first person. He opens his heart. He reveals what is going on inside while the fireworks are going off outside. We hold our breath on the brink of these most private revelations. We have been so often disappointed, even disillusioned, when we have gained access to the diaries, letters, tapes of great and admired people. How many public reputations can survive a thorough exposure of the inner life?[3]

Jeremiah's inner life is revealed in these confessions. We are surprised, but we are not disillusioned. When Jeremiah was out of the public eye he was passionate with God – he prayed. Jeremiah's secret life is a prayer life. The cellar reality of Jeremiah's towering humanity is prayer.

A look at Jeremiah in secret does not show him with a few cronies in a bull session swapping stories about God, catching up on the rumors of God. God is not someone or something to be talked *about*. Nor do we find Jeremiah in a library studying up on God. He did not pore over the volumes from Babylonia in order to analyze their beliefs. He did not examine the burial practices of the Egyptians to discover what might be learned about their concept of immortality. God is not an idea to be studied. And we don't find Jeremiah at his desk with pen and paper using his sharp mind and comprehensive intelligence to work out answers to the question of God ('How can it be that a good God permits an evil time?'). God is not a problem to be solved.

What we find is Jeremiah *praying:* addressing God, listening to God. Prayer is the act in which we approach God as living person, a *thou* to whom we speak, not an *it* that we talk about. Prayer is the attention that we give to the one who attends to us. It is the decision to approach God as the personal center, as our Lord and our Savior, our entire lives gathered up and expressed in the approach. Prayer is personal language raised to the highest degree. These seven confessional passages show Jeremiah in his unguarded and most personal times saying *I* and *Thou.*

The Intimacy of Prayer

Nearly everyone believes in God and throws casual offhand remarks in his general direction from time to time. But prayer is something quite different. Suppose yourself at dinner with a person whom you very much want to be with – a friend, a lover, a person important to you. The dinner is in a fine restaurant where everything is arranged to give you a sense of privacy. There is adequate illumination at your table with everything else in shadow. You are aware of other persons and other activity in the room, but they do not intrude on your intimacy. There is talking and listening. There are moments of silence, full of meaning. From time to time a waiter comes to your table. You ask questions of him; you place your order with him; you ask to have your glass refilled; you send the broccoli back because it arrived cold; you thank him for his attentive service and leave a tip. You depart, still in companionship with the person with whom you dined, but out on the street conversation is less personal, more casual.

That is a picture of prayer. The person with whom we set aside time for intimacy, for this deepest and most personal conversation, is God. At such times the world is not banished, but it is in the shadows, on the periphery. Prayer is never complete and unrelieved solitude; it is, though, carefully protected and skillfully supported intimacy. Prayer is the desire to listen to God firsthand, to speak to God firsthand, and then setting aside the time and making the arrangements to do it. It issues from the conviction that the living God is immensely important to me and that what goes on between us demands my exclusive attention.

But there is a parody of prayer that we engage in all too often. The details are the same but with two differences: the person across the table is Self and the waiter is God. This waiter-God is essential but peripheral. You can't have the dinner without him, but he is not an intimate participant in it. He is someone to whom you give orders, make complaints, and maybe, at the end, give thanks. The person you are absorbed in is Self – your moods, your ideas, your interests, your satisfactions or lack of them. When you leave the restaurant you forget about the waiter until the next time. If it is a place to which you go regularly, you might even remember his name.

The confessions of Jeremiah are no parody but the real thing – exclusive focus on God: intense, undivided preoccupation with God. This accounts for much that is powerful and attractive in Jeremiah. Here is the source of the personal intensity and incorruptible integrity that is so impressive in Jeremiah.

What goes on in these intimate exchanges between Jeremiah and God? We know who he is *with* in secret; what does he *say* in secret? The confession in Jeremiah 15 is a fair sample. Here some of us are in for another surprise, for the uninstructed idea of prayer is that it is accepting and soothing, that the person at prayer is the person at peace in the universe. But Jeremiah at prayer is scared, lonely, hurt and angry.

O Lord, thou knowest;
remember me and visit me,
and take vengeance for me on my persecutors.

Jeremiah was frightened. Cursed and hunted down, there was no secure place for him. The plots against his life and the physical beatings and cruel confinements that he suffered all come out in this prayer. He is speaking to God what he is experiencing. It is clear that he neither accepted it or liked it: 'God, you got me into this, now get me out!'

He continues by contrasting his own sense of urgency with God's deliberate patience.

> *In thy forbearance take me not away;*
> *know that for thy sake I bear reproach. (Jer 15:15)*

John Bright translates with more clarity: 'Do not through thy patience destroy me! Consider! For thy sake I suffer abuse.' Which seems to mean, 'Don't be so lenient with my persecutors that they have time to destroy me.'[4] There is desperation in that sentence. Jeremiah struggles to accommodate his awareness of God's unhurried, measured pace with the panicky fear that time is running out on him. The mills of God turn slowly while the engines of persecution run exceedingly swift. Our compulsive timetables collide with God's leisurely providence. We tell God not only what to do but when to do it. We take him seriously – why else would we be praying? – but we take ourselves more seriously, telling him exactly what he must do for us and when.

Loneliness

Jeremiah next prays his loneliness.

> *Thy words were found, and I ate them,*
> *and thy words became to me a joy*
> *and the delight of my heart;*
> *for I am called by thy name,*

O LORD, God of hosts.
I did not sit in the company of merrymakers,
nor did I rejoice;
I sat alone, because thy hand was upon me,
for thou hadst filled me with indignation. (Jer 15:16-17)

From the first Jeremiah received God's word with enthusiasm. There may be a reference here to the discovery of the Deuteronomy scroll in the temple which Jeremiah welcomed and then threw himself into the task of preaching as spokesman for the reform commanded by Josiah. It was delightful work but a lonely business. It meant years of solitude. The laughing, merrymaking majority went its way, and Jeremiah went his in lonely reflection, finding the meaning of God's word and preaching its lived truth. Jeremiah was constitutionally unable to say something just because he was told it was true: he *lived* the truth and then he spoke it. There was delight in living that way. He gave himself without reserve to this way of life that meant taking God's word more seriously than any human word. But having plunged into this way, he found that no one was with him. He was all by himself. What would he do? Go back to the party until others decided to come along? He couldn't do that. He was committed. Having acquired a taste for God's truth, he could not return to the bland diet of gossip and rumor. All the same it was a lonely business.

HURT

He goes on to pray his hurt.

Why is my pain unceasing,
my wound incurable,
refusing to be healed?

The sin of the people, the cruelty of the wicked, the giddy indifference of the everyday crowd – all this was a deep wound in Jeremiah. He hurt because he cared. He had undertaken to speak for God, to speak that eternal love to this fickle people. Now he felt in his own being all the aching hurt of unrequited love. Having identified so thoroughly with God's message, he also felt the rejection in every bone and muscle. Their blasphemies cut him; their clumsy rebellions bruised him; their thoughtless rituals salted his open wounds. And there was no cure in sight, for the only cure was a people who repent and trust God. He looked in vain for any intimation of that.

Anger

The prayer intensifies. Turning from his hurt, now, in an audacious burst, he prays his anger.

> *Wilt thou be to me like a deceitful brook,*
> *like waters that fail?*

He calls God to task. Once he had preached that God was 'the fountain of living waters' (Jer 2:13); now he accuses him of being a 'deceitful brook' – one of those stream beds in the desert that looks as if water should be flowing in it but when you arrive at its banks it is dry. Water only flows in it after a rain; it cannot be depended upon between times. What he says in effect is 'God, you have tricked me. You promised but you did not deliver.'

Jeremiah was not timid in his prayers. An even bolder accusation came later when he raged, 'You seduced me, Yahweh, and I let you; You seized and overcame me' (Jer 20:7 Bright's translation). A blunt but literal rendering is 'First you seduced me, then you raped me.' You lured me by enticing words, then you seized me by force and made me submit to your will.[5] Our anger can be a measure of our faith. Believers argue with God; skeptics argue with each other.

That is Jeremiah at prayer: scared, lonely, hurt, angry. A surprise? The indomitable Jeremiah praying like that? All of us experience these things. No one alive is a stranger to them. But do we pray them? Jeremiah prayed them. Everything he experienced and thought he set in relationship to a living, knowing, saving God. And the moment these things are set in relationship to God something begins to happen.

Repentance

Jeremiah stops speaking but the prayer continues, for prayer does not end when we end. In prayer God is not merely audience, he is partner. Jeremiah has spoken honestly, now he listens expectantly.

> *Therefore thus says the* LORD:
> *'If you return, I will restore you,*
> *and you shall stand before me.'* (Jer 15:19)

Return/repent. This is one of the key words in Jeremiah's preaching. Now the message that he has been delivering to the people is delivered to him. Could it be that his pouring out of pain is tinged with self-pity? God responds: 'The fright, the loneliness, the hurt, the anger – I understand that, Jeremiah, but I won't indulge you in it. Don't wallow in it. Turn away from it. Repent. If you turn (from such talk) then I will turn you (restore you) to the prophetic office.' Throughout this passage there is a play on the word *return/repent.*[6]

Jeremiah's part in the prayer was to be honest and personal; it is *God* with whom he has to do. The first requirement in a personal relationship is to be ourselves. Off with the masks. Away with the pretense. 'It's *me,* it's *me,* it's *me,* O Lord.' Jeremiah's prayer is not pious, not nice, not proper – he speaks what he feels, and he feels scared, lonely, hurt and angry. Well enough. *God's part* in the prayer is to restore and save. Before God in prayer we do not remain the same. The fright and loneliness and pain and accusation are all there, but they do not stay there. Part (not all) of what Jeremiah was doing was feeling sorry for himself on his knees. God feels our pains, but he does not indulge our self-pity. God is severe with Jeremiah as Jeremiah was severe with the people: 'Repent. Turn away from that kind of feeling for it is destructive. Then I will restore you, and you will stand upright, ready to serve again, in my presence.'

Re-establishing Priorities

God's response continues.

> *If you utter what is precious, and not what is worthless,*
> *you shall be as my mouth.*
> *They shall turn to you,*
> *but you shall not turn to them.*

Jeremiah was discouraged, understandably, because his words accomplished nothing. His preaching was futile. All he got for his pains was persecution and reproach. Should he change his tune and speak the trash the people loved to hear? God stiffens his resolve. Stick to your calling; you shall be as my mouth. 'Let *them* come over to you; don't *you* go over to them' (Bright's translation). Jeremiah was concerned about what people were saying; that is not his concern. *God* is his concern.

Priorities are re-established in prayer. It makes all the difference in the world whether God is in the first place or in the second. Who is in the first place here? God or the people? If it is God who is in first place, the complaints express only what is involved in a tough job. The job is either worth doing or it is not. What do I really want to do with my life, love others or flatter them, please others or please God?

The setting of priorities is not a once-for-all act. It has to be redone frequently. Balances shift. Circumstances change. Moods swing. Is it still God, in fact, with whom I have first of all to do, or is it not? Prayer is the place where the priorities are re-established.

Renewal

Jeremiah continues to listen. He hears this.

And I will make you to this people
a fortified wall of bronze;
they will fight against you,
but they shall not prevail over you,
for I am with you
to save you and deliver you, says the Lord.
I will deliver you out of the hand of the wicked,
and redeem you from the grasp of the ruthless.

He had heard these words once, in his youth (Jer 1:18-19). Everything God said then he says still. The promise is still in effect.

It is not enough to remember; we must *hear* it again. Prayer is the act in which we hear it again. It is not enough to carry memory verses around with us; we need daily encounter with the resonant voice of God. Prayer is that encounter. Situations change. Does God change? We pray. We listen. God speaks his word again – the same word! – and we are restored and renewed in our commitment.

Three words, somewhat synonymous, conclude: *save you . . . deliver you . . . redeem you.* 'The total picture of deliverance is many-sided and each verb provides a different emphasis.'[7] The live connection between God's call and Jeremiah's commitment is reaffirmed. The personal relationship, the covenant connection, has been subject to a thousand stresses and called into question a hundred times. What Walter Lippmann called the 'acids of modernity' eat away at the sinews and thongs that connect our lives with God's purposes.[8] Life is moving and dynamic, changing and growing. The world challenges and attacks. The word of God does not change and my call does not change, but the relationship is under constant assault and must be renewed constantly. Resolve is essential but not enough. In prayer God provides renewal. Prayer is not so much the place where we learn something new, but where God confirms anew the faith to which we are committed.

Running the Race

The marathon is one of the most strenuous athletic events in sport. The Boston Marathon attracts the best runners in the world. The winner is automatically placed among the great athletes of our time. In the spring of 1980, Rosie Ruiz was the first woman to cross the finish line. She had the laurel wreath placed on her head in a blaze of lights and cheering.

She was completely unknown in the world of running. An incredible feat! Her first race a victory in the prestigious Boston Marathon! Then someone noticed her legs – loose flesh, cellulite. Questions were asked. No one had seen her along the 26.2 mile course. The truth came out: she had jumped into the race during the last mile.

There was immediate and widespread interest in Rosie. Why would she do that when it was certain that she would be found out? Athletic performance cannot be faked. But she never admitted her fraud. She repeatedly said that she would run another marathon to validate her ability. Somehow she never did. People interviewed her, searching for a clue to her personality. One interviewer concluded that she really believed that she had run the complete Boston Marathon and won. She was analyzed as a sociopath. She lied convincingly and naturally with no sense of conscience, no sense of reality in terms of right and wrong, acceptable and unacceptable behavior. She appeared bright, normal and intelligent. But there was no moral sense to give coherence to her social actions.

In reading about Rosie I thought of all the people I know who want to get in on the finish but who cleverly arrange not to run the race. They appear in church on Sunday wreathed in smiles, entering into the celebration, but there is no personal life that leads up to it or out from it. Occasionally they engage in spectacular acts of love and compassion in public. We are impressed, but surprised, for they were never known to do that before. Yet, you never know. Better give them the benefit of the doubt. Then it turns out to be a stunt: no personal involvement either precedes or follows the act. They are plausible and convincing. But in the end they do not run the race, believing through the tough times, praying through the lonely, angry, hurt hours. They have no sense for what is *real* in religion. The proper label for such a person is *religiopath.*

No one becomes human the way Jeremiah was human by posing in a posture of victory. It was his prayers, hidden but persistent, that brought him to the human wholeness and spiritual sensitivity that we want. What we do in secret determines the soundness of who we are in public. Prayer is the secret work that develops a life that is thoroughly authentic and deeply human.

9

Twenty-Three Years . . . Persistently

For twenty-three years, from the thirteenth year of Josiah the son of Amon, king of Judah, to this day, the word of the LORD has come to me, and I have spoken persistently to you, but you have not listened. You have neither listened nor inclined your ears to hear, although the LORD persistently sent to you all his servants the prophets, saying, 'Turn now, every one of you, from his evil way and wrong doings, and dwell upon the land which the LORD has given to you and your fathers from of old and for ever.'

JEREMIAH 25:3-5

Experienced mountaineers have a quiet, regular, short step – on the level it looks petty; but then this step they keep up, on and on as they ascend, whilst the inexperienced townsman hurries along, and soon has to stop, dead beat with the climb. . . . Such an expert mountaineer, when the thick mists come, halts and camps out under some slight cover brought with him, quietly smoking his pipe, and moving on only when the mist has cleared away. . . . You want to grow in virtue, to serve God, to love Christ? Well, you will grow in and attain to these things if you will make them a slow and sure, an utterly real, a mountain stepplod and ascent, willing to have to camp for weeks or months in spiritual desolation, darkness and emptiness at different stages in your march and growth. All demand for constant light, for ever the best – the best to your own feeling, all attempt at eliminating or minimizing the cross and trial, is so much soft folly and puerile trifling.

BARON FRIEDRICH VON HÜGEL[1]

THE DIFFERENCE BETWEEN THE RIGHT WORD AND THE almost right word is, said Mark Twain, the difference between lightning and a lightning bug. A single word, if it is the right word, can illuminate and strike fire all at once. In Jeremiah 25 at the center of the book of Jeremiah and spoken at the midpoint of his prophetic career, there is one of these right words: persistently, *hashkem.*

The word has a picture behind it. *Shechem* means shoulder. At the center of Palestine there are two immense shoulder mountains, Ebal and Gerazim. The village nestled between these massive shoulders is named Shechem. When the Israelites first came into the land after their forty years of wandering in the wilderness, Joshua led them to Shechem, lined them up on the slopes of the two shoulder mountains, half on one slope and half on the other, and reviewed the word of God that had directed them there. From one shoulder the blessings that would come from a life of worshipful trust were called out; from the other shoulder the curses that would come from a life of rebellious self-centeredness were called out. Shechem – the center where the word of God was spoken and listened to.

Then, as words do, *shechem* developed another meaning. When you went on a trip in those days you loaded provisions for the journey on your donkey's shoulders, or put them on your own shoulders, and set out. So the noun, shoulder, developed into a verb that meant 'load the shoulders of beasts for a day's journey.'[2] In a hot country like Israel it was important to get in as many miles as possible before the sun came up and fatigued you, so such journeys characteristically began long before dawn. Eventually the word came to describe the activity of people who got up early before the sun and set out with heavy burdens on long journeys.[3] They got up early in order to have as many hours as possible to do what they intended to do.

This is the form of the word that is used here at the center of Jeremiah – the unwobbling pivot of his life and his book. 'For twenty-three years . . . the word of the LORD has come to me, and I have spoken persistently [*hashkem*] to you, but you have not listened.' For twenty-three years Jeremiah got up every morning and listened to God's word. For twenty-three years Jeremiah got up every morning and spoke God's word to the people. For twenty-three years the people slept in, sluggish and indolent, and heard nothing.

The word is not only at the center of Jeremiah's book and his life, it is spread out across his ministry. There are eleven instances:

> *7:13 And now, because you have done all these things, says the LORD, and when I spoke to you* persistently *you did not listen, and when I called you, you did not answer . . .*
>
> *7:25-26 From the day that your fathers came out of the land of Egypt to this day, I have* persistently *sent all my servants the prophets to them, day after day; yet they did not listen to me . . .*

11:7-8 For I solemnly warned your fathers when I brought them up out of the land of Egypt, warning them persistently, *even to this day, saying, Obey my voice. Yet they did not obey or incline their ear . . .*

25:3 For twenty-three years, from the thirteenth year of Josiah the son of Amon, king of Judah, to this day, the word of the LORD has come to me, and I have spoken persistently *to you, but you have not listened.*

25:4 You have neither listened nor inclined your ears to hear, although the LORD persistently *sent to you all his servants the prophets . . .*

26:5 . . . to heed the words of my servants the prophets whom I send to you urgently, *though you have not heeded . . .*

29:19 . . . because they did not heed my words, says the LORD, which I persistently *sent to you by my servants the prophets, but you would not listen, says the LORD.*

32:33 They have turned to me their back and not their face; and though I have taught them persistently *they have not listened to receive instruction.*

35:14 I have spoken to you persistently, *but you have not listened to me.*

35:15 I have sent to you all my servants the prophets, sending them persistently, *saying, 'Turn now every one of you from his evil way, and amend your doings . . .*

44:4 Yet I persistently *sent to you all my servants the prophets, saying, 'Oh, do not do this abominable thing that I hate!'*

Does that sound like a grim business? Tough sledding? There is no question but that it was difficult. We know that Jeremiah suffered an enormous amount of abuse across those years. He faced mockery and rejection and imprisonment. He wrestled with stretches of discouragement and pits of despair and thought of quitting. What difference did it make anyway? Why not adjust to the mediocrities of the age?

At one of those times God confronted Jeremiah: 'If you're tired from running a footrace, how will you race against horses?' (Jer 12:5 Bright's translation). What do you want, Jeremiah, a tame, domesticated life? A Sunday stroll with these bloated and cretinous people who are living like parasites? Or will you compete against horses? The confrontation galvanized Jeremiah out of his enervating despair: 'I want to run with the horses.' The next morning he was again up before dawn, living *persistently* and *urgently*.

A Ready Heart

The word *hashkem* ('persistently') has a sunrise in it. Jeremiah is up before the sun to do his work. He is no reluctant, bored drudge. There is an early morning lightness in him. Every day there is the anticipation of listening to God's word and then speaking God's word. Jeremiah almost certainly knew Psalm 108; it would have been entirely characteristic of him to use it as a morning prayer:

> *My heart is ready, O God,*
> *my heart is ready!*
> *I will sing, I will sing praises!*
> *Awake, my soul!*
> *Awake, O harp and lyre!*
> *I will awake the dawn!* (Ps 108:1-2 RSV, 1st ed.)

Jeremiah did not resolve to stick it out for twenty-three years, no matter what; he got up every morning with the sun. The day was God's day, not the people's. He didn't get up to face rejection, he got up to meet with God. He didn't rise to put up with another round of mockery, he rose to be with his Lord. That is the secret of his persevering pilgrimage – not thinking with dread about the long road ahead but greeting the present moment, every present moment, with obedient delight, with expectant hope: 'My heart is ready!'

We all know people who spend a lifetime at the same job, or the same marriage, or the same profession, who are slowly, inexorably diminished in the process. They are persistent in the sense that they keep doing the same thing for many years, but we don't particularly admire them for it. If anything, we feel sorry for them for having got stuck in such an uninteresting rut with neither the energy nor imagination to get out.

But we don't feel sorry for Jeremiah. He was not stuck in a rut; he was committed to a purpose. The one thing that Jeremiah shows no evidence of is bored drudgery. Everything we know of him shows that after the twenty-three years his imagination is even more alive and his spirit even more resilient than it was in his youth. He wasn't putting in his time. Every day was a new episode in the adventure of living the prophetic life. The days added up to a life of incredible tenacity, of amazing stamina.

Joel Henderson was once asked how he had managed to write all those books. He replied that he had never written a book. All he did was write one page a day. With his limited energy and restricted imagination, a page at a time was all that he could manage. But when a year was up he had a 365-page book.

Jeremiah's persistent faithfulness contrasts with the erratic and impulsive nature of the people with whom he lived. They were full of projects, wild with enthusiasms, but nothing ever added up. They were like a character in a John Fowles short story – 'he wanted Everest in a day; if it took two, he lost interest.'[4]

Jeremiah does his best to show them the shabby emptiness of such lives. In a bold, sexually explicit metaphor, he captures their attention and then dramatizes the futility of their days.

Look at your way in the valley;
know what you have done –
a restive young camel interlacing her tracks,
a wild ass used to the wilderness,
in her heat sniffing the wind!
Who can restrain her lust?

(Jer 2:23-24)

That is strong speech. Stand on a hill and look down in the valley at a young camel looking for a mate, back and forth, up and down. The record of her restless searching is in the footprints in the dust. All that movement and not going anywhere. Or look at the wild ass in heat out in the wilderness, sniffing the wind for the scent of a mate – no matter who – unrestrained and purposeless except for one thing, the satisfaction of desire.

That is what you look like, preaches Jeremiah. Dominated by appetite and impulse, your lives are empty of commitment, purpose, continuity. You are frantic and busy, rushing here and there, wherever there is the slightest suggestion that you might satisfy something or other. But you are not camels and donkeys in the rutting season; you are persons with a capacity for faithfulness. Isn't it time to start living like it?

Israel had a long history of unfaithfulness. Every attractively packaged promise distracted her from her God. Every new fad was taken up and tried in a burst of short-lived enthusiasm. For centuries it had been one lover after another.

In another sermon to the same effect Jeremiah used a different image: 'How lightly you gad about, changing your way! You shall be put to shame by Egypt as you were put to shame by Assyria' (Jer 2:36). Here he holds a mirror up to them, and they see the reflection of a fickle schoolgirl with a crush on the new boy who has just moved in down the street. All aflutter she can think of nothing but seeing him, attracting his attention, getting noticed. When she is jilted by him, she goes after the boy in the next block and the story begins all over again. Giddy and flirtatious, the girl flits from one boy to another, careless of all relationships, concerned only with making an impression. And the boys, of course, are only interested in using her. They deserve each other.

The message is clear enough. First you had a crush on Assyria and that was a waste. Now you have a crush on Egypt and that will turn out the same way. If you ever grow up, you will look back on those times in embarrassment and blush. Meanwhile God is loving you. And you once said you loved him! Your actions develop out of your silly fantasies. They have no basis in reality. Assyria never cared for you; Egypt will never care for you. *God* cares for you. And God will not permit the people he loves and the people he created for glory to live in such silliness and emptiness.

New Every Morning

Where did Jeremiah learn his persistence? How did he get the word into his vocabulary, into his life? Certainly not by observing the people around him. He learned it from God.

Jeremiah learned to live persistently toward God because God lived persistently toward him. The five poem-prayers in Lamentations (written in the tradition of Jeremiah) express the suffering God's people experienced during and after the fall of Jerusalem, the most devastating disaster in their history. At the very center of this dark time, and placed at almost the exact center of these five poems that lament the sin and suffering, there is this verse: 'The steadfast love of the Lord never ceases, his mercies never come to an end; they are new every morning; great is thy faithfulness' (Lam 3:22-23).

There it is – 'new every morning . . . great is thy faithfulness.' God's persistence is not a dogged repetition of duty. It has all the surprise and creativity, and yet all the certainty and regularity, of a new day. Sunrise – when the spontaneous and the certain arrive at the same time.

Does anyone ever get used to daybreak? Every night we are 'dissolved into darkness as we shall one day be dissolved into dust; our very selves, so far as we know, have been wiped out of the world of living things; and then we are raised alive like Lazarus, and found all our limbs and senses unaltered, with the coming of the day.'[5] We never get used to it. Daybreak is always a surprise. There are times, of course, when we fail to respond. But when that happens we instinctively know that it is due to a deficiency within ourselves, whether from disease or depression. If the repetitions in nature are never boring, how much less the repetitions in God.

That is the source of Jeremiah's living persistence, his creative constancy. He was up before the sun, listening to God's word. Rising early, he was quiet and attentive before his Lord. Long before the yelling started, the mocking, the complaining, there was this centering, discovering, exploring time with God.

'But,' Jeremiah said, '*you* have not listened. . . . *You* never listened or paid the slightest attention' (Jer 25:3-4, Bright's translation). Here, then, is the clue to our erratic life patterns, our inconstancy, our unfaithfulness, our stupid inability to distinguish between fashion and faith: we don't rise up early and listen to God. We don't daily find a time apart from the crowd, a time of silence and solitude, for preparing for the day's journey. 'A very original man,' says Garry Wills, 'must shape his life, make a schedule that allows him to reflect, and study, and create.'[6]

Jeremiah had a defined priority: persistently rising early, he listened to God, then spoke and acted what he heard. It was not because there were no other options open to him. It was not because he couldn't think of anything else to do. He had chosen what Jesus called 'the one thing needful' – listening, attentively and believingly, to God.

The mark of a certain kind of genius is the ability and energy to keep returning to the same task relentlessly, imaginatively, curiously, for a lifetime. Never give up and go on to something else; never get distracted and be diverted to something else. Augustine wrote fifteen commentaries on the book of Genesis. He began at the beginning and was never satisfied that he had got to the beginning. He never felt that he had got to the depths of the first book of the Bible, down to the very origins of life, the first principles of God's ways with us. He kept returning to those first questions. Beethoven composed sixteen string quartets because he was never satisfied with what he had done. The quartet form intrigued and challenged him. Perfection eluded him – he kept coming back to it over and over in an attempt at mastery. We think he did pretty well with them, but he didn't think so. So he persisted, bringing fresh, creative energy to each day's attempt. The same thing over and over, and yet it is never the same thing, for each venture is resplendent with dazzling creativity.

And Jeremiah: 'For twenty-three years . . . the word of the LORD has come to me, and I have spoken *persistently* to you.' There is only one thing needful. And there is only today in which to do it. Do it. Then do it again. And again. *Persistently.* Not mindlessly, but with all the exuberance of an encore.

10

Take a Scroll and Write on It

This word came to Jeremiah from the LORD: 'Take a scroll and write on it all the words that I have spoken to you against Israel and Judah and all the nations, from the day I spoke to you, from the days of Josiah until today. It may be that the house of Judah will hear all the evil which I intend to do to them, so that every one may turn from his evil way, and that I may forgive their iniquity and their sin.'

Then Jeremiah called Baruch the son of Neriah, and Baruch wrote upon a scroll at the dictation of Jeremiah all the words of the LORD which he had spoken to him.

JEREMIAH 36:1-4

Some people may wonder: why was the light of God given in the form of language? How is it conceivable that the divine should be contained in such brittle vessels as consonants and vowels? This question betrays the sin of our age: to treat lightly the ether which carries the light-waves of the spirit. What else in the world is as capable of bringing man and man together over the distances in space and in time? Of all things on earth, words alone never die. They have so little matter and so much meaning. . . . God took these Hebrew words and breathed into them

> *of His power, and the words became a live wire charged with His spirit. To this very day they are hyphens between heaven and earth. What other medium could have been employed to convey the divine? Pictures enameled on the moon? Statues hewn out of the Rockies?*
>
> ABRAHAM HESCHEL[1]

IN A LETTER FRANZ KAFKA WROTE, 'IF THE BOOK WE ARE reading does not wake us, as with a fist hammering on our skull, why then do we read it? . . . A book must be like an ice-axe to break the sea frozen inside us.'[2] There are two ice-axe books in Jeremiah's life, the one he read and the one he wrote.

THE ICE AXE OF DEUTERONOMY

The book Jeremiah read was Deuteronomy. Discovered in the course of the temple repairs, it was the handbook for Josiah's reform. Jeremiah grew up with the book. He pondered and absorbed its message. He didn't read the book as a scholar, analyzing and explaining it (although it is unlikely he would reject such concerns); he didn't read the book as a reformer, searching for the principles that could be applied to society to make it whole (although he participated in such search and application); he read it as a person addressed personally by God. Everything that Jeremiah preached and later wrote shows the influence of what he read. George Adam Smith wrote that 'Jeremiah heard in the heart of Deuteronomy the call of God [and] uttered his Amen to it.'[3] Three elements stand out in his reading.

Reading Deuteronomy Jeremiah acquired a memory. Deuteronomy recapitulates the totality of what it means to be a people of God. Written in the form of an address by Moses on the border between wilderness and promised land, it recollects the experience of being saved out of Egypt, preserved in the wilderness and promised a life of blessing. It collects the scattered and half-remembered experiences of the past and integrates them into the present. Life is more than the diary jottings of harassed individuals: there is pattern, every detail is part of the design. Daily life in constant flight from its origin is returned to its source in this act of recollection.

Reading Deuteronomy Jeremiah developed a theology. He learned to think of God in a comprehensive, ordered, relational way. Deuteronomy presents God in a loyal, committed relationship of love with his people. God is not a random thought. God is not a word to fill in the gaps of what we don't know. God is actively, energetically dealing with people in love. *Love* is the key and characteristic word in the book.[4] This love is both God's character and his command. Because we are under this kind of God, there is no living worth the name that is not a participation in that love.

Reading Deuteronomy Jeremiah became responsible. Deuteronomy is full of commands. A command is a word that calls us to live beyond what we presently understand or feel or want. 'The commandment pulls people up from animality to humanity.'[5] Life is not mechanistically determined. We are not swept along in sociological movements, fixed on economic grids. Everyone has choices to make. The choices are not trial-and-error guesses; they are informed by the commands of God. These commands do not restrict a natural freedom; they create the conditions of freedom. The first word addressed to Adam by his Creator is a command (Gn 1:28). Commands assume freedom and encourage response. Addressed by commands we are trained in response-ability.

The Ice Axe of Jeremiah

The book Jeremiah read developed into the book that Jeremiah wrote. Just as Deuteronomy *repreached* the message of Moses to a people who had lost touch with Moses, so Jeremiah *repreached* the message of Deuteronomy to a people who had drifted from its moorings. Josiah, the king with whom Jeremiah grew up and shared a life shaped by the book of Deuteronomy, was dead, killed in a battle at Megiddo. His son was on the throne and showed no sign that he had so much as heard of the book of Deuteronomy. Descent into laxity and corruption was swift. The Deuteronomy-inspired reform was in shreds.

'There is no other institution that suffers from time so much as religion,' wrote Charles Williams. 'At the moment when it is remotely possible that a whole generation might have learned something both of theory and practice, the learners and their learning are removed by death, and the Church is confronted with the necessity of beginning all over again. The whole labour of regenerating mankind has to begin again every thirty years or so.'[6] In this case, it was seventeen years.

Jeremiah was directed: 'Take a scroll and write on it all the words that I have spoken. . . . It may be that the house of Judah will hear all the evil which I intend to do to them, so that every one may turn from his evil way, and that I may forgive their iniquity and their sin' (Jer 36:2-3). God has something to say, and he wants us to know what it is. He is not secretive, delighting in keeping us in the dark; he reveals. He reveals in a form that is accessible to us: *take a scroll* – the word is to be written on everyday material, parchment or papyrus, the same kind of material we use for sending thank-you notes and making up shopping lists. Then the process is outlined: *write* develops into *hear* which develops into *turn* which develops into *forgive.*

Another book of Scripture is brought into existence. But this Scripture is not now a static phenomenon, a thing that we can handle at our pleasure or for our pleasure. It is a vortex of swiftly moving energies constituted by these five verbs *(take, write, hear, turn, forgive).* This vortex makes God's words visible and audible and draws human life into responsiveness. Abraham Heschel, a man great in learning and prayer, complained that some people hail the Bible as literature as if that were the highest praise they could give it, 'as if "literature" were the climax of spiritual reality.' Then he commented: 'What would Moses, what would Jeremiah have said to such praise? Perhaps the same as Einstein would have said, if the manuscript of his Theory of Relativity were acclaimed for its beautiful handwriting.'[7]

Jeremiah enlisted his friend Baruch in the work. Baruch wrote as Jeremiah dictated what he had been preaching and praying for twenty-three years: life-probing words, brilliant images, biting confrontations, profound analysis. His language, as described by George Adam Smith, is 'terse, concrete, poignant and graceful.'[8]

We live on the gossip of the moment and the rumors of the hour. It is not as if we never hear the truth at all, but we don't realize its overwhelming significance. It is an extra, an aside. We have no sense of continuity. We respond to whims, sometimes good, sometimes bad. Then Scripture is placed before us. Words are assembled and arranged, and powerful patterns of truth become visible. The sermon that moved us to repentance ten years ago but then was forgotten in the press of business, the prayer that lifted us to new hope at a time of crisis but has since been buried under failures and disappointments – these words, along with many others that we had never known before, come before us in such a way that everything becomes coherent in their presence. Amnesia is replaced by recognition. Distraction is gathered into attention. Jeremiah dictates. Baruch writes. The syntax gives shape and the metaphors give focus to God's word.

A Word in Crisis

Several months later the Babylonian armies were in the land, and news arrived that they had reduced the coast city of Ashkelon to rubble. The world powers, Egypt and Babylon, were at each other's throats. In the rapid shifts of power that were taking place, Jerusalem was dangerously vulnerable. The people feared that their lives were up for grabs in the contest between the great powers. A day of fasting was called in response to the crisis. The city was thronged with anxious and praying people.

The timing was propitious. The sense of crisis had drawn the nation to its knees before God; the largest congregation Jeremiah would ever get was assembled in the city. Though he himself was forbidden to speak in public (he was persona non grata to King Jehoiakim),[9] his message was now written so that it could be delivered by another. Baruch took the scroll to the temple and read it out before the people (Jer 36:4-10).

Micaiah, a young man in the congregation, heard Baruch read from Jeremiah's scroll and became a true listener. He had heard Jeremiah's words many times; now he heard *God's* word. He acted swiftly. He ran to his father and told him what he had heard. His father, a member of the king's cabinet, was meeting at that moment with four other government officials. They responded to the youth's urgency and sent for Baruch to come and read the scroll to them. Baruch came and read. The father was as impressed as his son had been. His associates were likewise moved. 'When they heard all the words, they turned one to another in fear; and they said to Baruch, "We must report all these words to the king"' (Jer 36:16).

They had heard the truth and were committed to it. They were responsible men and knew that their lives and the life of the nation were addressed by this word of God. And they knew that the king must be told. They also knew their king. The moment that he heard what had been written and read, Jeremiah and Baruch were as good as dead. They advised Jeremiah and Baruch to go into hiding. The king had already murdered one prophet, Uriah, who had dared confront him (Jer 26:20-33); he wouldn't hesitate to kill another.

Scripture's task is to tell people, at the risk of their displeasure, the mystery of God and the secrets of their own hearts – to speak out and make a clean breast. There are many ways to say and write these truths: in oracles, in poems, in novels, in sermons, in satire, in journalism, in drama. Honestly written and courageously presented words reveal reality and expose our selfish attempts to violate beauty, manipulate goodness and dominate people, all the while defying God. Most of us most of the time, whether consciously or not, live this way. Honest writing shows us how badly we are living and how good life is. Enlightenment is not without pain. But the pain, accepted and endured is not a maiming but a purging. 'Every significant utterance is a wound, but "faithful are the wounds of a friend."'[10]

The Burning of the Scroll

Now it was the king's turn to hear the scroll read. The king was in his winter room, specially constructed for the cold months (it was December), and there was a brazier of coals near him at which he was keeping himself warm. He sent a servant, Jehudi, to get the scroll and read it. The king had a penknife in his hand. When Jehudi had read three or four columns, the king, sneering and contemptuous, cut them off with his knife and tossed them into the fire. The smart-set advisors with whom he had surrounded himself joined in the joking and jeering. They all thought it was hilarious. The senior cabinet ministers who had called the king's attention to the scroll begged him to take what he heard seriously. The king was unreachable. The scroll was read and destroyed, column by column cut into strips and burned in the fire.

As this story unfolds before us we become aware of the contrast between son and father. Seventeen years before, the father, Josiah, was presented with a scroll by the state official Shaphan, and he asked that it be read aloud to him. His reaction was penitential – 'he rent his clothes.' He recognized the scroll as God's word and realized the sin in which they all had been ignorantly living. A prophetess, Huldah, responded to his repentant faith, 'Because your heart was penitent, and you humbled yourself before the LORD, when you heard how I spoke, . . . I also have heard you, says the LORD' (2 Kgs 22:19).

Now a generation later the scenario is repeated. Josiah's son, Jehoiakim, is presented with a scroll by Shaphan's son. Gemariah. Jehoiakim's reaction is also emotional, but in him it is the emotion of derision. Instead of tearing his garments in penitence as his father had, he tore up the book in ridicule. There is also a prophetic word to conclude the narration, but in contrast to the commendation of Huldah there is the condemnation of Jeremiah: 'You have burned this scroll. . . . Therefore thus says the LORD concerning Jehoiakim king of Judah. . . . His dead body shall be cast out to the heat by day and the frost by night' (Jer 36:29-30). The heat the scroll had radiated as he had warmed himself at its burning wouldn't last long – he would soon be a corpse, exposed to the 'frost by night'!

The key word of commendation to Josiah was 'you heard how I spoke'; the key word of condemnation to Jehoiakim and his offspring was 'they would not hear' (Jer 36:31). The father heard the word of God and obeyed it; the result was a surging new lease on life for the nation. The son heard the word of God and burlesqued it; the result was a precipitous fall into exile.

A Charade of Nonchalance

Jehoiakim's response to the reading of Scripture betrays excessive anxiety. Giggling in the presence of the holy, cheap joke making in the atmosphere of the sublime are defenses against an awareness that requires a change of life. He was trying desperately to keep the truth of Jeremiah's words and the reality of God's truth at bay. But the extravagant inappropriateness of his behavior shows that it was not out of simple ignorance that he was being silly, but out of a complex selfishness. Jehoiakim knew that he was hearing the word of God; but if he gave any indication he knew, he would be accountable for responding in obedience. So he gave an elaborate charade of non-chalance, casually and indifferently whittling away at the scroll, feeding the fire with the parings until it was gone.

Jehoiakim with his penknife is a parody of all who attempt to *use* Scripture, who attempt to bring it under control and reduce it to something manageable. Scripture cannot be *used*. It is God's word calling us to a personal response. The word of God addresses us, calls us into being. The only appropriate response is a reverent answering. It is always more than we are, always previous to us, always over us.

Wanting to maintain control over our lives, to keep the initiative in our own hands, we chop the word of God into little pieces so that we can control it and maybe even put it to practical use – like warming us on a cold winter day! We reduce Scripture to something impersonal that we can use for our purposes or discard at our pleasure. We dismember its organically developed parts so that it is no longer a complete representation of God's address to us to which we must respond.

Scripture can be burned, but God's word cannot be destroyed. It has been thrown into the fire many times, but no one has yet successfully suppressed it. Jeremiah and Baruch simply went back to work again, dictating and writing. This time there was more: 'And many similar words were added to them' (Jer 36:32).[11] Jehoiakim should have left well enough alone; now copies more extensive than the first edition were circulating through the shops and streets of Jerusalem.

I enjoy conversations that open with the gambit, 'If you were shipwrecked on a desert island, what single book would you most like to have?' I usually try to exclude the Bible from the answers to prevent pious cheating. In the answers I like to think that I can discern significant values and tastes. The person who chooses Shakespeare's *King Lear,* I think, is probably committed to an exploration of the depths of human relationships. A choice of the *Almanac* or the *Guinness Book of World Records* shows a mind that reduces all knowledge to impersonal information, preferring to get along with as little personal relationship as possible. A preference for Milton's *Paradise Lost* indicates a bent for theological meditation. The best answer to the question that I have ever heard was the surprising, but obvious, Butler's *Practical Guide to Boat-Building.*

The book that Jeremiah read and the book that Jeremiah wrote are both boat-building kinds of books. They are not pious books of meditation. They are not about ideas or about things, but about survival – getting back home. They show

how a life is constructed that gets us where we are supposed to be, to God. All of Scripture is similarly written. *Deuteronomy* was used to rebuild a society that had been shipwrecked by Manasseh's evil reign. *Jeremiah* was used to rebuild lives that suffered the shipwreck of exile. Along with the sixty-four other books that have been added to them, they continue to present the word of God to ship-wrecked people and to construct a way of salvation.

11

House of the Rechabites

'Go to the house of the Rechabites, and speak with them, and bring them to the house of the Lord *. . .'*

'We have obeyed the voice of Jonadab the son of Rechab, our father, in all that he commanded us, to drink no wine all our days, ourselves, our wives, our sons, or our daughters, and not to build houses to dwell in. We have no vineyard or field or seed; but we have lived in tents, and have obeyed and done all that Jonadab our father commanded us.'

'The sons of Jonadab the son of Rechab have kept the command which their father gave them, but this people has not obeyed me.'

Jeremiah 35:2, 8-10, 16

It is more than ever the task of the little teams and small flocks, to struggle most effectively for man and the spirit, and, in particular, to give the most effective witness to those truths for which men so desperately long and which are, at present, in such short supply. For only the little teams and small flocks are able to muster around something which completely escapes technique and the process of massification, and which is the love of wisdom and of the intellect and the trust in the invisible radiation of this love. Such invisible rays carry far; they have the same kind of incredible power in the realm of the spirit that atomic fission and the miracles of microphysics have in the world of matter.

JACQUES MARITAIN[1]

CROWDS LIE. THE MORE PEOPLE, THE LESS TRUTH.[2] INTEGRITY is not strengthened by multiplication. We can test this observation easily. Which promise is most likely to be kept: the promise spoken by a politician to a crowd of ten thousand or the promise exchanged between two friends?

Since we all have everyday experience of the unreliability of crowds to discern and reflect the truth, it is puzzling that the appeal to numbers continues to carry so much weight with us. The selling of a million copies of a book is accepted as evidence that the book is excellent and important. The engagement of a majority of people in a certain moral behavior is set forth as evidence of its legitimacy. Approval by the masses is accreditation. But a rudimentary knowledge of history corroborated by a few moments of personal reflection will convince us that truth is not statistical and that crowds are more often foolish than wise. In crowds the truth is flattened to fit a slogan. Not only the truth that is spoken but the truth that is lived is reduced and distorted by the crowd. The crowd makes spectators of us, passive in the presence of excellence or beauty. The crowd makes consumers of us, inertly taking in whatever is pushed at us. As spectators and consumers the central and foundational elements of our being human – our ability to create, our drive to excel, our capacity to commune with God – atrophy.

There is nothing wrong, of course, in being in a crowd, and often it is unavoidable. If I want to watch some highly skilled athletes play a game and 50,000 other people also want to watch, I can hardly avoid being in a crowd, nor does it damage my life. But if in addition to watching the game I parrot the profanity of the crowd and imitate the behavior of the crowd (because 50,000 people must be right), then my life is falsified.

We cannot avoid being in crowds. Can we keep from being crowd-conditioned? Can we keep from trading our name in for a number, from letting the crowd reduce us to mindless passivity?

UNCROWD-CONDITIONED

Jeremiah dealt with crowds most of his life. Unlike many of the prophets who were men of the desert, solitary and rustic, Jeremiah was a man of the city 'where cross the crowded ways of life.' Daily he walked its streets. Frequently he assembled in the temple courts. But while Jeremiah was often in crowds he was not crowd-conditioned. The crowd did not dictate his message. The crowd did not shape his values. Jeremiah did not commission a public opinion survey to find out what the Jerusalem crowds wanted to hear about God. He did not ask for a show of hands to determine what level of moral behavior to stress.

God shaped his behavior. God directed his life. God trained his perceptions. This shaping and directing and training took place as he listened to God and spoke to God. He meditated long and passionately on the word of God; he forged responses that were absolutely and intensely personal. Everything he lived and spoke issued from this inner action: 'There is in my heart as it were a burning fire shut up in my bones, and I am weary with holding it in, and I cannot' (Jer 20:9).

Jeremiah made his mark. He wanted everything God promises. He wanted to participate in all that God does. His spiritual intensity and prophetic passion set him apart. He became what Søren Kierkegaard, himself a strikingly Jeremiah-like figure, called, 'the single one, the individual.'[3]

Sometimes in the presence of a person of surpassing excellence we are stimulated to strive for a similar achievement. We see an athlete perform and decide to embrace the disciplines that will give poise and grace to our lives. We hear an artist play and determine never to be content with anything sloppy or ugly in our lives again. We observe a person live with courage and zest and decide that we also will pursue the very best that is in us. But other times we respond by being intimidated. We assume that no matter how much we try we could never approximate such a life. Our inadequacies are exposed in the comparison and we accommodate ourselves to getting along and getting by. The artist, the athlete and the saint are rejected as evidence and proof of what is possible and treated as diversions and entertainments for lazy spectators and bored consumers.[4]

This was Jeremiah's fate in Jerusalem. The crowd avoided dealing with his life by setting him apart. The crowds understood what he was saying and probably admired the way he was living, but their self-concepts were crowd-conditioned. They didn't disbelieve in God, but they disqualified themselves from strenuous, personal participation.

Biblical faith, however, has always insisted that there are no special aptitudes for a life with God – no required level of intelligence or degree of morality, no particular spiritual experience. The statement 'I'm not the religious type' is inadmissible. There are no religious types. There are only human beings, every one created for a relationship with God that is personal and eternal.

How can people who are conditioned to a life of distraction and indulgence be moved to live at their best, to be artists of the everyday, to plunge into life and not loiter on the fringes?

The Guild of Rechabites

One day some strange people appeared on the streets of Jerusalem. They were called Rechabites. The Rechabites led a wandering life and lived in tents. They were a guild of metalworkers involved in the making of chariots and other weaponry. They roamed the country, setting up camp outside villages and cities. If you had a javelin that needed straightening or a chariot wheel that needed mending, you put it aside for the time when the Rechabites would arrive. They were a small band and kept to themselves.[5]

The Rechabites traced their ancestry back 250 years, to one Jonadab ben Rechab in the time of Jehu. They accounted for their disciplined life and distinctive identity in terms of their obedience to the command given by their ancestor: 'We have obeyed the voice of Jonadab the son of Rechab, our father, in all that he commanded us, to drink no wine all our days, ourselves, our wives, our sons, or our daughters, and not to build houses to dwell in. We have no vineyard or field or seed; but we have lived in tents, and have obeyed and done all that Jonadab our father commanded us' (Jer 35:8-10).

Craftsmen in metal would have many trade secrets, tightly held. The abstinence from intoxicants followed from the well-known rule, 'loose lips sink ships.' Metallurgists in antiquity, as a rule, formed proud families with long genealogies. Marriages were carefully arranged within the guild, preventing the entrance of outsiders. The smith had to dispose of a formidable body of technical lore which was handed down and guarded jealously from generation to generation. The nature of his work prevented the smith from establishing a permanent residence. He remained in one locality from a few months to several years until the supply of ore and fuel at that place was exhausted. The smith's work required such skill and long practice that agricultural work was excluded.

The Babylonian invasion of Judah had made living in the country dangerous and so the Rechabites had come inside the city walls of Jerusalem for safety. They were an oddity in the city, conspicuous in their strangeness. They were, of course, noticed, commented on, gawked at. Within two or three days everyone would either have seen them or heard about them.

An Invitation to Lunch

Then this: 'The word which came to Jeremiah from the LORD: . . . "Go to the house of the Rechabites, and speak with them, and bring them to the house of the LORD, into one of the chambers; then offer them wine to drink"' (Jer 35:1-2).

But Rechabites don't drink wine. Everybody knows that. Why invite them to a wine party that they can't enjoy? Then it dawned on Jeremiah. Of course. The Rechabites were living evidence, right on the crowded streets of Jerusalem, of the two things the crowd-conditioned people assumed were impossible: They were evidence that everyday, ordinary people could live their entire lives directed by a personal command (and not the impersonal pressures of the crowd); they were evidence that it is possible to maintain persistently a distinctive way of life (and not assimilate to the fashions of the crowd). The people had already noticed the Rechabites – how could they miss them! – now if they could just be made to notice exactly what it was that set them apart and gave them their identity, then they themselves might realize that a personal identity and a disciplined distinctiveness were possible for them also.

Jeremiah saw the possibilities and went to work. He arranged for the use of a public room in the temple precincts – an open chamber where they would be seen both by the religious leaders and by the general populace. He invited the Rechabites – there couldn't have been very many, perhaps fifteen or twenty – for a luncheon. He placed pitchers of wine and large drinking bowls on the table.

A Disciplined People

Jeremiah was no novice at this business of using experiences from the streets in order to get people to pay attention to God. One day in the bazaar he had bought a fine linen garment, the kind worn for a wedding ceremony or a religious festival. I always imagine Jeremiah making a production out of the purchase, spending most of an afternoon bargaining with the shopkeeper (not in itself an unusual practice in the Middle East) so that a lot of people would know of the purchase. The word would get around: 'What is Jeremiah buying that fine linen garment for? What special event is coming up? What was he invited to that we weren't?'

Then Jeremiah made a show of wadding up this beautiful piece of clothing and sticking it in a rock crevice to keep it safe until the time that he was going to wear it. Later he went back to retrieve it, as if to wear it for the special occasion. It was rotten, in tatters because of exposure to the elements and the insects.

The people got the message: Israel was the fine garment that God wanted to wear, but she wasn't ready yet to be used for his purposes. She wanted to live an ordinary life first, so she wadded herself up and stuffed herself into the secure routines, separating herself from what God had at great cost purchased her for. But when that day comes it will turn out that she is good for nothing. The beautiful moral life that she set aside for a more convenient day will turn out, when she picks it up, to be mildewed and moth-eaten (Jer 13).

Another time Jeremiah staggered through the streets of Jerusalem with an ox yoke on his shoulders, telling the people that they were going to experience just such servitude under the approaching Babylonian rule, and that they should get used to the idea for it was far better than getting killed (Jer 27-28).

This day it was the talk-of-the-town Rechabites that Jeremiah used. Invited by Jeremiah, they were now at table with him. The wine was on the table. Jeremiah, a gracious and friendly host, lifted his glass in a toast: *L'Chaim!* Drink wine!

Did they join in? Did they relax their rule for the moment so as not to offend their new friend? Did they realize that they were living under emergency war conditions and that it was only courteous to adapt to the customs of their protectors? Did they take a realistic view of the situation and share the common cup, showing appreciation for being treated so generously?

They did not, as Jeremiah knew they would not. 'They answered, "We will drink no wine, for Jonadab the son of Rechab, our father, commanded us, 'You shall not drink wine'"' (Jer 35:6). The Rechabites lived life not on the basis of what was current with the crowd but on the basis of what had been commanded by their ancestor. Their way of life was not formed out of historical conditions but out of centuries of devotion. The ancient command, not the current headline, gave them their identity. That word shaped and preserved their proud traditions as skilled craftsmen. Neither the hospitality of a kind host nor the customs of the city where they had come for sanctuary could distract them from what was essential: that they were a commanded people, that they were a disciplined people. Jonadab's 250-year-old command carried far more weight with them than Jeremiah's immediate friendship. The discipline that made it possible for them to maintain their craft was far more important to them than making the commonsense adaptations that would have given them an easy rapport with their new neighbors.

Life in Relationship to God

Now Jeremiah had both his text and the attention of the crowds: 'Will you not receive instruction and listen to my words? says the LORD. The command which Jonadab the son of Rechab gave to his sons, to drink no wine, has been kept; and they drink none to this day, for they have obeyed their father's command. I have spoken to you persistently, but you have not listened to me. . . . The sons of Jonadab the son of Rechab have kept the command which their father gave them, but this people has not obeyed me' (Jer 35:13-14, 16).

Note well that Jeremiah did not say, 'You must sell your houses and live in tents; you must abandon your vineyards and roam the desert; you must abstain from wine and drink only water.' It was not the specific details of the Rechabite life that were held up but that they lived in obedience to a command and lived with integrity in a discipline.

The essence of Jeremiah's message here is this: You also have a father who has commanded you to live in total relationship to him. You know that he has set you apart for a life of love. Why don't you live in response to it? If you think it is because ordinary, mortal human beings can't do it, think again. The Rechabites are ordinary, mortal human beings, and they have been doing it for 250 years. You also have a way of life that requires certain disciplines to maintain its character. The disciplines involve you in making specific decisions about the way you live: regular worship, faithful prayer, tithing and caring for the poor, moral conduct and the pursuit of righteousness. Now, why don't you do it? If you think that is too rigorous a life for ordinary, mortal human beings, think again. The Rechabites are ordinary, mortal human beings, and they have been doing it for 250 years.

Don't just look at them. Don't just talk about them. Pay attention to what is distinctive about them. They are not entertainment, they are example. Let them show you how badly and boringly you live – and how well you can live.[6] Your problem is not that you are incapable but that you are lazy. There is not a single person in Jerusalem who is not up to living consciously and deliberately as a child of God, and then practicing the distinctive disciplines that support and preserve a life of faith. But you have let the crowd turn you into spectators and consumers. You have let your lives get flabby and indulgent. You have ignored the best things that have ever been said to you – God's word! – and let the chatter and gossip of the crowd fill your ears. You have abandoned the simple actions that people of faith have used for centuries to keep in touch with the truth of God, the beauty of creation and the reality of being human. Instead you have let the crowd distract you with frivolities and dehumanize you with propaganda.

Why will you not let God's command develop in you a life of holy obedience instead of letting the crowd drag you into a sloppy indolence? 'The sons of Jonadab the son of Rechab have kept the command which their father gave them, but this people has not obeyed me.'

Larger but Smaller

Jeremiah raises weighty objections to our unreflective ways of going about our well-defined jobs, jobs that become lives shaped and sanctioned by the crowd. The New York philosopher William Barrett objects: 'Modern civilization has raised the material level of millions of people beyond the expectations of the past, has it succeeded in making people happier? To judge by the bulk of modern literature, we would have to answer "No"; and in some respects we might even have to say it has accomplished the reverse.'[7]

The moral level of our society is shameful. The spiritual integrity of our culture is an embarrassment. Any part of our lives that is turned over to the crowd makes it and us worse. The larger the crowd, the smaller our lives. Pliny the Elder once said that the Romans, when they couldn't make a building beautiful, made it big. The practice continues to be popular: If we can't do it well, we make it larger. We add dollars to our income, rooms to our houses, activities to our schedules, appointments to our calendars. And the quality of life diminishes with each addition.

On the other hand, every time that we retrieve a part of our life from the crowd and respond to God's call to us, we are that much more ourselves, more human. Every time we reject the habits of the crowd and practice the disciplines of faith, we become a little more alive.

12

Letter to the Exiles

Thus says the LORD of hosts, the God of Israel, to all the exiles whom I have sent into exile from Jerusalem to Babylon: Build houses and live in them; plant gardens and eat their produce. Take wives and have sons and daughters. . . . Seek the welfare of the city where I have sent you into exile, and pray to the LORD on its behalf, for in its welfare you will find your welfare. . . . Do not let your prophets and your diviners who are among you deceive you, and do not listen to the dreams which they dream, for it is a lie which they are prophesying to you in my name; I did not send them, says the LORD. . . .

For I know the plans I have for you, says the LORD, plans for welfare and not for evil, to give you a future and a hope. Then you will call upon me and come and pray to me, and I will hear you. You will seek me and find me; when you seek me with all your heart, I will be found by you, says the LORD.

JEREMIAH 29:4-14

Christ is certainly no less concerned than Nietzsche that the personality should receive the fullest development of which it is capable, and be more and more of a power. The difference between them lies in the moral method by which the personality is put into possession of itself and its resources – in the one case by asserting self, in the other by losing it. . . . We complete our personality only as we fall into place and service in the vital movement of the society in which we live. Isolation means arrested development. The aggressive egotist is working his own moral destruction by stunting and shrinking his true personality. Social life, duty, and sympathy are the only conditions under which a true personality can be shaped. And if it be asked how a society so crude, imperfect, unmoral, and even immoral as that in which we live is to mould a personality truly moral, it is here that Christ comes to the rescue with the gift to faith both of an active Spirit and of a society complete in Himself.

PETER T. FORSYTH[1]

EXILE IS TRAUMATIC AND TERRIFYING. OUR SENSE OF WHO WE are is very much determined by the place we are in and the people we are with. When that changes, violently and abruptly, who are we? The accustomed ways we have of finding our worth and sensing our significance vanish. The first wave of emotion recedes and leaves us feeling worthless, meaningless. We don't fit anywhere. No one expects us to do anything. No one needs us. We are extra baggage. We aren't necessary.

Israel was taken into exile in 587 B.C.[2] The people were uprooted from the place in which they were born. The land that had been promised to them, which they had possessed, in which their identity as a people of God had been formed, was gone. They were forced to travel across the Middle Eastern desert seven hundred miles, leaving home, temple and hills. In the new land, Babylon, customs were strange, the language incomprehensible, and the landscape oddly flat and featureless. All the familiar landmarks were gone. The weather was different. The faces were unrecognized and unrecognizing.

Israel's exile was a violent and extreme form of what all of us experience from time to time. Inner experiences of exile take place even if we never move from the street on which we were brought up. We are exiled from the womb and begin life in strange and harsh surroundings. We are exiled from our homes at an early age and find ourselves in the terrifying and demanding world of school. We are exiled from school and have to make our way the best we can in the world of work. We are exiled from our hometowns and have to find our way in new states and cities.

These experiences of exile, minor and major, continue through changes in society, changes in government, changes in values, changes in our bodies, our emotions, our families and marriages. We barely get used to one set of circumstances and faces when we are forced to deal with another. The exile experienced by the Hebrews is a dramatic instance of what we all experience simply by being alive in this world. Repeatedly we find ourselves in circumstances where we are not at home. We are 'strangers in a strange land.'[3]

The essential meaning of exile is that we are where we don't want to be. We are separated from home. We are not permitted to reside in the place where we comprehend and appreciate our surroundings. We are forced to be away from that which is most congenial to us. It is an experience of dislocation – everything is out of joint; nothing fits together. The thousand details that have been built up through the years that give a sense of at-homeness – gestures, customs, rituals, phrases – are all gone. Life is ripped out of the familiar soil of generations of language, habit, weather, story-telling, and rudely and unceremoniously dropped into some unfamiliar spot of earth. The place of exile may boast a higher standard of living. It may be more pleasant in its weather. That doesn't matter. It isn't home.

But this very strangeness can open up new reality to us. An accident, a tragedy, a disaster of any kind can force the realization that the world is not predictable, that reality is far more extensive than our habitual perception of it. With the pain and in the midst of alienation a sense of freedom can occur.

False Dreams

The reason for Israel's exile is clear enough: Jeremiah and other prophets had preached that the nation's stability and security depended on a certain faithfulness to the love of God. That message had been scorned and rejected. The Babylonian army came one day and captured the city. After conquering Jerusalem the Babylonians selected the leading people of the city for deportation. The tactic was to remove all persons of influence and leadership – artisans, merchants, political leaders – so that the general populace would be dependent on and submissive to the invaders. Without leaders the people, like sheep, would submit to the puppet king and the occupying army with a minimum of hassle. Jeremiah, interestingly, was left behind. He had been ignored for so long as a leader by his own people that the Babylonians did not consider him important enough to exile.

How did these people in exile feel? How did they respond? If we imagine ourselves in a similar situation, remembering how we respond when we are forced to spend extended time with people we don't like in a place we don't like, we will not be far from the truth. Their experience can be expressed in a complaint: 'A terrible thing has happened to us. And it's not fair. I know we weren't perfect, but we were no worse than the rest of them. And here we end up in this Babylonian desert while our friends are carrying on life as usual in Jerusalem. Why us? We can't understand the language; we don't like the food; the manners of the Babylonians are boorish; the schools are sub-standard; there are no decent places to worship; the plains are barren; the weather is atrociously hot; the temples are polluted with immorality; everyone speaks with an accent.' They complained bitterly about the terrible circumstances in which they were forced to live. They longed, achingly, for Jerusalem. They wallowed in self-pity, what Robertson Davies calls the 'harlot emotion'.[4]

They had religious leaders with them who nurtured their self-pity. We know the names of three of them: Ahab, Zedekiah and Shemiah. These prophets called attention to the unfairness of their plight and stirred the pots of discontent: 'Yes, the old religion of Jerusalem is what we must get back to. Yes, it's worse luck that we are here when so many are enjoying the good life back in Jerusalem. But hang on a little longer and we'll get back. It can't last much longer. How can it? Not one of us deserves such a life. Justice will prevail.' These prophets described dreams, God-given they claimed, that revealed that the exile would end soon.

These three prophets made a good living fomenting discontent and merchandising nostalgia. But their messages and dreams, besides being false, were destructive. False dreams interfere with honest living. As long as the people thought that they might be going home at any time, it made no sense to engage in committed, faithful work in Babylon. If there was a good chance that they would soon get back all they had lost, there was no need to develop a life of richness, texture and depth where they were. Since their real relationships were back in Jerusalem, they could be casual and irresponsible in their relationships in exile – they weren't going to see these people much longer anyhow. Why bother planting gardens? That is backbreaking work, and they would probably be out of there before harvest time. Why learn the business practices of the culture? That is demanding; they would get along with odd jobs here and there. Why take on the disciplines of marriage and family? They would make do with casual sexual encounters until they got back to Jerusalem where they could settle down to serious family building.

The prophets manipulated the self-pity of the people into neurotic fantasies. The people, glad for a religious reason to be lazy, lived hand to mouth, parasites on society, irresponsible in their relationships, indifferent to the reality of their actual lives.

A Letter from Jeremiah

One day two men from Jerusalem appeared unannounced among the exiles: Elasah and Gemariah. They had come on official business, carrying a message to the king of Babylon. On their way to the palace they visited the community in exile. The air was charged with excitement. Everyone had questions: What was this one doing? What was that one doing? Elasah and Gemariah waved them silent. Before giving them the gossip they had a message from Jeremiah, a letter to the exiles.

'Thus says the LORD of hosts, the God of Israel, to all the exiles whom I have sent into exile from Jerusalem to Babylon: Build houses and live in them; plant gardens and eat their produce. Take wives and have sons and daughters.... Seek the welfare of the city.... Pray to the LORD on its behalf.... Do not let your prophets and your diviners who are among you deceive you, and do not listen to the dreams which they dream, for it is a lie which they are prophesying to you in my name.'

Build houses and live in them. You are not camping. This is your home; make yourself at home. This may not be your favorite place, but it is a place. Dig foundations; construct a habitation; develop the best environment for living that you can. If all you do is sit around and pine for the time you get back to Jerusalem, your present lives will be squalid and empty. Your life right now is every bit as valuable as it was when you were in Jerusalem, and every bit as valuable as it will be when you get back to Jerusalem. Babylonian exile is not your choice, but it is what you are given. Build a Babylonian house and live in it as well as you are able.

Plant gardens and eat their produce. Enter into the rhythm of the seasons. Become a productive part of the economy of the place. You are not parasites. Don't expect others to do it for you. Get your hands into the Babylonian soil. Become knowledgeable about the Babylonian irrigation system. Acquire skill in cultivating fruits and vegetables in this soil and climate. Get some Babylonian recipes and cook them.

Take wives and have sons and daughters. These people among whom you are living are not beneath you, nor are they above you; they are your equals with whom you can engage in the most intimate and responsible of relationships. You cannot be the person God wants you to be if you keep yourself aloof from others. That which you have in common is far more significant than what separates you. They are God's persons: your task as a person of faith is to develop trust and conversation, love and understanding.

Seek the welfare of the city where I have sent you into exile, and pray to the LORD on its behalf, for in its welfare you will find your welfare. Welfare: *shalom.* Shalom means wholeness, the dynamic, vibrating health of a society that pulses with divinely directed purpose and surges with life-transforming love. Seek the shalom and pray for it. Throw yourselves into the place in which you find yourself, but not on its terms, on God's terms. *Pray.* Search for that center in which God's will is being worked out (which is what we do when we pray) and work from that center.

Jeremiah's letter is a rebuke and a challenge: 'Quit sitting around feeling sorry for yourselves. The aim of the person of faith is not to be as comfortable as possible but to live as deeply and thoroughly as possible – to deal with the reality of life, discover truth, create beauty, act out love. You didn't do it when you were in Jerusalem. Why don't you try doing it here, in Babylon? Don't listen to the lying prophets who make an irresponsible living by selling you false hopes. You are in Babylon for a long time. You better make the best of it. Don't just get along, waiting for some miraculous intervention. Build houses, plant gardens, marry husbands, marry wives, have children, pray for the wholeness of Babylon, and do everything you can to develop that wholeness. The only place you have to be human is where you are right now. The only opportunity you will ever have to live by faith is in the circumstances you are provided this very day: this house you live in, this family you find yourself in, this job you have been given, the weather conditions that prevail at this moment.'

Living at Our Best

Exile (being where we don't want to be with people we don't want to be with) forces a decision: Will I focus my attention on what is wrong with the world and feel sorry for myself? Or will I focus my energies on how I can live at my best in this place I find myself? It is always easier to complain about problems than to engage in careers of virtue. George Eliot in her novel *Felix Holt* has a brilliantly appropriate comment on this question: 'Everything's wrong says he. That's a big text. But does he want to make everything right? Not he. He'd lose his text.'[5]

Daily we face decisions on how we will respond to these exile conditions. We can say: 'I don't like it; I want to be where I was ten years ago. How can you expect me to throw myself into what I don't like – that would be sheer hypocrisy. What sense is there in taking risks and tiring myself out among people I don't even like in a place where I have no future?'

Or we can say: 'I will do my best with what is here. Far more important than the climate of this place, the economics of this place, the neighbors in this place, is the God of this place. God is here with me. What I am experiencing right now is on ground that was created by him and with people whom he loves. It is just as possible to live out the will of God here as any place else. I am full of fear. I don't know my way around. I have much to learn. I'm not sure I can make it. But I had feelings like that back in Jerusalem. Change is hard. Developing intimacy among strangers is always a risk. Building relationships in unfamiliar and hostile surroundings is difficult. But if that is what it means to be alive and human, I will do it.'

Fenelon used to say that there are two kinds of people: some look at life and complain of what is not there; others look at life and rejoice in what is there.[6] Will we live on the basis of what we don't have or on what we do have?

Invitation and Promise

So much for the rebuke and counsel in Jeremiah's letter to the exiles. There is also invitation and promise in it, and this is what finally came to the center and shaped the exile experience: 'I know the plans I have for you, says the LORD, plans for welfare and not for evil, to give you a future and a hope. Then you will call upon me and come and pray to me, and I will hear you. You will seek me and find me; when you seek me with all your heart, I will be found by you, says the LORD.'

Jeremiah habitually used words greatly, but never more so than in these sentences.

A few people rejected the message out of hand. The three prophets, for instance, were furious. Shemiah wrote a sharp, angry letter back to the Jerusalem high priest, Zephaniah, and said, 'Can't you shut up Jeremiah? How long are you going to permit this crazy man to rant and rave and write letters telling us it is going to be a long exile? Do you realize what that will do to us? If people start feeling at home in Babylon, we will *never* get home to Jerusalem! Why have you not disciplined Jeremiah of Anathoth?' (Jer 29:24-28).

But others, maybe most, accepted the message. Jarred out of their everydayness by the exile, they embarked on 'the search'.[7] They settled down to find out what it meant to be God's people in the place they did not want to be – in Babylon. The result was that this became the most creative period in the entire sweep of Hebrew history. They did not lose their identity, they discovered it. They learned how to pray in deeper and more life-changing ways than ever. They wrote and copied and pondered the vast revelation that had come down to them from Moses and the prophets, and they came to recognize the incredible riches of their Scriptures. They found that God was not dependent on a place, that he was not tied to familiar surroundings. The violent dislocation of the exile shook them out of their comfortable but reality-distorting assumptions and allowed them to see depths and heights that they had never even imagined before. They lost everything that they thought was important and found what was important: they found God.

The exile tore the cover off their way of life and showed its emptiness. Never again could they live by bread alone. The word of God was essential nourishment. They realized that this extraordinary change of life could only take place in the structures of the everyday – houses and gardens, marriages and children. When Jeremiah directed them to build houses and plant gardens and raise families they did not misunderstand him to mean that they were to assimilate to Babylonia. That would be no more than to repeat the sins of Jerusalem in Babylonia. They embraced the everyday, but did not become absorbed in it. They did not let the duties and routines of life dull them: they prayed and they searched. The search paid off: they noticed the texture of life; they became responsive to the many subtleties just waiting for an eye to notice them, an ear to listen to them, a mind to find them worthy of attention.

The exile was the 'crucible of Israel's faith'.[8] They were pushed to the edge of existence where they thought they were hanging on by the skin of their teeth, and they found that in fact they had been pushed to the center, where God was. They experienced not bare survival but abundant life. Now they saw their previous life as subsistence living, a marginal existence absorbed in consumption and fashion, empty ritual and insensitive exploitation. Exile pushed them from the margins of life to the vortex where all the issues of life and death, love and meaning, purpose and value formed the dynamic everyday, participation-demanding realities of God's future with them.

It keeps on happening. Exile is the worst that reveals the best. 'It's hard believing,' says Faulkner, 'but disaster seems to be good for people.'[9] When the superfluous is stripped away we find the essential – and the essential is God. Normal life is full of distractions and irrelevancies. Then catastrophe: Dislocation. Exile. Illness. Accident. Job loss. Divorce. Death. The reality of our lives is rearranged without anyone consulting us or waiting for our permission. We are no longer at home.

All of us are given moments, days, months, years of exile. What will we do with them? Wish we were someplace else? Complain? Escape into fantasies? Drug ourselves into oblivion? Or build and plant and marry and seek the shalom of the place we inhabit and the people we are with? Exile reveals what really matters and frees us to pursue what really matters, which is to seek the Lord with all our hearts.

13

Sentry . . . King . . . Eunuch

When he was at the Benjamin Gate, a sentry there named Irijah the son of Shelemiah, son of Hananiah, seized Jeremiah the prophet, saying, 'You are deserting to the Chaldeans.' . . .

When Jeremiah had come to the dungeon cells, and remained there many days, King Zedekiah sent for him, and received him. The king questioned him secretly in his house, and said, 'Is there any word from the LORD*?' . . .*

When Ebedmelech the Ethiopian, a eunuch, who was in the king's house, heard that they had put Jeremiah into the cistern . . . Ebedmelech . . . said to the king, 'My lord the king, these men have done evil in all that they did to Jeremiah the prophet by casting him into the cistern; and he will die there of hunger.' . . . So Ebedmelech . . . drew Jeremiah up with ropes and lifted him out of the cistern.

JEREMIAH 37:13, 16-17; 38:7-13

> *I must register a certain impatience with the faddish equation, never suggested by me, of the term identity with the question, 'Who am I?' This question nobody would ask himself except in a more or less transcient morbid state, in a creative self-confrontation, or in an adolescent state sometimes combining both; wherefore on occasion I find myself asking a student who claims that he is in an 'identity crisis' whether he is complaining or boasting. The pertinent question, if it can be put into the first person at all, would be, 'What do I want to make of myself, and what do I have to work with?'*
>
> ERIK H. ERIKSON[1]

MOST FIGURES IN HISTORY BOOKS ARE FLASHES OF COLOR that illuminate an episode and are then forgotten. How many can recall ten years back the name of the Secretary of State – certainly one of the most prestigious positions in the world? Who can name the best-selling author of five years ago? But the significance of a few persons, instead of fading, blazes more brightly each century. Their significance blazes because they did not merely fulfill a prestigious role or get associated with a notable event. They became *human* in depth and thoroughness. These few, in R. P. Blackmur's words, 'show an attractive force, massive and inexhaustible, and a disseminative force which is the inexhaustible spring or constant declaration of value. Where your small man is a knoll to be smoothed away [such a person is] a mountain to be mined on all flanks.'[2]

Jeremiah is a 'mountain to be mined on all flanks.' He centers an epoch. He was a first-hand participant in the events which became the pivot for a millennium. The age of Jeremiah is a nodal ganglion that shoots out nerve endings in all directions of human existence: philosophy, religion, politics, art. In China, India, Israel and Greece the foundations are laid for universal history. Karl Jaspers describes Jeremiah's century as the 'axial time' *(Achsenzeit)*.[3]

The man made headlines. His theological perception, his religious sensibility, his rhetorical power, his emotional range, his confrontational courage – these all made their historical mark. But the primary interest of people of faith in Jeremiah is not in his historical impact but in his personal development.

Only a few people make the historical headlines, but anyone can become human. Is it possible to be great when you are taking out the garbage as well as when you are signing a peace treaty? Is it possible to exhibit grace in your conduct in the kitchen as well as in a nationally televised debate?

I once knew a man well who had a commanding public presence and exuded charm to all he met. What he said *mattered.* He had *influence.* He was always impeccably dressed and unfailingly courteous. But his secretary was frequently in tears as a result of his rudely imperious demands. Behind the scenes he was tyrannical and insensitive. His public image was flawless; his personal relationships were shabby.

How did Jeremiah deal with the people day by day? What was it like to be with him when he wasn't preaching a sermon, or polishing an oracle, or waging a confrontation? The sifted reflection of the centuries adds up to an impressive consensus: Jeremiah became human in a complex and developed *personal* sense. An examination of some of the persons with whom he had to do strengthens our estimation of his 'full humanness', Abraham Maslow's phrase for our rarely realized destinies.[4]

In chapters 37-39 of Jeremiah decisive historical events are taking place. World history is being shaped before our eyes.

The nation is being radically altered. Powerful theological realities are emerging. Jeremiah is in the middle of it all. But Jeremiah, while not oblivious to the big issues, is mostly dealing with *persons,* persons with *names.* Named persons formed the raw material for Jeremiah's daily life of faith. Every life of faith, whether it is conspicuous or obscure, is worked out in the context of persons not unlike the persons with whom Jeremiah rubbed shoulders. Quite apart from the big ideas we ponder, the important movements we participate in, the particular jobs we are given, named persons constitute most of the agenda of our lives. Three men on Jeremiah's agenda are representatively significant: Irijah the sentry, Zedekiah the king, Ebedmelech the eunuch.

Irijah the Sentry

The city was under final attack by the Babylonians. It would soon fall. Jeremiah had given counsel to the leaders and had preached to the people that the Babylonian presence was God's judgment: it should be accepted and submitted to. They had sinned and they were being judged. The judgment was God's way of restoring wholeness.

People didn't like that. They kept trying to find ways to avoid the reality of judgment, to think in other categories than those of right and wrong, sin and irresponsibility. One of their substitute ways of thinking was in terms of loyalty and disloyalty. Patriotism was used to muddle the sense of morality: 'Our beloved country is being attacked and we must be loyal to it; in times of crisis it is not right to criticize your leaders. It is disloyal, an act of treachery.'

Using jingoist language is far easier than taking responsibility for righteousness in the nation. Far easier to shout patriotic slogans than to work patriotically for justice.

One day Jeremiah was going out the city gate to his hometown of Anathoth, three miles away. Irijah, the sentry, arrested him on the grounds that he had caught him defecting to the enemy.

Jeremiah had lived in Jerusalem all his adult life. He had been a public figure for over thirty years. He had established credentials as a loyal friend and adviser to the great King Josiah. He had never for a moment rejected or repudiated his identity as a Jew or exempted himself from any of the obligations of membership in that community. To anyone who knew him he obviously was not a bystander criticizing and not a turncoat propagandizing, but an insider agonizing.

Irijah led the man he had arrested to his bosses, the princes, who beat him and imprisoned him. Apparently they had been waiting for any incident that they could use to pounce on him. Irijah, with the undiscriminating reflexes of a watchdog, pounced.

Irijah was a man who used his job to escape his responsibilities as a person. He was a bureaucrat in the worst sense of the word, a person who hides behind the rules and prerogatives of a job description to do work that destroys people. Without considering morality or righteousness, God or person, he did his job. We meet these people all the time. And there are more and more jobs like this all the time. Every day people are hurt and demeaned by office-holders who refuse to look us in the eye, shielding themselves behind regulations and paperwork, secretaries and committees.

Irijah was the kind of person that Melville, in his novel *The Confidence Man,* describes with great scorn as 'the moderate man, the invaluable understrapper of the wicked man. You, the moderate man, may be used for wrong, but you are useless for right.'[5] Irijah, no doubt, would have protested vehemently that he had nothing against Jeremiah personally, that he was just doing what he had been told to do.

The most famous twentieth-century instance of Irijah is Adolf Eichmann, key figure in the murder of six million Jews in Nazi Germany. At his trial in Jerusalem it became quite clear that he had nothing against the Jews; he was just doing his job. No great venom of hate flowed in him; he was simply being obedient to what his superiors told him. Hannah Arendt coined the phrase 'the banality of evil' to describe him.[6] Incalculable evil comes from these unlikely sources: quiet, efficient, little people doing their job, long since having given up thinking of themselves as responsible, moral individuals.

Jeremiah responded to Irijah with implacable endurance. He did not bluster and curse. He did not threaten and rail. Nor was he a lifeless doormat. He asserted his innocence and he endured; he accepted this banal stupidity with, it seems, equanimity, and persisted in his vocation.

Zedekiah the King

Zedekiah was not properly the king but a puppet king appointed by the Babylonians. The actual king, Jehoiachin, had been taken into exile in 598 B.C. along with most of the ruling class of the city. His uncle, Zedekiah, was appointed to rule in his place. Zedekiah was king for eleven years. All through those eleven years he had frequent conversations with Jeremiah. Jeremiah had been closely associated with his brother, the great Josiah, and with both his nephews, the kings Jehoiakim and Jehoiachin.

Zedekiah had mixed feelings about Jeremiah. He respected him. How could he not respect him? – his stature was immense, his integrity impressive, his courage legendary. But he was also an embarrassment, for Zedekiah permitted himself to be surrounded with the usual crowd of self-serving sycophants, who were trying to gain advantage from association with his kingship. He could well guess that Jeremiah had a quiet contempt for such persons.

A weak, vacillating person, Zedekiah was appointed to rule, we suspect, because the Babylonians knew that he had no will of his own and would submit to what was commanded. What they failed to anticipate was that he would do what he was told by anyone who happened to be in the room with him. When the Babylonians were gone and ultranationalists of the most reckless sort began showing up with elaborate plots to throw off the Babylonian rule with the help of an Egyptian alliance, he was easily swayed. Sometimes he would have qualms of conscience and call Jeremiah in for a consultation and, for a brief time, pay attention to the prophetic word. But nothing lasted long with Zedekiah. The man was a marshmallow. He received impressions from anyone who pushed hard enough. When the pressure was off, he gradually resumed his earlier state ready for the next impression. In contrast to Jeremiah, who was formed from within by obedience to God and faith in God (an iron pillar!), Zedekiah took on whatever shape the circumstances required.

Zedekiah shows that good intentions are worthless if they are not coupled with character development. We don't become whole persons by merely wanting to become whole, by consulting the right prophets, by reading the right book. Intentions must mature into commitments if we are to become persons with definition, with character, with substance.

After the princes threw Jeremiah into the dungeon at the time of his arrest by Irijah, Zedekiah secretly brought him to his palace for a conversation. Zedekiah would not do this openly for fear of the princes. But neither would he ignore him, fearing that he might not get in on an important truth that Jeremiah might provide. Later the princes, enraged at

Jeremiah preaching from his prison cell, threw him into a cistern. Zedekiah did nothing to prevent it.

Zedekiah was hardly a person at all. There was nothing to him. He fit into whatever plans stronger people had for him. He was not an evil person. There is no evidence that he premeditated wrongdoing. But, and this is the significant fact, neither did he premeditate goodness. And goodness does not just happen. It does not spring full-bodied out of the head of kingly intent. It requires careful nurture, disciplined training, long development. For this, Zedekiah had no stomach.

Zedekiah must have been one of the most difficult persons in all of Jeremiah's life. One king (Josiah) had been his close friend; one king (Jehoiakim) had been his implacable enemy. But this king was formless: he could never be counted on for anything, whether positive or negative. Meanwhile Jeremiah maintained his witness under the faithfulness of his God, quite apart from the fickleness of his king.

Ebedmelech the Eunuch

Ebedmelech was a foreigner, a black man from Ethiopia and an official in the administrative government. When he learned that Jeremiah was in the cistern, he knew that he would die quickly if not rescued. Although the cistern was without water, it was swampy with mud and Jeremiah was sinking into it. He must die soon, if not by suffocation, by exposure.

Ebedmelech went to the king and confronted him with the injustice that he had permitted. He got authority to carry out a rescue operation. He took three men with him, got ropes, went to the palace wardrobe and got rags, and then went to the cistern. He lowered the ropes to Jeremiah and instructed him to put the rags under his armpits so that the ropes would not cut into his flesh as they pulled him out. He rescued Jeremiah.

Jeremiah was never popular. He was never surrounded with applause. But he was not friendless. In fact, Jeremiah was extremely fortunate in his friends. Twenty years or so earlier, under King Jehoiakim, Jeremiah was almost murdered, but Ahikam ben Shaphan intervened and saved him (Jer 26:24). Baruch was his disciple and secretary, loyal and faithful, sticking with him through difficult times to the very end. And Ebedmelech, the Ethiopian eunuch, came to his aid. 'One friend in a lifetime is much,' wrote Henry Adams, 'two are many; three are hardly possible.'[7] Jeremiah had three.

Ebedmelech risked his life in rescuing Jeremiah. Being a foreigner he had no legal rights. He was going against popular opinion in a crisis that was hysterical with wartime emotion. That didn't matter. A friend is a friend. Ebedmelech didn't indulge in sentimental pity for Jeremiah, philosophically lamenting his fate; he went to the king, he got ropes, he even thought of getting rags for padding so that the ropes would not cut, he enlisted help, and he pulled him out of the cistern. He acted out his friendship.

Not everyone in Jerusalem that year was just doing his job. Not all were sailing under the winds of popular opinion. There were a few people for whom a friend was more significant than a job, for whom a friend was more significant than a calculated advantage, for whom a friend meant a commitment and was worth a risk.

The simple fact that he had friends says something essential about Jeremiah: he *needed* friends. He was well-developed in his interior life. It was impossible to deter him from his course by enmity or by flattery. He was habituated to solitude. But he needed friends. No one who is whole is self-sufficient. The whole life, the complete life, cannot be lived with haughty independence. Our goal cannot be to not need anyone. One of the evidences of Jeremiah's wholeness was his capacity to receive friendship, to let others help him, to be accessible to mercy. It is easier to extend friendship to others than to receive it ourselves. In giving friendship we share strength, but in receiving it we show weakness. But well-developed persons are never garrisoned behind dogmas or projects, but rather they are alive to a wide spectrum of relationships.

The theological ideas, historical forces and righteous causes that touched Jeremiah's life never remained or became abstract but were worked out with persons, persons with names. He never used labels that lumped people into depersonalized categories. It can come as no surprise to find that there are more personal names in the book of Jeremiah than in any other prophetic book.[8]

14

I Bought the Field at Anathoth

And I bought the field at Anathoth from Hanamel my cousin, and weighed out the money to him, seventeen shekels of silver. I signed the deed, sealed it, got witnesses, and weighed the money on scales. . . . For thus says the Lord *of hosts, the God of Israel: Houses and fields and vineyards shall again be bought in this land.*

After I had given the deed of purchase to Baruch the son of Neriah, I prayed to the Lord, *saying: 'Ah Lord* God! *It is thou who hast made the heavens and the earth by thy great power and by thy outstretched arm! Nothing is too hard for thee. . . . Behold, the siege mounds have come up to the city to take it, and because of sword and famine and pestilence the city is given into the hands of the Chaldeans who are fighting against it. What thou didst speak has come to pass, and behold, thou seest it. Yet thou, O Lord* God, *hast said to me, "Buy the field for money and get witnesses" – though the city is given into the hands of the Chaldeans.'*

The word of the Lord *came to Jeremiah: 'Behold, I am the* Lord, *the God of all flesh; is anything too hard for me?. . .*

'Just as I have brought all this great evil upon this people, so I will bring upon them all the good that I promise them. Fields shall be bought in this land of which you are saying, It is a desolation, without man or beast; it is given into the hands of the Chaldeans. Fields shall be bought for money, and deeds shall be signed and sealed and witnessed.'

JEREMIAH 32:9-10, 15-17, 24-27, 42-44

I can stick artificial flowers on this tree that will not flower; or I can create the conditions in which the tree is likely to flower naturally. I may have to wait longer for my real flowers; but they are the only true ones.

JOHN FOWLES[1]

THE WORD *PRACTICAL* HAS BEEN LIFTED FROM RUN-OF-THE-mill discourse and set apart as a virtue. To describe a person as practical is to give high praise. To name a person as impractical is to dismiss as irrelevant. Antique virtues, like justice and fortitude, love and faith, maintain a precarious half-life in obscurity while the parvenu virtue, practicality, preens itself at the apex of our values.

Americans have contributed in special ways to the honor of this adjective. The hallmark of America is the practical. Americans have made their mark in the world with their single-minded practicality. We are quick; we don't waste time. We are efficient; we don't waste energy. We are down-to-earth; we don't get taken in by harebrained schemes. We get things done. We make things happen. And if as individuals we don't act up to these high standards, we extravagantly admire those who do. We lead the world in knowing how to get things done.[2]

Biblical and Practical

I applaud the emphasis. This claim to be practical is a basic stance of biblical faith. It can be fairly stated, in fact, that *biblical* and *practical* are essentially synonymous. If it is practical, it is biblical; if it is biblical, it is practical. Biblical faith rejects, fiercely and unhesitatingly, any conduct or thinking that diminishes our ability to function as human beings in time and space. Ideas that drive a wedge between God and creation are false. Prayers or acts of devotion that divert or incapacitate us from the here and now are spurious. Biblical faith everywhere and always warns against siren voices that lead people away from specific and everyday engagement with weather and politics, dogs and neighbors, shopping lists and job assignments. No true spiritual life can be distilled from or abstracted out of this world of chemicals and molecules, paying your bills and taking out the garbage.[3]

But if I applaud the emphasis on the practical and find it deeply biblical, I find myself in frequent disagreement with what is supposed to be practical. We have great enthusiasm for the practical in our society, but much confusion and no little bit of ignorance surround what is in fact practical. In the confusion and ignorance great crowds of people live extremely impractical lives and engage in hopelessly impractical acts, all the while supposing themselves to be hard-headed, no-nonsense, practical people.

Jeremiah's Practicality

Jeremiah was one of the most practical persons who ever lived. All his ideas and beliefs got turned into actions, and his actions were so on target that the history of his century was in large measure the lengthened shadow of his personal history. One of the most practical things that he did was to buy a field for seventeen dollars. At the time he did it he was judged an impractical fool. People watching him buy that field thought that he was buying the Brooklyn Bridge.

Jeremiah's sense of the practical conflicted constantly with the impracticality of the people around him. Jeremiah was convinced that he lived in a creation that was made to work and work well – a *practical* creation. Everything mattered and what happened to everything – to people, to mountains, to flowers, whatever – mattered. It is an affront to God when things don't work, when people live badly. It is scandalous to substitute sham posturing in a place of worship for devout love and faith with God. Gaping wounds are opened in the body of creation when the poor and unfortunate, God's creatures every one, are cruelly exploited.

Jeremiah's sense of the practical was built on the belief that God is the most important reality with which he and the people with whom he lived had to deal. He said that insistently and persuasively all his life. He believed that every person is made for a relationship with God, and without that relationship acknowledged and nurtured we live falsely and therefore impractically. People try to be good without God and it doesn't work. We try to live the good life and not the God life, and it doesn't work. The waste of our underdimensioned lives is appalling, and Jeremiah was appalled. It is impossible to live thus without unfortunate consequences. Jeremiah pleaded: 'A voice on the bare heights is heard, the weeping and pleading of Israel's sons, because they have perverted their way, they have forgotten the LORD their God. "Return, O faithless sons, I will heal your faithlessness"' (Jer 3:21-22). Reality won't put up with unreality. Nature, including human nature, warned Coventry Patmore, 'will not bear any absolute and sustained contradiction. She must be converted, not outraged.'[4]

The pleadings were ignored and the judgment came. Babylonian armies captured the city and took the leaders of the people into exile. Eleven years (598 to 587 B.C.) followed in which the people who were left behind had a measure of personal freedom but were politically subject to Babylon. They could have continued decent lives in those conditions, but after several years of restlessness and agitation they plotted to throw off the Babylonian yoke by enlisting Egypt in an alliance. It didn't work. The conspiracy provoked a severe Babylonian reprisal. The Egyptians saw that they could get no profit out of the affair and abandoned the scene. Judah was hopelessly outclassed militarily by the Babylonians. It was the blackest time in their history. Doomsday was just around the corner. In a matter of weeks, maybe only days, the city would be plundered and everyone marched off to exile. There was absolutely no hope at all.

Jeremiah, during these weeks, was shut up in prison. He had been accused of collaboration with the enemy, a false charge, but in the war hysteria it stuck. He was an unpopular figure at best, and so, as far as the people were concerned, prison was not an inappropriate place for him. In this prison – we must imagine a kind of loose confinement in the palace court where he was openly visible and had access to visitors – Jeremiah did what at the time appeared absolutely crazy: he bought a field for seventeen dollars.

It was crazy because at the very moment that he was buying it, the Babylonian armies were camping on it. He himself was in prison with no prospects for getting out. The enemy was pounding the city walls and about to take the people off to exile. At that moment Jeremiah bought a field on which he would never plant an olive tree, prune a grapevine, or build a house – a field that in all probability he would never even see.

Why did he do it? For the most practical of reasons: he did it because he was convinced that the troubles everyone was experiencing were at that very moment being used by God in what would eventually turn out to be the salvation of that land. The essential reality for Jeremiah was not that the Babylonians were camped on that field in Anathoth (although there was no denial of that fact) but that God was using that ground to fulfill his promises. He bought the field as an investment in God's next project for Israel, an investment that, as we now know, paid off admirably. 'As long as matters are really hopeful,' wrote Chesterton, 'hope is mere flattery or platitude. It is only when everything is hopeless that hope begins to be a strength at all. Like all the Christian virtues, it is as unreasonable as it is indispensable.'[5]

Jeremiah had preached God's judgment for years. Now that the judgment is at hand he alertly directs attention to the purpose of the judgment, which is to prepare lives to receive the promise of salvation. He does not say, 'I told you so.' He does not smugly survey the unavoidable evidence that he had been right. He is not interested in building a reputation as an accurate forecaster. He is not interested in checking off a list of fulfilled predictions. He is a practical man, interested in how the purposes of God can fill the present, changing it from futility that envelops the city like fog to hope. He takes no time out to enjoy the discomfiture of his detractors. It is God and persons with whom he has to do.

So at the moment that judgment is at hand he speaks the word that evokes hope. There is more here than Babylonians at the gate; there is God in your midst. Judgment is here. But don't despair; it is God's judgment. Face it. Accept the suffering. Experience the chastening action. God is not against you; he is for you. God has not rejected you; he is working with you. 'It is a time of distress for Jacob; yet he shall be saved out of it' (Jer 30:7). 'Why do you cry out over your hurt?... For I will restore health to you, and your wounds I will heal, says the LORD' (Jer 30:15, 17).

Judgment is not the last word; it is never the last word. Judgment is necessary because of centuries of hardheartedness; its proper work is to open our hearts to the reality beyond ourselves, to crack the carapace of self-sufficiency so that we can experience the inrushing grace of the healing, merciful, forgiving God.

The people who survived the sword
found grace in the wilderness . . .
I have loved you with an everlasting love;
therefore I have continued my faithfulness to you.
Again I will build you, and you shall be built,
O virgin Israel!
Again you shall adorn yourself with timbrels,
and shall go forth in the dance of the merrymakers. (Jer 31:2-4)

This is not the cold language of the courtroom, nor is it the angry language of reprisal and revenge. It is the personal pathos of a parent.

Is Ephraim my dear son?
Is he my darling child?
For as often as I speak against him,
I do remember him still.
Therefore my heart yearns for him;
I will surely have mercy on him, says the LORD. (Jer 31:20)

When the people were prosperous, they supposed that nothing could interrupt or interfere with their self-satisfied careers. During those years Jeremiah preached judgment. Now that calamity is all around them they believe that nothing can make things better. While the Babylonian siege engines are pounding the walls and hourly reports on the encroaching Babylonian devastators are posted, Jeremiah from his prison in the palace court (a distinctly unhopeful place) pours out his message: 'There is hope for your future, says the LORD' (Jer 31:17).

But the message of hope is no more believed than the message of judgment had been, and for the same reason. Anything that isn't corroborated by daily press releases and news bulletins is dismissed as impractical.

THE FIELD AT ANATHOTH

One day while all this was going on, Jeremiah's cousin Hanamel came into the courtyard where Jeremiah was confined and offered to sell him a plot of ground out in Anathoth, Jeremiah's hometown, three miles northeast of Jerusalem. Was Hanamel serious? Was he mocking Jeremiah? Babylonian armies were camped all over Anathoth. It was as if someone told me that he believed that in our lifetime people on earth would inhabit Mars and I said, 'Terrific. Let me sell you an acre of land right on the main canal.' Or as if someone assured me of her confidence that before long there would be a stable, lasting peace in the Middle East, and I jumped in with an offer to sell her a franchise in Iranian oil wells.

Jeremiah had been saying, 'Keep your voice from weeping, and your eyes from tears. . . . There is hope for your future, says the LORD, and your children shall come back to their own country' (Jer 31:16-17). Immediately Hanamel stepped up and said, 'Buy my field which is at Anathoth in the land of Benjamin, for the right of possession and redemption is yours; buy it for yourself' (Jer 32:8).

What would a practical person do with such an offer? I imagine Jeremiah shuffling and temporizing: 'You don't quite understand, Hanamel, I'm speaking in symbols and metaphors.

I'm talking of your interior life, the way our unconscious is in touch with God's purpose. Don't be such a literalist. And don't try to unload that worthless piece of property in Anathoth on me. Just because I am a preacher doesn't mean that I'm stupid. I know the value of a buck just as well as the next man.' Saying that, all the bystanders would have cheered – maybe Jeremiah wasn't such a goose as they had thought.

But that is not what happened. What is reported is that Jeremiah, deeply in touch with a reality that most of us ignore and without anxiety about what people thought about him, promptly bought the field. He weighed out seventeen shekels of silver, got the required witnesses, signed and sealed the deeds. He then instructed his friend Baruch to put the official deeds in a pottery jar to preserve them 'that they may last for a long time. For thus says the LORD of hosts, the God of Israel: Houses and fields and vineyards shall again be bought in this land' (Jer 32:14-15).

Jeremiah knew that buying that field looked impractical and foolish. It was against history, against reason, against public opinion. But he didn't buy the field on the advice of his broker, but by the leading of God. He was not planning a retirement cabin on the property; he was witnessing an involvement in the continuity of God's promises. All the same, he couldn't have helped *feeling* foolish – and so he prayed, recentering himself in God's word: 'Ah Lord GOD! It is thou who has made the heavens and the earth by thy great power and by thy outstretched arm! Nothing is too hard for thee.... Behold, the siege mounds have come up to the city to take it, and because of sword and famine and pestilence the city is given into the hands of the Chaldeans who are fighting against it.... Yet thou, O Lord GOD, hast said to me, "Buy the field for money and get witnesses" – though the city is given into the hands of the Chaldeans' (Jer 32:17, 24-25).

As he prays the confirmation is provided: 'Behold, I am the LORD, the God of all flesh; is anything too hard for me? . . . Just as I have brought all this great evil upon this people, so I will bring upon them all the good that I promise them. Fields shall be bought in this land' (Jer 32:27, 42-43).

LIVING IN HOPE

Buying that field in Anathoth was a deliberate act of hope. All acts of hope expose themselves to ridicule because they seem impractical, failing to conform to visible reality. But in fact they are the reality that is being constructed but is not yet visible. Hope commits us to actions that connect with God's promises.

What we call hoping is often only wishing. We want things we think are impossible, but we have better sense than to spend any money or commit our lives to them. Biblical hope, though, is an act – like buying a field in Anathoth. Hope acts on the conviction that God will complete the work that he has begun even when the appearances, especially when the appearances, oppose it.

William Stringfellow, who has extensive personal experience with 'Babylon', agrees with Jeremiah: 'Hope is reliance upon grace in the face of death: the issue is that of receiving life as a gift, not as a reward and not as a punishment; hope is living constantly, patiently, expectantly, resiliently, joyously in the efficacy of the word of God.'[6] Every person we meet must be drawn into that expectation. Every situation in which we find ourselves must be included in the kingdom that we are convinced God is bringing into being. Hope is buying into what we believe. We don't turn away in despair. We don't throw up our hands in disgust. We don't write this person off as incorrigible. We don't withdraw from a complex world that is too much for us.

It is, of course, far easier to languish in despair than to live in hope, for when we live in despair we don't have to do anything or risk anything. We can live lazily and shiftlessly with an untarnished reputation for practicality, current with the way things appear. It is fashionable to espouse the latest cynicism. If we live in hope, we go against the stream.

Getting Practical

I find it bordering on the incomprehensible when someone says, 'Well, the Bible is all well and good in its place, but after all, when it comes down to the nitty-gritty, we have to get practical, don't we? Jeremiah, after all, never had to meet a payroll.' People like that remind me of George Eliot's Mr Tulliver, who 'considered that church was one thing and common sense another, and he wanted nobody to tell *him* what common sense was.'[7]

But the great looming fact is this: In the flurry and panic of that day in Jerusalem, not at all unlike any randomly selected day in anyone's week, with the populace divided between a dull acquiescence to the inevitable and wild schemes for escape, the single practical act that stands out from the historical record is that Jeremiah bought a field in Anathoth for seventeen shekels. That act made the word of God visible, made a foothold of it for anyone who wanted to make a way out of chaotic despair into the ordered wholeness of salvation. Many made their way out.

We have to get practical. Really practical. The most practical thing we can do is hear what God says and act in appropriate response to it. 'Arguments are ineffectual unless supported by events.'[8] Hope-determined actions participate in the future that God is bringing into being. These acts are rarely spectacular. Usually they take place outside sacred settings. Almost never are they perceived to be significant by bystanders. It is not easy to act in hope because most of the immediate evidence is against it. As a result, we live in one of the most impractical societies the world has ever seen. If we are to live practically, we must frequently defy the impracticalities of our peers. It takes courage to act in hope. But it is the only practical action, for it is the only action that survives the decay of the moment and escapes the scrapheap of yesterday's fashion.

15

Concerning the Nations

The word of the LORD which came to Jeremiah the prophet concerning the nations. About Egypt . . . concerning the Philistines . . . concerning Moab . . . concerning the Ammonites . . . concerning Edom . . . concerning Damascus . . . concerning Kedar and the kingdoms of Hazor . . . concerning Elam . . . concerning Babylon . . .

JEREMIAH 46:1-2; 47:1; 48:1; 49:1, 7, 23, 28, 34; 50:1

Were the Gentiles to be abandoned to their own myth and to their own fate and regarded from the viewpoint of their own religion, they would constitute no part of God's creation; they would stand outside, a total negation. That however is not, and never has been the case. They are not abandoned to their myth or their fate, but are involved from the outset in God's mighty acts of creation; they belong to the earth which the Lord has rescued out of the primeval ocean; they are 'the ends' towards which God's purpose is directed, the ultimate reason for the work which he has begun on his mountain of Zion, centre of the earth.

AREND TH. VAN LEEUWEN[1]

I GREW UP IN A SMALL WESTERN TOWN, AN OUT-OF-THE-WAY place that was of no consequence to anyone other than the people who lived there. No one in my family or among my acquaintances traveled. We were isolated and out of touch with great events and important people. The exceptions were peripheral. I had an uncle, for instance, who had served in the infantry in World War I and had been wounded in France. I heard his war stories. Several of my maternal uncles and aunts had come from Norway when they were young, and there were stories of the farms and fjords that gave color to holiday gatherings. My paternal grandfather carried the accents of Sweden in his daily speech, but he never talked about the land of his birth. That was about it. It was not a propitious place in which to acquire a realistic conception of the world's size and complexity.

Yet by the time I was ten years old I had a lively acquaintance with the great diversity of languages and customs, climate and terrain that the earth comprises. I didn't acquire this through school studies, although I am sure that attempts were made there to give it to me. I got it in church. There were frequent visitors from remote corners of the world who came to our church. Often they were given a place to sleep in our home. Conversation at our breakfast table included references to the elephants of Africa and the temples of India, the lakes of Finland and the jungles of Brazil, the dances in Indonesia and the songs of the Congo. These people carried artifacts with them and photographs. They overflowed with stories. My childhood memories are vivid with the impressions that these missionaries made on me with their stories and zest, their passion and their prayers. I did not so much grow up in a small town as in a global village.

Among Christians my experience is typical. For biblical religion is aggressively internationalist. People who participate in the community of faith find themselves in a company of men and women who have a passion for crossing boundaries – linguistic, racial, geographic, cultural – in order to demonstrate that there is no spot on earth and no person on earth that is not included in the divine plan.

A Global Village

This quality is not recent. It is original. It has nothing to do with the human curiosity to explore or the technology of the scientific age. It is rooted in the nature of God and the reality of faith. The missionary, not the media, gave us the global village. At the time of his call Jeremiah was designated 'prophet to the nations' (Jer 1:5). The word *nations (goyim)* specifically refers to the nations across the border, the others, the foreigners. He was not appointed as prophet to the Hebrews nor installed as chaplain to the court of Judah.

The title 'prophet to the nations' is a deliberate rejection of any understanding of the life of faith that is identified with a single nation or a particular culture. The human task is to grow in conscious and healthy relationship with all reality, and God is the largest part of reality. If God is understood as being local, a tribal deity, he is misunderstood, and our lives are correspondingly reduced. Jeremiah battled against small-minded religion all his life. He attacked every tendency to make the temple into a cozy place. He worked strenuously and imaginatively to show the people that they were not the only people that God had dealings with, and that the life of faith necessarily involves us in a worldwide community that includes strange-appearing, strange-acting and strange-sounding people.

Biblical faith always has and always will have this global dimension to it. The promise to Abraham was that in him 'all the families of the earth shall bless themselves' (Gn 12:3). D. T. Niles documents the biblical base: 'The God who chose Israel out of the nations and gave it a distinctive history remained also and always the God of the nations too. The same God who brought Israel from Egypt, brought the Philistines from Caphtor and the Syrians from Kir (Am 9:7). He is concerned with the life of the nations for He is their God (Jer 20:4; Is 10:5).'[2] The final vision of the Apocalypse shows the nations walking in the light of God's glory and eating of the tree of life (Rv 21:24; 22:2). God is not geographically restricted to Palestine; his mercy extends to the far corners of the earth. Jeremiah is named prophet to the nations because the God he proclaims is God of the nations. Since God is not confined in the local, the life of faith cannot be restricted to the local.

Religions that we make up for ourselves always reduce reality to what we feel comfortable with, or what makes us comfortable. We love being insiders. We feel secure when we are with cronies who talk our language and sing our songs and don't rock the boat. It hardly matters that such a life is banal. It is *safe*. 'Why does man accept to live a trivial life?' asks Ernest Becker. His answer: 'Because of the danger of a full horizon of experience, of course.'[3] The danger is not to our humanity, but to our sense of running life on our own terms, managing people and things with ourselves at the center. The larger the world, the less of it we can subject to our own control. But that is a miserable ambition and a certain prescription for boredom. It is God's world and God rules it. Our wholeness comes from participating in what God is doing, not manipulating what we can manage. So the Bible continually protests all forms of isolationism. The great missionary statesman John R. Mott said, 'The missionary activities of the church are the circulation of its blood, which would lose its vital power if it never flowed to the extremities.'[4]

Prophet to the Nations

But Jeremiah never left Jerusalem and its immediate environs.[5] At the end of his life he was taken against his will to Egypt, but that hardly justifies the title 'prophet to the nations'. How did Jeremiah carry out his appointment to the nations without ever leaving Jerusalem? He did it by composing oracles for ten different nations: Egypt, Philistia, Moab, Ammon, Edom, Damascus, Kedar, Hazor, Elam and Babylon. The geographical range represented by these nations is immense, from Egypt in the west to Elam in the east, a distance of about 1500 miles, and from Damascus in the north to Edom in the south, a distance of 500 miles - 750,000 square miles. He may never have left Jerusalem, but he was mentally and spiritually a world traveler. These oracles are collected in chapters 46-51 in the book of Jeremiah.

With a single exception we do not know how these messages were delivered. The exception is the message to Babylon. Jeremiah enlisted Seriah to take it with him on an official diplomatic journey and commissioned him to read it to the Babylonians. He also instructed him in its dramatic disposition. When he had completed reading it, Seriah was to take a stone and tie it to the scroll, throw it into the middle of the River Euphrates that flowed alongside Babylon and announce: 'Thus shall Babylon sink, to rise no more, because of the evil that I am bringing upon her' (Jer 51:64). The *way* the message was delivered was as important as *that* it was delivered.

For the other nations we have no information. Would those messages have been delivered similarly, by getting a traveling merchant or soldier or government official to take it? The conjecture is by no means implausible. But if we don't know how they were delivered, we do know that the messages were carefully and accurately prepared.

Jeremiah's messages to the ten nations were prepared with the same seriousness as the messages that he delivered personally in Jerusalem. Jeremiah preached with great power and poetic craft. He never spoke in clichés or slogans. He treated language with immense respect. Words had a holy quality; they were precious gifts treated with reverence and care. Marianne Moore wrote of the need for humility, concentration and gusto in the use of words. Humility she describes as the necessary armor. By concentration she means the intensity that makes for clear language; for her, gusto is the spontaneity which humility and skill make possible.[6] These qualities are evident in everything we have from Jeremiah. The messages to the nations exhibit the same exuberant yet controlled strength. John Bright values these messages as 'some of the finest poetry in the entire prophetic canon.'[7] They are not second-level works tossed off in a slovenly manner because they are for despised foreigners.

Jeremiah took as much care in proclaiming God's word to people he would never see as he did in addressing the people he grew up with and lived with. An examination of the messages shows that he cared enough about the ten nations to acquire thorough and detailed knowledge about them. We expect Jeremiah to take *God* seriously and to speak God's word with care, but it is a surprise to find that he has painstakingly studied these *peoples* that mean nothing to him personally. All of these oracles show an extraordinary knowledge of the geography, the history and the politics of these nations. He was not interested in them in general but in particular. He bothered to find out the details of their lives. He spoke God's word in relation to the actual conditions of their existence. This feature makes our understanding of the messages more difficult, for many of the geographical features and political allusions can no longer be determined. But every difficulty we encounter in reading the text represents a local detail in which the Philistine and the Babylonian recognized that they were being addressed with attentive and personal seriousness. The nations were not lumped together as 'pagans' or 'lost sinners' and then assaulted with stereotyped formulas.

I once knew a man who had come to this country after World War II as a displaced person. He had been a skilled cabinetmaker in his home country but after the war had to settle for a job as sexton in a church. Not long after I became a pastor in that same church I also became a father. Toys began to accumulate around the house. Knowing of his dexterity with tools and lumber, I asked Gus if he would throw together a toy box for me when he had a few minutes. I wanted a storage bin for the toys; I knew Gus could do it in an hour or so. Weeks later he presented our family with a carefully designed and skillfully crafted toy box. My casual request had not been treated casually. All I had wanted was a box; what I got was a piece of furniture. I was pleased, but also embarrassed. I was embarrassed because what I thought would be done in an off hour had taken many hours of work. I expressed my embarrassment. I laced my gratitude with apologies. His wife reproached me: 'But you must understand that Gus is a cabinetmaker. He could never, as you say, "throw" a box together. His pride would not permit it.' That toy box has been in our family for over twenty years now and rebukes me whenever I am tempted to do hasty or shoddy work of any kind.

In a similar way Jeremiah was a prophet. It didn't matter who he was speaking to, whether they were essential to his everyday life or a passing acquaintance, people he would live with for his entire life or someone he would never see: he was a prophet. He couldn't 'throw' an oracle together, 'toss off' a sermon. His commitment would not permit it. He took the ten nations, although they were a minor part of his everyday ministry, as seriously as he took his own nation.

Warning and Judgment

The content of the messages that Jeremiah preached to the nations was virtually the same as that preached to his own people: warning and judgment that anticipates salvation. Egypt is promised judgment: 'Prepare yourselves baggage for exile, O inhabitants of Egypt! For Memphis shall become a waste, a ruin, without inhabitant' (Jer 46:19). She is also promised salvation: 'Afterward Egypt shall be inhabited as in the days of old, says the LORD' (Jer 46:26).

Moab is lamented and mourned: 'The calamity of Moab is near at hand and his affliction hastens apace. Bemoan him, all you who are round about him, and all who know his name; say, "How the mighty scepter is broken, the glorious staff"' (Jer 48:16-17). But the last word is 'Yet I will restore the fortunes of Moab in the latter days, says the LORD' (Jer 48:47).

The Ammonites are addressed: 'Gird yourselves with sackcloth, lament, and run to and fro among the hedges! For Milcom [their god] shall go into exile, with his priests and his princes' (Jer 49:3). Still, the final word is 'But afterward I will restore the fortunes of the Ammonites, says the LORD' (Jer 49:6).

Elam is warned: 'I will break the bow of Elam, the mainstay of their might; and I will bring upon Elam the four winds from the four quarters of heaven; and I will scatter them to all those winds' (Jer 49:35-36). But the characteristic last word is 'But in the latter days I will restore the fortunes of Elam, says the LORD' (Jer 49:39).

The bulk of the material is devoted to judgment. The anticipation of salvation is, in each instance, a single line. But those spare lines prevent the messages from being understood as the vengeful anger of an outsider crying doom. The intimations of hope are not explicit in all the messages, but neither are they always expressed in messages to Israel. The fact that they are there at all shows that judgment is in the service of salvation, the salvation of the nations as well as of Israel. There is not one message for the insider and another for the outsider. The biblical message is the same for Jew and Gentile. As Paul puts it, 'Are we Jews any better off? No, not at all; for I have already charged that all men, both Jews and Greeks, are under the power of sin' (Rom 3:9).

CONCERNING THE NATIONS

Jeremiah wrote concerning the nations: specifically named, attentively described, seriously addressed. What anthropologists call ethnocentricity – the unthinking assumption that one's own people are the best while other people, especially those who constitute a threat, are considered inferior – he clearly rejected. Kenneth Cragg, reflecting on this reality and meditating on its implications through the centuries of faith experience, wrote: 'The Gospel as such has no native country. He who goes out humbly with Christ in the world of all races will perpetually discover the multiple, but constant, relevance of what he takes. It takes a whole world to understand a whole Christ.... Those who take are not vulgarly universalizing their own culture: they are conveying that by the apprehension of which both they and their hearers learn. If the claims of the Gospel are valid it could not be otherwise.'[8]

Reaching out is an act of wholeness, not only for others but for us: 'It takes a whole world to understand a whole Christ.' Crossing the boundaries and exploring the horizons (whether imaginatively like Jeremiah or bodily like Seriah) demonstrates God's universal love, but it also develops our own deepest health. For we cannot be whole enclosed in our own habits, even if they are pious habits. We cannot grow to maturity confined within our own coterie, even if it is a very orthodox coterie. We cannot grow an oak tree in a barrel; it needs acres of earth under it and oceans of sky above it. Neither can we grow a human being in a narrow sect, a ghettoized religion. The larger the world we live in, the larger our lives develop in response. At least one of the reasons for Jeremiah's heroic stature is his concern for the Elamites. We cannot be whole human beings if we cut ourselves off from the environment which God created and in which he is working. People of faith live in a far larger reality than people without faith. 'God so loved the *world.*'

We often betray this reality. We huddle and retreat. We ignore and even despise outsiders. We collect a few friends who look alike and think alike. We reject any suggestion that we transcend biological comforts and psychological securities. We barricade ourselves from visions that expose our prejudices, from people that challenge our narcissism.

André and Pierre-Emmanuel Lacocque, in a brilliant weaving of biblical, theological and psychological material, have called this the 'Jonah complex' – the clash between what I feel good about in myself and what I am under commission to do for God, the tension between coziness and character.[9] Jonah was torn between his desire for an undisturbed enjoyment of his personal potential and accumulated possessions, and the fulfillment of a vocation that smashed his preconceptions and interrupted his comfortable pursuit of happiness.

Meanwhile there is Jeremiah, and the people like him who keep showing up in our homes and communities and churches, who go beyond the boundaries of what is safe and comfortable, learn new languages, discover alien cultures, brave hostility and misunderstanding, and who have the scars and tell the stories that prove that the life of faith can be lived in every place and among all peoples – *must* be lived in every place, among all peoples.

16

In the Land of Egypt They Shall Fall

Hear the word of the L*ORD*, *O remnant of Judah. Thus says the* L*ORD of hosts, the God of Israel: If you set your faces to enter Egypt and go to live there, then the sword which you fear shall overtake you there in the land of Egypt; and the famine of which you are afraid shall follow hard after you to Egypt; and there you shall die.*

So Johanan the son of Kareah and all the commanders of the forces and all the people did not obey the voice of the L*ORD*, *to remain in the land of Judah. But Johanan the son of Kareah and all the commanders of the forces took all the remnant of Judah who had returned to live in the land of Judah from all the nations to which they had been driven – the men, the women, the children, the princesses, and every person whom Nebuzaradan the captain of the guard had left with Gedaliah the son of Ahikam, son of Shaphan; also Jeremiah the prophet and Baruch the son of Neriah. And they came into the land of Egypt, for they did not obey the voice of the* L*ORD*.

Therefore thus says the L*ORD of hosts, the God of Israel: Behold, I will set my face against you for evil, to cut off all Judah. I will take the remnant of Judah who have set their faces* *to come to the land of Egypt to live, and they shall all be consumed; in the land of Egypt they shall fall.*

JEREMIAH 42:15-16; 43:4-7; 44:11-12

Nothing could be farther from the truth than the facile belief that God only manifests Himself in progress, in the improvement of standards of living, in the spread of medicine and the reform of abuses, in the diffusion of organized Christianity. The reaction from this type of theistic meliorism, which a few years ago had almost completely supplanted the faith of Moses, and Elijah, and Jesus among modern Christians, both Protestant and Catholic, is now sweeping multitudes from their religious moorings. Real spiritual progress can only be achieved through catastrophe and suffering, reaching new levels after the profound catharsis which accompanies major upheavals. Every such period of mental and physical agony, while the old is being swept away and the new is still unborn, yields different social patterns and deeper spiritual insights.

WILLIAM FOXWELL ALBRIGHT[1]

EVERY ONCE IN A WHILE, WHEN I GET TIRED OF LIVING BY faith, I drive twenty-five miles southwest to Memorial Stadium in Baltimore and watch the Orioles play baseball. For a couple of hours I am in a world that is defined by exactly measured lines and precise, geometric patterns. Every motion on the playing field is graceful and poised. Sloppy behavior is not tolerated. Complex physical feats are carried out with immense skill. Errors are instantly detected and their consequences immediately experienced. Rule infractions are punished directly. Unruly conduct is banished. The person who refuses to play by the rules is ejected. Outstanding performance is recognized and applauded on the spot. While the game is being played, people of widely divergent temperaments, moral values, religious commitments, and cultural backgrounds agree on a goal and the means for pursuing it. When the game is over, everyone knows who won and who lost. It is a world from which all uncertainty is banished, a world in which everything is clear and obvious. Afterward the entire experience is summarized in the starkly unambiguous vocabulary of numbers, exact to the third decimal point.

The world to which I return when the game is over contains all the elements that were visible in the stadium – elegance and sloppiness, grace and unruliness, victory and defeat, diversity and unity, reward and punishment, boundary and risk, indolence and excellence – but with a significant difference instead of being sharply distinguished they are hopelessly muddled. What is going on at any particular time is almost never exactly clear. None of the lines are precise. The boundaries are not clear. Goals are not agreed upon. Means are in constant dispute. When I leave the world of brightly lighted geometric patterns, I pick my way through inkblots, trying to discern the significance of the shapes with all the help from Rorschach that I can get. My digital wristwatch, for all its technological accuracy, never tells me whether I am at the beginning or in the middle or near the end of an experience. At the end of the day – or the week, or the year – there is no agreement on who has won and who has lost.

The Egyptian Alternative

When the Israelites got tired of living by faith, they went 250 miles southwest to Egypt where everything was clear and precise. They took Jeremiah with them. All his life Jeremiah had preached a faith that was intensely personal; Egypt organized a religion that was impersonally bureaucratic. It is the supreme irony of Jeremiah's life that it ended in Egypt, the place that represented everything that he abhorred.

It was not the first time that Israel had done this. The Egyptian alternative to faith asserted itself over and over again. When Abraham, father of all who live by faith, got tired of living by faith he went to Egypt (Gn 12:10-20). He hoped to find security there, but instead he was plunged into deceit and compromise. Abraham's Egyptian experiment was a near disaster for the development of faith in which he was the God-selected pioneer.

At the time of the Exodus, after the Hebrews had been delivered out of Egyptian bondage and were being trained to live by faith in the desert, the pull back to Egypt was persistent. True, they had been slaves there, but at least they were secure. They knew what to expect. The pillar of the cloud was a flimsy successor to the solid, fixed pyramids.

Later, when the monarchy was at its apogee, Solomon imported Egyptian certainties into the life of faith by making a marriage alliance with the Egyptian Pharaoh's daughter (1 Kgs 9:16). It must have seemed like a marvelous idea at the time – to live by faith in the Promised Land but to build up a nest egg of Egyptian security on the side. The Egyptian marriage alliance was the first of many. Solomon, once having compromised the life of faith, found himself hopelessly entangled in attempts to secure his kingdom on all sides by marrying into all the surrounding kingdoms (1 Kgs 11:1-8).

And so it was not without precedent that Israel, in the enormous confusion and muddle following the fall of Jerusalem in 586 B.C., would succumb to the age-old attraction of Egypt.

There is nothing more difficult than to live spontaneously, hopefully, virtuously – by faith. And there was never a time when the external conditions were less conducive to living by faith than in those devastating and bewildering days following the Babylonian invasion. The temple, focus for worship for half a millennium, was in rubble. The ritual, rich in allusion and meaning, was wiped out. The priestly voices, who had spoken in reassuring tones for decades, were silent. Out of this traumatic dislocation Jeremiah told the people to set aside their fears and begin a new life of faith.

It was easier to go to Egypt. So they went to Egypt. In Egypt there were no uncertainties, no loose ends, no ambiguity. Every detail in this life and the next was accounted for in Egypt.

Egypt was clear geographically. The great Nile River, a line of green life across the sere desert, divided Egypt. Along the river was life; apart from the river was death. There were no mountainous mysteries, no surprising valleys, no unexpected bursts of streams. There was simply this great river flowing in measured pace, predictable in its seasonal rhythms. All life, animal and vegetable, was ordered in relation to the river.

Egypt was clear architecturally. The pyramids and temples stood out from the landscape in precise lines. The mathematical exactitude of their construction is a marvel still. Nothing was left unexpressed in those monuments looming up from the desert. The pyramids arranged and plotted the uncertainties of death. The statuary and structures of the temples resolved the ambiguities of life. Under the cloudless Egyptian sky and on the featureless Egyptian sand, quarried and carved forms structured reality with such megalomaniac arrogance that all anxiety was banished. If there were ever doubts about the significance of an enterprise, they were chased off by the bully expedient of making it bigger.

Egypt was clear theologically. The unseen was translated into the seen. All gods were made into images. Everything that might have been more than human was reduced to what was less than human: the cat, the hawk, the hyena, the bull, the ibis were the god-images of the Egyptians. Every image was stylized, and in those stylized images all wonder was eliminated. Spontaneity was unheard of. It was a religion of absolute control. All reality was rendered in the flat surface of stone, in the anonymous language of number.

Egypt was clear socially. Everyone's place was defined hierarchically. The king was at the apex and the slave-serf at the base, with all others ranged in between. The diminishment of people was compensated for by the clarity of knowing where they stood. If there was less honor, there was also less responsibility. If there was less to hope for, there was also less to have to deal with.

Egypt was the Memorial Stadium of the ancient world: clean boundaries, set rules, a clear separation between the players (the royal house) and the spectators (everyone else), all the gods in picture form so that everyone knew who was who (you can't tell the players without a program), and, above all, numbers – everything accounted for by geometry, trigonometry, arithmetic. Straight lines. Sharp angles. Statistics.

The Clarities of Faith

Not that there are no clarities in the life of faith. There are vast, soaring harmonies; deep, satisfying meanings; rich, textured experiences. But these clarities develop from within. They cannot be imposed from without. They cannot be hurried. It is not a matter of hurriedly arranging 'dead things into a dead mosaic, but of living forces into a great equilibrium.'[2] The clarities of faith are organic and personal, not mechanical and institutional. Faith *invades* the muddle; it does not eliminate it. Peace develops in the midst of chaos. Harmony is achieved slowly, quietly, unobtrusively – like the effects of salt and light. Such clarities result from a courageous commitment to God, not from controlling or being controlled by others. Such clarities come from adventuring deep into the mysteries of God's will and love, not by cautiously managing and moralizing in ways that minimize risk and guarantee self-importance.

These clarities can only be experienced in acts of faith and only recognized with the eyes of faith. Jeremiah's life was brilliantly supplied with such clarities, but they were always surrounded by hopeless disarray. Sometimes devout and sometimes despairing, Jeremiah doubted himself and God. But these internal agonies never seemed to have interfered with his vocation and his commitment. He argued with God but he did not abandon him. He was clear at the center: it was with God that he had to do. He was committed to the covenant of God. He was unwavering in his understanding of morality. He was steady in his hope in God's mercy. But just because he was sure of God did not mean that he was always sure of himself. Nor did the world around him ever become clear. The world remained a muddle – and it will.

There is a moment in this last chapter of Jeremiah's life when it looks as if the muddle will be banished. The moment occurs in the time after the fall of Jerusalem and just before the escape to Egypt. The environment is the blackest it has ever been. Then this single, luminous moment in Jeremiah's life is framed. Every detail of the life of faith is etched clearly against the dark disorder of the sin-ruined Jerusalem streets and the false-front neatness of the Egyptian alternative.

The city had fallen to the Babylonians as Jeremiah had long warned that it would. All the people were rounded up and herded into exile as Jeremiah had predicted. The lies of the false prophets and priests were mercilessly exposed. The integrity of Jeremiah's preaching was confirmed. Jeremiah was put into chains along with the rest. A few of the poorest people, seen as weak and worthless, didn't even qualify as prisoners and were left behind. The forced-march journey across the 700 miles of hot plains to Babylon was begun. They were five miles out of the city when the Babylonian captain Nebuzaradan got word from his king to stop the march and give Jeremiah the choice of whether to go or stay.

Imagine: Jeremiah singled out from that crowd with a personal message from the world-conquering King Nebuchadnezzar. In Jerusalem Jeremiah had been laughed at in the streets, thrown into a cistern to die, taunted in the courtyard prison, put in the stocks and ridiculed. Now, half a day into the long hard trip into exile, the action is suddenly arrested, Jeremiah is singled out, his chains are cut off him, and Nebuzaradan presents him with a choice. He can go to Babylon with the promise of special treatment – no chains, no deprivation, protective custody (so that he will never again have to endure the abuse of his fellow citizens) and a special allowance from the King. Or he can stay in Jerusalem, the city he has lived in and labored for all his life. A governor has just been appointed who has been Jeremiah's good, lifelong friend (Gedeliah, son of Shaphan). Jeremiah is welcome, if he chooses, to stay with him and be part of the tiny remnant community.

Life in Jerusalem would be starting over: in a brutal environment with the scantiest of resources, human and material, in the midst of a wrecked city with a few poor people who weren't even worth being made prisoners! Not, it would seem, a very happy prospect at age sixty-five.

Life in Babylon would be an easy retirement: honored by the Babylonian court, protected by a Babylonian bodyguard, living on a Babylonian pension. Jeremiah was ready for retirement and he deserved it. After a lifetime of ridicule and rejection, hungry for recognition, he was offered an honorary degree by the most powerful king in the world. This prophet, who was either ignored or laughed at by his own countrymen, was held in awe and respect by the Babylonians.

But Jeremiah wasn't ready for retirement. He wasn't tired of living by faith. He was used to starting over with nothing. He had been doing it for a long time. He had long since quit calculating his chances by counting his resources; his habit was to expect God's grace, 'new every morning'. His decision was unhesitating. He chose to stay in Jerusalem. He chose the rubble, the outcasts, the poor – the remnant out of whom he believed that God would build a people to his glory.

In judged Jerusalem it was impossible to confuse material prosperity with God's blessing. It was impossible to confuse social status with God's favor. It was impossible to confuse national pride with God's glory. It was impossible to confuse rituals of religion with God's presence. The clutter of possessions was gone; the trappings of status were gone; the pride of nation was gone; the splendor of religion was gone. And God was present. All the cultural and political and religious and social assumptions and presuppositions that interfered with the clear hearing of God's word in Jeremiah's preaching were taken away. Conditions had never been better for developing a mature community of faith. Out of the emptiness God would make a new creation.

Jeremiah's choice that day at Rama is the characteristic action of his life. He chose to be where God commanded, at the center of God's action, at the place of God's promise, in the midst of God's salvation in defiance of stereotyped conventions and popular opinions and self-aggrandizing flatteries. Jeremiah chose to live by faith. Living by faith does not mean living with applause; living by faith does not mean playing on the winning team; living by faith demands readiness to live by what cannot be seen or controlled or predicted. 'If we fix our eyes,' wrote Karl Barth, 'upon the place where the course of the world reaches its lowest point, where its vanity is unmistakable, where its groanings are most bitter and the divine incognito most impenetrable, we shall encounter there – Jesus Christ. . . . The transformation of all things occurs where the riddle of human life reaches its culminating point. The hope of His glory emerges for us when nothing but the existentiality of God remains, and He becomes to us the veritable and living God. He, whom we can apprehend only as against us, stands there – for us.'[3]

The abyss of obscurity and contradiction and paradox in Jeremiah's life is resolved in this moment. All the skeptical question marks that had been raised over Jeremiah throughout his life – was he a true or false prophet? was he a patriot or a traitor? was he clear-sighted or deluded? was he futile or effective? – are turned into affirmative exclamation marks. The truth of his preaching is vindicated. The integrity of his life is proved. His commitment to God's covenant is validated. Finally, a happy ending!

Not the End

Except that it is not the end. The perfectly shaped moment disintegrates into chaos. The dramatic resolution collapses into a moral muddle.

No sooner had Gedeliah been installed as governor and Jeremiah gone to work developing the life of the people of God than a terrorist outlaw, Ishmael, murdered governor

Gedeliah, slaughtered everyone in the vicinity and threw their corpses into a giant cistern. A real bloodbath. His action was countered by one Johanan who rallied the survivors, chased Ishmael out of the country and set about restoring order again.

The first and best thing that Johanan did was to ask Jeremiah to pray for God's guidance. Jeremiah prayed. God gave direction consistent with Jeremiah's previous decision: the people were to stay in Jerusalem. They were to be the remnant people out of whom God would develop his holy nation. They were, in other words, to live by faith. 'If you will remain in this land, then I will build you up and not pull you down; I will plant you, and not pluck you up. . . . I will grant you mercy' (Jer 42:10, 12).

Johanan and the people respected Jeremiah enough to ask for his prayers, but they didn't trust God enough to follow his counsel. They were tired of living by faith. They decided to go to Egypt. Fear was one motive. They feared Babylonian reprisal for Ishmael's terrorist assassination. But the big reason was a refusal to live by faith. They didn't want the risk and hazard of depending on an invisible God. They wanted the security and stability of a solid economy. They didn't want the hard work of rebuilding a life of faith in God. They wanted the soft life that they thought awaited them in Egypt: 'No, we will go to the land of Egypt, where we shall not see war, or hear the sound of the trumpet, or be hungry for bread, and we will dwell there' (Jer 42:14). They were looking for an easy way out.

Far too many people choose to live in Egypt instead of by faith. They go to religion the way I go to a baseball game – to escape the muddle, to have everything clear, to find a good seat from which they can see the whole scene at a glance, evaluate everyone's performance easily and see people get what they deserve. Moral box scores are carefully penciled in. Statistics are obsessively kept. Many religious meetings are designed to meet just such desires. The world is reduced to what can be organized and regulated; every person is clearly labeled as being on your side or on the other side; there is never any doubt about what is good and what is bad.

The only problem with such 'Egyptian' religion is that the clarity lasts only as long as the meeting. It is not a deepening of reality but a vacation from it. During that protected time and space, heroic performances are applauded and villains booed. There is a clear-cut opposition to hate. But back at work, at play, at home, the labels don't stick. Life outside the meeting is then resented as being hopelessly contaminated. It is understandable that people who embrace this kind of religious life go to as many meetings as possible in order to have the experience of clear and controlled order as frequently as possible.

Neither Shot nor Married

Flannery O'Connor once remarked that she had an aunt who thought that nothing happened in a story unless somebody got married or shot at the end of it.[4] But life seldom provides such definitive endings. As a consequence, the best stories, the stories that show us our true condition by immersing us in reality, don't provide them either. Life is ambiguous. There are loose ends. It takes maturity to live with the ambiguity and the chaos, the absurdity and the untidiness. If we refuse to live with it, we exclude something, and what we exclude may very well be the essential and dear – the hazards of faith, the mysteries of God.

Jeremiah ends inconclusively. We want to know the end, but there is no end. The last scene of Jeremiah's life shows him, as he had spent so much of his life, preaching God's word to a contemptuous people (Jer 44). We want to know that he was finally successful so that, if we live well and courageously, we also will be successful. Or we want to know that he was finally unsuccessful so that, since a life of faith and integrity doesn't pay off, we can get on with finding another means by which to live. We get neither in Jeremiah. He doesn't get married and he doesn't get shot.[5] In Egypt, the place he doesn't want to be, with people who treat him badly, he continues determinedly faithful, magnificently courageous, heartlessly rejected – a towering life terrifically lived.

Notes

CHAPTER 1

[1] William McNamara, *The Human Adventure* (Garden City, NY: Image Books, Doubleday, 1976), p. 9; and *Mystical Passion* (New York: Paulist Press, 1977), p. 3.

[2] Tom Howard, *Chance or Dance* (Carol Stream, IL: Harold Shaw Publishers, 1972), p. 104.

[3] Cleanth Brooks, *The Hidden God* (New Haven: Yale University Press, 1963), p. 4.

[4] 'Maslow wrote in 1968: "the only way we can ever know what is right for us is that it feels better subjectively than any alternative"; and again: "what tastes good is also, in the growth sense, 'better' for us." No position has been more damaging to modern society. The terms "feel" and "subjectivity" as criteria for "growth" are especially deceiving. It is simply contrary to truth that one "grows" by choosing "what tastes good." In many cases the opposite is true. If the Jew Abraham Maslow were right in this, there would have been no Israel in human history.' André Lacocque and Pierre-Emmanuel Lacocque, *The Jonah Complex* (Atlanta: John Knox Press, 1981), p. 106.

[5] 'The book of Jeremiah does not so much teach religious truths as present a religious personality. Prophecy had already taught its truths, its last effort was to reveal itself in a life.' A. B. Davidson, quoted in John Skinner, *Prophecy and Religion* (London: Cambridge University Press, 1963), p. 16.

[6] James Bentley, 'Vitezslav Gardavsky, Atheist and Martyr,' *The Expository Times,* June 1980, pp. 276-77.

[7] Erwin Chargaff, *Heraclitean Fire* (New York: The Rockefeller University Press, 1978), p. 122.

CHAPTER 2

[1] Eugen Rosenstock-Huessy, *Speech and Reality* (Norwich, VT: Argo Books, 1970), p. 167.

[2] Eugen Rosenstock-Huessy, *I Am an Impure Thinker* (Norwich, VT: Argo Books, 1970), pp. 41-42.

[3] Quoted by Skinner, *Prophecy and Religion,* p. 350.

[4] Rosenstock-Huessy, *I Am an Impure Thinker,* p. 66.

[5] Thomas Merton, *The New Man* (New York: Mentor-Omega Books, 1961), p. 120.

[6] George Herbert, *The Country Parson* (New York: Paulist Press, 1981), p. 85.

[7] William Faulkner, *The Town* (New York: Random House, 1957), p. 112ff.

[8] I have paraphrased. The verbatim question and answer are: 'When did you first realize that you wanted to be a poet?' 'I've thought about that and sort of reversed it. My question is "when did other people give up the idea of being a poet?" You know, when we were kids we make up things, we write, and for me the puzzle is not that some people are writing, the real question is why did the other people stop?' William Stafford, *Writing the Australian Crawl* (Ann Arbor: University of Michigan Press, 1978), p. 86.

[9] Stephen Spender, 'What I expected was,' in *The New Oxford Book of English Verse 1250-1950,* ed. Helen Gardner (New York: Oxford University Press, 1972), p. 930.

Chapter 3

[1] Pierre Teilhard de Chardin, *The Divine Milieu* (New York: Harper and Bros., 1960), pp. 48-49.

[2] 'Men are still men, and not keyboards of pianos over which the hands of Nature may play at their own sweet will.' Fyodor Dostoyevsky, *Letters from the Underworld* (New York: E. P. Dutton & Co., 1957), p. 36.

[3] Quoted by E. F. Schumacher, *A Guide for the Perplexed* (New York: Perennial Library, Harper & Row, 1977), p. 6.

Chapter 4

[1] J. R. R. Tolkien, *The Fellowship of the Ring* (Boston: Houghton Mifflin, 1965), p. 70.

[2] Schumacher, *A Guide for the Perplexed,* p. 38.

[3] William Barrett, *Irrational Man* (Garden City, NY: Doubleday Anchor Books, 1962), p. 3.

[4] W. H. Auden, 'Reflections in a Forest,' *Homage to Clio* (New York: Random House, 1960), p. 8.

[5] Blaise Pascal, *Pensées* (New York: The Modern Library, Random House, 1941), p. 273.

[6] Quoted by Maisie Ward, *Gilbert Keith Chesterton* (Baltimore: Penguin Books, 1958), p. 114.

[7] That is not to say that everybody admitted it. The false prophets throughout Jeremiah's lifetime reassured the people that everything would be all right. And the kings continued to arrange political alliances to stave off disaster. But the shrillness of the positive-thinking preaching and the desperation in the treaty making betrayed the knowledge that doomsday was threatening.

CHAPTER 5

[1] Thomas à Kempis, *The Imitation of Christ,* translated by Ronald Knox and Michael Oakley (New York: Sheed and Ward, 1959), pp. 76-77.

[2] Also see John Bright, *The Kingdom of God* (Nashville: Abingdon Press, 1953), p. 100.

[3] William Meredith, 'Chinese Banyan' quoted in Richard Howard, *Alone with America* (New York: Atheneum, 1969), p. 324.

[4] John Bright, *A History of Israel* (Philadelphia: Westminster Press, 1959), p. 299.

[5] Ibid., p. 297.

[6] Quoted by John W. Gardner, *Self-Renewal* (New York: Harper & Row, 1963), p. 96.

CHAPTER 6

[1] R. P. Blackmur, *The Lion and the Honeycomb* (New York: Harcourt, Brace & World, 1955), pp. 179-80.

[2] The line is not quite as clear as I have drawn it. Kathleen Kenyon's excavations of Jericho have shown the existence of city life previous to the invention of pottery – 'pre-pottery neolithic'. But granted Jericho and two or three other excavated sites as exceptions, the generalization still holds. See Kathleen Kenyon, *Digging Up Jericho* (London: Ernest Benn Ltd., 1957).

[3] George Herbert, 'The Bag,' *The Temple* (New York: Paulist Press, 1981), p. 276.

[4] John Bright, *Jeremiah* (Garden City, NY: Doubleday, 1965), p. 125.

CHAPTER 7

[1] Malcolm Muggeridge, *A Twentieth Century Testimony* (Nashville: Thomas Nelson, 1978), p. 72.

[2] F. O. Matthiessen, *American Renaissance* (New York: Oxford University Press, 1968), p. 182.

[3] Flannery O'Connor, *The Habit of Being*, Letters edited by Sally Fitzgerald (New York: Farrar, Straus & Giroux, 1979), p. 81.

[4] I have let my imagination roam rather freely in comparing and contrasting Pashhur and Jeremiah. Some of this comes from a textual detail that suggests that Pashhur is to be seen as a parody of Jeremiah – Pashhur the corruption of a life that Jeremiah maintains in integrity. Jeremiah was appointed as prophet to the nations ('See, I have set you this day over nations' – Jer 1:10). The verb 'I have set you' is *paqad*. The noun form of that verb is *paqid*, and appointed officer. Pashhur is such an appointee, a *paqid* ('officer in the house of the LORD' – Jer 20:1). So both men live out the role of *paqid*, Jeremiah as God's prophet, Pashhur as the temple's overseer. Pashhur, in irony, is exaggerated as *chief* appointee, *paqid nagid*. By using the same root word *(pqd)* in relation to their respective appointments, and describing the clash between them as they lived out their similar vocations in such very different ways, the text invites, it seems to me, this kind of reflection.

CHAPTER 8

[1] Therese of Lisieux, *Autobiography of a Saint*, trans. Ronald Knox (London: Fontana Books, Collins, 1960), p. 94.

[2] The passages are Jeremiah 8:18-9:3; 11:18-23; 12:1-6; 15:10-12, 15-21; 17:14-18; 18:18-23; 20:7-18.

[3] 'We have a record of one attempt to discover the operations of sanctity which is as diverting to us as it was frustrating to the watcher. The subject under investigation was Francis de Sales, and his arrogantly curious observer was Jean Pierre Camus, Bishop of Belley. There seems to have been no planned mischief in the trick the Bishop used, but there was certainly bad taste. For what he did was drill a hole in the wall of his bedroom in the episcopal residence so that he could spy on his host when Francis thought himself alone.... And what did Camus discover? That he crept out of bed early and quietly in the mornings so as not to wake his servant. That he prayed, wrote, answered his letters, read his office, slept, and prayed again.' Phyllis McGinley, *Saint-Watching* (New York: The Viking Press, 1969), pp. 17-18.

[4] Bright, *Jeremiah*, p. 110.

[5] John A. Thompson, *The Book of Jeremiah* (Grand Rapids: Eerdmans, 1980), p. 459.

[6] Ibid., p. 398.

[7] Ibid.

[8] Walter Lippmann, *A Preface to Morals* (New York: MacMillan, 1929), p. 56.

Chapter 9

[1] Baron Friedrich von Hügel, *Selected Letters 1896-1924,* edited by Bernard Holland (New York: E. P. Dutton, 1933), pp. 305, 266.

[2] Brown, Driver, Briggs, *Hebrew and English Lexicon of the Old Testament* (Oxford: Clarendon Press, 1957), p. 1014.

[3] Ibid.

[4] John Fowles, *The Ebony Tower* (Boston: Little, Brown & Co., 1974), p. 147.

[5] G. K. Chesterton, quoted in Ward, *Gilbert Keith Chesterton,* p. 397.

[6] Garry Wills, 'Hurrah for Politicians,' *Harper's Magazine,* September 1975, p. 53.

Chapter 10

[1] Abraham Heschel, *God in Search of Man* (New York: Farrar, Straus and Giroux, 1955), p. 244.

[2] Quoted by George Steiner, *Language and Silence* (New York: Atheneum, 1970), p. 67.

[3] George Adam Smith, *Jeremiah* (London: Hodder and Stoughton, 1923), p. 146.

[4] In S. R. Driver's list of the characteristic words and expressions in Deuteronomy, the best and most complete list that has been made, *love* heads the list. See *A Critical and Exegetical Commentary on Deuteronomy* (New York: Charles Scribner's Sons, 1895), pp. lxxviii-lxxxiv.

[5] André and Pierre-Emmanuel Lacocque, *The Jonah Complex,* p. 113.

[6] Charles Williams, *The Descent of the Dove* (New York: Meridian Books, 1956), p. 83.

[7] Heschel, *God in Search of Man,* p. 237.

[8] Smith, *Jeremiah,* p. 41.

[9] King Jehoiakim's antipathy to Jeremiah is understandable. Early in the king's reign Jeremiah had dressed him down for thinking that he was a king just because he spent money like a king ('Do you think you are a king because you compete in cedar?'). He compared him unfavorably with his father, Josiah, who had administered justice in the land and honored God, whereas the son was rapacious and plundering. He predicted a donkey's death for him on the city's garbage dump: 'With the burial of an ass he shall be buried, dragged and cast forth beyond the gates of

Jerusalem' (Jer 22:11-19). With such rebukes ringing in his ears it is no wonder that the king had forbidden Jeremiah to speak in public.

[10] R. E. C. Browne, *The Ministry of the Word* (Philadelphia: Fortress Press, 1976), p. 23.

[11] This scroll is probably chapters 1-25, the first step in the composition of the book of Jeremiah. The complete book was the result of a long and intricate process that would include Baruch's memoirs. The formation was extremely complex. A good description of the elements in the process can be found in Thompson, *The Book of Jeremiah,* pp. 56-59.

Chapter 11

[1] Jacques Maritain, *The Peasant of the Garonne* (New York: Holt, Rinehart and Winston, 1968), p. 172.

[2] Søren Kierkegaard insisted 'the crowd is untruth'. He explored the significance of this assertion in all of his writings. For instance: 'There is a view of life which conceives that where the crowd is, there is also the truth, and that in truth itself there is need of having the crowd on its side. There is another view of life which conceives that wherever there is a crowd there is untruth, so that (to consider for a moment the extreme case), even if every individual, each for himself in private, were to be in possession of the truth, yet in case they were to get together in a crowd – a crowd to which any sort of *decisive* significance is attributed, a voting, noisy, audible crowd – untruth would at once be in evidence.' But Kierkegaard also carefully qualifies his position: 'Perhaps it may be well to note here, although it seems to me almost superfluous, that it naturally could not occur to me to object to the fact, for example, that preaching is done or that the truth is proclaimed, even though it were to an assemblage of hundreds of thousands. Not at all; but if there were an assemblage even of only ten – and if they should put the truth to the ballot, that is to say if the assemblage should be regarded as the authority, if it is the crowd which turns the scale – then there is untruth.' *The Point of View* (London: Oxford University Press, 1939), p. 112.

[3] Kierkegaard, *The Point of View,* p. 131.

[4] When we 'admire and blubber' in the presence of superior human achievement, we turn ourselves, says Kierkegaard, into spectators and connoisseurs and neatly avoid the call to live as human beings ourselves. Admiration, in other words, can be a dodge. See Søren Kierkegaard, *Concluding Unscientific Postscript* (Princeton: Princeton University Press, 1941), pp. 320-22.

[5] The Rechabites have usually been described as a nomadic clan that lived a disciplined, ascetic life pasturing flocks in the wilderness. Their way of life was a protest against the decadence of civilization and an idealization of the forty wilderness years when religion was austere and untainted with the fertility rites of the agricultural communities and the immoralities associated with the cities. Recent studies have shown that there is no basis in biblical fact for that identification and argue a high degree of probability that the Rechabites were a guild of craftsmen in metal. See Frank S. Frick, 'The Rechabites Reconsidered,' *Journal of Biblical Literature,* 90 (1971):279-87; and 'Rechabites,' *Interpreter's Dictionary of the Bible, Supplement* (Nashville: Abingdon Press, 1976), pp. 726-28.

[6] Maxim Gorky said that he did not write to entertain; he wanted to show people how 'badly and boringly they lived their lives' so that they could then go on to live them well.

[7] William Barrett, *The Illusion of Technique* (Garden City, NY: Anchor Press/Doubleday, 1978), p. 219.

Chapter 12

[1] Peter T. Forsyth, *Positive Preaching and the Modern Mind* (London: Independent Press Ltd., 1907), pp. 178-79.

[2] The exile took place in two stages. King Jehoiachin, the queen mother, and most leaders were deported in 598 B.C. Most of the populace was left behind under the puppet king Zedekiah. Jeremiah, one of those left behind, wrote his letter in about 594. Eleven years after the first exile, provoked by plots and insurrectionist activity, Babylon returned in 587 and destroyed the city. At that time they took virtually everyone into exile. See John Bright, *A History of Israel* (Philadelphia: Westminster Press, 1959), pp. 302-10.

[3] Exodus 2:22. The phrase entered the popular speech of our century through the science-fiction novel of Robert A. Heinlein, *Stranger in a Strange Land* (New York: Avon Books, 1961).

[4] Robertson Davies, *Rebel Angels* (New York: Viking Press, 1981), p. 326.

[5] George Eliot, *Felix Holt* (New York: The Century Co., 1911), p. 301.

[6] His actual words: 'Sinners always want what is lacking to them, and souls full of God want only what they have.' Quoted by Thomas Merton, *Conjectures of a Guilty Bystander* (Garden City, NY: Image/Doubleday, 1968), p. 285.

[7] Walker Percy's Binx Bolling says, 'The search is what anyone would undertake if he were not sunk in the everydayness of his own life. . . . To become aware of the possibility of the search is to be onto something. Not to be onto something is to be in despair.' *The Moviegoer* (New York: Avon Books, 1980), p. 18.

[8] J. A. Sanders, *Interpreter's Dictionary of the Bible,* 2:188.

[9] *William Faulkner, Lion in the Garden,* Interviews edited by James B. Merriweather and Michael Millgate (New York: Random House, 1968), p. 108.

Chapter 13

[1] Erik H. Erikson, *Identity, Youth and Crisis* (New York: W. W. Norton and Co., 1968), p. 314.

[2] R. P. Blackmur, *Henry Adams* (New York: Harcourt Brace Jovanovich, 1980), p. 3.

[3] F. H. Heinemann, *Existentialism and the Modern Predicament* (London: Adam and Charles Black, 1954), p. 67. His contemporaries had no way of knowing it, but Jeremiah was the brightest star in what scholars centuries later would see as a constellation of religious leaders strategically placed across the world. The seventh and sixth centuries B.C. were renaissance centuries in matters of the soul and God. In other parts of the world Zarathustra was beginning a new religion in Persia; Lao-tse was formulating Taoism in China; the Buddha was beginning his great reform movement in India. In Greece the philosophers Thales and Anaximander were laying the foundations of Greek philosophy. All over the world there was yearning and hunger and thirst for righteousness. Deep thinking and ardent yearning seem to characterize what we know of the centers of civilization in China, India, Persia and Greece. In Palestine it was Jeremiah.

[4] Abraham Maslow, *The Farther Reaches of Human Nature* (New York: Viking Press, 1971), p. xvi.

[5] Herman Melville, *The Confidence Man* (New York: New American Library, Signet Classics, 1964), p. 119.

[6] Hannah Arendt, *Eichmann in Jerusalem* (New York: Viking Press, 1963).

[7] Henry Adams, *The Education of Henry Adams* (New York: Houghton Mifflin Co., 1918), p. 312.

[8] Counting only the names of Jeremiah's contemporaries who appear in the narrative, about sixty persons are named. It is not possible to be precise in the number as in two or three instances the names may be vari-

ants referring to the same person. Sixty names, plus or minus two or three, seems to me to be an extraordinary number in so brief a narrative.

CHAPTER 14

[1] John Fowles, *The Aristos* (Boston: Little, Brown and Co., 1964), p. 50.

[2] Even in the realm of philosophical discourse - not, it would seem, a highly practical field - we have made our distinctively American contributions in thinking about how to make things happen, in understanding how things get done. The pragmatism of William James and the instrumentalism of John Dewey steered a wide berth from anything resembling an ivory tower and have pursued the down-to-earth concerns of the practical person. 'It is no exaggeration to say that in American intellectual life irrelevant thinking has always been considered the cardinal sin.' John E. Smith, *The Spirit of American Philosophy* (New York: Oxford University Press, 1963), p. vii.

[3] 'I was talking to David Riesman a few weeks ago, and he was saying that apocalyptic solutions and apocalyptic analyses and diagnoses don't interest him, really, because it's the little things, day by day, picking up the garbage in this village, that makes life *work,* and the values will finally take their shape from these thousands of little efforts, of little decencies, little organizations that give the *ground* for social continuity.' *Robert Penn Warren Talking,* Interviews 1950-1978, edited by Floyd C. Watkins and John T. Hiers (New York: Random House, 1980), p. 192.

[4] Coventry Patmore, *The Rod, the Root and the Flower* (Freeport, NY: Books for Libraries Press, 1968), p. 52.

[5] G. K. Chesterton, *Heretics* (London: Bodley Head, 1905), p. 114.

[6] William Stringfellow, *An Ethic for Christians and Other Aliens in a Strange Land* (Waco, TX: Word Books, 1976), p. 138.

[7] George Eliot, *The Mill on the Floss* (New York: The Century Co., 1911), p. 409.

[8] Philip Reiff, *The Triumph of the Therapeutic* (New York: Harper & Row, 1966), p. 37.

CHAPTER 15

[1] Arend Th. Van Leeuwen, *Christianity in World History,* trans. H. H. Hoskins (London: Edinburgh House Press, 1964), p. 100.

[2] D. T. Niles, *Upon the Earth* (New York: McGraw Hill Co., 1962), p. 250.

[3] Ernest Becker, *The Denial of Death* (New York: The Free Press, 1973), p. 74.

[4] Quoted by Niles, *Upon the Earth,* p. 259.

[5] A possible, though not at all probable, exception is recorded in chapter 13 in the story of the linen waistcloth. Jeremiah is instructed to 'go to the Euphrates' to bury it, which he did. If, in fact, this is the River Euphrates, it was a 700-mile round trip. The word in Hebrew is *perath* and, though used often for the Euphrates River, more likely refers to Parah (modern Ain Farah) about four miles from Anathoth where there is an abundant supply of water. Since Parah and Euphrates were very similar in sound, the former could have stood symbolically for the latter. Indeed 'to Parah' and 'to the Euphrates' would be spelled identically in Hebrew. See Thompson, *The Book of Jeremiah,* p. 364, and Bright, *Jeremiah,* p. 96.

[6] Marianne Moore, *Predilections* (London: Faber & Faber, 1956), p. 12.

[7] Bright, *Jeremiah,* p. 307.

[8] Kenneth Cragg, *The Call of the Minaret* (London: Oxford University Press, 1952), p. 183.

[9] André and Pierre-Emmanuel Lacocque, *The Jonah Complex,* p. 30.

Chapter 16

[1] William Foxwell Albright, *From the Stone Age to Christianity* (Garden City, NY: Doubleday, Anchor Books, 1957), p. 402.

[2] Friedrich von Hügel, *Essays & Addresses on the Philosophy of Religion,* 2d series (London: J. M. Dent and Sons, Ltd., 1926), p. 54.

[3] Karl Barth, *Epistle to the Romans* (London: Oxford University Press, 1960), p. 327.

[4] Flannery O'Connor, *Mystery and Manners* (New York: Farrar, Straus and Giroux, 1961), p. 94.

[5] The tidy conclusion that the book of Jeremiah fails to give is supplied extra-biblically (as it usually is!) by the first-century *Lives of the Prophets.* A most satisfying ending is provided by combining a hero's honor among the Egyptians and a martyr's death at the hands of the Jews: 'He was of Anathoth, and he died in Taphenes in Egypt, stoned to death by the Jews. He is buried in the place where Pharaoh's palace stood; for the Egyptians held him in honor, because of the benefit which they received through him. For at his prayer, the serpents which the Egyptians called *epoth* departed from them; and even at the present day the faithful servants of God pray on that spot, and taking of the dust of the place they heal the bites of serpents.' Charles Cutler Torrey, *The Lives of the Prophets,* Greek Text and Translation (Philadelphia: Society of Biblical Literature and Exegesis, 1946), p. 35.

THE GIFT

REFLECTIONS ON A CHRISTIAN MINISTRY

For H. James Riddell

Contents

REDEFINITIONS

1

The Naked Noun

If I, even for a moment, accept my culture's definition of me, I am rendered harmless.

A HEALTHY NOUN DOESN'T NEED ADJECTIVES. ADJECTIVES clutter a noun that is robust. But if the noun is culture-damaged or culture-diseased, adjectives are necessary.

'Pastor' used to be that kind of noun – energetic and virile. I have always loved the sound of the word. From an early age, the word called to mind a person who was passionate for God and compassionate with people. And even though the pastors I knew did not embody those characteristics, the word itself held its own against its exemplars. Today still, when people ask me what I want to be called, I always say, 'Pastor'.

But when I observe the way the vocation of pastor is lived out in America and listen to the tone and context in which the word *pastor* is spoken, I realize that what I hear in the word and what others hear is very different. In general usage, the noun is weak, defined by parody and diluted by opportunism. The need for strengthening adjectives is critical.

I find I have to exercise this adjectival rehabilitation constantly, redefining by refusing the definitions of *pastor* that the culture hands me, and reformulating my life with the insights and images of Scripture. The culture treats me so amiably! It encourages me to maintain my orthodox creed; it commends me for my evangelical practice; it praises me for my singular devotion. All it asks is that I accept its definition of my work as an encourager of the culture's good will, as the priest who will sprinkle holy water on the culture's good intentions. Many of these people are my friends. None, that I am aware of, is consciously malign.

But if I, even for a moment, accept my culture's definition of me, I am rendered harmless. I can denounce evil and stupidity all I wish and will be tolerated in my denunciations as a court jester is tolerated. I can organize their splendid goodwill and they will let me do it, since it is only for weekends.

The essence of being a pastor begs for redefinition. To that end, I offer three adjectives to clarify the noun: *unbusy, subversive, apocalyptic.*

2

The Unbusy Pastor

How can I persuade a person to live by faith and not by works if I have to juggle my schedule constantly to make everything fit into place?

THE ONE PIECE OF MAIL CERTAIN TO GO UNREAD INTO MY wastebasket is the letter addressed to the 'busy pastor'. Not that the phrase doesn't describe me at times, but I refuse to give my attention to someone who encourages what is worst in me.

I'm not arguing the accuracy of the adjective; I am, though, contesting the way it's used to flatter and express sympathy.

'The poor man,' we say. 'He's so devoted to his flock; the work is endless, and he sacrifices himself so unstintingly.' But the word *busy* is the symptom not of commitment but of betrayal. It is not devotion but defection. The adjective *busy* set as a modifier to *pastor* should sound to our ears like *adulterous* to characterize a wife or *embezzling* to describe a banker. It is an outrageous scandal, a blasphemous affront.

Hilary of Tours diagnosed our pastoral busyness as *irreligiosa sollicitudo pro Deo,* a blasphemous anxiety to do God's work for him.

I (and most pastors, I believe) become busy for two reasons; both are ignoble.

I am busy because I am vain. I want to appear important. Significant. What better way than to be busy? The incredible hours, the crowded schedule, and the heavy demands on my time are proof to myself – and to all who will notice – that I am important. If I go into a doctor's office and find there's no one waiting, and I see through a half-open door the doctor reading a book, I wonder if he's any good. A good doctor will have people lined up waiting to see him; a good doctor will not have time to read a book. Although I grumble about waiting my turn in a busy doctor's office, I am also impressed with his importance.

Such experiences affect me. I live in a society in which crowded schedules and harassed conditions are evidence of importance, so I develop a crowded schedule and harassed conditions. When others notice, they acknowledge my significance, and my vanity is fed.

I am busy because I am lazy. I indolently let others decide what I will do instead of resolutely deciding myself. I let people who do not understand the work of the pastor write the agenda for my day's work because I am too slipshod to write it myself. The pastor is a shadow figure in these people's minds, a marginal person vaguely connected with matters of God and good will. Anything remotely religious or somehow well-intentioned can be properly assigned to the pastor.

Because these assignments to pastoral service are made sincerely, I go along with them. It takes effort to refuse, and besides, there's always the danger that the refusal will be interpreted as a rebuff, a betrayal of religion, and a calloused disregard for people in need.

It was a favorite theme of C. S. Lewis that only lazy people work hard. By lazily abdicating the essential work of deciding and directing, establishing values and setting goals, other people do it for us; then we find ourselves frantically, at the last minute, trying to satisfy a half dozen different demands on our time, none of which is essential to our vocation, to stave off the disaster of disappointing someone.

But if I vainly crowd my day with conspicuous activity or let others fill my day with imperious demands, I don't have time to do my proper work, the work to which I have been called. How can I lead people into the quiet place beside the still waters if I am in perpetual motion? How can I persuade a person to live by faith and not by works if I have to juggle my schedule constantly to make everything fit into place?

Much Ado about the Significant

If I'm not busy making my mark in the world or doing what everyone expects me to do, what do I do? What is my proper work? What does it mean to be a pastor? If no one asked me to do anything, what would I do?

Three things.

I can be a pastor who prays. I want to cultivate my relationship with God. I want all of life to be intimate - sometimes consciously, sometimes unconsciously - with the God who made, directs, and loves me. And I want to waken others to the nature and centrality of prayer. I want to be a person in this community to whom others can come without hesitation, without wondering if it is appropriate, to get direction in prayer and praying. I want to do the original work of being in deepening conversation with the God who reveals himself to me and addresses me by name. I don't want to dispense mimeographed hand-outs that describe God's business; I want to witness out of my own experience. I don't want to live as a parasite on the first-hand spiritual life of others, but to be personally involved with all my senses, tasting and seeing that the Lord is good.

I know it takes time to develop a life of prayer: set-aside, disciplined, deliberate time. It isn't accomplished on the run, nor by offering prayers from a pulpit or at a hospital bedside. I know I can't be busy and pray at the same time. I can be active and pray; I can work and pray; but I cannot be busy and pray. I cannot be inwardly rushed, distracted, or dispersed. In order to pray I have to be paying more attention to God than to what people are saying to me; to God than to my clamoring ego.

Usually, for that to happen there must be a deliberate withdrawal from the noise of the day, a disciplined detachment from the insatiable self.

I can be a pastor who preaches. I want to speak the Word of God that is Scripture in the language and rhythms of the people I live with. I am given an honored and protected time each week to do that. The pulpit is a great gift, and I want to use it well.

I have no interest in 'delivering sermons,' challenging people to face the needs of the day or giving bright, inspirational messages. With the help provided by scholars and editors, I can prepare a fairly respectable sermon of either sort in a few hours each week, a sermon that will pass muster with most congregations. They might not think it the greatest sermon, but they would accept it.

But what I want to do can't be done that way. I need a drenching in Scripture; I require an immersion in biblical studies. I need reflective hours over the pages of Scripture as well as personal struggles with the meaning of Scripture. That takes far more time than it takes to prepare a sermon.

I want the people who come to worship in my congregation each Sunday to hear the Word of God preached in such a way that they hear its distinctive note of authority as God's Word, and to know that their own lives are being addressed on their home territory. A sound outline and snappy illustrations don't make that happen.

This kind of preaching is a creative act that requires quietness and solitude, concentration and intensity. 'All speech that moves men,' contends R. E. C. Browne, 'was minted when some man's mind was poised and still.' I can't do that when I'm busy.

I can be a pastor who listens. A lot of people approach me through the week to tell me what's going on in their lives. I want to have the energy and time to really listen to them so that when they're through, they know at least one other person has some inkling of what they're feeling and thinking.

Listening is in short supply in the world today; people aren't used to being listened to. I know how easy it is to avoid the tough, intense work of listening by being busy – as when I let a hospital patient know there are ten more people I have to see. (Have to? I'm not indispensable to any of them, and I am here with this one.) Too much of pastoral visitation is punching the clock, assuring people we're on the job, being busy, earning our pay.

Pastoral listening requires unhurried leisure, even if it's only for five minutes. Leisure is a quality of spirit, not a quantity of time. Only in that ambiance of leisure do persons know they are listened to with absolute seriousness, treated with dignity and importance. Speaking to people does not have the same personal intensity as listening to them. The question I put to myself is not 'How many people have you spoken to about Christ this week?' but 'How many people have you listened to in Christ this week?' The number of persons listened to must necessarily be less than the number spoken to. Listening to a story always takes more time than delivering a message, so I must discard my compulsion to count, to compile the statistics that will justify my existence.

I can't listen if I'm busy. When my schedule is crowded, I'm not free to listen: I have to keep my next appointment; I have to get to the next meeting. But if I provide margins to my day, there is ample time to listen.

The Means to the Margins

'Yes, but how?' The appointment calendar is the tool with which to get unbusy. It's a gift of the Holy Ghost (unlisted by

St Paul, but a gift nonetheless) that provides the pastor with the means to get time and acquire leisure for praying, preaching, and listening. It is more effective than a protective secretary; it is less expensive than a retreat house. It is the one thing everyone in our society accepts without cavil as authoritative. The authority once given to Scripture is now ascribed to the appointment calendar. The dogma of verbal inerrancy has not been discarded, only re-assigned.

When I appeal to my appointment calendar, I am beyond criticism. If someone approaches me and asks me to pronounce the invocation at an event and I say, 'I don't think I should do that; I was planning to use that time to pray,' the response will be, 'Well, I'm sure you can find another time to do that.' But if I say, 'My appointment calendar will not permit it,' no further questions are asked. If someone asks me to attend a committee meeting and I say, 'I was thinking of taking my wife out to dinner that night; I haven't listened to her carefully for several days,' the response will be, 'But you are very much needed at this meeting; couldn't you arrange another evening with your wife?' But if I say, 'The appointment calendar will not permit it,' there is no further discussion.

The trick, of course, is to get to the calendar before anyone else does. I mark out the times for prayer, for reading, for leisure, for the silence and solitude out of which creative work – prayer, preaching, and listening – can issue.

I find that when these central needs are met, there is plenty of time for everything else. And there is much else, for the pastor is not, and should not be, exempt from the hundred menial tasks or the administrative humdrum. These also are pastoral ministry. But the only way I have found to accomplish them without resentment and anxiety is to first take care of the priorities. If there is no time to nurture these essentials, I become a busy pastor, harassed and anxious, a whining, compulsive Martha instead of a contemplative Mary.

A number of years ago I was a busy pastor and had some back trouble that required therapy. I went for one hour sessions three times a week, and no one minded that I wasn't available for those three hours. Because the three hours had the authority of an appointment calendar behind them, they were sacrosanct.

On the analogy of that experience, I venture to prescribe appointments for myself to take care of the needs not only of my body, but also of my mind and emotions, my spirit and imagination. One week, in addition to daily half-hour conferences with St Paul, my calendar reserved a two-hour block of time with Fyodor Dostoevsky. My spirit needed that as much as my body ten years ago needed the physical therapist. If nobody is going to prescribe it for me, I will prescribe it for myself.

The Poised Harpooner

In Herman Melville's *Moby Dick,* there is a turbulent scene in which a whaleboat scuds across a frothing ocean in pursuit of the great, white whale, Moby Dick. The sailors are laboring fiercely, every muscle taut, all attention and energy concentrated on the task. The cosmic conflict between good and evil is joined; chaotic sea and demonic sea monster versus the morally outraged man, Captain Ahab. In this boat, however, there is one man who does nothing. He doesn't hold an oar; he doesn't perspire; he doesn't shout. He is languid in the crash and the cursing. This man is the harpooner, quiet and poised, waiting. And then this sentence: 'To insure the greatest efficiency in the dart, the harpooners of this world must start to their feet out of idleness, and not out of toil.'

Melville's sentence is a text to set alongside the psalmist's 'Be still, and know that I am God' (Ps 46:10), and alongside Isaiah's 'In returning and rest you shall be saved; in quietness and in trust shall be your strength' (Is 30:15).

Pastors know there is something radically wrong with the world. We are also engaged in doing something about it. The stimulus of conscience, the memory of ancient outrage, and the challenge of biblical command involve us in the anarchic sea that is the world. The white whale, symbol of evil, and the crippled captain, personification of violated righteousness, are joined in battle. History is a novel of spiritual conflict. In such a world, noise is inevitable, and immense energy is expended. But if there is no harpooner in the boat, there will be no proper finish to the chase. Or if the harpooner is exhausted, having abandoned his assignment and become an oarsman, he will not be ready and accurate when it is time to throw his javelin.

Somehow it always seems more compelling to assume the work of the oarsman, laboring mightily in a moral cause, throwing our energy into a fray we know has immortal consequence. And it always seems more dramatic to take on the outrage of a Captain Ahab, obsessed with a vision of vengeance and retaliation, brooding over the ancient injury done by the Enemy. There is, though, other important work to do. Someone must throw the dart. Some must be harpooners.

The metaphors Jesus used for the life of ministry are frequently images of the single, the small, and the quiet, which have effects far in excess of their appearance: salt, leaven, seed. Our culture publicizes the opposite emphasis: the big, the multitudinous, the noisy. It is, then, a strategic necessity that pastors deliberately ally themselves with the quiet, poised harpooners, and not leap, frenzied, to the oars. There is far more need that we develop the skills of the harpooner than the muscles of the oarsman. It is far more biblical to learn quietness and attentiveness before God than to be overtaken by what John Oman named the twin perils of ministry, 'flurry and worry.' For flurry dissipates energy, and worry constipates it.

Years ago I noticed, as all pastors must, that when a pastor left a neighboring congregation, the congregational life carried on very well, thank you. A guest preacher was assigned to conduct Sunday worship, and nearby pastors took care of the funerals, weddings, and crisis counseling. A congregation would go for months, sometimes as long as a year or two, without a regular pastor. And I thought, *All these things I am so busy doing – they aren't being done in that pastorless congregation, and nobody seems to mind.* I asked myself, *What if I, without leaving, quit doing them right now? Would anybody mind?* I did, and they don't.

3

The Subversive Pastor

I am undermining the kingdom of self and establishing the kingdom of God. I am being subversive.

As a pastor, I don't like being viewed as nice but insignificant. I bristle when a high-energy executive leaves the place of worship with the comment, 'This was wonderful, Pastor, but now we have to get back to the real world, don't we?' I had thought we were in the most-real world, the world revealed as God's, a world believed to be invaded by God's grace and turning on the pivot of Christ's crucifixion and resurrection. The executive's comment brings me up short: he isn't taking this seriously. Worshiping God is marginal to making money. Prayer is marginal to the bottom line. Christian salvation is a brand preference.

I bristle and want to assert my importance. I want to force the recognition of the key position I hold in the economy of God and in *his* economy if only he knew it.

Then I remember that I am a subversive. My long-term effectiveness depends on my not being recognized for who I really am. If he realized that I actually believe the American way of life is doomed to destruction, and that another kingdom is right now being formed in secret to take its place, he wouldn't be at all pleased. If he knew what I was really doing and the difference it was making, he would fire me.

Yes, I believe that. I believe that the kingdoms of this world, American and Venezuelan and Chinese, will become the kingdom of our God and Christ, and I believe this new kingdom is already among us. That is why I'm a pastor, to introduce people to the real world and train them to live in it. I learned early that the methods of my work must correspond to the realities of the kingdom. The methods that make the kingdom of America strong – economic, military, technological, informational – are not suited to making the kingdom of God strong. I have had to learn a new methodology: truth-telling and love-making, prayer and parable. These are not methods very well adapted to raising the standard of living in suburbia or massaging the ego into a fashionable shape.

But America and suburbia and the ego compose my parish. Most of the individuals in this amalgam suppose that the goals they have for themselves and the goals God has for them are the same. It is the oldest religious mistake: refusing to countenance any real difference between God and us, imagining God to be a vague extrapolation of our own desires, and then hiring a priest to manage the affairs between self and the extrapolation. And I, one of the priests they hired, am having none of it.

But if I'm not willing to help them become what they want to be, what am I doing taking their pay? I am being subversive. I am undermining the kingdom of self and establishing the kingdom of God. I am helping them to become what God wants them to be, using the methods of subversion.

But isn't that dishonest? Not exactly, for I'm not misrepresenting myself. I'm simply taking my words and acts at a level of seriousness that would throw them into a state of catatonic disbelief if they ever knew.

The Pastor's Odd Niche

Pastors occupy an odd niche in American culture. Christian communities employ us to lead worship, teach and preach the Scriptures, and provide guidance and encouragement in the pilgrim way. Within our congregation, we experience a modest honor in our position. Occasionally one of us rises to national prominence and catches the attention of large numbers of people with the charisma of sunny, millennial cheerleading or (less often) the scary forecasts of Armageddon. But most of us are known by name only to our congregations and, except for ceremonial appearances at weddings, funerals, and bullroasts, are not in the public eye.

In general, people treat us with respect, but we are not considered important in any social, cultural, or economic way. In parody we are usually treated as harmless innocents, in satire as shiftless parasites.

This is not what most of us had in mind when we signed on. We had not counted on anything either so benign or so marginal. The images forming our pastoral expectations had a good deal more fierceness to them: Moses' bearding the Pharaoh; Jeremiah with fire in his mouth; Peter swashbucklingly reckless as the lead apostle; Paul's careering through prison and ecstasy, shipwreck and kerygma. The kingdom of God in which we had apprenticed ourselves was presented to us as revolutionary, a dangerously unwelcome intruder in the Old Boy Club of thrones, dominions, principalities, and powers.

The vocabulary we learned in preparation for our work was a language of battle ('We fight not against flesh and blood'), danger ('Your adversary the devil prowls around like a roaring lion, seeking some one to devour'), and austerity ('Take up your cross and follow me'). After arriving on the job, we find precious few opportunities to use our leadership language. And so, like the two years of Spanish we took in high school, it is soon nonfunctional from nonuse.

Did we learn the wrong language? Did we acquire the wrong images? Did we apprentice ourselves to the wrong master?

Everybody treats us so nicely. No one seems to think we mean what we say. When we say 'kingdom of God', no one gets apprehensive, as if we had just announced (which we thought we had) that a powerful army is poised on the border, ready to invade. When we say radical things like 'Christ', 'love', 'believe', 'peace', and 'sin' – words that in other times and cultures excited martyrdoms – the sounds enter the stream of conversation with no more splash than baseball scores and grocery prices.

It's hard to maintain a self-concept as a revolutionary when everyone treats us with the same affability they give the grocer.

Are these people right? Is their way of life in no danger from us? Is what we say about God and his ways among us not real in the same way that Chevrolets and basketball teams and fresh garden spinach are real? Many pastors, realizing the opinion polls overwhelmingly repudiate their self-concept, submit to the cultural verdict and slip into the role of chaplain to the culture. It is easy to do. But some pastors do not; they become subversives in the culture.

Virginia Stem Owens has written the most powerful evocation since *King Lear* of the subversive character of the person (and this certainly includes the pastor) who intends to convert the world by truth and not guns. Her book *And the Trees Clap Their Hands* is a dazzling performance on the parallel bars of anti-gnostic polemic and 'God's spy' intrigue. In the opening pages, Owens, accompanied by her pastor-husband, sets the scene.

> We sit in coffee shops and scan faces as they filter by unawares on the sidewalk. We are collecting, sorting, storing the data. But we do not call ourselves scientists; we cannot make controlled experiments. In life there can never be a control group. There is only what is – or what presents itself, at any given moment, for our perusal. And we, with our own limitations, can only be in one place and one time at any moment. For this reason we call ourselves spies, for we must strike a trail and stick to it. We must catch as catch can, life being no laboratory, spreading our senses wide and

drawing them in again to study what we have managed to snare in the wind.

We have several covers, my companion and I, business we appear to be about while we are actually always watching for signs of the invisible prey, which is our primary occupation. He, for example, balances church budgets, counsels divorcees and delinquents, writes sermons. But beneath it all is a constant watchfulness, a taking note. Even as he stands in the pulpit, he sifts the faces of the congregation for those fine grains, no larger than the dust of pollen, that carry the spoor of the trail he's on.

And I sit among them there, internally knitting them up like Madame Defarge, listening, recording, watching, remembering. Softly. Softly. The clues one must go on are often small and fleeting. A millimeter's widening of the eye, a faint contraction of the nostrils, a silent exhalation, the slight upward modulation of the voice. To spy out the reality hidden in appearances requires vigilance, perseverance. It takes everything I've got.

The kingdom of self is heavily defended territory. Post-Eden Adams and Eves are willing to pay their respects to God, but they don't want him invading their turf. Most sin, far from being a mere lapse of morals or a weak will, is an energetically and expensively erected defense against God. Direct assault in an openly declared war on the god-self is extraordinarily ineffective. Hitting sin head-on is like hitting a nail with a hammer; it only drives it in deeper. There are occasional exceptions, strategically dictated confrontations, but indirection is the biblically preferred method.

Jesus the Subversive

Jesus was a master at subversion. Until the very end, everyone, including his disciples, called him Rabbi. Rabbis were important, but they didn't make anything happen. On the occasions when suspicions were aroused that there might be more to him than that title accounted for, Jesus tried to keep it quiet – 'tell no one.'

Jesus' favorite speech form, the parable, was subversive. Parables sound absolutely ordinary: casual stories about soil and seeds, meals and coins and sheep, bandits and victims, farmers and merchants. And they are wholly secular: of his forty or so parables recorded in the Gospels, only one has its setting in church, and only a couple mention the name God. As people heard Jesus tell these stories, they saw at once that they weren't about God, so there was nothing in them threatening their own sovereignty. They relaxed their defenses. They walked away perplexed, wondering what they meant, the stories lodged in their imagination. And then, like a time bomb, they would explode in their unprotected hearts. An abyss opened up at their very feet. He *was* talking about God; they had been invaded!

Jesus continually threw odd stories down alongside ordinary lives (*para,* 'alongside'; *bole,* 'thrown') and walked away without explanation or altar call. Then listeners started seeing connections: God connections, life connections, eternity connections. The very lack of obviousness, the unlikeness, was the stimulus to perceiving likeness: God likeness, life likeness, eternity likeness. But the parable didn't do the work – it put the listener's imagination to work. Parables aren't illustrations that make things easier; they make things harder by requiring the exercise of our imaginations, which if we aren't careful becomes the exercise of our faith.

Parables subversively slip past our defenses. Once they're inside the citadel of self, we might expect a change of method, a sudden brandishing of bayonets resulting in a palace coup. But it doesn't happen. Our integrity is honored and preserved.

God does not impose his reality from without; he grows flowers and fruit from within. God's truth is not an alien invasion but a loving courtship in which the details of our common lives are treated as seeds in our conception, growth, and maturity in the kingdom. Parables trust our imaginations, which is to say, our faith. They don't herd us paternalistically into a classroom where we get things explained and diagrammed. They don't bully us into regiments where we find ourselves marching in a moral goose step.

There is hardly a detail in the gospel story that was not at the time (and still) overlooked because unlikely, dismissed because commonplace, and rejected because illegal. But under the surface of conventionality and behind the scenes of probability, each was effectively inaugurating the kingdom: illegitimate (as was supposed) conception, barnyard birth, Nazareth silence, Galilean secularity, Sabbath healings, Gethsemane prayers, criminal death, baptismal water, eucharistic bread and wine. Subversion.

The Assumptions of Subversives

Three things are implicit in subversion. One, the status quo is wrong and must be overthrown if the world is going to be livable. It is so deeply wrong that repair work is futile. The world is, in the word insurance agents use to designate our wrecked cars, totaled.

Two, there is another world aborning that is livable. Its reality is no chimera. It is in existence, though not visible. Its character is known. The subversive does not operate out of a utopian dream but out of a conviction of the nature of the real world.

Three, the usual means by which one kingdom is thrown out and another put in its place – military force or democratic elections – are not available. If we have neither a preponderance of power nor a majority of votes, we begin searching for other ways to effect change. We discover the methods of subversion. We find and welcome allies.

At a sixtieth birthday conversation in 1986, the poet A. R. Ammons was asked, 'Is poetry subversive?' He responded, 'Yes, you have no idea how subversive – deeply subversive. Consciousness often reaches a deeply intense level at the edges of things, questioning and undermining accepted ways of doing things. The audience resists change to the last moment, and then is grateful for it.'

These are the convictions implicit in the gospel. They are not, though, convictions commonly implicit in parish life. More frequently, there is the untested assumption that the congregation is close to being the kingdom already and that if we all pull together and try a little harder, it will be. Pastors especially seem to assume that everybody, or at least a majority, in a congregation can be either persuaded or pushed into righteousness and maybe even holiness, in spite of centuries of evidence to the contrary.

That pastors need an accurate knowledge of Christian doctrine is universally acknowledged; that they need practiced skill in the techniques of Christian subversion is a minority conviction. But Jesus is the Way as well as the Truth. The way the gospel is conveyed is as much a part of the kingdom as the truth presented. Why are pastors experts on the truth and dropouts on the way?

In acquiring familiarity and skill in pastoral subversion, we could do worse than to read spy novels and observe the strategies of communist infiltration, but the biblical passages are more than adequate if we will only pay attention to them:

- 'A great and strong wind rent the mountains, and broke in pieces the rocks before the Lord, but the Lord was not in the wind; and after the wind an earthquake, but the Lord was not in the earthquake; and after the earthquake a fire, but the Lord was not in the fire; and after the fire a still small voice' (1 Kgs 19:11-12).

- 'This is the word of the Lord to Zerubbabel: Not by might, nor by power, but by my Spirit, says the Lord of hosts' (Zec 4:6).
- 'You are the salt of the earth' (Mt 5:13).
- 'The kingdom of heaven is like a grain of mustard seed which a man took and sowed in his field; it is the smallest of all seeds' (Mt 13:31-32).
- 'For I decided to know nothing among you except Jesus Christ and him crucified. And I was with you in weakness and in much fear and trembling' (1 Cor 2:2-3).

Unfortunately, this unbroken biblical methodology of subversion is easily and frequently discarded by pastors in favor of assault or promotion. There are two likely reasons: vanity and naiveté.

Vanity. We don't like being wallflowers at the world's party. A recent study of the decline in white males' preparing for pastoral work concluded that a major reason is that there's no prestige left in the job. Interestingly, the slack is taken up by others (blacks, Asians, women) who apparently are not looking for prestige and have a history of working subversively. Neither was there prestige in Paul's itinerant tent-making.

Naiveté. We think the church is already the kingdom of God and, if only better organized and motivated, can conquer the world. But nowhere in Scripture or history do we see a church synonymous with the kingdom of God. The church in many instances is more worldly than the world. When we equate the church and the kingdom and the identity turns out to be false, we feel 'taken in'. Little wonder that anger and cynicism are epidemic behind the smiling veneer of American pastors. We need refresher courses in Barthian critiques of religion and Dantean analyses of sin, especially spiritual sin.

Tools of Subversion

Prayer and parable are the stock-in-trade tools of the subversive pastor. The quiet (or noisy) closet life of prayer enters into partnership with the Spirit that strives still with every human heart, a wrestling match in holiness. And parables are the consciousness-altering words that slip past falsifying platitude and invade the human spirit with Christ-truth.

This is our primary work in the real world. But we need continual convincing. The people for whom we are praying and among whom we are telling parables are seduced into supposing that their money and ambition are making the world turn on its axis. There are so many of them and so few of us, making it difficult to maintain our convictions. It is easy to be seduced along with them.

Words are the real work of the world – prayer words with God, parable words with men and women. The behind-the-scenes work of creativity by word and sacrament, by parable and prayer, subverts the seduced world. The pastor's real work is what Ivan Illich calls 'shadow work' – the work nobody gets paid for and few notice but that makes a world of salvation: meaning and value and purpose, a world of love and hope and faith – in short, the kingdom of God.

4

The Apocalyptic Pastor

With the vastness of the heavenly invasion and the urgency of the faith decision rolling into our consciousness like thunder and lightning, we cannot stand around on Sunday morning filling the time with pretentious small talk on how bad the world is and how wonderful this new stewardship campaign is going to be.

THE ADJECTIVE *APOCALYPTIC* IS NOT COMMONLY FOUND IN company with the noun *pastor*. I can't remember ever hearing them in the same sentence. They grew up on different sides of the tracks. I'd like to play Cupid between the two words and see if I can instigate a courtship.

Apocalyptic has a wild sound to it: an end-of-the-world craziness; a catastrophic urgency. The word is used when history seems out of control and ordinary life is hopeless. When you aren't sure whether it is bombs or stars that are falling out of the sky, and people are rushing toward the cliffs like a herd of pigs, the scene is 'apocalyptic'. The word is scary and unsettling.

Pastor is a comforting word: a person who confidently quotes the Twenty-third Psalm when you are shivering in the dark shadows. Pastors gather us in quiet adoration before God. Pastors represent the faithfulness and love of the eternal God and show up on time every Sunday to say it again – that God so loves the world. Pastors build bridges over troubled waters and guide wandering feet back to the main road. The word accumulates associations of security and blessing, solidity and peace.

But I have a biblical reason for bringing the two words together. The last book of the Bible was written by a pastor. And the book he wrote was an apocalypse. The St John who gave us the last words of the Bible was an apocalyptic pastor.

I am misunderstood by most of the people who call me pastor. Their misunderstandings are contagious, and I find myself misunderstanding: Who am I? What is my proper work? I look around. I ask questions. I scout the American landscape for images of pastoral work. What does a pastor do? What does a pastor look like? What place does a pastor occupy in church and culture? I get handed a job description that seems to have been developed from the latest marketing studies of religious consumer needs. But there are no images, no stories. St John gives me an image and a story – and a blessedly blank job description. He is my candidate for patron saint for pastors.

St John is the kind of pastor I would like to be. My admiration expands: he is also the kind of pastor I would like my colleagues to be. As I look to him, searching for the energy source that makes him a master and not one more religious hack, I find it is the apocalyptic element that is critical.

Ernst Käsemann captured what many think is *the* unique biblical stance in his sentence: 'Apocalyptic was the mother of all Christian theology.' Perhaps, then, the grandmother of all Christian pastoral work. Early church Christians believed that the resurrection of Jesus inaugurated a new age. They were in fact – but against appearances – living in God's kingdom, a kingdom of truth and healing and grace. This was all actually present but hidden from unbelieving eyes and inaudible to unbelieving ears.

Pastors are the persons in the church communities who repeat and insist on these kingdom realities against the world appearances, and who therefore must be apocalyptic. In its dictionary meaning, apocalypse is simply 'revelation', the uncovering of what was covered up so that we can see what is there. But the context in which the word arrives adds color to the black-and-white dictionary meaning, colors bright and dark – crimson urgency and purple crisis. Under the crisis of persecution and under the urgency of an imminent end, reality is revealed suddenly for what it is. We had supposed our lives were so utterly *ordinary*. Sin-habits dull our free faith into stodgy moralism and respectable boredom; then crisis rips the veneer of cliché off everyday routines and reveals the side-by-side splendors and terrors of heaven and hell. Apocalypse is arson – it secretly sets a fire in the imagination that boils the fat out of an obese culture-religion and renders a clear gospel love, a pure gospel hope, a purged gospel faith.

I have been a pastor for thirty years to American Christians who do their best to fireproof themselves against crisis and urgency. Is there any way that I can live with these people and love them without being shaped by the golden-calf culture? How can I keep from settling into the salary and benefits of a checkout clerk in a store for religious consumers? How can I avoid a metamorphosis from the holy vocation of pastor into a promising career in religious sales?

Here is a way: submit my imagination to St John's apocalypse – the crisis of the End combined with the urgencies of God – and let the energies of the apocalyptic define and shape me as pastor. When I do that, my life as pastor simplifies into prayer, poetry, and patience.

Apocalyptic Prayer

The apocalyptic pastor *prays*. St John's pastoral vocation was worked out on his knees. He embraced the act of prayer as pivotal in his work, and then showed it as pivotal in everyone's work. Nothing a pastor does is different in kind from what all Christians do, but sometimes it is more focused, more visible. Prayer is the pivot action in the Christian community.

After a few introductory sentences in the Revelation, we come upon St John in the place and practice of prayer (1:9-10). The place: 'on the island called Patmos.' The practice: 'in the Spirit on the Lord's Day.' In the intricate task of being pastor to his seven congregations, which in the case study we have before us involves composing this theological poem, *The Revelation,* he never leaves the place of prayer, never abandons the practice of prayer. At the end of the book he is still praying: 'Amen. Come, Lord Jesus!' (22:20). St John listens to God, is silent before God, sings to God, asks questions of God. The listening and silence, the songs and questions are wonderfully in touch with reality, mixing the sights and sounds of Roman affairs with the sights and sounds of salvation – angels and markets and Caesars and Jesus. St John doesn't miss much. He is an alert and alive pastor. He reads and assimilates the Scriptures; he reads and feels the impact of the daily news. But neither ancient Scripture nor current event is left the way it arrives on his doorstep; it is all turned into prayer.

St John lives on the boundary of the invisible world of the Holy Spirit and the visible world of Roman times. On that boundary he prays. The praying is a joining of realities, making a live connection between the place we find ourselves and the God who is finding us.

But prayer is not a work that pastors are often asked to do except in ceremonial ways. Most pastoral work actually erodes prayer. The reason is obvious: people are not comfortable with God in their lives. They prefer something less awesome and more informal. Something, in fact, like the pastor. Reassuring, accessible, easygoing. People would rather talk to the pastor than to God. And so it happens that without anyone actually intending it, prayer is pushed to the sidelines.

And so pastors, instead of practicing prayer, which brings people into the presence of God, enter into the practice of messiah: we will do the work of God for God, fix people up, tell them what to do, conspire in finding the shortcuts by which the long journey to the Cross can be bypassed since we all have such crowded schedules right now. People love us when we do this. It is flattering to be put in the place of God. It feels wonderful to be treated in this godlike way. And it is work that we are generally quite good at.

A sense of apocalypse blows the whistle on such messianic pastoring. The vastness of the heavenly invasion, the urgency of the faith decision, the danger of the impinging culture – with these pouring into our consciousness accompanied by thunder and lightning, we cannot stand around on the street corners of Sunday morning filling the time with pretentious small talk on how bad the world is and how wonderful this new stewardship campaign is going to be.

If we have even an inkling of apocalypse, it will be impossible to act like the jaunty foreman of a home-improvement work crew that is going to re-landscape moral (or immoral) garden spots. We must pray. The world has been invaded by God, and it is with God we have to do.

Prayer is the most thoroughly *present* act we have as humans, and the most energetic: it sockets the immediate past into the immediate future and makes a flexible, living joint of them. The Amen gathers what has just happened into the Maranatha of the about to happen and produces a Benediction. We pay attention to God and lead others to pay attention to God. It hardly matters that so many people would rather pay attention to their standards of living, or their self-image, or their zeal to make a mark in the world.

Apocalypse opens up the chasm of reality. The reality is God: worship or flee.

Apocalyptic Poet

The apocalyptic pastor is a *poet.* St John was the first major poet of the Christian church. He used words in new ways, making (*poétés* in Greek is *maker*) truth right before our eyes, fresh in our ears. The way a pastor uses the language is a critical element in the work. The Christian gospel is rooted in language: God *spoke* a creation into being; our Savior was the *Word* made flesh. The poet is the person who uses words not primarily to convey information but to *make* a relationship, *shape* beauty, *form* truth. This is St John's work; it is every pastor's work.

I do not mean that all pastors write poems or speak in rhyme, but that they treat words with reverence, stand in awe before not only the Word, but words, and realize that language itself partakes of the sacred.

If St John's Revelation is not read as a poem, it is virtually incomprehensible, which, in fact, is why it is so often uncomprehended. St John, playful with images and exuberant in metaphor, works his words into vast, rhythmic repetitions. The gospel has already been adequately proclaimed to these people to whom he is pastor; they have become Christians through preaching and teaching that originated with Peter and Paul, and was then passed on by canonical Gospel writers along with unnumbered deacons, elders, and martyrs. But there is more to St John's work than making a cognitive connection with the sources. As pastor he re-speaks, re-visions the gospel so that his congregations experience the *word*, not mere words. To do that he must be a poet.

The pastor's task is to shape the praying imagination before the gospel. This revelation of God to us in Jesus is a fact so large and full of energy, and our capacities to believe and love and hope are so atrophied, that we need help to hear the words in their power, see the images in their energy.

Isn't it odd that pastors, who are responsible for interpreting the Scriptures, so much of which come in the form of poetry, have so little interest in poetry? It is a crippling defect and must be remedied. The Christian communities as a whole must rediscover poetry, and the pastors must lead them. Poetry is essential to the pastoral vocation because poetry is original speech. The word is creative: it brings into being what was not there before – perception, relationship, belief. Out of the silent abyss a sound is formed: people hear what was not heard before and are changed by the sound from loneliness into love. Out of the blank abyss a picture is formed by means of metaphor: people see what they did not see before and are changed by the image from anonymity into love. Words create. God's word creates; our words can participate in the creation.

But poetry is not the kind of language that pastors are asked to use, except in quotation at funerals. Most pastoral work erodes poetry. The reason is obvious: people are not comfortable with the uncertainties and risks and travail of creativity. It takes too much time. There is too much obscurity. People are more comfortable with prose. They prefer explanations of Bible history and information on God. This is appealing to the pastor, for we have a lot of information to hand out and are adept at explanations. After a few years of speaking in prose, we become prosaic.

Then a dose of apocalyptic stops us in mid-sentence: the power of the word to create faith, the force of imagination to resist the rationalism of evil, the necessity of shaping a people who speak and listen personally in worship and witness. The urgencies of apocalyptic shake us down to the roots of language, and we become poets: pay attention to core language, to personal language, to scriptural language.

Not all words create. Some merely communicate. They explain, report, describe, manage, inform, regulate. We live in an age obsessed with communication. Communication is good but a minor good. Knowing about things never has seemed to improve our lives a great deal. The pastoral task with words is not communication but communion – the healing and restoration and creation of love relationships between God and his fighting children and our fought-over creation. Poetry uses words in and for communion.

This is hard work and requires alertness. The language of our time is in terrible condition. It is used carelessly and cynically. Mostly it is a tool for propaganda, whether secular or religious. Every time badly used and abused language is carried by pastors into prayers and preaching and direction, the word of God is cheapened. We cannot use a bad means to a good end.

Words *making* truth, not just conveying it: liturgy and story and song and prayer are the work of pastors who are poets.

Apocalyptic Patience

The apocalyptic pastor is *patient.* St John identified himself to his parishioners as 'your brother, who shares with you in Jesus the tribulation and the kingdom and the patient endurance' (1:9). The 'patient endurance,' what the Greeks called *hypomone* – the hanging in there, the sticking it out – is one of the unexpected but most notable achievements of apocalyptic.

The connection is not obvious. After all, if everything is falling apart, and the world about to come to an end, doesn't that mean the end of patience? Why not cut and run? Why not eat, drink, and be merry for tomorrow we die? Bastard apocalyptic, apocalyptic that has no parentage in biblical sources or gospel commitments, does promote a progeny of irresponsibility (and the brats are noisily and distressingly in evidence on every American street), but the real thing, the conceived-in-holy-wedlock apocalyptic, develops communities that are passionately patient, courageously committed to witness and work in the kingdom of God no matter how long it takes, or how much it costs. Typically, marginal, oppressed, and exploited groups are nurtured on apocalypse.

St John is terrifically urgent, but he is not in a hurry. Note his unhurried urgency in the book he wrote. It takes a long time to read *The Revelation*. It cannot be read quickly and requires repeated rereadings to enter into the subtle and glorious poem-vision. St John works with vast and leisurely repetitions, pulling us into ancient rhythms. An impatient person never finishes this book. We learn patience in the very act of reading/listening to St John's Apocalypse. If St John would have been impatient, he would have given us a slogan on a decal.

The reason St John insists on patience is that he is dealing with the vast mysteries of God and the intricacies of the messy human condition. This is going to take some time. Neither the mysteries nor the mess is simple. If we are going to learn a life of holiness in the mess of history, we are going to have to prepare for something intergenerational and think in centuries. The apocalyptic imagination gives us a facility in what geologists call 'deep time' – a sense of 'ages' that transcends the compulsions of time-management experts and at the same time dignifies the existence of the meanest fossil.

But the working environment of pastors erodes patience and rewards impatience. People are uncomfortable with mystery (God) and mess (themselves). They avoid both mystery and mess by devising programs and hiring pastors to manage them. A program provides a defined structure with an achievable goal. Mystery and mess are eliminated at a stroke. This is appealing. In the midst of the mysteries of grace and the complexities of human sin, it is nice to have something that you can evaluate every month or so and find out where you stand. We don't have to deal with ourselves or with God, but can use the vocabulary of religion and work in an environment that acknowledges God, and so be assured that we are doing something significant.

With programs shaping the agenda – not amazing grace, not stubborn sin – the pastor doesn't have to be patient. We set a goal, work out a strategy, recruit a few Christian soldiers, and go to it. If, in two or three years the soldiers haven't produced, we shake the dust off our feet and hire on as captain to another group of mercenaries. When a congregation no longer serves our ambition, it is abandoned for another under the euphemism of 'a larger ministry'. In the majority of such cases, our impatience is rewarded with a larger salary.

Apocalypse shows this up as inexcusable exploitation. Apocalypse convinces us that we are in a desperate situation, and in it together. The grass is not greener in the next committee, or parish, or state. All that matters is worshiping God, dealing with evil, and developing faithfulness. Apocalypse ignites a sense of urgency, but it quenches shortcuts and hurry, for the times are in God's hands. Providence, not the newspaper, accounts for the times in which we live.

Impatience, the refusal to *endure,* is to pastoral character what strip mining is to the land – a greedy rape of what can be gotten at the least cost, and then abandonment in search of another place to loot. Something like fidelity comes out of apocalyptic: fidelity to God, to be sure, but also to people, to parish – to *place.*

St John was patient, teaching the Christians in his seven less-than-promising congregations to be patient. But it is an apocalyptic patience – not acquiescence to boredom, not doormat submissiveness. It is giant sequoia patience that scorns the reduction of a glorious gospel to a fast-food religion. Mount Rainier patience that mocks the fast-lane frenzy for a weekend with the Spirit. How long did it take to grow the sequoia? How long did it take to build Rainier? Apocalypse ushers us into the long and the large. We acquire, with St John and his congregations, fidelity to place and people, the faithful endurance that is respectful of the complexities of living a moral, spiritual, and liturgical life before the mysteries of God in the mess of history.

American religion is conspicuous for its messianically pretentious energy, its embarrassingly banal prose, and its impatiently hustling ambition. None of these marks is remotely biblical. None is faintly in evidence in the gospel story. All of them are thoroughly documented diseases of the spirit. Pastors are in great danger of being undetected carriers of the very disease we are charged to diagnose and heal. We need the most powerful of prophylactics – something like the apocalyptic prayer and poetry and patience of St John.

BETWEEN SUNDAYS

5

Ministry Amid the Traffic

From Monday through Saturday, the vision of myself as pastor, so clear in Lord's Day worship, is now blurred and distorted as it is reflected back from the eyes of confused and hurting people.

SUNDAYS ARE EASY. THE SANCTUARY IS CLEAN AND ORDERLY, the symbolism clear, the people polite. I know what I am doing: I am going to lead this people in worship, proclaim God's word to them, celebrate the sacraments. I have had time to prepare my words and spirit. And the people are ready, arriving dressed up and expectant. Centuries of tradition converge in this Sunday singing of hymns, exposition of Scripture, commitments of faith, offering of prayers, baptizing, eating and drinking the life of our Lord. I love doing this. I wake up early Sunday mornings, the adrenaline pumping into my veins.

But after the sun goes down on Sunday, the clarity diffuses. From Monday through Saturday, an unaccountably unruly people track mud through the holy places, leaving a mess. The order of worship gives way to the disorder of argument and doubt, bodies in pain and emotions in confusion, misbehaving children and misdirected parents. I don't know what I am doing half the time. I am interrupted. I am asked questions to which I have no answers. I am put in situations for which I am not adequate. I find myself attempting tasks for which I have neither aptitude nor inclination. The vision of myself as pastor, so clear in Lord's Day worship, is now blurred and distorted as it is reflected back from the eyes of people who view me as pawn to their egos. The affirmations I experience in Sunday greetings are now precarious in the slippery mud of put-down and fault-finding.

Sundays are important – celebrative and essential. The first day defines and energizes our lives by means of our

Lord's resurrection and gives a resurrection shape to the week. But the six days between Sundays are just as important, if not so celebrative, for they are the days to which the resurrection shape is given. Since most pastoral work takes place on the six days, an equivalent attention must be given to them, practicing the art of prayer in the middle of the traffic.

6

Curing Souls: The Forgotten Art

BLESSED ARE THE POOR IN SPIRIT

A beech tree in winter, white
Intricacies unconcealed
Against sky blue and billowed
Clouds, carries in his emptiness
Ripeness: sap ready to rise
On signal, buds alert to burst
To leaf. And then after a season
Of summer a lean ring to remember
The lush fulfilled promises.
Empty again in wise poverty
That lets the reaching branches stretch
A millimeter more towards heaven,
The bole expand ever so slightly
And push roots into the firm
Foundation, lucky to be leafless:
Deciduous reminder to let it go.

A REFORMATION MAY BE IN PROCESS IN THE WAY PASTORS DO their work. It may turn out to be as significant as the theological reformation of the sixteenth century. I hope so. The signs are accumulating.

The Reformers recovered the biblical doctrine of justification by faith. The gospel proclamation, fresh and personal and direct, through the centuries had become an immense, lumbering Rube Goldberg mechanism: elaborately contrived ecclesiastical gears, pulleys, and levers rumbled and creaked importantly but ended up doing something completely trivial. The Reformers recovered the personal passion and clarity so evident in Scripture. This rediscovery of firsthand involvement resulted in freshness and vigor.

The vocational reformation of our own time (if it turns out to be that) is a rediscovery of the pastoral work of the cure of souls. The phrase sounds antique. It is antique. But it is not obsolete. It catches up and coordinates, better than any other expression I am aware of, the unending warfare against sin and sorrow and the diligent cultivation of grace and faith to which the best pastors have consecrated themselves in every generation. The odd sound of the phrase may even work to advantage by calling attention to how remote present-day pastoral routines have become.

I am not the only pastor who has discovered this old identity. More and more pastors are embracing this way of pastoral work and are finding themselves authenticated by it. There are not a lot of us. We are by no means a majority, not even a high-profile minority. But one by one, pastors are rejecting the job description that has been handed to them and are taking on this new one or, as it turns out, the old one that has been in use for most of the Christian centuries.

It is not sheer fantasy to think there may come a time when the number reaches critical mass and effects a genuine vocational reformation among pastors. Even if it doesn't, it seems to me the single most significant and creative thing happening in pastoral ministry today.

There's a distinction between what pastors do on Sundays and what we do between Sundays. What we do on Sundays has not really changed through the centuries: proclaiming the gospel, teaching Scripture, celebrating the sacraments, offering prayers. But the work between Sundays has changed radically, and it has not been a development but a defection.

Until about a century ago, what pastors did between Sundays was a piece with what they did on Sundays. The context changed: instead of an assembled congregation, the pastor was with one other person or with small gatherings of persons, or alone in study and prayer. The manner changed: instead of proclamation, there was conversation. But the work was the same: discovering the meaning of Scripture, developing a life of prayer, guiding growth into maturity.

This is the pastoral work that is historically termed the cure of souls. The primary sense of *cura* in Latin is 'care', with undertones of 'cure'. The soul is the essence of the human personality. The cure of souls, then, is the Scripture-directed, prayer-shaped care that is devoted to persons singly or in groups, in settings sacred and profane. It is a determination to work at the center, to concentrate on the essential.

The between-Sundays work of American pastors in this century, though, is running a church. I first heard the phrase just a few days before my ordination. After thirty years, I can still remember the unpleasant impression it made.

I was traveling with a pastor I respected very much. I was full of zest and vision, anticipating pastoral life. My inner conviction of call to the pastorate was about to be confirmed by others. What God wanted me to do, what I wanted to do, and what others wanted me to do were about to converge. From fairly extensive reading about pastor and priest predecessors, I was impressed that everyday pastoral life was primarily concerned with developing a life of prayer among the people. Leading worship, preaching the gospel, and teaching Scripture on Sundays would develop in the next six days into representing the life of Christ in the human traffic of the everyday.

With my mind full of these thoughts, my pastor friend and I stopped at a service station for gasoline. My friend, a gregarious person, bantered with the attendant. Something in the exchange provoked a question.

'What do you do?'

'I run a church.'

No answer could have surprised me more. I knew, of course, that pastoral life included institutional responsibilities, but it never occurred to me that I would be defined by those responsibilities. But the moment I became ordained, I found I was so defined both by the pastors and executives over me and by the parishioners around me. The first job description given me omitted prayer entirely.

Behind my back, while my pastoral identity was being formed by Gregory and Bernard, Luther and Calvin, Richard Baxter of Kidderminster and Nicholas Ferrar of Little Gidding, George Herbert and Jonathan Edwards, John Henry Newman and Alexander Whyte, Phillips Brooks and George MacDonald, the work of the pastor had been almost completely secularized (except for Sundays). I didn't like it and decided, after an interval of confused disorientation, that being a physician of souls took priority over running a church, and that I would be guided in my pastoral vocation by wise predecessors rather than contemporaries. Luckily, I have found allies along the way and a readiness among my parishioners to work with me in changing my pastoral job description.

It should be clear that the cure of souls is not a specialized form of ministry (analogous, for instance, to hospital chaplain or pastoral counselor) but is the essential pastoral work. It is not a narrowing of pastoral work to its devotional aspects, but it is a way of life that uses weekday tasks, encounters, and situations as the raw material for teaching prayer, developing faith, and preparing for a good death. Curing souls is a term that filters out what is introduced by a secularizing culture. It is also a term that identifies us with our ancestors and colleagues in ministry, lay and clerical, who are convinced that a life of prayer is the connective tissue between holy day proclamation and weekday discipleship.

A caveat: I contrast the cure of souls with the task of running a church, but I do not want to be misunderstood. I am not contemptuous of running a church, nor do I dismiss its importance. I run a church myself; I have for over twenty years. I try to do it well.

But I do it in the same spirit that I, along with my wife, run our house. There are many essential things we routinely do, often (but not always) with joy. But running a house is not what we do. What we do is build a home, develop in marriage, raise children, practice hospitality, pursue lives of work and play. It is reducing pastoral work to institutional duties that I object to, not the duties themselves, which I gladly share with others in the church.

It will hardly do, of course, to stubbornly defy the expectations of people and eccentrically go about pastoral work like a seventeenth-century curate, even if the eccentric curate is far more sane than the current clergy. The recovery of this essential between-Sundays work of the pastor must be worked out in tension with the secularized expectations of this age: there must be negotiation, discussion, experimentation, confrontation, adaptation. Pastors who devote themselves to the guidance of souls must do it among people who expect them to run a church. In a determined and kindly tension with those who thoughtlessly presume to write job descriptions for us, we can, I am convinced, recover our proper work.

Pastors, though, who decide to reclaim the vast territory of the soul as their preeminent responsibility will not do it by going away for job retraining. We must work it out on the job, for it is not only ourselves but our people whom we are desecularizing. The task of vocational recovery is as endless as theological reformation. Details vary with pastor and parish, but there are three areas of contrast between running a church and the cure of souls that all of us experience: initiative, language, and problems.

Initiative

In running the church, I seize the initiative. I take charge. I take responsibility for motivation and recruitment, for showing the way, for getting things started. If I don't, things drift. I am aware of the tendency to apathy, the human susceptibility to indolence, and I use my leadership position to counter it.

By contrast, the cure of souls is a cultivated awareness that God has already seized the initiative. The traditional doctrine defining this truth is prevenience: God everywhere and always seizing the initiative. He gets things going. He had and continues to have the first word. Prevenience is the conviction that God has been working diligently, redemptively, and strategically before I appeared on the scene, before I was aware there was something here for me to do.

The cure of souls is not indifferent to the realities of human lethargy, naive about congregational recalcitrance, or inattentive to neurotic cussedness. But there is a disciplined, determined conviction that everything (and I mean, precisely, everything) we do is a response to God's first work, his initiating act. We learn to be attentive to the divine action already in process so that the previously unheard word of God is heard, the previously unattended act of God is noticed.

Running-the-church questions are: What do we do? How can we get things going again?

Cure-of-souls questions are: What has God been doing here? What traces of grace can I discern in this life? What history of love can I read in this group? What has God set in motion that I can get in on?

We misunderstand and distort reality when we take ourselves as the starting point and our present situation as the basic datum. Instead of confronting the bogged-down human condition and taking charge of changing it with no time wasted, we look at divine prevenience and discern how we can get in on it at the right time, in the right way.

The cure of souls takes time to read the minutes of the previous meeting, a meeting more likely than not at which I was not present. When I engage in conversation, meet with a committee, or visit a home, I am coming in on something that has already been in process for a long time. God has been and is the central reality in that process. The biblical conviction is that God is 'long beforehand with my soul'. God has already taken the initiative. Like one who walks in late to a meeting, I am entering a complex situation in which God has already said decisive words and acted in decisive ways. My work is not necessarily to announce that but to discover what he is doing and live appropriately with it.

Language

In running the church I use language that is descriptive and motivational. I want people to be informed so there are no misunderstandings. And I want people to be motivated so things get done. But in the cure of souls I am far more interested in who people are and who they are becoming in Christ than I am in what they know or what they are doing. In this I soon find that neither descriptive nor motivational language helps very much.

Descriptive language is language *about* – it names what is there. It orients us in reality. It makes it possible for us to find our way in and out of intricate labyrinths. Our schools specialize in teaching us this language. Motivational language is language *for* – it uses words to get things done. Commands are issued, promises made, requests proffered. Such words get people to do things they won't do on their own initiative. The advertising industry is our most skillful practitioner of this language art.

Indispensable as these uses of language are, there is another language more essential to our humanity and far more basic to the life of faith. It is *personal* language. It uses words to express oneself, to converse, to be in relationship. This is language to and with. Love is offered and received, ideas are developed, feelings are articulated, silences are honored. This is the language we speak spontaneously as children, as lovers, as poets – and when we pray. It is also conspicuously absent when we are running a church – there is so much to say and do that there is no time left to be and no occasion, therefore, for the language of being there.

The cure of souls is a decision to work at the heart of things, where we are most ourselves and where our relationships in faith and intimacy are developed. The primary language must be, therefore, to and with, the personal language of love and prayer. The pastoral vocation does not take place primarily in a school where subjects are taught, nor in a barracks where assault forces are briefed for attacks on evil, but in a family – the place where love is learned, where birth takes place, where intimacy is deepened. The pastoral task is to use the language appropriate in this most basic aspect of our humanity – not language that describes, not language that motivates, but spontaneous language: cries and exclamations, confessions and appreciations, words the heart speaks.

We have, of course, much to teach and much to get done, but our primary task is to be. The primary language of the cure of souls, therefore, is conversation and prayer. Being a pastor means learning to use language in which personal uniqueness is enhanced and individual sanctity recognized and respected. It is a language that is unhurried, unforced, unexcited – the leisurely language of friends and lovers, which is also the language of prayer.

Problems

In running a church I solve problems. Wherever two or three are gathered together, problems develop. Egos are bruised, procedures get snarled, arrangements become confused, plans go awry. Temperaments clash. There are polity problems, marriage problems, work problems, child problems, committee problems, emotional problems. Someone has to interpret, explain, work out new plans, develop better procedures, organize, and administer. Most pastors like to do this. I know I do. It is satisfying to help make the rough places smooth.

The difficulty is that problems arrive in such a constant flow that problem solving becomes full-time work. Because it is useful and the pastor ordinarily does it well, we fail to see that the pastoral vocation has been subverted. Gabriel Marcel wrote that life is not so much a problem to be solved as a mystery to be explored. That is certainly the biblical stance: life is not something we manage to hammer together and keep in repair by our wits; it is an unfathomable gift. We are immersed in mysteries: incredible love, confounding evil, the creation, the cross, grace, God.

The secularized mind is terrorized by mysteries. Thus it makes lists, labels people, assigns roles, and solves problems. But a solved life is a reduced life. These tightly buttoned-up people never take great faith risks or make convincing love talk. They deny or ignore the mysteries and diminish human existence to what can be managed, controlled, and fixed. We live in a cult of experts who explain and solve. The vast technological apparatus around us gives the impression that there is a tool for everything if we can only afford it. Pastors cast in the role of spiritual technologists are hard put to keep that role from absorbing everything else, since there are so many things that need to be and can, in fact, be fixed.

But 'there are things,' wrote Marianne Moore, 'that are important beyond all this fiddle.' The old-time guide of souls asserts the priority of the 'beyond' over 'this fiddle'. Who is available for this work other than pastors? A few poets, perhaps; and children, always. But children are not good guides, and most of our poets have lost interest in God. That leaves pastors as guides through the mysteries. Century after century we live with our conscience, our passions, our neighbors, and our God. Any narrower view of our relationships does not match our real humanity.

If pastors become accomplices in treating every child as a problem to be figured out, every spouse as a problem to be dealt with, every clash of wills in choir or committee as a problem to be adjudicated, we abdicate our most important work, which is directing worship in the traffic, discovering the presence of the cross in the paradoxes and chaos between Sundays, calling attention to the 'splendor in the ordinary,' and, most of all, teaching a life of prayer to our friends and companions in the pilgrimage.

7

Praying with Eyes Open

BLESSED ARE THOSE WHO MOURN

Flash floods of tears, torrents of them,
Erode cruel canyons, exposing
Long forgotten strata of life
Laid down in the peaceful decades:
A badlands beauty. The same sun
That decorates each day with colors
From arroyos and mesas, also shows
Every old scar and cut of lament.
Weeping washes the wounds clean
And leaves them to heal, which always
Takes an age or two. No pain
Is ugly in past tense. Under
The Mercy every hurt is a fossil
Link in the great chain of becoming.
Pick and shovel prayers often
Turn them up in valleys of death.

Writer Annie Dillard is an exegete of creation in the same way John Calvin was an exegete of Holy Scripture. The passion and intelligence Calvin brought to Moses, Isaiah, and Paul, she brings to muskrats and mockingbirds. She reads the book of creation with the care and intensity of a skilled textual critic, probing and questioning, teasing out, with all the tools of mind and spirit at hand, the author's meaning.

Calvin was not indifferent to creation. He frequently referred to the world around us as a 'theater of God's glory.' He wrote of the Creator's dazzling performance in arranging the components of the cosmos. He was convinced of the wide-ranging theological significance of the doctrine of creation and knew how important the understanding of that doctrine was to protect against the gnosticism and Manichaeism that are everpresent threats to the integrity of the incarnation.

Matter is real. Flesh is good. Without a firm rooting in creation, religion is always drifting off into some kind of pious sentimentalism or sophisticated intellectualism. The task of salvation is not to refine us into pure spirits so that we will not be cumbered with this too solid flesh. We are not angels, nor are we to become angels. The Word did not become a good idea, or a numinous feeling, or a moral aspiration; the Word became flesh. It also becomes flesh. Our Lord left us a command to remember and receive him in bread and wine, in acts of eating and drinking. Things matter. The physical is holy. It is extremely significant that in the opening sentences of the Bible, God speaks a world of energy and matter into being:

light, moon, stars, earth, vegetation, animals, man, woman (not love and virtue, faith and salvation, hope and judgment, though they will come soon enough). Apart from creation, covenant has no structure, no context, no rootage in reality.

Calvin knew all this, appreciated it, and taught it. But, curiously, he never seemed to have purchased a ticket to the theater, gone in, and watched the performance himself. He lived for most of his adult ministry in Geneva, Switzerland, one of the most spectacularly beautiful places on the earth. Not once does he comment on the wild thrust of the mountains into the skies. He never voices awe at the thunder of an avalanche. There is no evidence that he ever stooped to admire the gem flowers in the alpine meadows. He was not in the habit of looking up from his books and meditating before the lake loaded with sky that graced his city. He would not be distracted from this scriptural exegesis by going to the theater, even the legitimate theater of God's glory.

Aisle Seat at God's Glory

Annie Dillard has a season ticket to that theater. Day after day she takes her aisle seat and watches the performance. She is caught up in the drama of the creation. *Pilgrim at Tinker Creek* is a contemplative journal of her attendance at the theater over the course of a year. She is breathless in awe. She cries and laughs, and in turn, she is puzzled and dismayed. She is no uncritical spectator. During intermissions, she does not scruple to find fault with either writer or performance. All is not to her liking, and some scenes bring her close to revulsion. But she always returns to the action and ends up on her feet applauding, 'Encore! Encore!'

> I think that the dying pray at the last not 'please', but 'thank you' as a guest thanks his host at the door. Falling

from air-planes, the people are crying thank you, thank you, all down the air; and the cold carriages draw up for them on the rocks. Divinity is not playful. The universe was not made in jest but in solemn incomprehensible earnest. By a power that is unfathomably secret, and holy, and fleet. There is nothing to be done about it, but ignore it, or see. And like Billy Bray I go my way, and my left foot says 'Glory,' and my right foot says 'Amen': in and out of Shadow Creek, upstream and down, exultant, in a daze, dancing, to the twin silver trumpets of praise.

Pilgrim at Tinker Creek was published in 1974 when Dillard was 28 years old. It won the Pulitzer Prize and brought widespread but short-lived acclaim. Nothing she has written since has commanded an equivalent attention. This is unfortunate, because American spirituality needs her.

Her unpretentiousness (the telephone call that told her she had won the Pulitzer pulled her out of a softball game in which she was playing second base) and her youthful beauty (she has long yellow hair and smiles winningly) account, perhaps, for the failure to take her seriously as a mystical theologian, which she most certainly is.

Subsequent books have developed the articulation of her spirituality. *Holy the Firm* (1977) wrestles pain to the mat in a wild, unforgettable agony. *Teaching a Stone to Talk* (1982) takes up listening posts and watchtowers from Atlantic to Pacific coasts and in both American hemispheres, contemplatively alert for the sacred voice and presence. *Living by Fiction* (1982) shifts ground slightly, searching for meaning in what people create with words (fictions), using the same critical and contemplative disciplines with which she examines what God creates with word. Her early volume of poems, *Tickets for a Prayer Wheel,* provides many of the texts and images that are developed in the prose works.

God's World at Tinker Creek

Shadow Creek. It started out as Tinker Creek, burgeoning with life: 'The creator goes off on one wild, specific tangent after another, or millions simultaneously, with an exuberance that would seem to be unwarranted, and with an energy sprung from an unfathomable font. What is going on here that it all flows so freely wild, like the creek, that it all surges in such a free, fringed tangle? Freedom is the world's water and weather, the world's nourishment freely given, its soil and sap: and the creator loves pizzazz.'

Then one night when she was out walking, Tinker Creek vanished and Shadow Creek blocked its banks. The meaning leaked out of the creek. Imbecility replaced beauty. She praises anyway. Dark shapes intruded: the giant water bug, the dragonfly's terrible lip, the mantis's jaw, the parasites that make up 10 percent of living creatures (she calls them 'the devil's tithe'). Brutality, pain, mindlessness, waste. 'Shadow is the blue patch where the light doesn't hit.'

It is child's play to 'appreciate nature' when the sun is shining and the birds are singing. Something far more strenuous is involved when we face and deal with the cruelty and terror that the creation also deals out in spades. How we handle 'the blue patch where the light doesn't hit' is the wilderness test for creation-exegesis. It is this test that pushes Dillard into a religious vocation, into holy orders.

Annie Dillard does not go in for nature appreciation; she is no gossip of the numinous. Nor is she an explainer, flattening existence into what will fit a rationalizing diagram. 'These things,' she says, 'are not issues; they are mysteries.' She is after bigger game: after meaning, after glory, after God. And she will not, as a shortcut in her pursuit, brush aside a single detail of the appalling imbecility she meets in the shadows.

Here is where she parts company with most of her contemporaries and becomes such a valuable ally in Christian pilgrimage. Avoiding the camps of neo-pagan humanists who go to the wilderness to renew their spirits, and neo-Darwinian scientists who drag specimens into the classroom to explain them, she explores the world's text with the ancient but unfashionable tools of sacrifice and prayer. She embraces spiritual disciplines in order to deal with a Creator and a creation: 'Then we can at least wail the right question into the swaddling band of darkness, or, if it comes down to that, choir the proper praise.'

Persons in the Middle Ages who withdrew from the traffic of the everyday to contemplate the ways of God and the mysteries of being, giving themselves to a life of sacrifice and prayer, were called anchorites (from the Greek, *anachoreo,* to withdraw to a place apart). They often lived in sheds fastened to the walls of a church. These spare shacks commonly had a world-side window through which the nun or monk received the sights and sounds of the creation as data for contemplation. These barnacle-like rooms were called anchorholds. Dillard calls her cabin on Tinker Creek an anchorhold, and plays with the word: 'I think of this house clamped to the side of Tinker Creek as an anchorhold. It holds me at anchor to the rock bottom of the creek itself, and it keeps me steadied in the current, as a sea anchor does, facing the stream of light pouring down. It's a good place to live; there's a lot to think about.'

She announces her exegetical agenda. First, the active mystery of creeks: 'Theirs is the mystery of the continuous creation and all that providence implies: the uncertainty of vision, the horror of the fixed, the dissolution of the presence, the intricacy of beauty, the nature of perfection.' And then the passive mystery of the mountains: 'Theirs is the one simple mystery of creation from nothing, of matter itself, anything at all, the given. Mountains are giant, restful, absorbent. You can heave your spirit into a mountain and the mountain will keep it, folded, and not throw it back as some creeks will. The creeks are the world with all its stimulus and beauty; I live there. But the mountains are home.'

It is clear now that this is not academic exegesis, weighing and measuring, sorting and parsing. This is contemplative exegesis, receiving and offering, wondering and praying. She describes her vocation as a blend of nun, thinker, and artist: 'A nun lives in the fires of the spirit, a thinker lives in the bright wick of the mind, an artist lives jammed in the pool of materials. (Or, a nun lives, thoughtful and tough, in the mind, and with that special poignancy peculiar to religious, in the exile of materials; and a thinker, who would think of something, lives in the clash of materials, and in the world of spirit where all long thoughts must lead; and an artist lives in the mind, that warehouse of forms, and an artist lives, of course, in the spirit.)'

Her vocational self-understanding is most explicit in *Holy the Firm,* written in three parts as the contemplative result of three consecutive days in her life when she lived on an island in Puget Sound.

On November 18, she wakes. The world streams in through her world-side window ('I live in one room, one long wall of which is glass') and she is stunned by divinity: 'Every day is a god, each day is a god, and holiness holds forth in time.' She 'reads' the world as a sacred script: 'The world at my feet, the world through the window, is an illuminated manuscript whose leaves the wind takes, one by one, whose painted illuminations and halting words draw me, one by one, and I am dazzled in days and lost.'

She seeks orientation. She draws a map of the islands visible on the horizon, fixing their locations, giving them names.

She is looking around, seeing, smelling, listening: 'All day long I feel created . . . created gulls pock the air, rip great curved seams in the settled air: I greet my created meal, amazed.'

Even so, all is not well. She remembers a night in the mountains of Virginia when she was reading by candlelight and moths kept flying into the candle. One incinerated moth served the candle as a wick, and the flame soared through it, 'a saffron-yellow flame that robed her to the ground like any immolating monk.' There is pain out there. And death. There is also an immense mystery in it, something that has to do with sacrifice: the death gives light. The book she is reading is about the poet Rimbaud who burned himself out in the life of art, word-flames that illuminate the world.

Still, the day is, incredibly, fresh and full of promise. She notes that Armenians, Jews, and Catholics all salt their newborn. And all the first-offerings that Israel brought to the Lord were 'a covenant of salt' preserved and savory. And the 'god of today is a child, a baby new and filling the house, remarkably here in the flesh. He is day.' She salts the day, as she salts her breakfast eggs, anticipating delight, exultant.

On November 19, an airplane crashes in a nearby field. She hears the sound of the crash. The pilot pulls his 7-year-old daughter from the wreckage, and as he does, a gob of ignited fuel splashes her face and burns her horribly. On November 18, she wrote, 'I came here to study hard things, rock mountain and salt sea and to temper my spirit on their edges. "Teach me thy ways, O Lord" is, like all prayers, a rash one, and one I cannot but recommend.' She hadn't bargained on having to deal with a 7-year-old girl with a burnt-off face.

On November 18, God 'socketed into everything that is, and that right holy.' Now, on November 19, a child is in the hospital with her grieving parents at her side and 'I sit at the window, chewing the bones in my wrist and pray for them. Who will teach us to pray? The god of today is a glacier. We live in his shifting crevasses, unheard. The god of today is delinquent, a barn-burner, a punk with a pittance of power in a match.'

What is God up to? What is real? What is illusion? She asks all the hard questions: 'Has God a hand in this? Is anything firm, or is time on the loose? Did Christ descend once and for all to no purpose, in a kind of divine and kenotic suicide, or ascend once and for all, pulling his cross up after him like a rope ladder home?' And she faces the worst: 'We're logrolling on a falling world, of time released from meaning and rolling loose, like one of Atalanta's golden apples, a bauble flung and forgotten, lapsed, and the gods on the lam.'

She looks out of her world-side window and sees an island on the horizon that she hadn't noticed before. She names it God's Tooth.

On November 20, she walks to the store to buy the Communion wine in preparation for Sunday worship at the white frame Congregational church in the fir trees. Is there any accounting for this juxtaposition of the best and worst, this grandeur and this obscenity of the past two days? She recalls and meditates on the medieval idea that there is a created substance at the absolute base of everything, deep down 'in the waxy deepness of planets, but never on the surface of planets where men can discern it; and it is in touch with the Absolute, at base . . . the name of this substance is: Holy the Firm.' Everything eventually touches it. Something that touches something that touches Holy the Firm is in touch with the Absolute, with God. Islands are rooted in it, and trees, and the little girl with the slaughtered face.

Two weeks before, the little girl's parents had invited sixteen neighbors to their farm to make cider. Dillard brought her cat, and the girl played with it all afternoon. 'All day long she was dressing and undressing the yellow cat, sticking it into a black dress long and full as a nun's.' She and the girl resembled each other in appearance.

She names her little look-alike friend Julie Norwich. Juliana of Norwich was a fourteenth-century English nun, an anchorite, who steadily and courageously, through a suffering lifetime, looked the world's pain full in the face, and summed up her contemplation in the remarkable sentence, 'And all shall be well, and all shall be well, and all manner of things shall be well.' From anyone else that sentence would risk ridicule as glib gibberish, but from this nun, 'thoughtful and tough ... in the exile of materials,' it is tempered truth, flexible and hard.

Dillard gives the name of the nun whose life of prayer transmuted pain to wellness to the girl whose face two weeks before was much like her own, but now puts every concept of beauty and meaning and God to hazard, and in mediatory prayer addresses her: 'Held fast by love in the world like the moth in wax, your life a wick, your head on fire with prayer, held utterly, outside and in, you sleep alone, if you call that alone, you cry God.' She invites her into the full goodness of life in the years ahead of her healing: 'Mornings you'll whistle, full of the pleasure of days, and afternoons of this or that, and nights cry love. So live.'

Then an abrupt turning, returning to her own vocation. Earlier she observed that 'a life without sacrifices is abomination.' Now she embraces this sacrifice, burning in a life of art and thought and prayer through the canonical hours. While 'elsewhere people buy shoes,' she kneels at the altar rail, holding on for dear life in the dizzying swirl of glory and brutality, and calls Julie Norwich. The last words of the book: 'I'll be the nun for you. I am now.'

A World of Scripture

Even though her field is creation, not Scripture exegesis, Calvin would not, I think, be displeased with Dillard's competence in Scripture. She has assimilated Scripture so thoroughly, is so saturated with its cadences and images, that it is simply at hand, unbidden, as context and metaphor for whatever she happens to be writing about. She does not, though, use Scripture to prove or document; it is not a truth she 'uses' but one she lives. Her knowledge of Scripture is stored in her right brain rather than her left; nourishment for the praying imagination rather than fuel for apologetic argument. She seldom quotes Scripture; she alludes constantly. There is scarcely a page that does not contain one or several allusions, but with such nonchalance, not letting her left hand know what her right is doing, that someone without a familiarity with Scripture might never notice the biblical precept and story.

The verbal word of Scripture is the wide world within which she gives her attention to the non-verbal word of creation. The revealed world of Torah and Gospel is the spacious environment in which she works out the localized meanings of sycamore, weasels, eclipses, and sunlighted minnows. A sense of proportion develops out of her Scripture reading in which the so-called 'general' revelation is subordinate to and enclosed by the 'special' revelation of Scripture. She would agree, I think, with P. T. Forsyth: 'It is a vast creation, but a vaster salvation.'

One example: the title essay in *Teaching a Stone to Talk*, where I count seventeen allusions to Holy Scripture (not counting repeats) and three quotations. She tells the story of Larry, her neighbor on a Puget Sound island, who is trying to teach a stone to talk. He keeps the stone on his mantle, 'protected by a square of untanned leather, like a canary asleep under its cloth. Larry removes the cover for the stone's lessons.' The quirky story of the island crank is representational: 'Nature's silence is its one remark.' We are restive with the silence and are trying to raise a peep out of mute mother nature.

She finds the orienting background to the story of Larry in the story of Israel, scared witless at Sinai with its thunder and lightning, asking Moses to beg God, 'Please, never speak to them directly again.'

Now the entire non-human world is silent. We told God, like we tell a child who is annoying us, to shut up and go to his room. He heard our prayer. After these many centuries, we are bored and fitful with the unrelieved patter of human speech. Even our scientists, who earlier seemed to be the most determined of all to confine speech to the human, are trying to teach chimpanzees to talk, decipher the language of whales, and listen for messages from some distant star.

The island in Puget Sound on which Larry is trying to teach a stone to talk is one result of Israel's prayer; the Galapagos Islands are another. Since Darwin's time, scientists have treated the islands as a laboratory in which to find meaning in a world dissociated from the living voice of God, to study the process of evolution, to unravel the biological story of the race. Dillard goes there reading a different text, a creation text encompassed by a biblical text. She calls the Galapagos a 'kind of metaphysics laboratory.' She might as well have called them a prayer laboratory.

The sea lion is the most popular resident of the Galapagos, gregarious and graceful, welcoming and sportive, 'engaged in full-time play.' Visitors joke that when they 'come back' they would like to come as a sea lion. 'The sea lion game looked unbeatable.' After long reflection and another visit to the island, she made a different choice: the palo santo tree.

She had hardly noticed them on her first visit. The trees were thin, pale, wispy miles of them, half dead, the stands looking like blasted orchards. She chose the palo santo because even though 'the silence is all there is,' it is not a silence of absence but of presence. It is not a sterile silence, but a pregnant silence. The non-human silence is not because there is nothing to say but because, in disobedience or unbelief or sheer terror, we asked God not to speak and God heard our prayer. But though unspeaking, God is still there. What is needed from us is witness. The palo santo is a metaphor for witness.

The premier biblical witness, John the Baptist, said, 'He must increase, but I must decrease.' The witness does not call attention to itself; what it points to is more important. Being takes precedence over using, explaining, possessing. The witness points, mute, so as not to interfere with the sound of silence: the palo santos 'interest me as emblems of the muteness of the human stance in relation to all that is not human. I see us all as palo santo trees, holy sticks, together watching all that we watch, and growing in silence.'

Witness is the key word in all this. It is an important biblical word in frequent contemporary use. It is a modest word saying what is there, honestly testifying to exactly what we see, what we hear. But when we enlist in a cause, it is almost impossible to do it right: we embellish, we fill in the blanks, we varnish the dull passages, we gild the lily just a little to hold the attention of our auditors. Sea lion stuff. Important things are at stake – God, salvation – and we want so much to involve outsiders in these awesome realities that we leave the humble ground of witness and use our words to influence and motivate, to advertise and publicize. Then we are no longer witnesses, but lawyers arguing the case, not always with scrupulous attention to detail. After all, life and death issues are before the jury.

Dillard returns us to the spare, simple, modest role of witness. We live in a time when the voice of God has been extinguished in the creation. We want the stones to talk, the heavens to declare the glory of God, but 'the very holy mountains are keeping mum. We doused the burning bush and cannot rekindle it; we are lighting matches in vain under every green tree. Did the wind used to cry, and the hills shout forth praise? Now speech has perished from among the lifeless things of earth, and living things say very little to very few.'

Our necessary and proper work in such a world is witness like the palo santo trees.

The World in a Church

The American writers with whom Dillard is often grouped – Henry Thoreau, Waldo Emerson, John Muir – didn't go to church. They distanced themselves from what they saw as the shabbiness and hypocrisy of institutional religion and opted for the pine purity of forest cathedrals. Emily Dickinson gave them their text: 'Some worship God by going to church/I worship him staying at home/with a bobolink for a chorister/ and an orchard for a throne.' Their numerous progeny spend Sunday mornings on birdwatching field trips and Sierra Club walks. Annie Dillard goes to church: 'I know only enough of God to want to worship him, by any means ready to hand.... There is one church here, so I go to it.' It doesn't matter that it is out of fashion, she goes anyway: 'On a big Sunday there might be twenty of us there; often I am the only person under sixty, and feel as though I'm on an archaeological tour of Soviet Russia.'

It is unfashionable because it is ridiculous. How can searchers after God and seekers after beauty stomach the 'dancing bear act' that is staged in Christian churches, Protestant and Catholic alike, week after week? Dillard, cheerfully and matter-of-factly, goes anyway. Her tour de force on worship, 'An Expedition to The Pole,' provides the image and rationale. Wherever we go, to the pole or the church, 'there seems to be only one business at hand: that of finding workable compromises between the sublimity of our ideas and the absurdity of the fact of us.'

In *Pilgrim,* she wrote, 'These northings drew me, present northings, past northings, the thought of northings. In the literature of polar exploration, the talk is of northing. An explorer might scrawl in his tattered journal, "Latitude 82 + 15′ N. We accomplished 20 miles of northing today, in spite of the shifting pack." Shall I go northing? My legs are long.' She describes the parallel goals. The pole of Relative Inaccessibility is 'that imaginary point on the Arctic Ocean farthest from land in any direction.' Reading the accounts of polar explorers, one is impressed that at root they were seeking the sublime. 'Simplicity and purity attracted them; they set out to perform clear tasks in uncontaminated lands.... They praised the land's spare beauty as if it were a moral or a spiritual quality: "icy halls of cold sublimity," "lofty peaks perfectly covered with eternal snow."' That is geography. There is an equivalent pole in worship: 'the Absolute is the pole of Relative Inaccessibility located in metaphysics. After all, one of the few things we know about the Absolute is that it is relatively inaccessible. It is the point of spirit farthest from every accessible point of spirit in all directions. Like the others, it is a pole of the Most Trouble. It is also, I take this as a given, the pole of great price.'

She quotes Fridtjof Nansen on polar exploration, referring to 'the great adventure of the ice, deep and pure as infinity ... the eternal round of the universe and its eternal death' and notes that everywhere 'polar prose evokes these absolutes, these ideas of "eternity" and "perfection" as if they were some perfectly visible part of the landscape.' And she quotes Pope Gregory, who calls us to Christian worship 'to attain to somewhat of the unencompassed light, by stealth, and scantily.'

She tells the comic-tragic stories of polar explorers who 'despite the purity of their conceptions . . . manhauled their humanity to the poles.' The Franklin Expedition in 1845, with 138 officers and men, carried a '1,200 volume library, a hand-organ playing fifty tunes, china place settings for officers and men, cutglass wine goblets, sterling silver flatware, and no special clothing for the Arctic, only the uniforms of Her Majesty's Navy.' It was a noble enterprise, and they were nobly dressed for it. They all died. Their corpses were found with pieces of backgammon board and a great deal of table silver engraved with officers' initials and family crests. Dignity was all.

Sir Robert Falcon Scott had a different kind of dignity: he thought the purity of polar search dictated a purity of effort unaided by dogs or companions. He also died. 'There is no such thing as a solitary polar explorer, fine as the conception is.' Some of the most moving documents of polar writing, expressing his lofty sentiments, his purity and dignity and self-control, were found under his frozen carcass.

The explorers who made it weren't so fussy. They abandoned their roles, their privileges, their preconceived notions, and adapted to the conditions of pack ice and glaciers in the light-drenched land.

Annie Dillard going to worship – 'a kind of northing is what I wish to accomplish, a single-minded trek toward that place' – faces equivalent difficulties. Her experiences in the church's worship are interweaved with commentary on polar explorations. The amateurism is distressing: 'A high school stage play is more polished than this service we have been rehearsing since the year one. In two thousand years we have not worked out the kinks.'

The attempts to be relevant are laughable: 'I have overcome a fiercely anti-Catholic upbringing in order to attend Mass simply and solely to escape Protestant guitars.'

The blithe ignorance is frightening: 'Why do we people in churches seem like cheerful, brainless tourists on a packaged tour of the Absolute? . . . On the whole, I do not find Christians, outside the catacombs, sufficiently sensible of conditions. Does anyone have the foggiest idea what sort of power we so blithely invoke? Or, as I suspect, does not one believe a word of it? The churches are children playing on the floor with their chemistry sets, mixing up a batch of TNT to kill a Sunday morning. It is madness to wear ladies' straw hats and velvet hats to church; we should all be wearing crash helmets. Ushers should issue life preservers and signal flares: they should lash us to our pews.' Explorers unmindful of 'conditions' died. Why don't similarly unprepared worshipers perish on the spot?

Never mind. She sheds her dignity, sloughs off schooling and scruples, abandons propriety. 'I would rather, I think, undergo the famous dark night of the soul than encounter in church the dread hootenanny, but these purely personal preferences are of no account, and maladaptive to boot.' So she manhauls her humanity to her pew, gives up her personal dignity, and throws in her lot with random people. She realizes that one can no more go to God alone than go to the pole alone. She further realizes that even though the goal is pure, the people are not pure, and if we want to go to the Land we must go with the people, even when they are playing banjos, singing stupid songs, and giving vacuous sermons. 'How often have I mounted this same expedition, has my absurd barque set out half-caulked for the pole?'

So she worships. Weekly she sets out for the pole of Relative Inaccessibility, 'where the twin oceans of beauty and horror meet.' Dignity and culture abandoned, silence and solitude abandoned, she joins the motley sublime/ludicrous people who show up in polar expeditions and church congregations. 'Week after week we witness the same miracle: that God, for reasons unfathomable, refrains from blowing our dancing bear act to smithereens. Week after week, Christ washes the disciples' dirty feet, handles their very toes, and repeats, "It is all right, believe it or not, to be people."'

The spiritualities involved in going to the pole and to church are essentially the same. Dillard embraces both. And she deals with the hard things in both ventures, the absurd vanities in the explorers and the embarrassing shabbiness in the worshipers, with immense charity. She is blessedly free, whether in the wilderness or at worship, of sentimentalism and snobbery (the twin sins of touristy aesthetes). She is as accepting of absurdities in Christian worship as she is of absurdities in polar exploration. She is saying, I think, that we have put up with nature sentimentalism and liturgical snobbery long enough. If there are difficulties in going to church, they are no greater than those encountered in going to the pole. As she says, 'Nobody said things were going to be easy.'

Prayer: Eyes Open or Shut?

There are two great mystical traditions in the life of prayer, sometimes labeled kataphatic and apophatic. Kataphatic prayer uses icons, symbols, ritual, incense; the creation is the way to the Creator. Apophatic prayer attempts emptiness; the creature distracts from the Creator, and so the mind is systematically emptied of idea, image, sensation until there is only the simplicity of being. Kataphatic prayer is 'praying with your eyes open'; apophatic prayer is 'praying with your eyes shut.'

At our balanced best, the two traditions intermingle, mix, and cross-fertilize. But we are not always at our best. The Western church is heavily skewed on the side of the apophatic. The rubric for prayer when I was a child was, 'Fold your hands, bow your head, shut your eyes, and we'll pray.' My early training carries over into my adult practice. Most of my praying still is with my eyes shut. I need balancing.

Annie Dillard prays differently: Spread out your hands, lift your head, open your eyes, and we'll pray. 'It is still the first week in January, and I've got great plans. I've been thinking about seeing. There are lots of things to see, unwrapped gifts and free surprises.' We start out with her on what we suppose will be no more than a walk through the woods. It is not long before we find ourselves in the company of saints and monks, enlisted in the kind of contemplative seeing 'requiring a lifetime of dedicated struggle.'

She gets us into the theater that Calvin told us about, and we find ourselves in the solid biblical companionship of psalmists and prophets who watched the 'hills skip like lambs' and heard the 'trees clap their hands', alert to God everywhere, in everything, praising, praying with our eyes open: 'I leap to my feet; I cheer and cheer.'

8

First Language

BLESSED ARE THE MEEK

Moses, by turns raging and afraid,
Was meek under the thunderhead whiteness,
The glorious opacity of cloudy pillar.
Each cloud is meek, buffeted by winds
It changes shape but never loses
Being: not quite liquid, hardly
Solid, in medias res. Like me.
Yielding to the gusting spirit
All become what ministering angels
Command: sign, promise, portent.
Vigorous in image and color, oh, colors
Of earth pigments mixed with sun
Make hues that raise praises at dusk,
At dawn, collect storms, release
Rain, filter sun in arranged
And weather measured shadows.
Sunpatches.

I ENTERED INTO MY PASTORAL CALLING WITH A GREAT CHARGE of educational zest. My mind fairly tumbled with stories and facts, insights and perspectives, that give the life of faith such richness and texture. I had been on an exuberant foray into the country of Scripture and theology in my years of study and was eager to take others on safari with me. I knew I could rescue the Arian controversy from textbook dullness and present the decipherment of Ugaritic in such ways that would enhance appreciation for the subtle elegances of biblical language and story. I couldn't wait to get started.

No place seemed to me better suited to such endeavors than the Christian congregation. It was far better than any school. People came to church not because they had to but because they willed it. They brought a level of motivation to learning that was far higher than in any academic assembly. Nobody was there just to get a grade or a diploma. They came together in a community of faith wanting to love the Lord with both mind and heart. And they had called me to help them do it.

So I taught. I taught from pulpit and lectern. I taught in home and classroom. I taught adults and youth and children. I formed special groups, arranged mini-courses, conducted seminars. The ones who loitered and held back I promoted and persuaded. I had people studying Isaiah and Mark, Reformation theology and Old Testament archaeology, who hadn't used their minds in a disciplined way since they got their high school diplomas or college degrees. I didn't, of course, get everyone, but by and large I was not disappointed. I had a wonderful time.

What Is My Educational Task?

After a few years of this, I noticed how different my teaching was from that of early generations of pastors. My secularized schooling had shaped my educational outlook into something with hardly any recognizable continuities with most of the church's history. I had come into the parish seeing its great potential as a learning center, a kind of mini-university in which I was the resident professor.

And then one day, in a kind of shock of recognition, I saw that it was in fact a worship center. I wasn't prepared for this. Nearly all my preparation for being a pastor had taken place in a classroom, with chapels and sanctuaries ancillary to it. But these people I was now living with were coming, with centuries of validating precedence, not to get facts on the Philistines and Pharisees but to pray. They were hungering to grow in Christ, not bone up for an examination in dogmatics. I began to comprehend the obvious: that the central and shaping language of the church's life has always been its prayer language.

Out of that recognition a conviction grew: that my primary educational task as pastor was to teach people to pray. I did not abandon, and will not abandon, the task of teaching about the faith, teaching the content of the gospel, the historical backgrounds of biblical writings, the history of God's people. I have no patience with and will not knowingly give comfort to obscurantist or anti-intellectual tendencies in the church. But there is an educational task entrusted to pastors that is very different from that assigned to professors. The educational approaches in all the schools I attended conspired to ignore the wisdom of the ancient spiritual leaders who trained people in the disciplines of attending to God, forming the inner life so that it was adequate to the reception of truth, not just the acquisition of facts. The more I worked with people at or near the centers of their lives where God and the human, faith and the absurd, love and indifference were tangled in daily traffic jams, the less it seemed that the way I had been going about teaching made much difference, and the more that teaching them to pray did.

Help Available

It is not easy to keep this conviction in focus, for the society in which I live sees education primarily as information retrieval. But there is help available.

Most of mine came from making friends with some ancestors long dead. Gregory of Nyssa and Teresa of Avila got me started. I took these masters as my mentors. They expanded my concept of prayer and introduced me into the comprehensive and imaginative and vigorous language of prayer. They convinced me that teaching people to pray was my best work.

Other help has come from an unexpected quarter among my contemporaries, the philosophers of language (especially Ludwig Wittgenstein and Eugen Rosenstock-Huessy). Under their influence I came to be in awe of the way language works and to realize the immense mysteries that surround speech. I started paying attention to the way I used language both as a person and as a pastor. These philosophers gave me a compass that showed me the way to recover the kind of language that seemed more or less native to earlier generations in the faith, the language that was required if I were to keep faith with my pastoral vocation and teach people to pray.

I have reduced and simplified and summarized what I have learned in these respects into a kind of rough language map showing three sections: Language I, Language II, and Language III.

Three Types of Language

Language I is the language of intimacy and relationship. It is the first language we learn. Initially, it is not articulate speech. The language that passes between parent and infant is incredibly rich in meaning but less than impressive in content. The coos and cries of the infant do not parse. The nonsense syllables of the parent have no dictionary definitions. But in the exchange of gurgles and out-of-tune hums, trust develops. Parent whispers transmute infant screams into grunts of hope. The cornerstone words in this language are names, or pet names: mama, papa. For all its limited vocabulary and butchered syntax, it seems more than adequate to bring into expression the realities of a complex and profound love. Language I is primary language, the basic language for expressing and developing the human condition.

Language II is the language of information. As we grow, we find this marvelous world of things surrounding us, and everything has a name: rock, water, doll, bottle. Gradually, through the acquisition of language, we are oriented in a world of objects. Beyond the relational intimacy with persons with which we begin, we find our way in an objective environment of trees and fire engines and weather. Day after day words are added. Things named are no longer strange but familiar. We make friends with the world. We learn to speak in sentences, making connections. The world is wonderfully various and our language enables us to account for it, recognizing what is there and how it is put together. Language II is the major language used in schools.

Language III is the language of motivation. We discover early on that words have the power to make things happen, to bring something out of nothing, to move inert figures into purposive action. An infant wail brings food and a dry diaper.

A parental command arrests a childish tantrum. No physical force is involved. No material causation is visible. Just a word: stop, go, shut up, speak up, eat everything on your plate. We are moved by language and use it to move others. Children acquire a surprising proficiency in this language, moving people much bigger and more intelligent than themselves to strenuous activity (and often against both the inclination and better judgment of these people). Language III is the predominant language of advertising and politics.

Languages II and III are, clearly, the ascendant languages of our culture. Informational language (II) and motivational language (III) dominate our society. We are well schooled in language that describes the world in which we live. We are well trained in language that moves people to buy and join and vote. Meanwhile Language I, the language of intimacy, the language that develops relationships of trust and hope and understanding, languishes. Once we are clear of the cradle, we find less and less occasion to use it. There are short-lived recoveries of Language I in adolescence when we fall in love and spend endless hours talking on the telephone using words that eavesdroppers would characterize as gibberish. In romantic love, we find that it is the only language adequate to the reality of our passions. When we are new parents, we relearn the basic language and use it for a while. A few people never quit using it – a few lovers, some poets, the saints – but most let it slide.

Converting Language

When I first started listening to language with these discriminations, I realized how thoroughly culture-conditioned I was. Talk about being conformed to this world! My use of language in the community of faith was a mirror image of the culture: a lot of information, a lot of publicity, not much intimacy. My ministry was voiced almost entirely in the language of description and of persuasion – telling what was there, urging what could be. I was a great explainer. I was a pretty good exhorter. I was duplicating in the church what I had learned in my thoroughly secularized schools and sales-saturated society, but I wasn't giving people much help in developing and using the language that was basic to both their humanity and their faith, the language of love and prayer.

But this is my basic work: on the one hand to proclaim the word of God that is personal – God addressing us in love, inviting us into a life of trust in him; on the other hand to guide and encourage an answering word that is likewise personal – to speak in the first person to the second person, I to Thou, and avoid third-person commentary as much as possible. This is my essential educational task: to develop and draw out into articulateness this personal word, to teach people to pray. Prayer is Language I. It is not language *about* God or the faith; it is not language in the service *of* God and the faith; it is language *to* and *with* God in faith.

I remembered a long-forgotten sentence by George Arthur Buttrick, a preacher under whom I sat for a year of Sunday morning sermons while in seminary: 'Pastors think people come to church to hear sermons. They don't; they come to pray and to learn to pray.' I remembered Anselm's critical transition from talking about God to talking to God. He had written his *Monologion,* setting forth the proofs of God's existence with great brilliance and power. It is one of the stellar theological achievements in the West. Then he realized that however many right things he had said about God, he had said them all in the wrong language. He re-wrote it all in a *Proslogion,* converting his Language II into Language I: first-person address, an answer to God, a personal conversation with the personal God. The *Proslogion* is theology as prayer.

If the primary preaching task of the pastor is the conversion of lives, the primary teaching task is the conversion of language. I haven't quit using the languages of information and motivation, nor will I. Competency in all languages is necessary in this life of faith that draws all levels of existence into the service and glory of God. But I have determined that the language in which I must be most practiced and for which I have a primary responsibility for teaching proficiency in others is Language I, the language of relationship, the language of prayer – to get as much language as possible into the speech of love and response and intimacy.

'Abba! Father!'

9

Is Growth a Decision?

BLESSED ARE THOSE WHO HUNGER AND THIRST AFTER RIGHTEOUSNESS

Unfeathered unbelief would fall
Through the layered fullness of thermal
Updrafts like a rock; this red-tailed
Hawk drifts and slides, unhurried
Though hungry, lazily scornful
Of easy meals off carrion junk,
Expertly waiting elusive provisioned
Prey: a visible emptiness
Above an invisible plenitude.
The sun paints the Japanese
Fantail copper, etching
Feathers against the big sky
To my eye's delight, and blesses
The better-sighted bird with a shaft
Of light that targets a rattler
In a Genesis-destined death.

THE PEOPLE WITH WHOM I GREW UP TALKED A LOT ABOUT 'breaking the will'. The task of every devout parent was to 'break the will' of the child. I don't remember ever hearing it used by adults on one another, but that may be a more or less willful defect in my memory.

The assumption underlying this linchpin in the program for Christian development in our church was, apparently, that the will, especially a child's will, is contrary to God's will. A broken will presumably left one open to the free play of God's will.

Fifty years later, I recall my now grown-up friends who were enrolled in this school of childhood spirituality and along with me got their wills broken with regularity. By my observations, we all seem to have passed through the decades every bit as pigheaded and stiff-necked as any of our uncircumcised Philistine companions who never went to church, or at least not to churches that specialized in breaking the wills of little kids. Apparently broken wills mend the same way that broken arms and legs do, stronger at the line of fracture.

At the same time, I also recall a lot of emphasis in our church on 'making a decision for the Lord', and exercising my willpower in saying no to the temptations that surrounded me in school and neighborhood. I had many occasions to do that, making repeated decisions for Christ as evangelists and pastors took turns at sowing doubts about the validity of my last decision and urging me to do it again. My schoolmates provided daily practice in exercising my nay-saying willpower as they offered up the attractions of world, flesh, and devil.

Hung on the wall of my room at home was a framed picture of a three-masted ship with wind-filled sails on a blue background. Under the picture was a verse:

Ships sail East, and ships sail West,
while the selfsame breezes blow.
It's the set of the sail, and not the gale
that determines the way they go.

I could see the picture and verse as I laid in bed. I learned the use of the rudder and how to tack before the wind by pondering that rectangle of blue. The doggerel embedded itself in me. The picture became a kind of mandala that gathered the energies of will – my childhood yea-saying at the altar calls and nay-saying on the playgrounds – into visual form. The verse took on the force of a mantra. Together, picture and verse confirmed with the force of Scripture the capacity of my will to determine the direction of my life, which I never doubted was a life following Christ.

These two approaches to the will, breaking it and exercising it, existed alongside each other through my childhood and youth. It never occurred to me to see them in contradiction, canceling each other out. Nor does it now. But in adulthood I did become puzzled by their apparent dissonance.

I set off in search of counsel that had more wisdom than the simplistic slogan (break the will) and doggerel verse (It's the set of the sail) that seemed to serve well enough as I grew up.

Human Will and God's Will

I found, early in my search, that I was not the first to be puzzled. I found a large company of men and women scratching their heads over these matters. I found myself, in fact, in the middle of a centuries-long discussion that is still in progress.

Hamlet's question, *To be or not to be?* is not ours. Being is not in question. Willing is. *To will or not to will?*

In a gospel of divine grace, what place does the human will play? In a world in which God's will initiates everything, does our will only get in the way? In a creation brought into being by God's will and in a salvation executed by Christ's will, what is left for a human will?

On the positive side, willing is the core of my being. If my will is broken, am I myself? Am I complete? Am I not a cripple, limping along on a crutch? The capacity to make a decision, to direct life, to exercise freedom is the very thing that needs developing if I am to make a decision for Christ – which I grew up believing to be the most important act of will there is. I still believe that.

Without an exercised will, I am a dishrag, limp in a dirty sink. If I am anemic in will, the imperatives that are staccato stabs throughout the gospel message (come, follow, rise, love) sink into marshmallow piety without drawing one drop of red blood.

But the moment I begin exercising my will, I find that I have put a fox in charge of the chicken coop. That is the negative side. The poor Rhode Island Reds that had been laying so well – humility, trust, mercy, patience, kindness, hope – are doomed. It is a heady experience to find that I am in charge of my life and, although I wouldn't think of dismissing God, no longer have the need to depend wimpily upon him.

My will is my glory; it is also what gives me the most trouble. There is something deeply flawed in me that separates me from the God who wills my salvation; that 'something' seems to be located in and around my will. I ponder St Paul, 'I do not understand my own actions. For I do not do what I want, but I do the very thing I hate' (Rom 7:15), and I pray with my Lord, 'Not as I will but as thou wilt' (Mt 26:39).

To will or not to will, that is the question.

Searching the Intersection

I prayed and pondered. I asked questions and read books. I looked around. It wasn't long before I realized I had set up shop at heavily trafficked crossroads.

Not only were God and my consequent spirituality at issue, but nearly everything that was distinctively human about me – the way I worked, the way I talked, the way I loved. Standing in the presence of these mysteries – work, language, love – I found insights developing and experiences occurring that were convergent with the greatest mystery: God and my relationship to him in prayer and belief and obedience.

The question at the heart of the intersection of God's will and human wills is apparently at the heart of everything. The relation of God's will and my will is not a specialized religious question; it is *the* question. The way we answer it shapes our humanity in every dimension.

Whenever I paid attention to what was happening in my life that was beyond biology – beyond, that is, getting fed and clothed – this strange issue of will was involved, and in a way not at all obvious or simple. Always other wills were involved in ways that defied simple alternatives of either asserting my will or acquiescing to another will.

The three areas of experience where I have paid particular attention are common to all: we all work; we all use language; we all love and are loved (even if only intermittently).

Work: Negative Capability

I entered the world of work at an early age in my father's butcher shop. This was a privileged world, this adult world of work, and when I was working in it I was, in my own mind anyway, an adult. When I was 5 years old, my mother made me a white butcher's apron. Every year, as I grew, she made another to size. To this day, I picture the linen ephod that Hannah made for the boy Samuel cut on the pattern of, and from similar material as, my butcher's apron.

I was started out on easy jobs of sweeping and cleaning display windows. I graduated to grinding hamburger. One of the men would pick me up and stand me on an upended orange crate before the big, red Hobart meat grinder, and I in my linen ephod would push the chunks of beef into its maw. The day I was trusted with a knife and taught to respect it and keep it sharp, I knew adulthood was just around the corner.

'That knife has a will of its own,' old Eddie Nordham, one of my dad's butchers, used to say to me. 'Get to know your knife.' If I cut myself, he would blame me not for carelessness but for ignorance – I didn't 'know' my knife.

I also learned that a beef carcass has a will of its own – it is not just an inert mass of meat and gristle and bone, but has character and joints, texture and grain. Carving a quarter of beef into roasts and steaks was not a matter of imposing my knife-fortified will on dumb matter, but respectfully and reverently entering into the reality of the material.

'Hackers' was my father's contemptuous label for butchers who ignorantly imposed their wills on the meat. They didn't take into account the subtle differences between pork and beef. They used knives and cleavers inappropriately and didn't keep them sharp. They were bullies forcing their wills on slabs of bacon and hind quarters of beef. The results were unattractive and uneconomical. They commonly left a mess behind that the rest of us had to clean up.

Real work always includes a respect for the material at hand. The material can be a pork loin, or a mahogany plank, or a lump of clay, or the will of God, but when the work is done well there is a kind of submission of will to the conditions at hand, a cultivation of humility. It is a noticeable feature in all skilled workers – woodworkers, potters, poets, and prayers. I learned it in the butcher shop.

'Negative capability' is the phrase the poet John Keats coined to refer to this experience in work. He was impressed by William Shakespeare's work in making such a variety of characters in his plays, none of which seemed to be a projection of Shakespeare's ego. Each had an independent life of his or her own. Keats wrote, 'A poet has no Identity ... he is continually ... filling some other Body.' He believed that the only way real creative will matured was in a person who was not hell-bent on imposing his or her will on another person or thing but 'was capable of being in uncertainties, mysteries, doubts, without any irritable searching after fact and reason.' Interesting: Shakespeare, the poet from whom we know the most about people, is the poet about whom we know next to nothing.

Adolescents are workers bent on self-expression. The results are maudlin. Simpering songs. Sprawling poems. Banal letters. Bombastic reforms. Bursts of energy that run out of gas (the self tank doesn't hold that much fuel) and litter house and neighborhood with unfinished models, friendships, and projects. The adolescent, excited at finding the wonderful Self, supposes that life now consists in expressing it for the edification of all others. Most of us are bored.

Real work, whether it involves making babies or poems, hamburger or holiness, is not self-expression, but its very opposite. Real workers, skilled workers, practice negative capability – the suppression of self so that the work can take place on its own. St John the Baptist's 'I must decrease, but he must increase' is embedded in all good work. When we work well, our tastes, experiences, and values are held in check so that the nature of the material or the person or the process or our God is as little adulterated or compromised by our ego as possible.

The worker in the work is a self-effacing servant. If the worker shows off in his or her work, the work is ruined and becomes bad work – a projection of ego, an indulgence of self.

St Paul's description of Jesus, 'emptied himself' (Phil 2:7), is often cited as the center point in the work of Incarnation, the making of our salvation. *Kenosis.* Emptying is prelude to filling. The Son of God empties himself of prerogative, of divine rights, of status and reputation, in order to be the one whom God uses to fill up creation and creatures with the glory of salvation. A bucket, no matter what wonderful things it contains, is of no use for the next task at hand until it is emptied. Negative capability.

I now see that all the jobs I have ever been given have been apprenticeships in the work of God. What I experience in kitchen, bedroom, workshop, athletic arena, studio, and sanctuary trains me in the subtleties of negative capability. I will to not will what I am already good at in order that what is more than me and beyond me, the will of God, can come into existence in my willing work.

Language: The Middle Voice

Five hundred miles farther west and ten years later, another strand of experience entered my life, sat alongside the butcher's knife for a few years, and then converged with it to provide insight into the nature of the praying will.

For four years, minus vacations, I made a daily descent into a basement room in MacMillan Hall at the foot of Queen Anne Hill in Seattle. Light came uncertainly through Venetian blinds from shallow windows high in the walls. I was learning Greek. I puzzled over many strange things those years under the soft-spoken patience of my professor, Dr Winifred Weter.

I puzzled longest over the middle voice. It was a small class, five of us I think, and I was the last to get it. In a class that size slowness is conspicuous, and I was unhappy with my growing reputation as the class tortoise. Then one day, a winter afternoon of Seattle drizzle, the room filled with light, or at least my corner of it did. We were about two-thirds of the way through Xenophon's *Anabasis* when I got the hang of the mysterious middle voice.

At the time I thought only that I had nailed down an elusive piece of Greek grammar. Years later I realized that I had grasped a large dimension of being and a way of prayer. I was the slowest in my class but by no means the only person to have difficulty coming to terms with the middle voice. Active and passive voices I understood, but middle was a new kid on the block. When I speak in the active voice, I initiate an action that goes someplace else: 'I counsel my friend.' When I speak in the passive voice, I receive the action that another initiates: 'I am counseled by my friend.' When I speak in the middle voice, I actively participate in the results of an action that another initiates: 'I take counsel.' Most of our speech is divided between active and passive; either I act or I am acted upon. But there are moments, and they are those in which we are most distinctively human, when such a contrast is not satisfactory: two wills operate, neither to the exclusion of the other, neither canceling out the other, each respecting the other.

My grammar book said, 'The middle voice is that use of the verb which describes the subjects as participating in the results of the action.' I read that now, and it reads like a description of Christian prayer – 'the subject as participating in the results of the action.' I do not control the action; that is a pagan concept of prayer, putting the gods to work by my incantations or rituals. I am not controlled by the action; that is a Hindu concept of prayer in which I slump passively into the impersonal and fated will of gods and goddesses. I enter into the action begun by another, my creating and saving Lord, and find myself participating in the results of the action. I neither do it, nor have it done to me; I will to participate in what is willed.

Prayer and spirituality feature participation, the complex participation of God and the human, his will and our wills. We do not abandon ourselves to the stream of grace and drown in the ocean of love, losing identity. We do not pull the strings that activate God's operations in our lives, subjecting God to our assertive identity. We neither manipulate God (active voice) nor are manipulated by God (passive voice). We are involved in the action and participate in its results but do not control or define it (middle voice). Prayer takes place in the middle voice.

Now comes a most fascinating sentence in my grammar: 'Nothing is more certain than that the parent language of our family possessed no passive, but only active and middle, the latter originally equal with the former in prominence, though unrepresented now in any language, save by forms which have lost all distinction of meaning.' No passive! Think of it: back at the origins of our language, there was no way to express an action in which I was not somehow, in some way, involved as a participant.

But the farther we travel from Eden, the less use we have for the middle voice, until it finally atrophies for lack of use. We either take charge of our own destinies (active voice) or let others take charge and slip into animal passivity before forces too great for us (passive voice). The gospel restores the middle voice. We learn to live with praying-willing involvement in an action that we do not originate. We become subjects in an action in which we are personally involved. In the middle voice objects take second place to subjects – everyone and everything becomes subject.

Eden pride and disobedience delete the middle and reduce us to two voices, active and passive. We end up taking sides. We don't have enough (or any!) verbal experience in this third voice, this voice that is fine-tuned to the exquisitely and uniquely human venture of entering into and responding to God. But no friendship, no love affair, no marriage can exist with only active and passive voices. Something else is required, a mode of willingness that radiates into a thousand subtleties of participation and intimacy, trust and forgiveness and grace.

At our human and Christian best we are not fascists barking our orders to God and his creatures. At our human and Christian best we are not quietists dumbly submissive before fate. At our human and Christian best we pray in the middle voice at the center between active and passive, drawing from them as we have need and occasion but always uniquely and artistically ourselves, creatures adoring God and being graced by him, 'participating in the results of the action.'

And to think I got my start in learning this during that long winter of Seattle rain while reading Xenophon!

Love: Willed Passivity

After another decade and a few years into marriage, I was surprised to find myself at the center of what has turned out to be the richest experience yet in my will and God's will. I had supposed when I entered marriage that it was mostly about sexuality, domesticity, companionship, and children. The surprise was that I was in a graduate school for spirituality – prayer and God – with daily assignments and frequent exams in matters of the will.

(What I have learned in marriage can be just as well, maybe better, learned in friendship. The unmarried have just as much experience to work with as the married. But since my primary experience has been in marriage, I will write of it.)

It goes without saying that in marriage two wills are in operation at the same time. Sometimes, and especially in the early months of marriage, the two wills are spontaneously congruent and experienced as one. But as time goes by and early ecstasies are succeeded by routines and demands, what was experienced as a gift must be developed as an art.

The art is willed passivity. The phrase sounds self-contradictory, but it is not, and converges with what I started out learning in my father's butcher shop and continued in Professor Weter's Greek class.

Learning the art of willed passivity begins with appreciating the large and creative part passivity plays in our lives. By far the largest part of our life is experienced in the mode of passivity. Life is undergone. We receive. We enter into what is already there. Our genetic system, the atmosphere, the food chain, our parents, the dog – they are there, in place, before we exercise our will.

'Eighty percent of life,' says Woody Allen, 'is just showing up.' Nothing we do by the exercise of our wills will ever come close to approximating what is done to us by other wills. Our lives enter into what is already done; most of life is not what we do but what is done to us. If we deny or avoid these passivities, we live in a very small world. The world of our activities is a puny enterprise; the world of our passivities is a vast cosmos. We experience as happening to us weather, our bodies, our parents, much of our government, the landscape, much of our education.

But there are different ways of being passive: there is an indolent, inattentive passivity that approximates the existence of a slug; and there is a willed and attentive passivity that is something more like worship.

St Paul's famous 'Wives, be subject to your husbands. Husbands, love your wives, as Christ loved the church and gave himself up for her' (Eph 5:22-25) sets down the parallel operations of willed passivity.

An earlier sentence establishes the necessary context, apart from which the dual instructions can only be misunderstood. The sentence is: 'Be subject to one another out of reverence for Christ' (Eph 5:21).

Reverence is the operative word – *en phobo Christou* – awed, worshipful attentiveness, ready to respond in love and adoration. We do not learn our relationship with God out of a cocksure, arrogant knowledge of exactly what God wants (which then launches us into a vigorous clean-up campaign of the world on his behalf, in the course of which we shout orders up at him, bossing him around so that he can assist us in accomplishing his will). Nor do we cower before him in a scrupulous anxiety that fears offending him, only venturing a word or an action when explicitly commanded and at all other times worrying endlessly of what we might have done to offend him.

No, gospel reverence, Christ reverence, spouse reverence is a vigorous (but by no means presumptuous) bold freedom, full of spontaneous energy. This is the contextual atmosphere in which we find ourselves loved and loving before God.

We are more than ready to bow down before Christ unafraid that we will be tyrannized, for Christ has already laid down his life for us on the cross, pouring himself out and holding nothing back. Willed passivity.

St Paul teaches husbands and wives how their wills can become the means for love and not the weapons of war. He counsels willed passivity in both marriage partners as an analogy of Christ's willingness to be sacrificed. Love is defined by a willingness to give up my will ('not my will but thine be done'), a voluntary crucifixion.

Marriage provides extensive experience in the possibilities of willed passivity. We find ourselves in daily relationship with a complex reality we did not make – this *person* with functioning heart and kidneys, with glorious (and not so glorious) emotions, capable of interesting us profoundly one minute and then boring us insufferably the next, and most mysterious of all, with a will, the freedom to choose and direct and intend a shared life intimacy.

And all the time I am also all those things, also with a will. When we are doing it right, and not always knowing how we are doing it right, the two wills enhance and glorify each other. We learn soon that love does not develop when we impose our will on the other, but only when we enter into sensitive responsiveness to the will of the other, what I am calling willed passivity. If the operation is mutual, which it sometimes is, a great love is the consequence. The high failure rate in marriage is the sad statistical witness to the difficulties involved. We would rather operate as activists in our love, commanding our beloved in actions that please us, which reduces our partner's options to indolent passivity or rebellion.

No ambiguities in either case. But also no love – and no faith.

'I no longer call you servants; I call you friends,' said Jesus (Jn 15:15). Is it not quite obvious that this is the model by which we understand our growing intimacy with God? Not as abject, puppy-dog submission, and certainly not as manipulative priest-craft, but as willed passivity, in imitation of and matched by the willed passivity of him who 'did not count equality with God a thing to be grasped but emptied himself, being born in the likeness of men' (Phil 2:6-7).

Willfulness or Willingness?

Gerald May, in his book *Will and Spirit,* distinguishes between willfulness and willingness. Every act of intimacy, whether in work or language or marriage or prayer, suppresses willfulness and cultivates willingness.

All of us, in the act of creation, suppress willfulness and cultivate willingness. There is a deep sense of being involved in something more than the ego, better than the self. The 'more' and the 'better' among Christians has a personal name, *God.*

One of the qualities of will in its freedom is knowing the nature and extent of the necessities in which it works. Unmindful of necessities, the will becomes arrogant and liable to hubris (which the Greeks saw as inevitably punished with tragedy) or timidly declines to couch-potato lethargy indistinguishable from vegetation. Humble boldness (or, bold humility) enters into a sane, robust willing – free willing – and finds its most expressive and satisfying experience in prayer to Jesus Christ, who wills our salvation.

10

The Ministry of Small Talk

Blessed are the Merciful

A billion years of pummeling surf,
Shipwrecking seachanges and Jonah storms
Made ungiving, unforgiving granite
Into this analgesic beach:
Washed by sea-swell rhythms of mercy,
Merciful relief from city
Concrete. Uncondemned, discalceate,
I'm ankle deep in Assateague sands,
Awake to rich designs of compassion
Patterned in the pillowing dunes.
Sandpipers and gulls in skittering,
Precise formation devoutly attend
My salt and holy solitude,
Then feed and fly along the moving,
Imprecise ebb- and rip-tide
Border dividing care from death.

MY PASTOR, DURING MY ADOLESCENT YEARS, CAME OFTEN to our home. After a brief and awkward interval, he always said, 'And how are things in your SOUL today?' (He always pronounced 'soul' in capital letters.)

I never said much. I was too intimidated. The thoughts and experiences that filled my life in those years seemed small potatoes after that question. I knew, of course, that if I ever wanted to discuss matters of SOUL, I could go to him. But for everything else, I would probably do better with someone who wouldn't brush aside as worldly vanity what it felt like to get cut from the basketball varsity, someone who wouldn't pounce with scary intimations of hellfire on the thoughts I was having about Marnie Schmidt, the new girl from California.

Pastoral work, I learned later, is that aspect of Christian ministry that specializes in the ordinary. It is the nature of pastoral life to be attentive to, immersed in, and appreciative of the everyday texture of people's lives – the buying and selling, the visiting and meeting, the going and coming. There are also crisis events to be met: birth and death, conversion and commitment, baptism and Eucharist, despair and celebration. These also occur in people's lives and, therefore, in pastoral work. But not as everyday items.

Most people, most of the time, are not in crisis. If pastoral work is to represent the gospel and develop a life of faith in the actual circumstances of life, it must learn to be at home in what novelist William Golding has termed the 'ordinary universe' – the everyday things in people's lives – getting kids off to school, deciding what to have for dinner, dealing with the daily droning complaints of work associates, watching the nightly news on TV, making small talk at coffee break.

Small talk: the way we talk when we aren't talking about anything in particular, when we don't have to think logically, or decide sensibly, or understand accurately. The reassuring conversational noises that make no demands, inflict no stress. The sounds that take the pressure off. The meandering talk that simply expresses what is going on at the time. My old pastor's refusal (or inability) to engage in that kind of talk implied, in effect, that most of my life was being lived at a sub-spiritual level. Vast tracts of my experience were 'worldly', with occasional moments qualifying as 'spiritual'. I never questioned the practice until I became a pastor myself and found that such an approach left me uninvolved with most of what was happening in people's lives and without a conversational context for the actual undramatic work of living by faith in the fog and the drizzle.

Impatient with the Ordinary

Given a choice between heated discussion on theories of the Atonement and casual banter over the prospects of the coming Little League season, I didn't hesitate. It was the Atonement every time. If someone in the room raised questions of eschatology, it wasn't long before I was in the thick of the talk, but if conversation dipped to the sale on radial tires at the local dealer's, my attention flagged. I substituted meaningless nods and grunts while looking for a way to disengage myself and get on to a more urgent and demanding meeting of souls. What time did I have for small talk when I was committed to the large message of salvation and eternity? What did I have to do with the desultory gossip of weather and politics when I had 'fire in my mouth'?

I know I am not the only pastor who has been ill at ease and impatient with small talk. And I know I am not the only pastor who has rationalized impatience by claiming big-talk priorities of Sermons and Apologetics and Counsel.

The rationalization seems plausible. After spending so much time learning the subtleties of supralapsarianism, surely it is wasteful to talk of the Pittsburgh Pirates. 'Redeem the time!' With warehouses of knowledge stored in our brain cells, what business do we have chatting about Cabbage Patch dolls? If we have any chance at all in setting the agenda for conversation, are we not obligated to make it something spiritually important? And if we can't set the agenda, isn't it our task to work the conversation around to what our calling and training have equipped us to bring home to people's hearts?

The practice of manipulating conversation was widely used among people I respected in my college and seminary years, and I was much influenced by them. Their conviction was that every conversation could be turned, if we were sharp enough, into witness. A casual conversation on an airplane could be turned into an eternity-fraught conversation on the soul. A brief interchange with a filling-station attendant could yield the opening for a 'word for Christ'.

Such approaches to conversation left no room for small talk – all small talk was manipulated into big talk: of Jesus, of salvation, of the soul's condition.

Small Talk: A Pastoral Art

But however appropriate such verbal strategies are for certain instances of witness (and I think there are such instances), as habitual *pastoral* practice they are wrong. If we bully people into talking on our terms, if we manipulate them into responding to our agenda, we do not take them seriously where they are in the ordinary and the everyday.

Nor are we likely to become aware of the tiny shoots of green grace that the Lord is allowing to grow in the backyards of their lives. If we avoid small talk, we abandon the very field in which we have been assigned to work. Most of people's lives is not spent in crisis, not lived at the cutting edge of crucial issues. Most of us, most of the time, are engaged in simple, routine tasks, and small talk is the natural language. If pastors belittle it, we belittle what most people are doing most of the time, and the gospel is misrepresented.

'Lord, how I loathe big issues!' is a sentence I copied from one of C. S. Lewis's letters and have kept as a reminder. He was reacting to pretentiousness that only sees significance in the headlines – in the noisy and large. Lewis warned of the nose-in-the-air arrogance that is oblivious to the homely and the out-of-the-way, and therefore misses participating in most of the rich reality of existence.

Pastors especially, since we are frequently involved with large truths and are stewards of great mysteries, need to cultivate conversational humility. Humility means staying close to the ground *(humus)*, to people, to everyday life, to what is happening with all its down-to-earthness.

I do not want to be misunderstood: pastoral conversation should not bound along on mindless clichés like gutter water. What I intend is that we simply be present and attentive to what is there conversationally, as respectful of the ordinary as we are of the critical. Some insights are only accessible while laughing. Others arrive only by indirection.

Art is involved here. Art means that we give ourselves to the encounter, to the occasion, not condescendingly and not grudgingly but creatively. We're not trying to make something happen but to be part of what is happening – without being in control of it and without it being up to the dignity of our office.

Such art develops better when we are convinced that the Holy Spirit is 'beforehand' in all our meetings and conversations. I don't think it is stretching things to see Jesus – who embraced little children, which so surprised and scandalized his followers – also embracing our little conversations.

We mount our Sinai pulpits week by week and proclaim the gospel in what we hope is the persuasive authority of 'artful thunder' (Emerson's phrase). When we descend to the people on the plain, a different artfulness is required, the art of small talk.

11

Unwell in a New Way

BLESSED ARE THE PURE IN HEART

Austere country, this, scrubbed
By spring's ravaging avalanche.
Talus slope and Appekunny
Mudstone make a meadow where
High-country beargrass gathers light
From lichen, rock, and icy tarn,
Changing sun's lethal rays
To food for grizzlies, drink for bees –
Heart-pure creatures living blessed
Under the shining of God's face.
Yet, like us the far-fallen,
Neither can they look on the face
And live. Every blossom's a breast
Holding eventual sight for all blind and
Groping newborn: we touch our way
Through these splendors to the glory.

A TUG OF WAR TAKES PLACE EVERY WEEK BETWEEN PASTOR and people. The contest is over conflicting views of the person who comes to church. The result of the struggle is exhibited in the service of worship, shaping sermon and prayers, influencing gesture and tone.

People (and particularly people who come to church and put themselves in touch with pastoral ministry) see themselves in human and moral terms: they have human needs that need fulfilling and moral deficiencies that need correcting. Pastors see people quite differently. We see them in theological terms: they are sinners – persons separated from God who need to be restored in Christ.

These two views – the pastor's theological understanding of people and the people's self-understanding – are almost always in tension.

Seeing People as Sinners

The word *sinner* is a theological designation. It is essential to insist on this. It is *not* a moralistic judgment. It is not a word that places humans somewhere along a continuum ranging from angel to ape, assessing them as relatively 'good' or 'bad'. It designates humans in relation to God and sees them separated from God. *Sinner* means something is awry between humans and God. In that state people may be wicked, unhappy, anxious, and poor. Or, they may be virtuous, happy, and affluent. Those items are not part of the judgment. The theological fact is that humans are not close to God and are not serving God.

To see a person as sinner, then, is not to see him or her as hypocritical, disgusting, or evil. Most sinners are very nice people. To call a man a sinner is not a blast at his manners or his morals. It is a theological belief that the thing that matters most to him is forgiveness and grace.

If a pastor finds himself resenting his people, getting petulant and haranguing them, that is a sign that he or she has quit thinking of them as sinners who bring 'nothing in themselves of worth' and has secretly invested them with divine attributes of love, strength, compassion, and joy. They, of course, do not have these attributes in any mature measure and so will disappoint him or her every time. On the other hand, if the pastor rigorously defines people as fellow sinners, he or she will be prepared to share grief, shortcomings, pain, failure, and have plenty of time left over to watch for the signs of God's grace operating in this wilderness, and then fill the air with praises for what he discovers.

An understanding of people as sinners enables a pastoral ministry to function without anger. Accumulated resentment (a constant threat to pastors) is dissolved when unreal – that is, untheological – presuppositions are abandoned. If people are sinners then pastors can concentrate on talking about God's action in Jesus Christ instead of sitting around lamenting how bad the people are. We already know they can't make it. We already have accepted their depravity. We didn't engage to be pastor to relax in their care or entrust ourselves to their saintly ways. 'Cursed be he that trusteth in man, even if he be a pious man, or, perhaps, particularly if he be a pious man' (Reinhold Niebuhr). We have come among the people to talk about Jesus Christ. Grace is the main subject of pastoral conversation and preaching. 'Where sin increased, grace abounded all the more' (Rom 5:20).

But a pastor is not likely to find this view of people supported by the people themselves. They ordinarily assume that everyone has a divine inner core that needs awakening. They're Emersonian in their presuppositions, not Pauline. They expect personal help from the pastor in the shape of moralistic, mystic, or intellectual endeavors. People don't reckon with sin as that total fact that characterizes them; nor do they long for forgiveness as the effective remedy. They yearn for the nurture of their psychic life, for a way in which they may bypass grace and walk on their own. They are frequently noble and sincere in their approach as they ask the pastor to believe in them and their inner resources and possibilities. The pastor can easily be moved to accommodate such self-understanding. But it is a way without grace. The pastor must not give in. This road must be blocked. The Word of God to which pastoral ministry is committed loses propinquity the moment a person is not understood as a sinner.

The happy result of a theological understanding of people as sinners is that the pastor is saved from continual surprise that they are in fact sinners. It enables us to heed Bonhoeffer's admonition: 'A pastor should not complain about his congregation, certainly never to other people, but also not to God. A congregation has not been entrusted to him in order that he should become its accuser before God and men.' So *sinner* becomes not a weapon in an arsenal of condemnation, but the expectation of grace. Simply to be against sin is a poor basis for pastoral ministry. But to see people as sinners – as rebels against God, missers of the mark, wanderers from the way – *that* establishes a basis for pastoral ministry that can proceed with great joy because it is announcing God's great action in Jesus Christ 'for sinners'.

Discerning Sin's Particular Forms

There is more to it, though, than establishing a theological viewpoint. If the pastor first of all has to be a theologian in order to see people accurately, he or she must quickly acquire pastoral insights into the particular way sin expresses itself. Sin, for pastors, does not remain a theological rubric; it takes on specific human forms that call out specific pastoral responses. There is a great peril in conveying too abstract an idea of it. Sin is not simply a failure in relation to God that can be studied lexically; it is a personal deviation from God's will. Pastors deal with stories, not definitions, of sin. The pastor enters the world of the local and the personal. He or she seeks to establish in the language and images of everyday life the bare fact that the Christian life is possible within the chronological boundaries of a person's life and in the geographical vicinity of his or her street address.

So however necessary it is to have a theological understanding of people as sinners, the pastor is not ready for ministry until he or she finds the particular forms that sin takes in individual histories. The pastor presses for details. He (or she) is interested in exactly *how* people are sinners. *That* they are sinners he accepts as a presupposition – he wouldn't be preaching the 'foolishness of the cross' if he hadn't accepted that. But there are different ways of being a sinner. Pastoral ministry increases in effectiveness as it discerns and discriminates among the forms of sin, and then loves, prays, witnesses, converses, and preaches the details of grace appropriate to each human face that takes shape in the pew.

Episodes of Adolescence

Each generation is, in poet John Berryman's words, 'unwell in a new way'. The way in which the present generation is unwell – that is, the forms under which it experiences sin – is through episodes of adolescence. There was a time when ideas and living styles were initiated in the adult world and filtered down to youth. Now the movement goes the other way: life-styles are generated at the youth level and pushed upward. Dress fashions, hair styles, music, and morals that are adopted by youth are evangelically pushed on an adult world, which in turn seems eager to be converted. Youth culture began as a kind of fad and then grew into a movement. Today it is nearly fascist in its influence, forcing its perceptions and styles on everyone whether he likes it or not.

This observation helps plot a pastoral understanding of people. There is a miasmic spread of the adolescent experience upward through the generations. Instead of being over and done with when the twenty-first birthday is reached, it infects the upper generations as well. It is common to see adults in their thirties, forties, and fifties who have not only adopted the external trappings of the youth culture but are actually experiencing the emotions, traumas, and difficulties typical of youth. They are experiencing life under its adolescent forms. The sins of the sons, it seems, are being visited upon the fathers.

Reference to two adolescent characteristics will illustrate this way of understanding people in pastoral ministry.

The Sense of Inadequacy

The first is a sense of inadequacy. People don't feel they are very good at the Christian life. They are apologetic and defensive about their faith.

A feeling of inadequacy is characteristic of adolescent life. When a person is growing rapidly on all fronts – physical, emotional, mental – he or she is left without competence in anything. Life doesn't slow down long enough for him to gain a sense of mastery. The teenager has a variety of devices to disguise this feeling: he can mask it with braggadocio, submerge it in a crowd of peers, or develop a subcult of language and dress in which he maintains superiority by excluding the larger world from his special competence. The variations are endless; the situation is the same: the adolescent is immature, and therefore inadequate. And he is acutely self-conscious about this inadequacy.

This is exactly what the pastor meets in people of all ages in the church. They feel they aren't making it as Christians. This is a bit of surprise because in the past the Christian church has more often had to deal with the Pharisee – the person who feels he achieved adequacy long ago. People today are much more apt to be uneasy and fearful about their Christian identity.

The ostensible reason is that the new world is changing so fast that no one gets a chance to feel at home in it. The adult, like the adolescent, is confronted with a new world every week or so and doesn't feel that he or she can cope. When this adult enters the church, he or she looks at the pastor and supposes that the *minister,* at least, has feet on the ground and knows where things are. People look at the pastor as the person with competence in things that have to do with God and cast him or her in the role of expert. That process seems natural and innocent – as natural and innocent as the feelings of inadequacy in the adolescent and his consequent admiration of competence. It is more likely, though, a new disguise for an old sin – the ancient business of making idols. God calls people to himself, but they turn away to something less than God, fashioning a religious experience but avoiding God. The excuse is that they are 'inadequate' for facing the real thing. They proceed with the awareness that, far from sinning, they have acquired the virtue of humility. But the theological nose smells idolatry.

Some pastors take deliberate steps to counteract their image as substitute God by sprinkling profanity through their syntax and quoting *Playboy* magazine. They say, in effect, to the people, 'I am no more adequate than you are. Don't look to me as any kind of saint; don't model your life on what I am doing.' But pastoral ministry must consist of something other than disclaimers.

There is a Pauline technique for dealing with this sense of inadequacy. Writing to the Ephesians, Paul says: 'For this reason, because I have heard of your faith in the Lord Jesus and your love toward all the saints, I do not cease to give thanks for you, remembering you in my prayers' (Eph 1:15-16). Assuming that the Ephesian church had the same percentage of sinners in it as modern ones do (namely, 100 percent), it would be a mistake to envy Paul his congregation, a congregation that it was possible to address so gratefully. It is better to admire Paul's ability to see God's action in those people. Paul had a meticulous eye for the signs of grace. He was God's spy, searching out the congregational terrain for evidence that the Holy Spirit had been there. Paul knew the people were sinners. But his passion was for describing grace and opening their eyes to what his eyes were open to – the activity of God in their lives, 'his power in us who believe' (Eph 1:19).

If the pastor sees inadequacy as an unfortunate feeling, he or she will use psychological and moral means to remove it. If he sees it as a sign of sin – an avoidance of personal responsibility in the awesome task of facing God in Christ – he will respond by kindly and gently presenting the living God, pointing out the ways in which God is alive in the community. The instances of courage and grace that occur every week in any congregation are staggering. Pastoral discernment that sees grace operating in a person keeps that person in touch with the living God.

Historical Amnesia

Another characteristic of the adolescent that has spread into the larger population is the absence of historical sense. The adolescent, of course, has no history. He or she has a childhood, but no accumulation of experience that transcends personal details and produces a sense of history. His world is highly personal and extremely empirical.

As a consequence, the teenager is incredibly gullible. We suppose that a person educated in fine schools by well-trained teachers would not be in any danger of superstition. We further suppose that the fact-demanding, scientific-oriented education that prevails in our schools would have sharpened the minds of the young to be perceptive in matters of evidence and logic. It doesn't happen. The reason it doesn't happen is that they have no feeling for the past, for precedents and traditions, and so have no perspective in making judgments or discerning values. They may know the facts of history and read historical novels by the dozen, but they don't feel history in their bones. It is not *their* history. The result is that they begin every problem from scratch. There is no feeling of being part of a living tradition that already has some answers worked out and some procedures worth repeating.

This state of mind, typical in adolescence, is, within certain parameters, accepted. The odd thing today is that there is no change when a person reaches adult years. The way this ahistorical anemia has become an adult trait was evident in the first landing on the moon. Everyone was caught up in a rush of historical speculation, including President Nixon himself, who rather recklessly declared it to be the most important day in human history, thereby scandalizing his spiritual director Billy Graham by forgetting so easily the birth of Christ. When these same people come to church, the pastor discovers that they have little consciousness of being part of a community that carries in its Scriptures, its worship, and its forms of obedience a life twenty and more centuries in the making.

Such people are subject to consistent trivialization. They find it impossible to tell what may be important. They buy things, both material and spiritual, that they will never use. They hear the same lies over and over again without ever becoming angry. They are led to entertain, and for brief times practice, all kinds of religious commitment from magazine moralisms to occultic séances. In none of it do they show any particular perseverance. But neither do they show much sign of wising up – of developing a historical sense, of becoming conscious that they are part of a continuing people of God and growing beyond the adolescent susceptibilities to novelty and fantasy.

If the pastor interprets this as a form of cultural deprivation, he or she will become a pedagogue, trying to teach the people who they are as Christians, extending their memory backward. But that would be a mistake, for it is not basically a cultural condition. What begins as a normal characteristic of adolescence, when stretched into Christian adulthood, becomes a clever ruse (largely unconscious) for masking sin: the sin is a denial of dependence on God and interdependence among neighbors, a refusal to be a *people* of God and a counter-insistence that the individual ego be treated as something god-like. In the Garden of Eden the decision to substitute firsthand experience for obedience to the command of God produced in a single generation a murder that revealed its loss of history and community in the flip but exceedingly lonely question, 'Am I my brother's keeper?'

Ezekiel was pastor to a similarly constituted people, who by refusing to be responsible to God and each other had lost a sense of history. His ministry provides insight into a style of pastoral response. Israel was severed from its roots, the old rituals and traditions didn't appear to have relevance in the land of exile, and people were easy prey to their heathen environment. Everyone was subject to the temptation to try to make it on his or her own, fashioning a religion out of personal basic survival needs. In this time of need, what Ezekiel did *not* do was start a school and teach history lessons. Rather he preached a new life, exposed the nature of the people's sin, and appealed to their conscience to be made into a new people by God's grace. A foundation was established in the covenant life of the people of God that, in contrast to the cultural and economic conceptions of the ancient East (and modern West!), protected the divine value of every person, showing a way of salvation and promising a future. People were asked to let themselves be taken into personal relationships of service and loyalty to the God who releases them from the chain of guilt down the generations and gives them a new start by forgiving them and then guaranteeing them a life and a future. They were reinserted into a community with a history.

Undoubtedly this development first took place in the prophet's own house where the elders (Ez 8:1; 12:9; 14:1; 20:1; 24:19) and other members of the colony in Babylon (33:30-33) gathered in order to hear some word from God or obtain advice about various problems. Many were superficial and came merely out of curiosity, but that did not prevent the prophet from finding some who responded to his appeal for a decision to repent and be made new by God. As a result, in meetings that had previously been held in order to keep up and preserve ancient, inherited spiritual possessions, hopelessly trying to defend against the loss of history that the exile produced, the Holy Spirit brought new expectations and resolutions to life. A new community was established with a lively sense of the past recast in bright visions of the future (chaps. 40-48). Ezekiel saw that the problem among the people was not historical ignorance, although they were ignorant that way. Perceptively, he diagnosed the sin that was using 'loss of history' as a front, and convincingly preached a word of grace.

The Quick Theological Eye

The people encountered in pastoral ministry today are sinners. But they don't look like it, and many of them don't even act like it. They rather look and act and feel like the youth they admire so much, struggling for 'identity' and searching for 'integrity'. A quick theological eye that is able to pick up the movements of sin hiding behind these seemingly innocent characteristics will keep a pastor on track, doing what he or she was called to do: sharing a ministry of grace and forgiveness centered in Jesus Christ.

12

Lashed to the Mast

BLESSED ARE THE PEACEMAKERS

Huge cloud fists assault
The blue exposed bare midriff of sky:
The firmament doubles up in pain.
Lightnings rip and thunders shout;
Mother nature's children quarrel.
And then, as suddenly as it began,
It's over. Noah's heirs, perceptions
Cleansed, look out on a disarmed world
At ease and ozone fragrant. Still waters.
What barometric shift
Rearranged these ferocities
Into a peace-pulsating rainbow
Sign? My enemy turns his other
Cheek; I drop my guard. A mirror
Lake reflects the filtered colors;
Breeze-stirred pine trees quietly sing.

Anne Tyler, in her novel *Morgan's Passing*, told the story of a middle-aged Baltimore man who passed through people's lives with astonishing aplomb and expertise in assuming roles and gratifying expectations.

The novel opens with Morgan's watching a puppet show on a church lawn on a Sunday afternoon. A few minutes into the show, a young man comes from behind the puppet stage and asks, 'Is there a doctor here?' After thirty or forty seconds with no response from the audience, Morgan stands up, slowly and deliberately approaches the young man, and asks, 'What is the trouble?' The puppeteer's pregnant wife is in labor; a birth seems imminent. Morgan puts the young couple in the back of his station wagon and sets off for Johns Hopkins Hospital. Halfway there the husband says, 'The baby is coming!'

Morgan, calm and self-assured, pulls to the curb, sends the about-to-be father to the corner to buy a Sunday paper as a substitute for towels and bed sheets, and delivers the baby. He then drives to the emergency room of the hospital, sees the mother and baby safely to a stretcher, and disappears. After the excitement dies down, the couple asks for Dr Morgan to thank him. But no one has ever heard of a Dr Morgan. They are puzzled – and frustrated that they can't express their gratitude.

Several months later they are pushing their baby in a stroller and see Morgan walking on the other side of the street. They run over and greet him, showing him the healthy baby that he brought into the world. They tell him how hard they had looked for him, and of the hospital's bureaucratic incompetence in tracking him down. In an unaccustomed gush of honesty, he admits to them that he is not really a doctor. In fact, he runs a hardware store. But they needed a doctor, and being a doctor in those circumstances was not all that difficult. It is an image thing, he tells them: You discern what people expect and fit into it. You can get by with it in all the honored professions. He has been doing this all his life, impersonating doctors, lawyers, pastors, counselors as occasions present themselves.

Then he confides, 'You know, I would never pretend to be a plumber or impersonate a butcher – they would find me out in twenty seconds.'

Morgan knew something that most pastors catch on to early in their work: the image aspects of pastoring, the parts that require meeting people's expectations, can be faked. We can impersonate a pastor without being a pastor. The problem, though, is that while we can get by with it in our communities, often with applause, we can't get by with it within ourselves.

At least, not all of us can. Some of us get restive. We feel awful. No level of success seems to be insurance against an eruption of *angst* in the middle of our applauded performance.

The restiveness does not come from puritanical guilt; we *are* doing what we're paid to do. The people who pay our salaries are getting their money's worth. We are 'giving good weight' – the sermons are inspiring, the committees are efficient, the morale is good. The restiveness comes from another dimension – from a vocational memory, a spiritual hunger, a professional commitment.

The Danger of Doing the Job

Being a pastor who satisfies a congregation is one of the easiest jobs on the face of the earth – *if* we are satisfied with satisfying congregations. The hours are good, the pay is adequate, the prestige considerable. Why don't we find it easy? Why aren't we content with it?

Because we set out to do something quite different. We set out to risk our lives in a venture of faith. We committed ourselves to a life of holiness. At some point we realized the immensity of God and of the great invisibles that socket into our arms and legs, into bread and wine, into our brains and our tools, into mountains and rivers, giving them meaning, destiny, value, joy, beauty, salvation. We responded to a call to convey these realities in Word and sacrament. We offered ourselves to give leadership that connects and coordinates what the people in this community of faith are doing in their work and play, with what God is doing in mercy and grace.

In the process, we learned the difference between a profession, a craft, and a job.

A job is what we do to complete an assignment. Its primary requirement is that we give satisfaction to whoever makes the assignment and pays our wage. We learn what is expected and we do it. There is nothing wrong with doing jobs. To a lesser or greater extent, we all have them; somebody has to wash the dishes and take out the garbage.

But professions and crafts are different. In these we have an obligation beyond pleasing somebody; we are pursuing or shaping the very nature of reality, convinced that when we carry out our commitments, we benefit people at a far deeper level than if we simply did what they asked of us.

In crafts we are dealing with visible realities, in professions with invisible. The craft of woodworking, for instance, has an obligation to the wood itself, its grain and texture. A good woodworker knows his woods and treats them with respect. Far more is involved than pleasing customers; something like integrity of material is involved.

With professions the integrity has to do with the invisibles: for physicians it is health (not merely making people feel good); with lawyers, justice (not helping people get their own way); with professors, learning (not cramming cranial cavities with information on tap for examinations). And with pastors, it is God (not relieving anxiety, or giving comfort, or running a religious establishment).

We all start out knowing this, or at least having a pretty good intimation of it. But when we entered our first parish, we were given a job.

Most of the people we deal with are dominated by a sense of self, not a sense of God. Insofar as we deal with their primary concern – the counseling, instructing, encouraging – they give us good marks in our *jobs* as pastors. Whether we deal with God or not, they don't care over much. Flannery O'Connor describes one pastor in such circumstances as one part minister and three parts masseur.

It is very difficult to do one thing when most of the people around us are asking us to do something quite different, especially when these people are nice, intelligent, treat us with respect, and pay our salaries. We get up each morning and the telephone rings, people meet us, letters are addressed to us – often at a tempo of bewildering urgency. All these calls and letters are from people who are asking us to do something for them, quite apart from any belief in God. That is, they come to us not because they are looking for God but because they are looking for a recommendation, or good advice, or an opportunity, and they vaguely suppose we might be qualified to give it to them.

A number of years ago, I injured my knee. According to my self-diagnosis, I knew all it needed was some whirlpool treatments. In my college years we had a whirlpool in the training room, and I had considerable experience with its effectiveness in treating my running injuries as well as making me feel good. In my present community, the only whirlpool was at the physical therapist's office. I called to make an appointment. He refused; I had to have a doctor's prescription.

I called an orthopedic physician, went in for an examination (this was getting more complicated and expensive than I had planned), and found he wouldn't give me the prescription for the whirlpool. He said it wasn't the proper treatment for my injury. He recommended surgery. I protested: a whirlpool certainly can't do any harm, and it might do some good. His refusal was adamantine. He was a professional. His primary commitment was to some invisible abstraction called health, healing. He was not committed to satisfying my requests. His integrity, in fact, forbade him to satisfy my requests if they encroached on his primary commitment.

I have since learned that with a little shopping around, I could have found a doctor who would have given me the prescription I wanted.

I reflect on that incident occasionally. Am I keeping the line clear between what I am committed to and what people are asking of me? Is my primary orientation God's grace, his mercy, his action in Creation and covenant? And am I committed to it enough that when people ask me to do something that will not lead them into a more mature participation in these realities, I refuse? I don't like to think of all my visits made, counseling given, marriages performed, meetings attended, prayers offered – one friend calls it sprinkling holy water on Cabbage Patch dolls – solely because people asked me to do it and it didn't seem at the time that it would do any harm and, who knows, it might do some good. Besides, I knew there was a pastor down the street who would do anything asked of him. But his theology was so wretched he would probably do active harm in the process. My theology, at least, was orthodox.

How do I keep the line sharp? How do I maintain a sense of pastoral vocation in a community of people who hire me to do religious jobs? How do I keep professional integrity in the midst of a people long practiced in comparative shopping, who don't get overly exercised on the fine points of pastoral integrity?

Entering the Wreckage

An illusion-bashing orientation helps. Take a long look at the sheer quantity of wreckage around us – wrecked bodies, wrecked marriages, wrecked careers, wrecked plans, wrecked families, wrecked alliances, wrecked friendships, wrecked prosperity. We avert our eyes. We try not to dwell on it. We whistle in the dark. We wake up in the morning hoping for health and love, justice and success; build quick mental and emotional defenses against the inrush of bad news; and try to keep our hopes up.

And then another kind of crash puts us or someone we care about in a pile of wreckage. Newspapers document the ruins with photographs and headlines. Our own hearts and journals fill in the details. Are there any promises, any hopes exempt from the general carnage? It doesn't seem so.

Pastors walk into these ruins every day. Why do we do it? What do we hope to accomplish? After all these centuries, things don't seem to have gotten much better; do we think another day's effort is going to stay the avalanche to doomsday? Why do we not all become cynics? Is it sheer naiveté that keeps some pastors investing themselves in acts of compassion, inviting people to a life of sacrifice, suffering abuse in order to witness to the truth, stubbornly repeating an old, hard-to-believe, and much-denied story of good news in the midst of bad news?

Is our talk of citizenship in a kingdom of God anything that can be construed as the 'real world'? Or are we passing on a spiritual fiction analogous to the science fictions that fantasize a better world than we will ever live in? Is pastoral work mostly a matter of putting plastic flowers in people's drab lives – well-intentioned attempts to brighten a bad scene, not totally without use, but not real in any substantive or living sense?

Many people think so, and most pastors have moments when they think so. If we think so often enough, we slowly but inexorably begin to adopt the majority opinion and shape our work to the expectations of a people for whom God is not so much a person as a legend, who suppose that the kingdom will be wonderful once we get past Armageddon, but we had best work right now on the terms that *this* world gives us, and who think that the Good News is nice – the way greeting card verse is nice – but in no way necessary to everyday life in the way that a computer manual or a job description is.

Two facts: the general environment of wreckage provides daily and powerful stimuli to make us want to repair and fix what is wrong; the secular mindset, in which God/kingdom/gospel are not counted as primary, living realities, is constantly seeping into our imaginations. The combination – ruined world, secular mind – makes for a steady, unrelenting pressure to readjust our conviction of what pastoral work is. We're tempted to respond to the appalling conditions around us in terms that make sense to those who are appalled.

Ministering as People Set Apart

The definition that pastors start out with, given to us in our ordination, is that pastoral work is a ministry of Word and sacrament.

Word. But in the wreckage, all words sound like 'mere words'.

Sacrament. But in the wreckage, what difference can water, a piece of bread, a sip of wine make?

Yet century after century, Christians continue to take certain persons in their communities, set them apart, and say, 'You are our shepherd. Lead us to Christlikeness.'

Yes, their actions will often speak different expectations, but in the deeper regions of the soul, the unspoken desire is for more than someone doing a religious job. If the unspoken were uttered, it would sound like this:

'We want you to be responsible for saying and acting among us what we believe about God and kingdom and gospel. We believe that the Holy Spirit is among us and within us. We believe that God's Spirit continues to hover over the chaos of the world's evil and our sin, shaping a new creation and new creatures. We believe that God is not a spectator, in turn amused and alarmed at the wreckage of world history, but a participant.

'We believe that the invisible is more important than the visible at any one single moment and in any single event that we choose to examine. We believe that everything, especially everything that looks like wreckage, is material God is using to make a praising life.

'We *believe* all this, but we don't *see* it. We see, like Ezekiel, dismembered skeletons whitened under a pitiless Babylonian sun. We see a lot of bones that once were laughing and dancing children, adults who once aired their doubts and sang their praises in church – and sinned. We don't see the dancers or the lovers or the singers – or at best catch only fleeting glimpses of them. What we see are bones. Dry bones. We see sin and judgment on the sin. That is what it *looks* like. It looked that way to Ezekiel; it looks that way to anyone with eyes to see and brain to think; and it looks that way to us.

'But we *believe* something else. We believe in the coming together of these bones into connected, sinewed, muscled human beings who speak and sing and laugh and work and believe and bless their God. We believe it happened the way Ezekiel preached it, and we believe it still happens. We believe it happened in Israel and that it happens in church. We believe we are a part of the happening as we sing our praises, listen believingly to God's Word, receive the new life of Christ in the sacraments. We believe the most significant thing that happens or can happen is that we are no longer dismembered but are remembered into the resurrection body of Christ.

'We need help in keeping our beliefs sharp and accurate and intact. We don't trust ourselves; our emotions seduce us into infidelities. We know we are launched on a difficult and dangerous act of faith, and there are strong influences intent on diluting or destroying it. We want you to give us help. Be our pastor, a minister of Word and sacrament in the middle of this world's life. Minister with Word and sacrament in all the different parts and stages of our lives – in our work and play, with our children and our parents, at birth and death, in our celebrations and sorrows, on those days when morning breaks over us in a wash of sunshine, and those other days that are all drizzle. This isn't the only task in the life of faith, but it is your task. We will find someone else to do the other important and essential tasks. This is *yours:* Word and sacrament.

'One more thing: We are going to ordain you to this ministry, and we want your vow that you will stick to it. This is not a temporary job assignment but a way of life that we need lived out in our community. We know you are launched on the same difficult belief venture in the same dangerous world as we are. We know your emotions are as fickle as ours, and your mind is as tricky as ours. That is why we are going to *ordain* you and why we are going to exact a *vow* from you. We know there will be days and months, maybe even years, when we won't feel like believing anything and won't want to hear it from you. And we know there will be days and weeks and maybe even years when you won't feel like saying it. It doesn't matter. Do it. You are ordained to this ministry, vowed to it.

'There may be times when we come to you as a committee or delegation and demand that you tell us something else than what we are telling you now. Promise right now that you won't give in to what we demand of you. You are not the minister of our changing desires, or our time-conditioned understanding of our needs, or our secularized hopes for something better. With these vows of ordination we are lashing you fast to the mast of Word and sacrament so you will be unable to respond to the siren voices.

'There are many other things to be done in this wrecked world, and we are going to be doing at least some of them, but if we don't know the foundational realities with which we are dealing – God, kingdom, gospel – we are going to end up living futile, fantasy lives. Your task is to keep telling the basic story, representing the presence of the Spirit, insisting on the priority of God, speaking the biblical words of command and promise and invitation.'

That, or something very much like that, is what I understand the church to say – even when the people cannot articulate it – to the individuals it ordains to be its pastors.

13

Desert and Harvest: A Sabbatical Story

BLESSED ARE THOSE WHO ARE PERSECUTED

Unfriendly waters do a friendly
Thing: curses, cataract-hurled
Stones, make the rough places
Smooth; a rushing whitewater stream
Of blasphemies hate-launched,
Then caught by the sun, sprays rainbow
Arcs across the Youghiogeny.
Savaged by the river's impersonal
Attack the land is deepened to bedrock.
Wise passivities are earned
In quiet, craggy, occasional pools
That chasten the wild waters to stillness,
And hold them under hemlock green
For birds and deer to bathe and drink
In peace – persecution's gift:
The hard-won, blessed letting be.

We were both apprehensive, my wife and I. We had been away from our congregation for twelve months, a sabbatical year, and we were on our way back. It had been a wonderful year, soaking in the silence, gulping down great drafts of high-country air. Could we handle the transition from the solitude of the Montana Rockies to the traffic of Maryland?

Being a pastor is a difficult job, maybe no harder than any other job – any job done well requires everything that is in us – but hard all the same. For a year we had not done it: no interruptive phone calls, no exhilarating/exhausting creativity at pulpit and lectern, no doggedly carried out duties. We played and we prayed. We split wood and shoveled snow. We read and talked over what we read. We cross-country skied in the winter and hiked in the summer.

Every Sunday we did what we had not done for thirty years: we sat together and worshiped God. We went to the Eidsvold Lutheran Church in Somers with seventy or eighty other Christians, mostly Norwegians, and sang hymns that we didn't know very well. Pastor Pris led us in prayer and preached rich sermons.

Comfortable in the pew on an April Sunday, I had an inkling of what the pastor had been doing that week – the meetings he had attended and the crises he had endured. While the Spirit was using his sermon to speak quite personally to me, at the edges of my mind I was admiringly aware of the sheer craft, exegetically and homiletically, behind it. Then, as people who sit in church pews often do, I mentally wandered. *How does he do that week after week? How does he stay so fresh, so alert, so on target, so alive to people and Christ? And in the midst of all this stress and emotion and study and ecclesiastical shopkeeping? That's got to be the toughest job on earth – I could never do that. I'm glad I don't have a job like that.*

And then I realized, *But I* do *have a job like that; that is my job – or will be, again, in a few months.*

Those 'few months' were now whittled down to 'next week'. We weren't sure we were up to it. Maybe the sabbatical, instead of refreshing us, had only spoiled us. Instead of energizing, maybe it had enervated us. For thirty years we had lived a hundred or so feet down in the ocean of parish life (how much pressure per square inch is that?) and for a year of sabbatical we had surfaced, basking in the sun, romping in the snow. Deep-sea divers enter decompression chambers as they leave the depths, lest they get the bends. We felt an equivalent need for a 'recompression chamber' as we returned to the depths.

From Montana to the East Coast, Interstate 90 stretches out an inviting beeline, nearly straight, with a couple of sweeping curves (but bees also buzz curves). But we veered off on a detour south to the high desert of Colorado for a four-day retreat at a monastery. The monastery, we hoped, would be our recompression chamber. It was not as if we hadn't had time for prayer. We had never had so much time for it. But we sensed the need for something else now – a community of prayer, some friends with a vocation for prayer among whom we could immerse our vocation as pastor.

So for four days we prayed in a community that prayed. The days had an easy rhythm: morning prayers in the chapel with the monks and other retreatants at 6 o'clock; evening prayers at 5 o'clock; before and after and in between, silence – walking, reading, praying, emptying. The rhythm broke on Sunday. After morning prayers and the Eucharist, everyone met for a noisy and festive breakfast. The silence had dug wells of joy that now spilled into the community in artesian conversation and laughter.

When we left the monastery, the Montana sabbatical year was, as we had intended in our praying, behind us emotionally as well as geographically. Three days later we arrived in Maryland, focused and explosive with energy.

Stimulus for Sabbatical

The idea for a sabbatical developed from a two-pronged stimulus: fatigue and frustration. I was tired. That's hardly unusual in itself, but it was a tiredness that vacations weren't fixing – a tiredness of spirit, an inner boredom. I sensed a spiritual core to my fatigue and was looking for a spiritual remedy.

Along the way as a pastor, I had also become a writer. I longed for a stretch of time to express some thoughts about my pastoral vocation, time that was never available while I was in the act of being a pastor.

A sabbatical year seemed to serve both needs perfectly. But how would I get it? I serve a single-pastor church, and there was no money to fund a sabbatical: Who would replace me while I was away? How would I pay for the venture? The two difficulties seemed formidable. But I felt that if the sabbatical was in fact the spiritual remedy to a spiritual need, the church ought to be able to come up with a solution.

I started by calling several of the leaders in the congregation and inviting them to my home for an evening. I told them what I felt and what I wanted. I didn't ask them to solve the problem, but asked them to enter into seeking a solution with me. They asked a lot of questions; they took me seriously; they perceived it as a congregational task; they started to see themselves as pastor to me. When the evening ended, we had not solved the difficulties, but I knew I had allies praying, working, and thinking with me. The concept of 'sabbatical' filled out and developed momentum. Over a period of several months, the 'mountains' moved.

Replacement: This turned out to be not much of a difficulty at all. My denomination offered help in locating an interim pastor – there are quite a few men and women who are available for just such work. We decided finally to call a young man who had recently served as an intern for a year with us.

Funding: We worked out a plan in which the church paid me one-third of my salary, and I arranged for the other two-thirds. I did this by renting out my house for the year and asking a generous friend for assistance. We had a family home on a lake in Montana where my parents, now deceased, had lived and we had always vacationed. It was suited to our needs for solitude, and we could live there inexpensively.

Detail after detail fell into place, not always easily or quickly, but after ten months the sabbatical year was agreed upon and planned. I interpreted what we were doing in a letter to the congregation:

'Sabbatical years are the biblically based provision for restoration. When the farmer's field is depleted, it is given a sabbatical – after six years of planting and harvesting, it is left alone for a year so that the nutrients can build up in it. When people in ministry are depleted, they also are given a sabbatical – time apart for the recovery of spiritual and creative energies. I have been feeling the need for just such a time of restoration for about two years. The sense that my reserves are low, that my margins of creativity are crowded, becomes more acute each week. I feel the need for some 'desert' time – for silence, for solitude, for prayer.

'One of the things I fear most as your pastor is that out of fatigue or sloth I end up going through the motions, substituting professional smoothness for personal grappling with the life of the Spirit in our life together. The demands of pastoral life are strenuous, and there is no respite from them. There are not many hours in any day when I am not faced with the struggle of faith in someone or another, the deep, central, eternal energies that make the difference between a life lived to the glory of God and a life wasted in self-indulgence or trivialized in diversions. I want to be ready for those encounters. For me, that is what it means to be a pastor: to be in touch with the Lord's Word and presence, and to be ready to speak and act out of that Word and presence in whatever I am doing – while leading you in worship, teaching Scripture, talking and praying with you individually, meeting with you in groups as we order our common life, writing poems and articles and books.

'It is in this capacity for intensity and intimacy, staying at the center where God's Word makes things alive, that I feel in need of repletion. The demands are so much greater today than they were in earlier years. One of the things that twenty-three years of pastoral life among you means is that there is a complex network of people both within and without the congregation with whom I am in significant relationship. I would not have it otherwise. But I must also do something to maintain the central springs of compassion and creativity lest it all be flattened out into routines.

'Parallel with this felt need for "desert" time, I feel the need for "harvest" time. These twenty-three years with you have been full and rich. I came here inexperienced and untutored. Together, taught by the Spirit and by each other, we have learned much: You have become a congregation; I have become a pastor. During this time, I realized that writing is an essential element in my pastoral vocation with you. All the writing comes out of the soil of this community of faith as we worship together, attend to Scripture, seek to discern the Spirit's presence in our lives. As I write, a growing readership expresses appreciation and affirms me in the work. Right now, so much that is mature and ripe for harvest remains unwritten. I want to write what we have lived together. I don't want to write on the run, hastily, or carelessly. I want to write this well, to the glory of God.

'Jan and I talked about this, prayed together, and consulted with persons whom we hold to be wise. The obvious solution was to accept a call to another congregation. That would provide the clean simplicity of new relationships uncomplicated by history and the stimulus of new beginnings. But we didn't want to leave here if we could find another way; the life of worship and love that we have developed together is a great treasure that we will part with only if required. We arrived at the idea of the sabbatical, a year away for prayer and writing so that we would be able to return to this place and this people and do our very best in ministry with you.

'So, a desert time and a harvest time, time for prayer and time for writing, the two times side by side, contrasting, converging, cross-fertilizing. Many of you have already given your blessing and encouragement in this venture, affirming our resolve in taking this faith-step, being obedient to God in our lives.'

Structure for the Sabbatical

And so it happened. Twelve months away from my congregation. Twelve months to pray and write, to worship and walk, to converse and read, to remember and revision.

From the outset we had conceived of the sabbatical as a joint enterprise, meeting a spiritual need in both pastor and congregation. We didn't want the year to be misinterpreted as an escape: we didn't want to be viewed as 'off doing their own thing.' We were committed to this congregation. The sabbatical was provided to deepen and continue our common ministry. How could we convey that? How could we cultivate our intimacy in the faith and not have the geographic separation separate us spiritually?

We decided to write a monthly 'Sabbatical Letter' in two parts, 'Jan's side' and 'Eugene's side'. We sent a roll of film along with the letter; a friend developed the pictures of our life that month and displayed them in the narthex. The letters and pictures did exactly what we had hoped. But only one side of the letters seems to have been read closely – Jan's. I couldn't quit preaching. She conveyed the sabbatical experience.

Brita Stendahl wrote once that the sabbatical year she and her husband, Krister, had in Sweden 'gave us our lives back'. Jan's side of the sabbatical letters revealed that dimension of our year for our worshiping and believing friends at home. She set the tone in the first letter:

'Separated from us by 2,500 miles, my mother-in-law was always pleased to get a letter from us. Because Eugene was her eldest and out "seeking adventures" both physically and ideologically, she was always glad to be stretched by his cosmic and theological letters. He would share with her all the *Big Ideas.* But being a mother and homemaker, she especially liked to hear from me because I would tell her what we were having for dinner, the latest troubles or triumphs of her grandchildren, the rips in their clothing, and the precocious oracles from their mouths. You can read the *Big Ideas* on the other side of the page, but here is my mother-in-law letter to you, our dear family at Christ Our King.

'The trip across the country was good. We camped out a couple of nights on the way. We took to heart most of the well-wishing advice you gave us as we left, but the numerous admonitions to dress warmly didn't "take". Our first night in Montana we camped at the headwaters of the Missouri River and managed to freeze the particular extremity that it isn't proper to mention in a church newsletter. We brought the dog into the tent for added warmth, but she wasn't as much help as we needed. The night sky was stunning with its brilliant stars all the way down to the horizon. (I never knew stars went all the way down to the horizon!) The tent was ice coated in the morning.

'The first week here has been spent cleaning, rearranging, and trying to get the house warm enough. I think I am finally getting the knack of building a wood fire. We have interspersed our settling in with walks in the woods and reading aloud to each other (Garrison Keillor right now).

'One day we took off for Glacier Park to see dozens of bald eagles fishing for the salmon spawning in MacDonald Creek. Last year on the peak day, over five hundred were sighted. After our birding we hiked to Avalanche Lake, two and one-half miles up into a glacial cirque. It was a day marvelous in weather – snow flurries, sun, wind, clouds.

'We have about thirty ducks swimming around our bay here on the lake. Last Sunday we returned from worship and saw a furry creature on our dock licking himself dry and realized it was a mink.

'Eric and Lynn came over from Spokane for the weekend. We had Eugene's brother and sister and their families for a potluck Friday evening. That was a happy reunion and a good time. One of our prayers for this year is that our family gatherings will be rich and full.

'One of the last things that we asked Mabel Scarborough to do for us before leaving Bel Air was to update a church directory so that we could pray for you, our faith family, each day. Be assured of our love and our prayers. We feel very close to you. For supper tonight we had creamed tuna over sourdough biscuits.'

Such was the nature of our time. Once we arrived in Montana, we established a routine to support our twin goals of desert and harvest so that we would not fritter away the year. We agreed on a five-day work week, with Saturday and Sunday given to playing and praying. I worked hard for about five hours a day at my writing desk and then relaxed. We had evening prayers in the late afternoon and followed that by reading aloud to each other and fixing supper. After nine months of this, I had the two books written that I had set out to complete (the 'harvest'). From then on it was all 'desert' – reading and praying and hiking.

Refit for Ministry

Everything I had hoped for came to pass: I returned with more energy than I can remember having since I was fifteen years old. I have always (with occasional, but brief, lapses) enjoyed being a pastor. But never this much. The experience of my maturity was now coupled with the energy of my youth, a combination I had not thought possible. The parts of pastoral work I had done out of duty before, just because somebody had to do them, I now embraced with delight. I felt deep reservoirs within me, capacious and free flowing. I felt great margins of leisure around everything I did – conversations, meetings, letter writing, telephone calls. I felt I would never again be in a hurry. The sabbatical had done its work.

A benefit I had not counted on was a change in the congregation. They were refreshed and confident in a way I had not observed before. One of the dangers of a long-term pastorate is the development of neurotic dependencies between pastor and people. I had worried about that from time to time: *Was it healthy of me to stay in this congregation for so long? Had I taken the place of God for them?*

Those fears became more acute when I proposed the sabbatical year, for many people expressed excessive anxiety – anxiety that I would not return, anxiety that the church could not get along without me, anxiety that the life of faith and worship and trust that we had worked so hard to develop would disintegrate in my absence. None of these fears was realized. Not one. Not even a little bit. The congregation thrived. They found they did not need me at all. They discovered they could be a church of Jesus Christ with another pastor quite as well as they could with me. I returned to a congregation confident in its maturity as a people of God.

A recent incident, seemingly trivial, illustrates the profound difference that keeps showing up in a variety of situations. About twenty-five of us were going on an overnight leadership retreat. We had agreed to meet in the church parking lot at 5:45 to car-pool together. I made a hospital visit that took longer than planned and arrived five minutes late – to an empty parking lot. They had left me. Before the sabbatical, that would never have happened; now that kind of thing happens all the time. They can take care of themselves and know that I can take care of myself. Maturity.

We are both, the congregation and I, experiencing a great freedom in this: neither of us neurotically *needs* each other. I am not dependent on them; they aren't dependent on me. That leaves us free to appreciate each other and receive gifts of ministry from each other.

THE WORD MADE FRESH

14

Poets and Pastors

Is it not significant that the biblical prophets and psalmists were all poets?

PASTORS AND POETS DO MANY THINGS IN COMMON: USE words with reverence, get immersed in everyday particulars, spy out the glories of the commonplace, warn of illusions, attend to the subtle interconnections between rhythm and meaning and spirit. I think we ought to seek each other out as friends and allies.

Poets are caretakers of language, the shepherds of words, keeping them from harm, exploitation, misuse. Words not only mean something; they are something, each with a sound and rhythm all its own.

Poets are not primarily trying to tell us, or get us, to do something. By attending to words with playful discipline (or disciplined playfulness), they draw us into deeper respect both for words and for the reality they set before us.

Pastors are also in the word business. We preach, teach, and counsel using words. People often pay particular attention on the chance that God may be using our words to speak to them. We have a responsibility to use words accurately and well. But it isn't easy. We live in a world where words are used carelessly by some, cunningly by others.

It is so easy for us to say whatever comes to mind, our role as pastor compensating for our inane speech. It is easy to say what either flatters or manipulates and so acquire power over others. In subtle ways, being a pastor subjects our words to corruption. That is why it is important to frequent the company of a poet friend – Gerard Manley Hopkins, George Herbert, Emily Dickinson, Luci Shaw are some of mine – a person who cares about words and is honest with them, who respects and honors their sheer overwhelming power. I leave such meetings less careless, my reverence for words and the Word restored.

Is it not significant that the biblical prophets and psalmists were all poets? It is a continuing curiosity that so many pastors, whose work integrates the prophetic and psalmic (preaching and praying), are indifferent to poets. In reading poets, I find congenial allies in the world of words. In writing poems, I find myself practicing my pastoral craft in a biblical way.

The following poems work off of the pivot of the incarnation, the doctrine closest to pastoral work. *Caro salutis est cardo,* wrote Tertullian. 'The flesh is the pivot-point of salvation.'

15

Poems

The Greeting

Hail, O favored one,
the Lord is with you!
Luke 1:28

My mail carrier, driving his stubby white
Truck, trimmed in blue and red, wingless
But wheeled, commissioned by the civil service
Daily delivers the Gospel every Advent.

This Gabriel, uniformed in gabardine,
Unsmiling descendant of his dazzling original,
Under the burden of greetings is stoical
But prompt: annunciations at ten each morning.

One or two or three a day at first;
By the second week momentum's up,
My mail box is stuffed, each card stamped

With the glory at a cost of only twenty-five cents,
(Bringing the news that God is here with us)
First class, personally hand addressed.

THE TREE

There shall come forth a shoot from the stump of Jesse,
and a branch shall grow out of his roots.

ISAIAH *11:1*

Jesse's roots, composted with carcasses
Of dove and lamb, parchments of ox and goat,
Centuries of dried up prayers and bloody
Sacrifice, now bear me gospel fruit.

David's branch, fed on kosher soil,
Blossoms a messianic flower, and then
Ripens into a kingdom crop, conserving
The fragrance and warmth of spring for winter use.

Holy Spirit, shake our family tree;
Release your ripened fruit to our outstretched arms.

I'd like to see my children sink their teeth
Into promised land pomegranates

And Canaan grapes, bushel gifts of God,
While I skip a grace rope to a Christ tune.

THE STAR

I see him, but not now; I behold him, but not nigh:
a star shall come forth out of Jacob.

NUMBERS 24:17

No star is visible except at night,
Until the sun goes down, no accurate north.
Day's brightness hides what darkness shows to sight,
The hour I go to sleep the bear strides forth.

I open my eyes to the cursed but requisite dark,
The black sink that drains my cistern dry,
And see, not nigh, not now, the heavenly mark
Exploding in the quasar-messaged sky.

Out of the dark, behind my back, a sun
Launched light-years ago, completes its run;

The undeciphered skies of myth and story
Now narrate the cadenced runes of glory.

Lost pilots wait for night to plot their flight,
Just so diurnal pilgrims praise the midnight.

The Candle

The people who walked in darkness have seen a great light:
Those who dwelt in a land of deep darkness, on them has light shined.

Isaiah 9:2

Uncandled menorahs and oilless lamps abandoned
By foolish virgins too much in a hurry to wait
And tend the light are clues to the failed watch,
The missed arrival, the midnight might-have-been.

Wick and beeswax make a guttering protest,
Fragile, defiant flame against demonic
Terrors that gust, invisible and nameless,
Out of galactic ungodded emptiness.

Then deep in the blackness fires nursed by wise
Believers surprise with shining all groping derelicts

Bruised and stumbling in a world benighted.
The sudden blazing backlights each head with a nimbus.

Shafts of storm-filtered sun search and destroy
The Stygian desolation: I see. I see.

The Time

When the time had fully come, God sent forth his Son, born of a woman, born under the law, to redeem those who were under the law, so that we might receive adoption

Galatians 4:4-5

Half, or more than half, my life is spent
In waiting: waiting for the day to come
When dawn spills laughter's animated sun
Across the rim of God into my tent.

In my other clock sin I put off
Until I'm ready, which I never seem
To be, the seized day, the kingdom dream
Come true. My head has been too long in the trough.

Keeping a steady messianic rhythm,
Ocean tides and woman's blood fathom

The deep that calls to deep, and bring to birth
The seeded years, and grace this wintered earth

Measured by the metronomic moon.
Nothing keeps time better than a womb.

The Dream

. . . an angel of the Lord appeared to him in a dream.

Matthew 1:20

Amiably conversant with virtue and evil,
The righteousness of Joseph and wickedness
Of Herod, I'm ever and always a stranger to grace.
I need this annual angel visitation

– sudden dive by dream to reality –
To know the virgin conceives and God is with us.
The dream powers its way through winter weather
And gives me vision to see the Jesus gift.

Light from the dream lasts a year. Impervious
To equinox and solstice it makes twelve months

Of daylight by which I see the crèche where my
Redeemer lives. Archetypes of praise take shape

Deep in my spirit. As autumn wanes I count
The days 'til I will have the dream again.

The Cradle

And she gave birth to her first-born son and wrapped him in swaddling clothes, and laid him in a manger.

Luke 2:7

For us who have only known approximate fathers
And mothers manqué, this child is a surprise:
A sudden coming true of all we hoped
Might happen. Hoarded hopes fed by prophecies,

Old sermons and song fragments, now cry
Coo and gurgle in the cradle, a babbling
Proto-language which as soon as it gets
A tongue (and we, of course, grow open ears)

Will say the big nouns: joy, glory, peace;
And live the best verbs: love, forgive, save.
Along with the swaddling clothes the words are washed

Of every soiling sentiment, scrubbed clean of
All failed promises, then hung in the world's
Backyard dazzling white, billowing gospel.

The Pain

. . . and a sword will pierce through your own soul also,
that thoughts out of many hearts may be revealed.

Luke 2:35

The bawling of babies, always in a way
Inappropriate – why should the loved and innocent
Greet existence with wails? – is proof that not all
Is well. Dreams and deliveries never quite mesh.

Deep hungers go unsatisfied, deep hurts
Unhealed. The natural and gay are torn
By ugly grimace and curse. A wound appears
In the place of ecstasy. Birth is bloody.

All pain's a prelude: to symphony, to sweetness.
'The pearl began as a pain in the oyster's stomach.'

Dogwood, recycled from cradle to cross, enters
The market again as a yoke for easing burdens.

Each sword-opened side is the matrix for God
To come to me again through travail for joy.

The War

And the dragon stood before the woman who was about to bear a child, that he might devour her child. . . . Now war arose in heaven.

Revelation 12:4, 7

This birth's a signal for war. Lovers fight,
Friends fall out. Merry toasts from flagons
Of punch are swallowed in the maw of dragons.
Will mother and baby survive this devil night?

I've done my share of fighting in the traffic:
Kitchen quarrels, playground fisticuffs;
Every cherub choir has its share of toughs,
And then one day I learned the fight was cosmic.

Truce: I lay down arms; my arms fill up
With gifts: wild and tame, real and stuffed

Lions. Lambs play, oxen low,
The infant fathers festive force. One crow

Croaks defiance into the shalom whiteness,
Empty, satanic bluster against the brightness.

The Carol

Glory to God in the highest, and on earth peace
among men with whom he is pleased.

Luke 2:14

Untuned, I'm flat on my feet, sharp with my tongue,
A walking talking dischord, out of sorts,
My heart murmurs are entered in lab reports.
The noise between my ears cannot be sung.

Ill-pleased, I join a line of hard-to-please people
Who want to exchange their lumpy bourgeois souls
For a keen Greek mind with a strong Roman nose,
Then find ourselves, surprised, at the edge of a stable.

Caroling angels and a well-pleased God
Join a choir of cow and sheep and dog

At this barnyard border between wish and gift.
I glimpse the just-formed flesh, now mine. They lift

Praise voices and sing twelve tones
Of pleasure into my muscles, into my bones.

The Feast

He who is mighty has done great things for me. . . .
He has filled the hungry with good things.

Luke 1:49, 53

The milkful breasts brim blessings and quiet
The child into stillness, past pain: El Shaddai
Has done great things for me. Earth nurses
Heaven on the slopes of the Grand Tetons.

Grown-up, he gives breakfasts, breaks bread,
Itinerant host at a million feasts.
His milkfed bones are buried unbroken
In the Arimethean's tomb.

The world has worked up an appetite:
And comes on the run to the table he set:
Strong meat, full-bodied wine.

Wassailing with my friends in the winter
Mountains, I'm back for seconds as often
As every week: drink long! drink up!

THE DANCE

When the voice of your greeting came to my ears,
the babe in my womb leaped for joy.

LUKE 1:44

Another's heart lays downs the beat that puts
Me in motion, in perichoresis, steps
Learned in the womb before the world's foundation.
It never misses a beat: praise pulses.

Leaping toward the light, I'm dancing in
The dark, touching now the belly of blessing,
Now the aching side, ready for birth,
For naming and living love's mystery out in the open.

The nearly dead and the barely alive pick up
The chthonic rhythms in their unused muscles

And gaily cartwheel three hallelujahs.
But not all: 'Those who are deaf always despise

Those who dance.' That doesn't stop the dance:
All waiting light leap at the voice of greeting.

The Gift

For to us a child is born, to us a son is given . . . and his name will be called 'Wonderful Counselor, Mighty God, Everlasting Father, Prince of Peace.'

Isaiah 9:6

Half-sick with excitement and under garish lights
I do it again, year after year after year.
I can't wait to plunder the boxes, then show
And tell my friends: Look what I got!

I rip the tissues from every gift but find
That all the labels have lied. Stones.
And my heart a stone. 'Dead in trespasses
And sin.' The lights go out. Later my eyes,

Accustomed to the dark, see wrapped
In Christ-foil and ribboned in Spirit-colors

The multi-named messiah, love labels
On a faith shape, every name a promise

And every promise a present, made and named
All in the same breath. I accept.

THE OFFERING

May the kings of Tarshish and of isles render him tribute,
may the kings of Sheba and Seba bring gifts!
Long may he live,
may gold of Sheba be given to him!

PSALM 72:10, 15

Brought up in a world where there's no free lunch
And trained to use presents for barter, I'm spending
The rest of my life receiving this gift with no
Strings attached, but not doing too well.

Three bathrobed wise men with six or seven
Inches of jeans and sneakers showing, kneel,
Offering gifts that symbolize the gifts
That none of us is ready yet to give.

A few of us stay behind, blow out the candles,
Sweep up the straw and put the creche in storage.

We open the door into the world's night
And find we've played ourselves into a better

Performance. We leave with our left-over change changed
At the offertory into kingdom gold.

We want to hear from you. Please send your comments about this book to us in care of the address below. Thank you.

ZONDERVAN™

GRAND RAPIDS, MICHIGAN 49530

WWW.ZONDERVAN.COM